Black Baseball
Players in Canada

Black Baseball Players in Canada

A Biographical Dictionary, 1881–1960

BARRY SWANTON *and*
JAY-DELL MAH

Foreword by Tom Hawthorn

McFarland & Company, Inc., Publishers
Jefferson, North Carolina, and London

ALSO OF INTEREST

The ManDak League: Haven for Former Negro League Ballplayers, 1950–1957 by Barry Swanton (McFarland, 2006)

LIBRARY OF CONGRESS CATALOGUING-IN-PUBLICATION DATA

Swanton, Barry, 1938–
Black baseball players in Canada : a biographical dictionary, 1881–1960 / Barry Swanton and Jay-Dell Mah ; foreword by Tom Hawthorn.
    p.   cm.
Includes bibliographical references and index.

ISBN 978-0-7864-4468-7
softcover : 50# alkaline paper ∞

1. African American baseball players—Canada—Biography—Dictionaries. 2. Baseball—Canada—History. 3. Discrimination in sports—United States—History. I. Mah, Jay-Dell. II. Title.

GV865.A1S945   2009   796.357092'396073071—dc22 [B]   2009017355

British Library cataloguing data are available

©2009 Barry Swanton and Jay-Dell Mah. All rights reserved

No part of this book may be reproduced or transmitted in any form or by any means, electronic or mechanical, including photocopying or recording, or by any information storage and retrieval system, without permission in writing from the publisher.

On the cover: Chet Brewer painting ©Jacqueline Jolles; background images ©2009 Shutterstock

Manufactured in the United States of America

McFarland & Company, Inc., Publishers
Box 611, Jefferson, North Carolina 28640
www.mcfarlandpub.com

To all those who've survived a prairie winter
to experience the warmth and joy
of baseball in the spring

Contents

Foreword by Tom Hawthorn 1

Preface 5

Introduction 11

THE PLAYERS 15

Bibliography 193

Index 195

Foreword by Tom Hawthorn

Baseball is a sport for storytelling. The game is famously played without a clock, which means the first pitch might be followed by two, or three, or four, or more hours of baseball. The game comes with natural pauses in the action after every three outs. Toss in batters stepping out of the box, pitchers talking to catchers, pitchers being sent to the showers, runners dusting off pants after a slide—why, there's plenty of time to gab about the great summer game.

At some point, a batter steps towards home, taps dirt from his cleats, tightens his batting gloves, adjusts his helmet. Your neighbor in the stands asks, "Who's this guy?" You can answer with statistics, but that's only part of the story. A better question might be, "Where's this guy from?" Is he a promising rookie on his way up to The Show, or is he a declining veteran hanging on in hopes of returning to the bigs? Who is he and how did he get here?

You appreciate the game more when you know the story behind the number on the uniform.

Many who have taken to the field in Canada were imports from the south—a left-handed college kid earning a few bucks under the table in summer, or a slugger seeking to put up big numbers in hopes a scout might sign him to a good contract. This steady trickle became a deluge after 1947, when the great Jackie Robinson broke the modern color barrier in the major leagues by taking to the field with the Brooklyn Dodgers.

This created a labor problem. Major league teams began to pluck the finest African-American talent from the Negro Leagues, the beginning of a steep decline and inglorious end to a circuit so rich in baseball lore. Lesser players faced a tough decision: Stay in black ball though the future looked bleak, or sign a contract to a minor-league team and face the possibility of having to play in the Jim Crow South.

Dozens of black athletes found well-paying and altogether more comfortable employment in Canada, where the pay was good and the reception, for the most part, welcoming.

Many headed north to find seasonal work on the wind-blown grass fields of Canada's three Western provinces. They wore uniforms with such names as Oilers, Eskimos and Combines spilling across the chest in Coca-Cola script.

These men played in the cities, as well as in whistle stop prairie hamlets in which a semi-professional team was the community's claim to fame. From Vulcan, Alta., to Indian Head, Sask., to Carman, Man., the hard-working people of a hardscrabble land eagerly flocked to watch a superior brand of baseball than that to which they had become accustomed.

The new recruits had nicknames like Baldy and Buddy, Pappy and Pepper, Doc and Ducky. They had baseball names like Lefty and Fireball and Pee Wee and Home Run. Even the family names had poetry, as there was a Coffee and a Colas and even one unfortunate stuck with the tag of Harry Butts.

They came from Cuba, Panama and, of course, the United States. Some had been playing on such barnstorming clubs as the Indianapolis Clowns, New York Komedy Kings, and Ligon's Colored All-Stars. Their resumes included stints with the Cuban Giants and the Elite Giants and the Colored Giants.

Seven players who came north in the 40s and 50s went on to bring integration to major-league clubs—from Jackie Robinson with Brooklyn to Pumpsie Green with the Red Sox, Boston being the last club to hire an African-American athlete, 12 full years after Robinson had been hired. Shoot, Robinson had been retired three years before Pumpsie joined the Scarlet Hose.

Earlier pioneers tried to earn a living in the sport they loved, only to be barred for the basest of reasons. By posing as a native Indian, Dick Brookins earned a spot at third base with the Regina Bone Pilers back in 1910. He would be kicked out of the game when other owners protested his ethnic ancestry.

The authors Barry Swanton and Jay-Dell Mah have compiled an informative, entertaining and, ultimately, inspiring series of thumbnail sketches of ball players who found a welcome home in Canada.

So, who are these guys?

Barry Swanton remembers awaiting his father's daily return home from his job as a postal clerk. "Go get the gloves," his father would say, the boy fetching two baseball mitts. On some days, his father, Cecil, brought with him a special delivery—two tickets to a game at Osborne Stadium in Winnipeg. They would ride the streetcar south from the North End to the ball park opposite the Manitoba Legislative Building. The stadium was the home of the Winnipeg Buffaloes and the Elmwood Giants. For a boy, it was a field upon which trod giants in stature as well as name.

The father treated the son to a 25-cent scorecard on which he could record the outcome of each confrontation between batter and pitcher. After the game, the boy liked to hang around the clubhouse entrance to beg for autographs and coax playing tips from savvy veterans. The players were willing to entertain a star-struck lad.

"They weren't in a hurry to get back to their rooming house, or the YMCA," Swanton says.

The following day, the boy would clip a game report and boxscore from either the Winnipeg Tribune or Winnipeg Free Press. He then placed these inside the scorecard, which was tucked away for keeps.

Years passed and the boy became a man, following his father into the post office. He never left the baseball diamond, coaching boys as wide-eyed as he was once himself. While preparing to move to British Columbia almost 20 years ago, Barry came across the box holding his yellowing scorecard collection.

A forgotten box also held the boyhood mementoes of Jay-Dell Mah. The CBC's Toronto city hall reporter was preparing to retire some years ago when he discovered a trove placed in safekeeping decades earlier—an autograph book, a signed baseball, assorted newspaper clippings, and two thick scrapbooks.

The two men, who both came to baseball through their fathers, each embarked on separate projects to revive interest in the baseball of their youth on the prairies. Mah built a comprehensive Web site—www.attheplate.com—about the history of baseball in Western Canada in the 1950s and 1960s. Swanton wrote a history of the ManDak (Manitoba-Dakota) League profiling the circuit that provided work for Cubans, Canadians and American players while entertaining fans in prairie cities on both sides of the border.

The two men struck a long-distance friendship. They share a passion, but not an area code.

Swanton lives in the Vancouver suburb of Surrey, while Mah (a long-time Toronto resident) now resides in Nakusp, a village in southeastern British Columbia.

Mah grew up in Lloydminster, where he "slept in Saskatchewan and ate breakfast in Alberta." The family home was on one side of the 4th Meridian, while the family restaurant was on the other. His father, Jimmy Mah, who had come to Canada from Canton in about 1911, when he was still known as Mah Doo-wing, owned the Elite Cafe. The restaurant became a hangout for mercenary ballplayers and the cafe owner's son, Harvey, became something of a mascot. (Harvey was nicknamed Jazz by his brothers, later shortened to Jay. When he launched his radio career, he called himself Jay Dell. The chosen name was later grafted onto his family name, becoming Jay-Dell Mah.) When he was old enough, Harvey became bat boy for the Lloydminster Meridians.

On the field, he fetched bats for the players and balls for the umpire. Off the field, he washed socks and shined shoes for tips. On one glorious day, when he was a bit older, a pitcher with speed but little accuracy asked the boy to catch his pitches. The first six stung his hand so much he could barely endure the pain. Then, his catching hand became so numb as to dull the pain. The next morning, he awoke with a left hand as swollen as a catcher's glove. Though painful, it was a temporary souvenir he displayed with pride.

One of his favorite players was Benny Lott, a slick-fielding second baseman whose panache on the field was matched by his stylish wardrobe. Lott's swing was so elegant, so sweet, he was nicknamed Honey. The infielder presented his No. 1 fan with an autographed five-dollar bill—a small fortune at the time—with the inscription: "To the best bat boy in the world." Somehow, the bill got mixed with the float in the restaurant till and was unceremoniously handed to a customer as change.

Lott came to the prairies after employment with the Indianapolis Clowns and New York Black Yankees. Only later as an adult would the bat boy realize the players he idolized had minor roles in a social revolution, ending segregation by playing sports in circumstances where the only color that mattered was that found on a uniform.

Both Mah and Swanton pursue forgotten players of the era with the same enthusiasm as a fielder chasing a hapless baserunner.

Tom Hawthorn is a veteran freelance reporter who lives in Victoria, B.C. His work has appeared in a wide variety of newspapers and magazines across Canada and he has won 16 journalism awards and citations.

Preface

Ten years ago, the co-authors—one beginning work on a book about the ManDak Baseball League, the other in the early stages of a web site on the Western Canada Baseball League—bumped into one another on the internet as both were chasing information on baseball players, especially imports, who had graced the diamonds of Western Canada.

The two were especially interested in those from the Negro Leagues and the Caribbean as there was so little information available at the time. Many had become popular visitors to Canada while on barnstorming teams and now were suiting up in the leagues and tournaments of the late 1940s through the early 1960s.

Over the years, the pair tucked away hundreds of notes as they chased leads through published material, personal interviews and emerging on-line sources. This effort is a result of that interest and research and a response to the many, many enquiries from friends and family of the players, former colleagues and people just inquisitive about them. For us, the journey itself has been quite a reward and a learning experience.

Little did we appreciate, as youngsters at the time, the impact of Jackie Robinson.

> When you look at the history of our game, Jackie Robinson coming into baseball—there's no question in my mind that April 15, 1947, was the most powerful moment in baseball history..... It transcended baseball. It was a precursor to the civil rights movement by 15 or 16 years.

Baseball Commissioner Bud Selig made the comment on April 15, 2004, in announcing the dedication of April 15th as Jackie Robinson Day. In 2008, the Baseball Hall of Fame re-installed the Robinson plaque with revised wording to recognize his considerable achievements in establishing and promoting civil rights.

> "A Player of Extraordinary Ability Renowned for His Electrifying Style of Play," the words on the new plaque begin before reciting several ... statistics. They then conclude, thankfully, with, "Displayed Tremendous Courage and Poise in 1947 When He Integrated the Modern Major Leagues in the Face of Intense Adversity." In a very real sense, Jackie Robinson also integrated America [Dave Anderson in the *New York Times*, June 26, 2008].

However, in Negro League baseball, there was a sacrifice to be made for the progress achieved. As the first Negro to be allowed into organized baseball—the Major League clubs and the associated minor leagues and teams—in half a century, Robinson not only made it possible for blacks to begin to challenge for major league and minor league jobs, but set in motion the rapid decline of the Negro Leagues. While star players and the best of the "up and comers" could visualize buttoning up a major league jersey one day, many other black players, primarily veterans, faced dwindling opportunities in the United States.

With baseball flourishing north of the border, Canada became an attractive option for many Negro and Caribbean players. For a few, it was a beginning, as opportunities for blacks in Canada attracted some younger athletes not yet experienced enough to win jobs in the remnants of the Negro Leagues or to gain the attention of the farm systems in organized ball. For some, signed to pro contracts, an assignment to a Canadian team often meant fewer hassles for the player and the club.

There was a history of integrated teams in the West, even in small communities such as Broadview, Saskatchewan which brought in Negro imports in the mid and late 1930s. In 1925 John Donaldson, one of the greatest Negro players, had been a part of an integrated team in Saskatchewan. Winnipeg was a regular stop for black and other barnstorming teams, including the famous Bismarck, North Dakota club of 1935 which featured Satchel Paige, Quincy Trouppe, Hilton Smith, Double Duty Radcliffe, among others. The integrated Bismarck semi-pro team was a familiar sight at Osborne Stadium in Winnipeg especially in the period just before and after their triumph at the inaugural National Baseball Congress Tournament in 1935.

Marvin Ligon, whose uncle operated the Ligon Colored All-Stars, a regular barnstorming feature on the prairies in the late 1940s and early 1950s, found color to be quite an attraction.

> We could come and go and stay in the hotels and things without any problem in Canada.... A black face was somewhat unique out there on the prairies. We'd go into areas there where they had never seen one and so they were coming out to see the black faces as much as the baseball game.

What follows is an encyclopedia of African-American and Caribbean players, mainly those who came to Canada in the late 1940s up to 1960 (when all the major league teams had finally been integrated), the "after Robinson" period with the most noticeable influx of dark-skinned athletes on baseball rosters in Canada. Past 1960, we've included notes on a few players who suited up on semi-pro teams in Canada as the Great White North seemed to be one of few alternatives when even the barnstorming teams began to close shop. And, we couldn't ignore Coco Laboy, even though his tenure was a tad outside the guideline. If we've missed anyone, we apologize and ask for any information you can provide on missing players (email: info@attheplate.com).

You will note the inclusion of several black athletes of the late 1800s and early 1900s. They were among the players affected as baseball closed the door to blacks and bricked up the entranceway. And there is note of players who integrated baseball in Quebec and the prairies in the mid 1930s.

The year 1881 is noted as the "beginning" as, no other than Bud Fowler, known as the first black professional baseball player, was forced to give up on baseball in Canada because of racial attitudes. Ontario's Guelph Maple Leafs recruited him but teammates refused to play if he were on the team. Signed by the nearby Petrolia Imperials, Fowler's new teammates spoke volumes with their gloves. In the new pitcher's first start, they booted the ball on 19 occasions. Fowler got the message and moved on, again.

Our research led to some of the same difficulties in categorization which had earlier baffled baseball and other reporters. In the period before Jackie Robinson integrated organized ball, many Cubans, light-skinned Cubans, had been allowed to play, even in the major leagues. For some, it wasn't primarily about color, but ethnicity.

> Renowned black sportswriter and editor Art Rust, Jr., was one of the earliest to question a well-established historical myth: "I have always been convinced that Jackie Robinson was not the first black man in the modern major leagues," wrote Rust. "The Washington Senators in the mid-thirties and forties were loaded with Latin players of darker hue, who because they spoke Spanish got away with it" [quoted by Rogosin, *Invisible Men*, 159]. Negro-league historian Donn Rogosin struck a similar note in suggesting that big-league scouts bypassed the "Black Babe Ruth,"

Cristobal Torriente, only because of unacceptable kinky hair and a flat African nose and that Negro-leaguer Quincy Trouppe was once told by scouts that he might be signable if only he would learn Spanish so that he might pass for a "foreigner" instead of an American black [*Baseball with a Latin Beat*, Peter C. Bjarkman, p.203].

Cleveland Grant, a star on the Ligon All-Stars, says the team took advantage of the differences:

Felix Valdez and Chino Valdez from Cuba ... they were brothers, one was light skinned the other was dark and had kinky hair and one had kind of straight hair. We'd play in Louisiana sometimes and the light skinned one could go into places and get food and bring it out to his brother because he had the darker skin they wouldn't let him in there. In Canada we had no problems whatsoever. It was a big change.

This compilation likely includes a few players who, according to the precedents of organized baseball at the time, might have been eligible to sidestep the color bar, but for the most part you'll find players who just found a level of opportunity in Canada where it did not exist south of the border. Keep in mind that it took the Boston Red Sox until 1959, 12 years after Robinson's debut with Brooklyn, to field its first black player.

Not all who came north were on the downside of their careers. Of those individuals who were the first to integrate the then sixteen major league teams, seven arose from baseball backgrounds in Canada.

Following are the Canadian leagues and teams in which Black and Caribbean players, mainly on integrated teams, competed.

British Columbia

Vancouver Canadians (Pacific Coast League)
Vancouver Capilanos (Western International League)

Alberta

Edmonton Eskimos (Western International League)
Calgary Bronchos/Stampeders (Western International League)
Western Canada League
Canadian-American League
Southern Alberta League
Big Six League
Foothills League
Wheat Belt League
Foothills—Wheat Belt League

Saskatchewan

Western Canada League
Canadian-American League
Saskatchewan League
Southern League

Preface

Manitoba-Saskatchewan League
Saskatoon & District League
Northern Saskatchewan League
Indian Head Rockets
Florida Cubans
Ligon's Colored All-Stars

Manitoba

Winnipeg Goldeyes (Northern League)
ManDak (Manitoba-Dakota) League
Northern Senior League
Manitoba Senior Baseball League
Manitoba-Saskatchewan League

Ontario

Ottawa Nationals/Senators (Border League)
Ottawa Athletics (International League)
Toronto Maple Leafs (International League)
Kingston Colonials (Border League)
Intercounty League

Quebec

Montreal Royals (International League)
Quebec Provincial League

New Brunswick

Semi Pro teams

Nova Scotia

Halifax and District League

Several of the teams were all-black or nearly so. The Indian Head Rockets, representing the small Saskatchewan community near Regina, were an all-black American team—the Jacksonville, Florida, Eagles—in new uniforms. The Florida Cubans were a barnstorming team which settled down for a season (1953) to be the Indian Head Rockets as most of the Rockets of 1952 moved on to Regina in 1953 to play as the Regina Caps. In 1950 the Winnipeg Buffaloes captured the title in the inaugural year of the ManDak League with an all-black import roster with the exception of cameo appearances by one or two local players. Victoria, B.C. had the Brown Bombers and Halifax, Nova Scotia and London and Chatham, Ontario, had well regarded all-black squads (in 2002, the Toronto Blue Jays wore replica jerseys of the Chatham All-Stars in a regular American League game to commemorate Negro baseball).

Many small towns would hire a couple of imports to help their town teams in the very competitive tournaments which became a staple of a summer on the prairies. It was not unusual to have several all-black or mainly black barnstorming teams entered in the competitions.

We've attempted to include statistics and highlights of play in Canada or with Canadian teams. The categories are familiar. Among those used for hitters are batting average, doubles, triples, home runs, runs batted in and stolen bases. For pitchers, we've tried to compile statistics on games pitched, games started, games completed, wins, losses, and earned run average.

Growing up in Lloydminster (on the Alberta-Saskatchewan border) Jay-Dell (Harvey in those days) became a fan of the Western Canada League. As a youngster he was the bat boy, clubhouse boy, reporter, and stats guy for the Lloydminster Meridians. His dad's restaurant, the Elite Café, was a central gathering spot for players and fans and the family became close to many of the players. Several stayed with the family during their Canadian tours.

Barry's dad was a big baseball fan and would take him to many a ManDak League game or he would jump on the street car with friends and head down town to Osborne Stadium in Winnipeg. When the game was over we would wait for the players to come out and get autographs.

The players left lasting memories for both.

In the early stages of our research, we were fortunate to make contact with Bill Guenthner who had some of the same interests as he began a project on his old hometown team, the Minot, North Dakota, Mallards. We were eager to assist each other and when we discovered information, particularly on the Negro Leaguers and Caribbean players it was shared.

We have had so many contribute to our research and we are most appreciative of their generosity. Among the players profiled here who responded to our appeals for assistance were Nat Bates, Lyman Bostock Sr., Sherwood Brewer, Sherman Cottingham, Wilmer Fields, Dirk Gibbons, Cleveland Grant, Pumpsie Green, Marvin Ligon, Walter McCoy, Ira McKnight, Modie Risher, Ron Teasley, Len Tucker, Armando Vasquez, Jimmy Wilkes, Willie "Curly" Williams, and Roberto Zayas. Sadly, several have since passed away. In addition, we were pleased to have made contact with the families of Frazier Robinson, Cowan "Bubba" Hyde, Curtis Tate and Ike Jackson.

Many other former players provided significant assistance along the way. They include, in alphabetical order, Jack Altman, Barry Arnett, Brack Bailey, Charlie Beene, Tom Bergeron, Tedd Bogal, Len Breckner, Mark Cameron, Reg Chopp, Gordon Elliott, Al Endriss, Mark Flynn, Johnny Ford, Emile Francis, Jim Garrett, Bill Gatenby, Leroy Gregory, Gary Harrison, Hub Kittle, Jim Lester, Dr. Andrew Lillie, Bob Linck, Chuck McGuigan, Jim Miller, Steve Molinari, David Moriarty, Tom Mulcahy, Conrad "Connie" Munatones, John Noce, Cliff Pemberton, Clark Rex, Phil Risinger, Bill Schulz, Gladwyn Scott, Greg Seastrom, Sterling Slaughter, Wayne Stephenson, Don Stewart, Ron Stillwell, Jules Swick, Roy Taylor, Roger Tomlinson, Bill "Willie" Walasko, Joe Weremy, Gord Wesley, Ed Williams, Bill Young, John Zeeben, and Dale Zeigler.

And, we've been blessed to have such a responsive public from fellow researchers and journalists to family members of former players to librarians and archivists, to just a lot of folks interested in our project. We extend our deep thanks to: Lois Bentley, Leola Brost, Tony Campos Jr., Doug Culbreth, Keith Davidson, Jan Derwores, Phil Dixon, Dan Doyle, Pat Doyle,

Stephen Harding, Tom Hawthorn, Bill Hoover, Marlene Isnor, Dave Kemp, Bill Kirwin, Neil Lanctot, Cesar Lopez, Lil Lowe, Ken McCabe, Kevin McCann, Lil McLean, Rodney McLean, Kyle McNary, T. Kent Morgan, Arch Mullin, Rich Necker, Ray Nemec, Tim Novak, Art Olyslager, Royse Paar, Daniel Papillon, Joan Parker, Armand Peterson, Lorne Plaxin, Kelly Powell, Joshua Raisen, Gary Reed, Dr. Layton Revel, Neill Sanders, Dave and Jane Shury, Paul Spyhalski, Wayne Stivers, Norman Thorpe, Christian Trudeau, Eleanor Williams, Lorna Wilson, Lyle Wilson, Bernie Wyatt, and Bill Wynn.

BARRY SWANTON *and* JAY-DELL MAH

Introduction

It was a few minutes past three o'clock as the 5-11½", 190 pound second baseman came to the plate for his first at bat in professional baseball, at least in official "organized ball." Jackie Robinson was old for a rookie having turned 27 at the end of January.

Now, on this sunny, Thursday, April 18th, he faced a big lefty, a recent cut from the New York Giants spring training camp, as the Montreal Royals opened their 1946 International League season at Roosevelt Stadium at Jersey City. It was the first game of a 13-game road trip for the Royals.

Opening Day was a festive occasion in Jersey City. Mayor Frank Hague, near the end of a record 8th consecutive term as the head of the civic government, threw out the ceremonial first pitch. The flamboyant and controversial Hague, the "Boss" of Jersey City for nearly 30 years, treated Opening Day as a civic duty for Jersey City citizens. Schools were closed for the afternoon and city employees were required to purchase tickets for the game. 51,872 tickets were sold. The stadium had seats for just 24,500.

Years later, Jackie's wife, Rachel, noted, "The carnival atmosphere enhanced the excitement and the stress" ("50 Years Ago: Robinson's Jersey Debut," *New York Times*, April 18, 1996).

There was a "slight round of applause" as the rookie began his approach to the batters' box with one out in the top of the first inning (Associated Press, April 19, 1946).

Batting second in the Royals' lineup behind center fielder Marv Rackley, Robinson took the first five pitches from 6'4" Warren Sandel before grounding out to the shortstop, Jaime Almendro. It was a "scorching grounder," according to one story or he "grounded weakly to shortstop" according to another.

Sandel, a four-year pro at age 24, was returning to baseball after a three year stint in the military. The game and the season would be among his worst as he finished the campaign with just one win and eight losses and an earned run average of 6.51.

The Canadian squad scored a pair in the second inning to take the lead. In the third, Robinson came up with two men on base. On the first pitch from Sandel, Robinson drove the ball over the 340 foot sign in left field for a three-run homer.

> It was as if a dam had burst. Roosevelt Stadium exploded with a roar than shook the old park to its foundations [*The Dodgers Encyclopedia*, second ed., William F. McNeil, p. 373].

George Shuba, who followed Robinson in the batting order, was waiting with outstretched hand to congratulate a smiling Robinson as he crossed home plate.

The former U.C.L.A. football star wasn't done. In the fifth inning, the noticeably pigeon-toed infielder beat out a bunt down the third base line. Promptly, he stole second and moved to third on an infield out. With relief pitcher Phil Oates keeping a close watch, Robinson feigned a dash home on the first pitch. As he stopped and returned to third the crowd roared.

> Robinson's dancing up and down the basepath so unsettled Oates that the pitcher hesitated in his delivery and Robinson was awarded home plate on a balk. The stadium erupted once more,

as fans laughed, screamed and stamped their feet [William Brown, *Baseball's Fabulous Montreal Royals*, p. 102].

In the 7th inning, with the Royals comfortably ahead, Robinson came to the plate for his fourth time at bat. He belted a single to right, again stole second, and scored on a triple by John "Spider" Jorgenson.

The next frame, Robinson again pushed a bunt to the third base side, just out of the reach of pitcher Herb Andrews. He moved around to third on infield outs and then began to pester Andrews. A big lead, a dash down the line, an abrupt stop. A feint here and move there. He was so convincing a flustered Andrews was called for a balk and Robinson scored his fourth run.

In five trips, Robinson made four hits, one a three-run homer, scored four times, drove in four runs and stole two bases as the Royals clobbered the hometown Giants 14–1.

Robinson had broken baseball's color barrier with a sensational display. The first black in organized baseball in the modern era, had, under intense scrutiny, made it look easy.

> Remnants of a crowd of more than 25,000 almost pulled the shirt off Robinson's back as the game ended as the young second baseman was kept busy for several minutes shaking hands and autographing score cards. The Royals' clubhouse was a mad scene after the final out with well-wishers fighting to get in to congratulate Robinson, who was so excited he had to tie his necktie three or four times [Associated Press, April 19, 1946].

When Robinson had signed with the Dodgers in the fall of 1945, *The Sporting News*, the "Bible of baseball," wasn't impressed.

> "It is quite conceivable," the paper wrote, "that the story has received far more attention than it is worth." Noting the technicality that Robinson had been signed by the Montreal Royals, Brooklyn's top farm club, the weekly paper said "Robinson has not been signed by the Dodgers, and insofar as can be discerned, never will play for the Brooklyn club in the National League [*The Sporting News*, November 1, 1945, p. 4].

Robinson had stunning debut season. With just one summer of professional baseball experience (with the Negro League Kansas City Monarchs) he not only survived, but excelled in leading the Montreal Royals to 100 wins, the team's best-ever finish. They captured the International League pennant as Robinson won the batting title with a .349 average. He led the league in runs, 113, and was the runner-up in stolen bases with 40.

In the playoffs, the Royals topped Newark, then Syracuse to win the right to compete in the Junior World Series against a team from the south, the Louisville Colonels, winners in the American Association. Royals won the opener in Louisville, but dropped the next two to return to Delorimier Stadium facing an uphill battle.

In the first of three games in Montreal, Robinson scored the tying run in the 9th inning then drove in the winner with the bases loaded in the 10th as the Royals notched a 6–5 triumph. The next night, Robinson again was the star in a 5–3 victory. He doubled and scored in the 1st inning, tripled and scored what proved to be the winner in the 7th and knocked in an insurance run in the 8th. Then, in a win which touched off a scene of Robby-mania, the self-professed "guinea pig" had two hits and was central in double plays in the 6th and 9th innings to preserve a 2–0 win and the championship.

"We want Robinson, we want Robinson" cheered the crowd which refused to leave the stadium. It was a celebration, a scene of adoration, never before seen in the city.

> Jackie came out and the crowd surged on him. Men and women of all ages threw their arms around him, kissed him, pulled and tore at his clothes, and then carried him around the infield

on their shoulders shouting themselves hoarse ... Jackie ran out with the mob running after him ... for three blocks they chased him, until a car pulled up ... and brought him safely to the hotel.... To the large group of Louisville fans who came here with their team, it may be a lesson of goodwill among men. That it's the man and not his color, race or creed. They couldn't fail to tell others down South of the "riots," the chasing of a Negro—not because of hate but because of love [Sam Maltin, *The Pittsburgh Courier*, Oct 12, 1946, p. 24].

Six months later, he took to the field as a Brooklyn Dodger against the Boston Braves. He was a major leaguer. Jackie Robinson was the first black player in the "bigs" since Fleetwood Walker and his brother Welday had brief major league appearances in 1884.

The integration of organized baseball had, for many, an unintended consequence. It was the beginning of the end of the Negro Leagues. As Robinson drew fans to Brooklyn's games at home and on the road, and baseball on radio and television became more than a novelty, attendance at Negro League parks dropped sharply. After the 1947 season, the Newark Eagles and New York Black Yankees called it quits and the Homestead Grays dropped out of league play to return to the road as barnstormers. The Negro National League was through. The Negro American League tried to carry on, but by 1952 there were just six teams and a year later, only four.

The diamonds of the north beckoned. Canada had not always put out the welcome mat for players of color. In 1881, as noted earlier, Bud Fowler found his skin color to be a barrier to playing ball in Canada. Hipple Galloway was a Canadian who played in 1899 with Woodstock, but racial taunts drove him to play in the United States. In 1910 the Western Canada League dumped Dick Brookins, "on the ground that the blood of African chieftains courses through his veins." The Winnipeg Free Press reported most of the teams had objected to Brookins because "a dusky player has no place in organized baseball" (*Winnipeg Free Press*, May 16, 1910, p. X).

In 1911, following complaints about an influx of black immigrants from Oklahoma to the Canadian prairies, the Edmonton Board of Trade urged the Canadian government to put a halt on further immigration.

> We submit that the advent of such negroes as are now here was most unfortunate for the country, and that further arrivals in large numbers would be disastrous.... It is a matter of common knowledge that it has been proved in the United States that negroes and whites cannot live in proximity without the occurrence of revolting lawlessness and the development of bitter race hatred [*Edmonton Capital*, April 25, 1911].

In Ontario, even as late as the 1950s, there were some obvious barriers to blacks.

> [Gentry Jessup] one of the most popular [Galt] Terriers at the time, was almost thwarted when he went to buy a house in town. An old city law forbade land ownership by blacks. When city fathers discovered the antiquated law on the books they quickly had it quashed [David Menary, *Terrier Town: Summer of '49*].

In 1948, Brandon, one of the cities involved in the 1910 Brookins affair in the Western Canada League, applauded its five Negro imports as the Grays marked a return to semi-professional baseball with a championship in the newly formed Manitoba Senior League. A year later, with nine black imports, the Grays had a magical season with 87 wins and 3 ties in a 108-game summer.

It was the beginning of a rush of colored players, from those for whom there's little more than a name, all the way to Hall of Famers.

Of the players to be the first to integrate the sixteen major league teams of the day, seven had roots in Canadian baseball. Robinson (Brooklyn) and Sam Jethroe (Boston Braves) had graduated from Montreal, Bob Trice, the first black on the Philadelphia A's, suited up in both Farnham and St. Hyacinthe, Quebec. Tom Alston (St. Louis Cardinals) attracted notice in the uniform of the Indian Head, Saskatchewan, Rockets. Elston Howard, who integrated the Yankees, polished his catching skills in Toronto, John Kennedy (Philadelphia Phillies) flashed leather in the ManDak League with Winnipeg and Pumpsie Green (Boston Red Sox) spent his summers in the early 1950s in Medicine Hat, Alberta and Indian Head.

For Walter McCoy, a former Negro Leaguer, the Canadian experience was unforgettable.

> The fans were nicer than I ever encountered anywhere. They were so nice, they really treated the ballplayers like human beings, you know, as compared to here in the United States at that time.

McCoy and Jesse Douglas, another former Negro League player, were driving up to Winnipeg for the 1952 season and were approaching Pembina Crossing, north of Fargo, North Dakota.

> As soon as we crossed the border and headed toward Winnipeg, Jesse says, "Homie, you're in God's country now." And, oddly enough, you could feel something different. It seemed like the air was different. There was just a slight breeze in the air, you know. And I know we passed through wheat fields and there was a little bit of rustle of the wheat you know with the wind blowing over the tops and I was saying this is beautiful, really beautiful. There was nothing else in sight, except a highway and wheat fields on both sides. It was the best time of my life, because, in addition to everything else that happened to me, I got married there. I married a girl there in Winnipeg [Walter McCoy Interview, 2008].

> I owe more to Canadians than they'll ever know. In my baseball career they were the first to make me feel my natural self [Jackie Robinson, quoted in *A Sporting Chance*, William Humber, Spider Jones, p. 50].

The Players

Jose Acosta—Pitcher, 5'7", 140 lbs. Batted right, threw right

Acosta, "the half-pint hurling demon," was an accomplished pitcher early in the last century (*Washington Post*, August 28, 1920, p. 8). July 14, 1914, while pitching for the Long Branch Cubans, he fired a no-hitter against the American League's St. Louis Browns. The story of the game, which circulated for months in newspapers across the county, said only twelve pitches were called balls the entire game (*Fort Wayne Journal-Gazette*, July 21, 1914, p. 12).

Acosta was a light-skinned Cuban who played for the New Jersey based Long Branch Cubans when the team played in organized ball in 1914 and the following season when they played as an independent club. Then, for two seasons, he performed in Canada for the Vancouver Beavers of the Class-B, Northwestern League and by 1920 had won a spot in the major leagues with the Washington Senators. Acosta played parts of three seasons in the majors although most of his time was spent in the International League and American Association. His last professional season was 1929 for High Point Pointers in the Piedmont League. During his career he also pitched in Cuba.

A family tragedy? A chart-topping whopper? A Spring Training prank?

March 9, 1917, the *New Castle News* carried a report of a delay, by one of the Washington Senators' Cuban players, in reporting to Spring Training. A letter, reportedly from Jose Acosta, was delivered, by hand, from Cuba, by Yankee outfielder Angel Aragón. It was during the 1917 Cuban insurrection.

> I kiss your hand, but I cannot report for a week, as my venerated father is with the insurrection and may be hanged next week. If my papa is to be hanged I feel that it is my duty to be present as an affectionate son ... my venerable parent is now well along in years, and to be hanged without the presence of his affectionate son might impair his health and hasten his end. As soon as my father is happily hanged I will hasten to report to you. Until then, adios. Jose Acosta.

The newspaper report said the message was from outfielder Jose Acosta. While Jose made it to Washington as a pitcher in 1920, it was his brother Merito who was with Washington as an outfielder 1913–1916 and 1918.

Jose Acosta died in 1977 in Havana. He was 86.

1916 Vancouver Beavers—Won 17, Lost 16
1917 Vancouver Beavers—Won 11, Lost 7

Canadian Highlights: In 1916, he logged 262 innings for Vancouver but, perhaps surprisingly, wasn't the leader. He was seventh behind William Rose of Seattle Giants who put in 319 innings.

"Smokey" Joe Adams—Pitcher. Threw left

Smokey Joe came to Canada with some pretty heady credentials.

> Adams, the most sensational pitcher to cross the colored baseball horizon since Satchel Paige was a rookie ... record indicates he is destined to become one of the great Negro hurlers of all time [*Traverse City Record-Eagle*, July 6, 1949, p. 13].

In 1949, Adams pitched in the Toledo, Ohio, City League and for the barnstorming Komedy Kings of New York. June 19, Adams registered a no-hitter with 20 strikeouts. It brought his strikeout total for his last five games to 84, slightly less than 17 per game. He was up in the ManDak League with Carman Cardinals in 1950 winning just two of six decisions. His career appears to have ended with the 1950 season.

1950 Carman Cardinals—Won 2, Lost 4, G 8, GS 6, CG 3

Canadian Highlights: July 1, Adams fired a six-hitter as Carman shaded Omaha Rockets 2–1 to take top money in the Carman Invitational Tournament. August 24, Adams pitched even better, a three-hitter, only to lose to Brandon as the Cardinal defense committed five errors.

Hank Adkins—Pitcher, 215 lbs. Threw right

A mid-season addition to the 1949 Brandon Greys of the Manitoba Senior League, Adkins was a significant force for a team which stampeded through league, exhibition and tournament play for 87 wins in 108 games. He finished with a pitching mark of 8–0 in 11 starts and a batting average of .294 in 15 games overall. He (originally identified as Leo, or Leon, Adkins) was reported to have come to the Greys from the camp of the Indianapolis Clowns (*Winnipeg Free Press*, June 29, 1949, p. 21).

1949 Brandon Greys—Won 8, Lost 0, 11 GS, 8 CG, .294

Canadian Highlights: In his first game, Adkins pitched in the Brandon Kinsmen Tournament on July 1 and went the distance in beating the touring St. Louis Black Cardinals 6–2. July 4 at Neepawa, Adkins fired a one-hitter to lead the Greys to a 14–1 exhibition win. July 25, he beat the Carman Cardinals 5–4 at the Carman Invitational Tournament. He was the hitting star of the game with two doubles and a single.

Ted "Red" Alexander—Pitcher, 5'10", 220 lbs. Batted right, threw right

The stocky right-handed flinger had a decade of Negro League experience (including stints with the New York Black Yankees, Chicago American Giants, Newark Eagles, Kansas City Monarchs, Homestead Grays and Birmingham Black Barons). His pro career dated back to 1936 with the Miami Clowns and the following season with Chicago's Palmer House Stars. During a 1949 season in which Alexander played for at least four teams (including clubs in the Michigan-Indiana League and the South Minny loop) he ended up with the barnstorming New Orleans Creoles. The London Majors of the Ontario Intercounty League were next, in 1950. He made an immediate impression.

> Mendham [Coach Dan "Uncle Buck" Mendham] described Alexander as "a happy-go-lucky guy, a bit of a showman, yakking all the time." He was real heavy, and the Majors didn't have a uniform big enough to fit him. That's why he started the season in his Homestead Grays outfit [Dan Mendham, *The 1948 London Majors: A Great Canadian Team*].

Alexander pitched in 1950 and most of the 1951 season in London, Ontario and had a brief stay in the ManDak League in 1952 with Brandon. He had the distinction of having played on two of the greatest teams of the Negro Leagues—the Kansas City Monarchs and the Homestead Grays. In a stroke of fortune, he won a championship with each club.

Canadian Highlights: June 16, 1951, Alexander fired a two-hit shutout over ten innings as London shaded Guelph 1–0.

Wally Alexander—Outfield, 5'11", 185 lbs. Batted right, threw right

Signed to a pro contract by the Cardinals, Alexander played four seasons in the St. Louis farm system. 1955 and 1956 were spent with Mexicali in the Arizona-Mexico League before a season in Canada with the Winnipeg Goldeyes. He led Winnipeg with 12 home runs and was second in runs batted in, with 86. Out of organized ball for two summers, he returned for a brief trial in 1960 with Billings of the Pioneer League.

1957 Winnipeg Goldeyes—.267, 18 D, 3 T, 12 HR, 86 RBI

Canadian Highlights: May 17, 1957, Alexander led the offense with a triple, double and single and two runs scored in a 4–0 Winnipeg victory. June 14, the left fielder knocked in five runs with a grand slam homer and two singles in a 7–6 victory over Eau Claire.

Harold Allan—Pitcher. Threw right

The right-hander was a key member of the 1950 Regina Caps of the Southern League in Saskatchewan.

1950 Regina Caps—Won 3, Lost 1, 4 G, 4 GS, 4 CG

Canadian Highlights: July 7, 1950, Allan fired a four-hitter in going the distance against Swift Current. The teams tied 1–1 in a game called because of darkness. July 24, it was a five-hitter as the Caps blasted Notre Dame 16–1. Allan also led the offense with three hits.

Lou Almendariz—Shortstop

Almendariz, a Cuban, played briefly with the Brandon Greys in 1954 and had a three-game fling in organized ball in 1956 in the California League.

Thomas Edison Alston—First Base, 6'5", 210 lbs. Batted left, threw right

Alston was one of seven players with roots in Canadian baseball who won distinction by being the first Afro-Americans to integrate major league teams.

After high school and a stint in the Navy, the tall first-baseman began his career in Negro ball with Goshen/Greensboro (NC) Red Wings and later suited up with the Jacksonville Eagles, a touring club which was enticed to come to Canada in 1950 to play under the banner of the Indian Head Rockets. After two seasons with the Rockets (1950–1951), Alston kicked off his career in organized baseball in the Southwest International League, and quickly made his way up to the San Diego Padres of the Pacific Coast circuit. With a strong 1953 season behind him, the Padres sold his contract to the St. Louis Cardinals in January, 1954.

April 13, 1954, he became the first Afro-American to suit up with St. Louis (two others who played in Western Canada figured in the Cardinals' plans to integrate—Len Tucker had been the first black signed by the Cards and Eloyd Robinson the third).

In 1952, his initial season of pro ball, Alston must have thought he had never left Canada as nearly a dozen of his teammates with Porterville, California of the Southwest International League had played on the prairies (including Jesse Blackman, Walt Tyler, Les Witherspoon and the team's manager, Chet Brewer). He was the Southwest's All-star first-baseman.

Alston died in December, 1993 in Winston-Salem, North Carolina after a troubled life following his baseball career. He was 67.

1950 Indian Head Rockets—Statistics not available
1951 Indian Head Rockets—.330 (incomplete)

The Indian Head Tournament was a magnet for barnstorming teams in the late 1940s and early 1950s. Ligon's Colored All-Stars captured the inaugural event in 1947. The Indian Head Rockets took top prize money in 1950 and the Florida Cubans took the crown in 1952 over Hardwood Sports of Baton Rouge in what the National Baseball Congress called the first "all–Negro" final in tournament history (photograph courtesy Ken McCabe, Indian Head Sports Hall of Fame and Museum).

Canadian Highlights: August 3, 1950, Alston went four for five to lead Indian Head to a 17–6 win over North Battleford to take top prize in the Rosetown Tournament. July 3, in a tie game with Regina, Alston punched out four hits.

July 7, 1951, in the second game of a twin-bill, Alston belted a pair of home runs and started a triple play as Indian Head trounced Swift Current 13–5. July 14, Alston and Bobby Prescott (who, like Alston, advanced to the major leagues) each had three hits to pace the Rockets to a 21–0 demolishing of Estevan. July 19, he was named as the All-star first baseman at the Indian Head Tournament. July 21, Alston and Prescott again each had three hits as Indian Head stretched its league winning streak to 18 games in an 11–2 win over Moose Jaw Canucks. July 25, Alston, the Rockets' cleanup hitter, had two hits and drove in a pair as Indian Head captured its 21st consecutive win in league play, 10–0 over Moose Jaw.

Higinio Alvarez—Outfield

The Cuban outfielder was a major offensive force for the Regina Braves of the Western Canada League in 1958. He tied for the league lead in home runs, with 10, finished 5th in the batting race, at .351, and was among the leaders in runs batted in, with 45. He led outfielders in assists with 13, nearly twice the number of the next best. Alvarez came to Canadian ball after brief stints in the Mexican League and with Havana Sugar Kings of the International League.

1958 Regina—.351, 10 HR, 45 RBI

Canadian Highlights: July 1, 1958, Alvarez had three hits in the first game and a two-run homer in the second as Regina trounced Moose Jaw 18–7 and 8–6. July 8, Alvarez took over the lead in the batting race with a .420 average. July 26, he knocked in four runs with a pair of homers and a single in an 8–6 win over Williston.

Mario Amaro—Pitcher, 6'0", 170 lbs. Batted right, threw right

The right-hander was barely out of his teens when he arrived in Canada from Cuba in 1952. Amaro joined the Brandon Greys for the first of two seasons in the ManDak League. Later, he advanced to organized ball for two years of play in the Arizona–New Mexican League.

1952 Brandon Greys—Won 5, Lost 3
1953 Brandon Greys—Won 2, Lost 6

Canadian Highlights: June 18, 1952, on loan to Winnipeg for tournament play, Amaro went 12 innings to down Brandon 4–3 and advance the Giants to the tourney final. June 24, he fanned nine in a 4–2 win over Carman. July 3, Amaro held Winnipeg to seven hits in Brandon's 3–1 triumph. July 31, he singled in the winning run, after pitching a seven-hitter, to beat Winnipeg 5–3.

1952 Brandon Greys pitcher Mario Amaro (left), outfielder Joe Mitchell and playing-manager Willie Wells, Sr. (photograph courtesy Lois Bentley).

Edmundo "Sandy" Amoros—Outfield, 5'8", 170 lbs. Batted left, threw left

Amoros made the most famous catch in Brooklyn history. It led to the Dodgers first ever World Series victory.

October 4, 1955, the Dodgers had charged back from a 2-0 game deficit to tie the series with the Yankees at three games each. In the bottom of the 6th inning, in the decisive seventh game, the Yankees had runners on first and second with none out. Billy Martin had walked and Gil McDougald reached on a bunt single. Dodger manager Walter Alston had made what turned out to be a brilliant defensive substitution sending Sandy Amoros to left field.

A tiring Johnny Podres faced Yankee catcher Yogi Berra and the Brooklyn outfield shifted way over to right, with Amoros nearly in center field. On an outside pitch from Podres, Berra sliced one to the left field corner, looking good for at least a game-tying double. But, the fleet Cuban sped to the ball, making a sensational catch with his right arm fully extended. He turned and fired to shortstop Pee Wee Reese who relayed to Gil Hodges at first to double up McDougald and end the Yankee threat. Three innings later, "Dem Bums" had their first World Series title.

> Frequently asked about his famous catch, Mr. Amoros always tried to oblige, but as he once put it in broken English that drew no argument in Brooklyn, "It really too good to describe" [*New York Times*, June 28, 1992].

Amoros played with the Dodgers in parts of seven seasons. His best year was in 1956 when he hit .260 with 16 home runs in just 292 at bats. He ended his pro career in the Mexican League in 1962. He had begun his career in the Negro League in 1950 with the New York Cubans. Signed by the Dodgers he spent parts of four seasons with the club's top farm team, the Montreal Royals.

Amoros died in 1992 at the age of 62.

1953 Montreal Royals—.353, 40 D, 11 T, 23 HR, 100 RBI
1954 Montreal Royals—.352, 5 D, 4 T, 14 HR, 50 RBI
1958 Montreal Royals—.260, 29 D, 2 T, 16 HR, 62 RBI
1959 Montreal Royals—.301, 33 D, 5 T, 26 HR, 79 RBI

Bill Anderson—Pitcher, 5'10", 185 lbs. Batted right, threw right

Anderson came to Brandon in 1951 from eight years of Negro League experience mainly with the New York Cubans and Homestead Grays.

1951 Brandon Greys—Won 2, Lost 1, 7 G, 3 GS, 1 CG

Canadian Highlights: May 22, Anderson went the distance pitching Brandon to a 5-2 win over Carman for their first win of the season. He helped at the plate with a homer and single.

Orinthal "Andy" Anderson—Outfield/Pitcher, 6'0", 170 lbs. Batted left, threw right

The versatile Anderson split the 1951 season between Carman of the ManDak League and the Negro League's Chicago American Giants.

Before first coming to Canada in '51, Anderson had experience in South Bend, Indiana in 1950. He moved into organized ball in 1952 playing mainly in the Class-A, Western League to 1955. His best pro season may have been the 1953 campaign with Denver Bears of the Pittsburgh farm system where he hit .305 with 18 home runs. He also played in the semi-pro Southern Minny League with Rochester in 1955 and had a 7-2 pitching record and a .305 batting average. In 1956 and 1957, he was with the Minot Mallards in the ManDak League.

1951 Carman Cardinals—.273, 1 HR, 6 RBI, Won 0, Lost 2
1956 Minot Mallards—.262, 7 D, 7 HR, 18 RBI, Won 0, Lost 1
1957 Minot Mallards—.248, 11 D, 4 T, 4 HR, 37 RBI, Won 1, Lost 0

Stanley Robert "Gabby" Anderson—Center Field, 5'11", 175 lbs. Batted left

Born in Detroit, Anderson's family came to London, Ontario when he was just a few months old. He grew up in a baseball family as his father and uncle were prominent on a Negro team in the London area. He played junior ball in London and signed a contract in 1950 to play in organized ball.

In a five-year pro career, interrupted by service in the U.S. Army, Anderson's batting marks included seasons of .335, .355 and .394. In 1951 in the PONY League he drove in 124 runs. He returned to London in 1957 to begin a 10-year stint in local ball. He won batting titles in 1957 and 1960, and was runner-up in 1958 and 1959, when he also won MVP honors. He was an all-star selection eight times. Gabby's number 5 was retired by the London club.

1957 London—.403
1958 London—.398
1959 London—.420
1960 London—.391

Curly Andrews—Second Base

Andrews joined the Estevan Maple Leafs of the Western Canada League in 1951 after first coming to Canada with Ligon's Colored All-Stars, a barnstorming team from Texas and California. He had played for and managed teams in Galveston, Texas and was back in 1953 to play for the Indian Head Rockets.

1951 Estevan Maple Leafs—.200 (incomplete)

John "Sonny" Andrews—Shortstop/Outfield, 5'7", 175 lbs. Threw right

After playing for Negro teams in the Detroit area (including time as the "sensational shortstop" of the Toledo Cubs) Andrews traveled north to Canada (*Traverse City Record Eagle*, May 29, 1946, p. 10).

In 1949, he suited up for the Carman Cardinals in the Manitoba Senior Baseball League and ended up playing another four seasons with the Cardinals when they were in the more advanced ManDak League. On July 29, 1950, Maurice Smith, writing in the Winnipeg Free Press, noted, "You won't see any better plays in the major leagues then what were made by Carman's shortstop Sonny Andrews. They were really gems." In 1955 Andrews played for Galt in the Intercounty League.

1949 Carman Cardinals—.366
1950 Carman Cardinals—.333, 19 D, 2 HR, 25 RBI
1951 Carman Cardinals—.264, 4 HR, 24 RBI
1952 Carman Cardinals—.280, 4 HR, 30 RBI
1953 Carman Cardinals—.268, 5 HR, 29 RBI

Canadian Highlights: June 11, 1949, Andrews had five hits and drove in three as Carman walloped Brandon 17–8.

June 23, 1950, Andrews punched out four hits and had a steal of home in Carman's 6–5 win over Winnipeg. July 10, he led the Cardinals to a 14–8 trouncing of Minot with a homer and two doubles. August 6, Andrews went 4 for 5 in an 8–7 loss to Minot. August 21, Andrews had three hits and scored three runs in a 12–1 trouncing of Elmwood. In 1950 he led the circuit in doubles with 19 and won a free suit of clothes, when he slammed a ball off an Osborne Stadium billboard advertising the free garb.

June 12, 1951, outstanding in the field, Andrews had five hits, including a triple to drive in all the Carman runs in a 4–0 shutout over Brandon. July 25, Andrews' three-run homer was the winning blow as Carman stopped Elmwood 6–2. August 3, Andrews drove in four runs with a triple and two singles in an 11–4 rout of Minot. In 1951 the squat shortstop—outfielder was described as "sensational both on the basepaths and in the outer pastures" and "mercury-footed" as he registered four steals, including one of home in a September 2nd playoff game (*Winnipeg Free Press*, September 3, 1951, p. 15).

June 4, 1952, He drove in three runs with a triple, double and a single in a 12–6 victory over Winnipeg. August 16, he had four singles in a win over Minot.

May 31, 1953, Andrews punched out three hits in a 7–6 win over Minot. He followed that the next day with three more hits as Carman beat Brandon 11–6. July 29, fans and players held Sonny Andrews Night in Carman to show their appreciation for Andrews.

July 1, 1955, Andrews belted a two-run homer in an 11–3 win for Galt over London. August 1, Andrews had three hits in a 10–4 win over Oshawa. August 24, he had four hits for Galt in a losing cause to St. Thomas.

Orlando Andux—Shortstop, 5'8", 150 lbs. Batted right

The agile shortstop came north from Cuba in 1951 for a stint in the Border League and moved on to join Drummondville of the Quebec Provincial League in 1952. After his season with the Brandon Greys in the ManDak League, in 1953, he played briefly with Lancaster of the Piedmont League the following summer.

> 1952 Drummondville Cubs—.179, 3 HR, 24 RBI
> 1953 Brandon Greys—.245, 0 HR, 17 RBI

Canadian Highlights: June 6, 1953, Andux had a triple and double in a loss to Carman. June 17, he belted two doubles and a single in a win over Winnipeg. July 13, the Cuban shortstop laid down two bunt singles and clouted a triple in Brandon's 10–3 win over Minot. September 2, Andux belted a two-run homer to give Brandon a 4–2 win over Carman. September 12, Andux had three hits in a 9–8 loss to Minot.

Tex Anthony—Outfield

Anthony, who had played for the Louisiana Black Travelers in the late 1940s and toured in Western Canada as the manager with the Muskogee Cardinals in 1949, returned in 1950 to suit up with the Estevan Maple Leafs of the Western Canada League. He was a mid-season addition to the club which, just a month into the season, had only one player remaining from the season-opening roster.

Orlando Arango—Pitcher. Threw right

The Cuban pitcher spent two seasons in Canada, in 1952 with the Florida Cubans and 1954 in the livery of the Indian Head Rockets.

Canadian Highlights: May 2, 1952, in a warm-up for the Cubans' Canadian tour, Arango fired a five-hitter and went 3 for 3, with a pair of doubles at the plate, as the Cubans topped Galveston, Texas, Seals 7–1. Arango, who fanned eight, allowed a run in the opening frame then pitched shutout ball the rest of the way.

Dionisio Cesar Argudin—Second Base, 5'9", 160 lbs. Batted right

The Cuban import joined the Brandon Greys for a month of the 1952 season before being released. Argudin then signed with the St. Louis Cardinals and played three seasons in organized ball, including one back in Canada, in 1956, with the Winnipeg Goldeyes of the Class-C, Northern League.

> 1952 Brandon Greys—.293, 0 HR, 2 RBI
> 1956 Winnipeg Goldeyes—.211, 0 HR, 5 RBI

Canadian Highlights: Known for his defensive ability, Argudin received particular praise for a May 5, 1956, game with the Goldeyes in which he made several glittering stops, one of which was compared to the best of any major league player. He made seven putouts and figured in fourteen plays, not bad for a second sacker.

Rudy Arias—Pitcher, 5'10", 165 lbs. Batted left, threw left

The Cuban lefthander had an 11-year career, including 34 games (2–0, 4.09) in the majors with the White Sox in 1959. He spent most of his time in Triple-A, including a "cup of coffee" with the Toronto Maple Leafs in 1956.

> 1956 Toronto Maple Leafs—Won 0, Lost 1, 5.40

Juan "Army" Armenteros—Catcher/Third Base, 5'11", 190 lbs. Batted right, threw right

A 19-year-old Armenteros began his baseball travels in 1952 as a member of the touring Havana Cubans where his play attracted the notice of Negro League legend Buck O'Neill, then managing the Kansas City Monarchs. The Havana native then spent three years with the Monarchs often drawing flattering reviews. In a 1953 newspaper report, the Monarchs were said to have three young players certain to receive big league tryouts. First mentioned was the young catcher.

> Armenteros, 21 year old Cuban catcher, is the top prospect with no less than seven clubs bidding for his services. He is said to

be the best catcher to play in the Negro major league since Roy Campanella played with the Newark Eagles [*Charleston Daily Mail*, August 18, 1953, p. 9].

The second player noted was shortstop Ernie Banks.

Armenteros moved into organized ball in 1956 with the El Paso Texans of the Southwestern League. The St. Louis Cardinals noticed his .317, 17 home run, season and took him aboard with an assignment to the Class-C, Winnipeg Goldeyes for 1957. He did okay, .251, 10 homers, and moved up to Class-B the next season and Class-A in 1958 which turned out to be his final year in pro ball.

1957 Winnipeg Goldeyes—.251, 12 D, 3 T, 10 HR, 46 RBI

Canadian Highlights: May 13, Armenteros had two key hits and two RBI in a 5–3 win over Wausau. May 24, his three hits led the Goldeyes to a 9–3 win over Duluth-Superior. June 10, the Winnipeg Free Press reported that "Army" continued to be a bright spot for the Goldeyes defensive unit. In the game against Wausau he had picked a runner, Don Mincher, off third base. It was noted "Army" loved to throw the ball and the result was few stolen bases against the Goldeyes.

Alfred "Buddy" Armour—Infield/Outfield, 5'9", 170 lbs. Batted left, threw right

From 1936 to 1948, Armour had a productive career in the Negro League. Three times he was chosen as an all-star. In 1949, he toured with the New Orleans Creoles and played for Farnham in the Quebec Provincial League. His last two seasons were spent in Canada with the Granby Red Sox. He died, at age 58, in 1974 at Carbondale, Illinois.

1949 Farnham Black Sox—.348, 8 HR, 67 RBI
1950 Granby Red Sox—.290, 10 D, 4 T, 2 HR, 29 RBI
1951 Granby Red Sox—.262, 28 D, 3 T, 6 HR, 59 RBI

Canadian Highlights: His .348 batting average in 1949 led the Provincial League. He played under the name of "Buddy Wilson" that season to protect his college football eligibility.

Marcelino Arozarena—Utility

A Cuban import, Arozarena played for three summers in Canada. He arrived with the Florida Cubans in 1952 and stayed on to play with the Indian Head Rockets in 1953 and 1954.

Canadian Highlights: June 5, 1952, Arozarena belted a homer and triple as the Florida Cubans upset Indian Head 8–0. June 12, he bashed a grand slam homer as the Cubans advanced the final of the Lloydminster Tournament with a 10–5 win over North Battleford.

June 13, 1954, playing shortstop and hitting leadoff, Arozarena had a double and two singles to lead Indian Head over North Battleford 4–2. The next day he had to be carried from the field after being struck in the head by a thrown ball while running the bases. July 16, Arozarena chipped in with two doubles and a single in a loss to Saskatoon.

Earl Ashby—Catcher, 5'11", 185 lbs. Batted right, threw right

The Cuban backstop once was considered as a replacement for Negro League legend Josh Gibson. Ashby had Negro League experience with the Cleveland Buckeyes, Homestead Grays, Birmingham Black Barons and Newark Eagles from 1945 to 1948 and added winter ball tours in Mexico and Panama. In 1947 the Grays put Ashby behind the plate as Gibson, at age 35, had died of a stroke shortly before the start of the 1947 season. However, Ashby hit just .254 with no homers. In 1950 he was up in Canada to play in the Quebec Provincial League and hit .292 in 22 games.

1950 Drummondville/St. Jean—.292, 2 HR, 9 RBI

Joe Atkins—Outfield, 6'1", 190 lbs. Batted right, threw right

Atkins had three years in the Negro League, from 1945 to 1947, with the Pittsburgh Crawfords and Cleveland Buckeyes before a 1948 stint with Farnham in the Quebec Provincial League. For the next six seasons he played in organized or semi-pro ball in the United States or Canada. In 1951 he was with Drummondville in the Quebec Provincial League. In 1953 he joined the Carman Cardinals in the Man-Dak League and in 1954 played briefly with Ottawa in the International League.

> 1949 Farnham Red Sox—.253, 21 HR, 71 RBI
> 1951 Drummondville Cubs—.268, 18 HR, 73 RBI
> 1953 Carman Cardinals—.294, 7 HR, 40 RBI
> 1954 Ottawa A's—.154, 1 HR, 3 RBI

Canadian Highlights: Merritt Clifton, in his book on the Provincial League, wrote that Atkins was one of the best players in the league.

June 22, 1953, Atkins' three-run homer was a spark as Carman whipped Winnipeg 15–8. June 28, another three-run homer was the big blow in the Cardinals' 10–2 win over Winnipeg. August 31, his two-run, four-bagger was the difference as Carman edged Winnipeg 3–2 in a sudden-death playoff.

Frank Austin—Shortstop, 5'7", 168 lbs. Batted right, threw right

Austin, one of few players from Panama, played in the Negro League from 1944 to 1948 with the Philadelphia Stars. In 1949, he started the season in Triple-A with Newark in the International League and ended up in the Pacific Coast loop. He spent eight seasons in the Pacific circuit, including one in Vancouver. Austin died in 1960 in Panama.

> 1956 Vancouver Mounties—.285, 14 D, 0 T, 0 HR, 27 RBI

Andy/Aquillon "A.Q." Bailey—Utility

Bailey toured Western Canada as a member of Ligon's Colored All-Stars in 1949 and 1950 before jumping to the North Battleford Beavers during the 1950 season. He was among the top hitters in the Saskatoon and District Baseball League

> 1949–1950 Ligon All-Stars—Statistics not available
> 1950 North Battleford Beavers—.341

Canadian Highlights: June 15, 1949, in a twin-bill at Regina, Bailey had two hits as the Ligon catcher in the first game and three safeties as the second baseman in the nightcap.

June 14, 1950, Bailey punched out three hits as the Ligons whipped a Saskatoon all-star squad 14–3. July 19, with his new team—the North Battleford Beavers—he had a triple, double and single in a 12–9 win over Saskatoon Legion. In mid-August, baseball was put on hold as Bailey received notice of his call up into military service.

Miguel "Pedro" Ballestro (Ballester)—Infield, 5'8", 160 lbs. Batted right, threw right

In 1885, Keokuk, Iowa, of the Western League had the distinction of featuring the first Afro-American professional baseball player—John W. "Bud" Fowler. In 1952 it had another—Miguel Ballestro. He had played in the Negro League in 1948 as a shortstop with the New York Cubans and came north in 1951 to join the Sherbrooke Athletics of the Quebec Provincial League. In 1952 he was in organized ball at Keokuk, Iowa, the city which had hosted Fowler nearly seventy years previous. A disappointing season (a batting mark of just .220) led to a demotion to Class-D ball in 1953 in the Wisconsin State League where he rebounded with a .315 average and 18 homers. Ballestro was back in Canada in the Provincial League in 1954 dividing the season between Drummondville and St. Jean. The little infielder played in Mexico in 1955.

> 1951 Sherbrooke Athletics—.282, 24 D, 3 T, 23 HR, 93 RBI
> 1954 Drummondville/St. John—.285, 34 D, 2 T, 12 HR, 60 RBI

Dan Bankhead—Pitcher/Outfield, 6'1", 184 lbs. Batted right, threw right

It was a family affair for the Bankheads. Dan was one of five baseball-playing brothers. He pitched and played the outfield in the Negro League from 1940 to 1947 with the Chicago American Giants, Birmingham Black Barons and Memphis Red Sox and had made stops in Winnipeg in 1942 and 1943 with the Ethiopian Clowns and Black Barons. He went straight from the Negro League to the majors joining the Brooklyn Dodgers on August 26, 1947 to pitch at Ebbets Field. He was the first black pitcher to appear in a major league game. Although he had little success on the mound that day he went into the record book with a home run in his first at bat. That fall, he and Jackie Robinson became the first black players to appear in the World Series. Back in the minors in 1948, he had an outstanding season winning 24 games between Nashua and St. Paul. He followed with a 20–6 campaign in Montreal in 1949, but shoulder woes soon made Bankhead a part-time pitcher. In 1953 he signed with Drummondville, Quebec as a position player. In 1954 he traveled south to Mexico and played another twelve seasons. He died in 1976 in Houston.

> 1949 Montreal Royals—Won 20, Lost 6, 3.76 ERA, .323, 1 HR, 26 RBI
> 1951 Montreal Royals—Won 2, Lost 6, 3.91 ERA, .364, 1 HR, 2 RBI
> 1952 Montreal Royals—Won 0, Lost 1, 6.92 ERA
> 1953 Drummondville Royals—.275, 3 HR, 28 RBI, Won 0, Lost 0

Fred Bankhead—Second Base, 5'11", 170 lbs. Batted right, threw right

After a dozen years in Negro League ball mainly with the Memphis Red Sox, Bankhead was a star with the Ligon Colored All-Stars in their 1949 summer in Western Canada. He had some barnstorming experience in the fall of '48 with the Jackie Robinson All-Stars.

Canadian Highlights: June 13, 1949, Bankhead clicked for three hits in a 10–8 win over Regina Caps.

Sam Bankhead—Infield/Pitcher/Manager, 5'8", 175 lbs. Batted right, threw right

After an outstanding Negro League career, Bankhead put his name in the record book as the first black manager in professional baseball. From 1930 to 1950 he played in the Negro League, including all-star appearances in 1933 and 1936. In a Pittsburgh Courier poll in 1952, he was selected as the first-team utility player on the All-Time, Negro League All-Stars. In 1951 Bankhead was the playing-manager of the Farnham Pirates of the Quebec Provincial League. It marked the first time an African-American had managed a team in organized baseball. At age 45, Bankhead hit .274. He died in 1976 in Pittsburgh.

> 1951 Farnham Pirates—.274, 2 HR, 51 RBI

Jim Banks—Pitcher/Outfield

Banks played the 1950 Negro League season with the Baltimore Elite Giants. In 1952 and 1953 he suited up with the Brandon Greys of the ManDak League.

> 1952 Brandon Greys—Statistics not available
> 1953 Brandon Greys—.276, 1 HR, 18 RBI Won 0, Lost 1, 14 G, 3 GS, 1 CG

Canadian Highlights: July 7, 1952, Banks hit two home runs in an exhibition game win over Indian Head, Saskatchewan.

July 4, 1953, Banks had four hits and knocked in three runs in a 5–4 victory over Moose Jaw.

Norman Banks—Second Base

Banks had Negro League experience with the 1945 Newark Eagles. The light-hitting infielder resurfaced in 1952 in Canada playing in the Saskatchewan Baseball League with the Regina Caps and with Brandon in the ManDak League.

Quincy "Bud" Barbee—Outfield/First Base/Pitcher, 6'0", 195 lbs. Batted right, threw right

Quincy "Bud" Barbee (not to be confused with his older brother Lamb "Bud" Barbee) put in a few games in the Negro League in 1949 with the Louisville Buckeyes and Kansas City Monarchs, but spent most of the season with the St. Jean Braves when they were a non-affiliated club in the Quebec Provincial League. He impressed with a .342 average and 23 home runs. Barbee returned to St. Jean in 1950 when the club lined up in organized ball in a Class-C circuit. His third season in the Provincial League was with the Granby Red Sox in 1951 and in 1952 he moved west to the ManDak League where he batted .279 with the Minot, North Dakota, Mallards.

He showed up in parts of the next three seasons in organized ball with his best effort in 1953 with Pampa of the West Texas–New Mexico League. Barbee put up some big numbers, a .371 average, 34 doubles, 19 homers, 112 runs batted in. But, in that high-octane environment, he was barely among the leaders in any category (.426 was the top batting mark, the leader in doubles had 66, homers 50, RBI 174). One pitcher, with an ERA over 5.00, recorded 25 wins. Barbee closed out his career in 1955 in the Big State League. He died in January 2000 at the age of 85.

   1949 St. Jean Braves—.342, 26 HR, 86 RBI, Won 4, Lost 1
   1950 St. Jean Braves—.284, 11 HR, 35 RBI
   1951 Granby Red Sox—.289, 8 HR, 79 RBI
   1954 Thetford Mines—.286, 3 HR, 14 RBI

Canadian Highlights: Barbee's 26 home runs led the league in 1949.

Roberto "Chico" Barbon—Pitcher/Utility, 5'11", 160 lbs. Batted right, threw right

The barnstorming Florida Cubans had the nineteen year old pitcher/utility player aboard when the club visited in 1952. Barbon returned to Saskatchewan the following season to join another traveling club, the Indian Head Rockets. After a brief stint in organized ball in the United States he became the first Cuban to play in Japan and had a successful eleven-year career in Japanese baseball (10 years with Hankyu Braves, one season with Kintetsu Buffaloes) mainly as a second baseman. He led the country's Pacific League in stolen bases three straight seasons from 1958 to 1960 and compiled a total of 308 steals in his Japanese career.

Canadian Highlights: In 1952, Barbon was "the man" as the Florida Cubans won first prize at the Camrose Tournament. In the final, he drove in two runs and scored another. In winning the semi-final, Barbon went 3 for 3, with a two-run homer, triple and single and registered the pitching victory. Less than three weeks later, he was the top hitter in the Lethbridge Rotary Tournament as the Cubans again took top money.

Frank Barnes—Pitcher, 6'0", 170 lbs. Batted right, threw right

Barnes was a good pitcher with the Kansas City Monarchs at the beginning of the end of the Negro leagues. He had three seasons with the fabled club, 1948 to 1950.

In July 1950, the Yankees, still without a player of color, announced they had purchased two players from the Monarchs, outfielder Elston Howard and Barnes. Both were assigned to the New York farm club at Muskegon in Class-A.

While Howard, converted to a catcher, went on to 9 all-star selections, an MVP award and four World Series, Barnes managed all of one victory in 15 games over three seasons in the majors with the Cardinals. He played for twenty years, wrapping up his career in the Mexican League in 1967.

His second year in organized ball and his second last were among his best. In 1951 in A-Ball, Barnes went 15–6, 3.22. In 1966 with Reynosa in Mexico he finished 17–8, 2.10. 1957 might have been his most satisfying as it prompted his elevation to the majors. His 2.41 ERA for Triple-A, Omaha was best in the American Association and led to a September call up to the Cardinals. Barnes fired six shutouts in Triple-A and set a league record with 41⅓ consecutive scoreless innings. In 1958 he tossed a no-hitter for Omaha, the second of his career. He played parts of five years with Toronto in the International League.

   1951 Toronto Maple Leafs—Won 0, Lost 1
   1952 Toronto Maple Leafs—Won 0, Lost 0
   1954 Toronto Maple Leafs—Won 9, Lost 8, 4.22
   1955 Toronto Maple Leafs—Won 2, Lost 2
   1956 Toronto Maple Leafs—Won 0, Lost 0

Canadian Highlights: May 8, 1954, Barnes fired a four-hitter in a 9–1 win over Montreal. June 30, he turned in a spectacular relief effort as Toronto beat Richmond 11–4. Barnes took over with one out in the first inning and allowed just one hit, with ten strikeouts, the rest of the way.

Tom Barnes—Pitcher/Outfield. Batted right, threw right

After a season in Negro ball for the Memphis Red Sox, Barnes came to Drummondville of the Quebec Provincial League in 1951. In 1952 he played for Three Rivers, an independent team in Quebec, before returning to Memphis for two more seasons of Negro League baseball.

> 1951 Drummondville Cubs—Won 5, Lost 6, 2.32 ERA
> 1952 Three Rivers Yankees—Won 1, Lost 4, 4.97 ERA

Herbert Barney Barnhill—Catcher, 6'0", 175 lbs. Batted right, threw right

Barnhill joined Chet Brewer's Indian Head Rockets in 1951 after a catching career in the Negro League which included stops with the Jacksonville Red Caps, Cleveland Bears, Kansas City Monarchs and Chicago American Giants.

> 1951 Indian Head Rockets—.255 (incomplete)

Wes Barrow—Manager

Barrow managed the New Orleans Black Pelicans (1945), Portland Rosebuds and Nashville Cubs (1946), Baltimore Elite Giants (1947) and New Orleans Creoles in 1950. The veteran manager was hired to guide the Elmwood Giants in the ManDak League in 1951. However, the Giants got off to a slow start and he was replaced by the legendary "Double Duty" Radcliffe after just fourteen games.

Lloyd "Pepper" Bassett—Catcher, 6'3", 220 lbs. Batted both, threw right

Bassett had a lengthy Negro League career from 1936 to 1949 and 1952 to 1954 highlighted by his play in four East-West All-Star games. Bassett was known as the "rocking chair" catcher. In the early 1940s, Bassett perfected his routine while catching for the Ethiopian and Cincinnati Clowns. Even when with the Homestead Grays and Pittsburgh Crawfords he would catch a few innings sitting in a rocking chair, much to the delight of the fans. In 1950 he caught for the New Orleans Crescents and came to Canada in 1951 to join the Brandon Greys in the ManDak League. After that it was back to the Negro League to finish out his career.

> 1951 Brandon Greys—.252, 2 HR, 23 RBI

Canadian Highlights: June 28, 1951, Bassett had a most unusual triple as Brandon came from behind to beat Elmwood 7–6. Down 6–5 with two on in the bottom of the 9th inning, Bassett clouted one way out to right field. Clearly heading out of the park, the ball hit a guy wire and fell back onto the playing field. He was awarded a triple. July 14, Bassett punched out four hits in a 13–3 win over Elmwood. July 30, he had three safeties in a loss to Minot. In playoff action, September 4, Bassett doubled and scored the winner in the 10th as Brandon edged Carman 2–1. September 14, he was behind the plate as Armando Suarez beat the Winnipeg Buffaloes 5–3 to give the Greys the championship.

Nathaniel "Nat" Bates—Pitcher, 6'0". Threw right

Bates (also a high school and college basketball star) was one of a quartet of friends and high school teammates from Richmond, California who ventured north to play for the Medicine Hat Mohawks in 1951 and the Indian Head Rockets in 1952. Bates, Pumpsie Green, Winters Calvin and Willie Reed were neighborhood chums who attended El Cerrito High School and West Contra Costa Junior College. Into 2008, they still kept in touch, living within six or seven miles of each other in Richmond.

"We were treated exceptionally well" said Bates, "people were always respectful. It was a wonderful experience. There were people who had never seen an African-American in person. So we were pioneers to a large extent as we went from town to town."

"Initially, it was a little bit uncomfortable as people would say, "How are you darkie?" Bates said, "It took us time for us to recognize that it was not derogatory but it was just a way of expression. Once we got passed that in terms of their hospitality and their friendliness there was no problem. They were just insensitive in how to approach us. Maybe somehow it got around that it was not necessarily appropriate slang to use and it diminished."

"One of the things we experienced was trying to get a haircut," said Bates, "most barbers didn't know how to cut the African-American's hair and we just took our chances. Some did a good job and some didn't."

In 1953 Bates was drafted into the military and served in Korea. After a lengthy career as a probation department counselor and administrator, Bates began a political career which has included two terms as mayor and nearly three decades of service on Richmond City Council.

> 1951 Medicine Hat Mohawks—Won 7, Lost 4, 13 G, 12 GS, 9 CG

Canadian Highlights: June 27, 1951, Bates fired a five-hit shutout as Medicine Hat blanked Estevan 5–0. July 5, Bates held Regina to six hits as Mohawks notched a 5–1 victory. July 10, Bates held the powerful Estevan Maple Leafs to seven hits as the Medicine Hat Mohawks upset the Leafs 3–2. July 25, Bates had a no-hitter for six innings, finishing with a three-hit performance as Medicine Hat topped Swift Current. August 17, Bates fired a six-hitter, losing his shutout in the 9th in a 16–2 win over Moose Jaw.

Charlie Beamon—Pitcher, 5'11", 195 lbs. Batted right, threw right

The Oakland product advanced to the major leagues for 27 games over parts of three seasons with Baltimore. In his major league debut, September 26, 1956, Beamon fired a four-hitter to beat Whitey Ford 1–0 and deprive the Yankee legend of his 20th win.

He worked his way up from a 1953 beginning in Class-A with Wenatchee in the Western International League. In 1955 Beamon gained considerable attention with a 16–0 record for Stockton in the California League. He had a 1.36 ERA. Beamon, whose son followed him to the majors, was well recognized in Vancouver in the 50s, having spent four seasons with the Triple-A, Mounties.

> 1956 Vancouver Mounties—Won 13, Lost 6, 3.54
> 1957 Vancouver Mounties—Won 12, Lost 10, 3.60
> 1958 Vancouver Mounties—Won 2, Lost 0, 0.00
> 1959 Vancouver Mounties—Won 1, Lost 5, 5.06

August 1, 1956, Beamon stole home, on the front end of a triple steal, in a win over Hollywood. August 3, 1956, he held Hollywood to five hits in notching a 5–1 win. August 12, he captured his fifth straight win, 3–2 over Seattle. August 26, the 21-year-old notched his seventh consecutive triumph, a 3–2, 10-inning triumph over Portland as he knocked in the winning run.

May 26, 1957, in a relief role, Beamon hurled eleven scoreless innings as Vancouver beat Seattle 6–4 in an eighteen-inning thriller. June 22, 1957, he pitched his first shutout of the season blanking Seattle 4–0 allowing just four hits. August 4, he tossed another shutout, 1–0 over San Diego.

Julio Becquer—First Base, 5'11½", 178 lbs. Batted left, threw left

The Havana-born Becquer signed with the Washington Senators in early 1952 and won an assignment to Drummondville in the Quebec Provincial League. He was up with Washington by 1955 and had a seven year major league career. Among his accomplishments, Becquer had 63 pinch hits and was involved in the first all–Cuban triple play. Whitey Herzog hit a ball to pitcher Pedro Ramos, who threw to first baseman Becquer, who relayed the ball to shortstop Jose Valdivielso for the third out. He finished his major league career with a .244 batting average.

> 1952 Drummondville Cubs—.292, 2 HR, 41 RBI

Baldy Benson—Catcher/Manager

Benson, touted as the "Ol' Rocking Chair Catcher" on his visits to Canada with barnstorming teams, had made Western Canadian stops for at least five years before managing the Estevan Maple Leafs for two seasons, 1950 and 1951. Benson, playing-manager of the San Francisco Sea Lions, San Francisco Tigers and Magic City Stars (Minot, North Dakota), often would put on an exhibition of catching (and throwing out runners) while seated in a rocking chair.

Carlos Bernier—Outfield, 5'9", 180 lbs. Batted right, threw right

Bernier, from Puerto Rico, began his professional baseball career in 1948 with Chester,

New York in the Colonial League. He started the following season with Indianapolis in Triple-A, but was released and headed back to the Colonial League to join the Bristol Owls. He led the league with 67 stolen bases. He was in Bristol to start the 1950 season, but the circuit folded in July and Bernier traveled north to the Provincial League in Quebec with St. Jean. Between the two leagues he had 94 stolen bases. He played with the Tampa Smokers in the Florida International League in 1951 and that December was drafted by the Pittsburgh Pirates. He won a spot with the Pirates in 1953 batting .213 with 5 HR and 48 RBI. It was his only season in the major leagues. He went on to an eleven year career in Triple-A. In 2004 he was elected to the Pacific Coast League Hall Of Fame. Over his career he was noted for his base stealing ability.

> Bernier put on his "act" in the first, stealing second on the first pitch and third on the next one.... Bernier is a hard running, aggressive ball player on the diamond, but off the field is one of the nicest young men you'd want to meet [*The Kingston Daily Freeman*, June 20, 1950, p. 13].

He died in 1989 at the age of 62.

1950 St. Jean Braves—.335, 15 HR, 39 RBI, 41 SB

Canadian Highlights: In 1950 Bernier scored 69 runs in 64 games and stole 41 bases.

Mike "Red" Berry—Pitcher, 5'11", 170 lbs. Batted right, threw right

In the fall of 1946, Berry joined Abe Saperstein's All-Stars and followed that with a tour in the Negro League in 1947 with the Kansas City Monarchs. He also suited up with the Harlem Globetrotters traveling team and had experience with clubs in the San Francisco area, including the Sea Lions. In 1951 it was up to Canada to join the Elmwood Giants in the ManDak League. He appeared in just three games.

1951 Elmwood Giants—Won 0, Lost 1

Bill "Fireball" Beverley—Pitcher/Outfield/First Base, 6'0", 182 lbs. Batted right, threw right

The right-hander played in the Negro League from 1950 to 1957 for five different teams. In 1951 Curly Haas, the general manager of the Elmwood Giants in the ManDak League announced that Beverley had signed and was on his way to the Giants, but he never did appear. He pitched in 36 games in the Quebec Provincial League in 1953 with Thetford Mines.

1953 Thetford Mines Miners—Won 7, Lost 10, 4.67 ERA

Joe Black—Pitcher, 6'2", 220 lbs. Batted right, threw right

Before entering organized ball in 1951, Black pitched in the Negro American League for the Baltimore Elite Giants. He split the '51 season between the Dodgers' Triple-A teams, St. Paul Saints of the American Association and Montreal Royals of the International League compiling an 11–12 record. At age 28, he made his major league debut the following season. He broke in with a splash, winning 15 and losing just 4, with a 2.15 ERA. He was selected as National League Rookie of the Year. After a lackluster 1953 season, Black was back in Montreal in 1954. He pitched in three more seasons in the majors, but not again with the success he had in his rookie year. Black died in 2002. He was 78.

1951 Montreal Royals—Won 7, Lost 9, 3.85 ERA
1954 Montreal Royals—Won 12, Lost 10, 3.60 ERA

Jesse James Blackman—Pitcher/Utility. Batted both, threw right

Blackman was born in Goldsboro, North Carolina, and began his career in the Carolina Negro League in 1947 and 1948 after he returned from three years military service. He joined the Jacksonville Eagles of the Southern Negro League in 1949 and came north the following season when the American club switched their Eagles' uniforms for those of the Indian Head Rockets and represented the small Saskatchewan community for two seasons. After a year in organized ball, Blackman returned to the prairies to join the North Battleford Beavers of the Western Canada League.

1950 Indian Head Rockets—Statistics not available
1951 Indian Head Rockets—.217, Won 4, Lost 4, 16 G, 6 GS, 3 CG
1953 North Battleford Beavers—Won 7, Lost 6, .294
1954 North Battleford Beavers—Won 6, Lost 6, 14 G, 11 GS, 10 CG, .278, 8 HR, 42 RBI
1955 North Battleford Beavers—Statistics not available
1956 North Battleford Beavers—.260, 3 D, 5 T, 8 HR, 30 RBI

Canadian Highlights: August 2, 1950, Blackman hurled nine superb frames, allowing just an unearned run, as Indian Head topped Swift Current 2–1 at the Rosetown Tournament.

July 26, 1951 the pitcher-infielder belted a pair of homers to give Indian Head a 7–5 win over Regina, the Rockets 22nd consecutive victory.

July 25, 1953, Blackman tossed a seven-hit shutout as North Battleford beat Saskatoon 4–0 to take over sole possession of first place.

In a July 2, 1956 tilt, Blackman paced the Beavers to a double-header sweep of Moose Jaw with two homers and a single in the first game and a homer and two singles in the second contest. September 3, Blackman led the Beavers to the Western Canada League title bashing a homer, double and single as North Battleford beat Ron Perranoski (later to become a renown major league closer) and the Lloydminster Meridians 9–1 to capture the championship. He was a key member of the Beavers' club which represented Canada at the Global World Series in Milwaukee.

Heberto "Henry" Blanco—Second base, 5'7", 165 lbs. Batted right, threw right

The middle infielder from Cuba played for the New York Cubans in 1941 and 1942 before moving his game to Mexico for several seasons. Blanco was an all-star in the Mexican League in 1946. In 1949, he joined the Sherbrooke Athletics, a non-affiliated team, in the Quebec Provincial League. He returned to the Mexican League and in 1956 spent his last season in the Southwest League.

Jim "Fireball" Bolden—Pitcher. Threw right

Bolden played in the Negro League in the 1946 and 1947 seasons with the Cleveland Buckeyes and Birmingham Black Barons. He toured with the New Orleans Creoles in 1949 and the Brooklyn Cuban Giants in 1950. The following year he came to Canada and joined the Elmwood Giants in the ManDak League. He was back in the Negro League in 1952 with the Birmingham Black Barons.

1951 Elmwood Giants—Won 4, Lost 8, 16 G, 12 GS, 6 CG

Canadian Highlights: August 9, 1949, Bolden came on in relief with one out in the second inning and blanked Elmwood Giants the rest of the way as New Orleans Creoles won an exhibition match 10–6.

In a game not for the superstitious, May 25, 1951, Bolden allowed 13 hits, walked 13 and hit a batter in a 10–3 loss to Brandon. June 20, Bolden was in total command firing a three-hitter to lead Elmwood to a 9–1 win over Carman. June 30, Bolden scatted nine hits in going the distance in a 10–3 win over Winnipeg. He helped at the plate with two hits, one a double, and drove in a pair.

Monte Bond—Shortstop/Outfield, 6'0", 175 lbs. Batted right, threw right

A high school star in Ohio, Bond had two solid seasons, 1958 and 1959, with the Lloydminster-North Battleford Combines of the Western Canada Baseball League. After signing a professional contract with the Chicago White Sox, Bond had three seasons in the lower ranks of professional ball, including a summer in the New York–Penn League where he hit .320 with 7 home runs and drove in 71. He also put in a season with the legendary Kansas City Monarchs (1961). He was killed in a highway accident in 1973.

1958 Lloydminster–N.Battleford—.305, 2 HR, 6 T, 21 RBI
1959 Lloydminster–N.Battleford—.302, 2 HR, 20 RBI

Canadian Highlights: July 23, 1958, Bond clubbed a triple, double and single and knocked in three runs as the Lloydminster–North Battleford Combines trounced Moose Jaw 16–3. Two days later, his two-run homer propelled the Combines to an 8–3 win over the Mallards and on July 27, Bonds had three hits as Moose Jaw went down 13–2. August 22, a run-scoring double by Bond in the 3rd inning proved decisive as Lloydminster–North Battleford advanced to the Western Canada Baseball League final with a 4–3 win over Edmonton in the ninth and deciding game of their semi-final series.

August 7, 1959, Bond clouted a two-run homer and a single to account for all three runs in the Combines' 3–2 win over Saskatoon. September 10, Bond, acquired by Edmonton Eskimos for the playoff final, belted a first-inning homer to send the Eskimos to a 14–4 win and a four-game sweep for the Canadian-American Baseball League title.

Marshall Boney—Catcher

Marshall Boney, or was it Boney Marshall? The latter came out of high school in Wilmington, North Carolina and the Danville All-Stars to line up with the barnstorming Brooklyn Cuban Giants in 1949. *(The Winona Republican-Herald, July 6, 1949, p.12)* When the catcher left the Cuban Giants to join the Elmwood Giants in the Manitoba Senior Baseball League in '49 he was identified as Marshall Boney. He returned for a second season in 1950 and then returned to the United States.

> 1949 Elmwood Giants—Statistics not available
> 1950 Elmwood Giants—.237, 1 HR, 28 RBI

Canadian Highlights: June 5, 1950, he hit three singles to lead the Giants to a 7–4 victory over the Winnipeg Buffaloes. Boney had four hits on June 10, as Elmwood whipped the Winnipeg Buffaloes 18–6 and July 26, he was the hitting star driving in 7 runs with a home run, double and single in a 9–2 win over Brandon.

Julio Bonilla—Second Base

Bonilla was among the Cuban imports who suited up as the Florida Cubans in 1952.

Canadian Highlights: On June 5, 1952, Bonilla poked out 3 hits in an 8–0 win over Indian Head.

Nathaniel "Legs" Booker—Pitcher

The Louisiana native suited up with the Prince Albert Bohemians of the Northern Saskatchewan League in 1951. He returned to Canada the following season with a barnstorming team, the Baton Rouge Hardwood Sports, which took second money at the famous Indian Head Tournament.

> 1951 Prince Albert Bohemians—Won 2, Lost 6, 12 G, 8 GS, 7 CG

Lyman Bostock—First Base, 6'1", 215 lbs. Batted right, threw right

The first sacker played with five clubs in a Negro League career which stretched from 1938 to 1949. He played for the Brooklyn Royal Giants, Birmingham Black Barons, Chicago American Giants, New York Cubans and Cincinnati Crescents. In 1950 he was enticed to join the Winnipeg Buffaloes for their inaugural season in the ManDak (Manitoba-Dakota) League. He had four productive seasons, two with the Buffaloes and two with the Carman Cardinals and was a fan favorite during his stay in Canada.

His son, Lyman Jr., made the major leagues as an outfielder with the Minnesota Twins. His promising career ended in 1978 when he was shot and killed in Gary, Indiana.

Lyman Sr. died in 2005.

> 1950 Winnipeg Buffaloes—.306, 1 HR, 31 RBI
> 1951 Winnipeg Buffaloes—.288, 17 D, 2 HR, 34 RBI
> 1952 Carman Cardinals—.328, 11 D, 1 T, 5 HR, 36 RBI
> 1953 Carman Cardinals—.316, 62 R, 16 D, 4 T, 2 HR, 55 RBI

Canadian Highlights: June 10, 1950, Bostock had three hits and drove in a pair in a 9–5 win over Brandon. August 29, Bostock knocked in Butch Davis and Leon Day with the tying and winning runs in a 3–2 victory over Minot. September 14, Bostock sacrificed a runner from second to third base in what resulted in the only run as the Buffaloes captured the ManDak championship in a 17-inning thriller.

May 24, 1951, he punched out two doubles and a single in a 14–10 win over Carman. June 23, Bostock had another three hit game to lead the Buffaloes to a ten inning 5–3 win over Brandon.

June 4, 1952, Bostock had three hits in a Carman victory over the Winnipeg Giants.

June 12, 1953, he had another three hit game in a 9–5 win over Regina. August 29, 1953, he had four hits in 8–7 Carman win over the Winnipeg Royals.

Roberto Bouza — Pitcher. Threw left

The southpaw was one of a group of Cuban players who joined the Regina Braves of the Western Canada League in 1957.

    1957 Regina — Won 1, Lost 0, 4.50 ERA

Chico Bowen — Second Base/Catcher

In 1935, Bowen was one of three black players in Quebec's Provincial League playing for Sorel. *(Integration in Quebec, Dominion Ball, SABR, 2005)*

Lincoln Boyd — First Base/Outfield, 6'3", 180 lbs. Batted right, threw right

Boyd parlayed his brief Negro League experience (Louisville Buckeyes, Atlanta Stars, Indianapolis Clowns, Brooklyn Cuban Giants) to some impressive days in Western Canada and a few exceptional seasons in lower levels of organized ball.

He played partial seasons in Canada with the Brandon Greys of the Manitoba Senior League in 1949 and Brandon and the Regina Caps of the Southern Saskatchewan League in 1950. Later, in three professional seasons with Clovis, New Mexico in Class-D and Class-B leagues he hit .314, .340 and .302 and belted a total of 95 home runs and knocked in 338 runs. In 1955, he led the league in home runs, with 44, and runs batted in, 157. April 30, 1956, Boyd likely had his best day on the diamond with consecutive grand slam homers and a triple, good for eleven runs batted in as Clovis won a slugfest 17–12.

    1949 Brandon Greys — .300, 0 HR, 10 RBI
    1950 Indian Head Rockets — Statistics not available
        Regina Caps — .436, 5 T, 3 HR

Canadian Highlights: July 22, 1949, Boyd had five hits as the Cuban Giants and Southern League All-Stars fought to a 2–2 tie. On August 27 and 28, Boyd had two hits and scored four runs to lead Brandon to the final of the Minot Tournament in North Dakota. He duplicated the performance, double and single, four runs, in the final as the Greys won top money with an 11–2 win over the host Minot club. September 6, Boyd drove in the tying run as Brandon shaded Elmwood 2–1 in fifteen innings to capture the 1949 title in the Manitoba Senior League. He added three hits in Brandon's last home game against the St. Louis Black Cardinals, September 7, and another three hits in the final game of the season, September 10, as Brandon defeated Minot to win the Mallot Trophy given to the winner of the Manitoba–North Dakota competition.

June 24, 1950, Boyd led Indian Head to a double-header sweep of Swift Current with two hits in the first game and three in the second. July 10 :

> Boyd's catch of Barnett's long fly was really a dandy. The ball, heading for the corner of the football grandstand, appeared well out of the reach of the Cap outfielders, but Lincoln Boyd, after racing a country mile, made a sensational one-handed catch [*The Leader-Post*, Regina, July 11, 1950].

July 21, Boyd took a turn on the mound and "fans were really surprised to see Boyd stroll to the mound in the first inning. His changeups, curves and slow balls were working to perfection." *(The Leader-Post, Regina, July 22, 1950).* Boyd continued his hitting tear with four straight hits as Regina Caps dumped Notre Dame 8–2. The outburst extended Boyd's consecutive hit streak to eleven games and boosted his average to .553. He had three doubles, five triples and three homers among his twenty one hits. August 12, Boyd had triple and single in the semi-final and two more hits in the final as Regina took top prize in the Regina Exhibition Tournament.

Luther Branham — Infield/Outfield, 5'6½", 160 lbs. Batted right, threw right

Branham was from California and in 1948, played for the San Francisco Sea Lions, who toured Western Canada. He then played in the Negro League from 1949 to 1950 with the Birmingham Black Barons and Chicago American Giants. In 1951 he played in the Quebec Provincial League with Drummondville and followed that by signing with Victoria (British Columbia) Tyees in the Western International League. Newspapers in Victoria described Branham as a speedster.

> 1951 Drummondville Cubs—.204, 5 D, 0 T, 0 HR, 10 RBI
> 1952 Victoria Tyees—.288, 16 D, 2 T, 3 HR, 41 RBI
> 1953 Victoria Tyees—.266, 24 D, 4 T, 2 HR, 43 RBI

Hiram Alonso Brathwaite—Outfield/First Base, 5'11", 174 lbs. Batted right, threw right

Brathwaite played in the Negro League from 1944 to 1948 with the Newark Eagles and Philadelphia Stars. He also played in Mexico. From 1951 to 1954, Brathwaite was in Quebec in the Provincial League with Farnham, St. Hyacinthe, Drummondville and St. Jean. From there he played in organized ball from 1955 to 1959.

> 1951 Farnham Pirates—.270, 17 D, 3 T, 3 HR, 39 RBI
> 1952 St. Hyacinthe A's—.256, 27 D, 1 T, 12 HR, 75 RBI
> 1953 St. Hyacinthe/Drummondville—.247, 13 D, 9 T, 2 HR, 48 RBI
> 1954 Drummondville/St. Jean—.200, 5 D, 1 T, 1 HR, 7 RBI

Canadian Highlights: In 1952 Brathwaite set a Provincial League record for most at bats with 531 official trips to the plate.

Jabe Brazzle—Pitcher. Threw right

The Texas native pitched for Central Texas Vocational College of Waco in 1948 tournaments before moving to the barnstorming Ligon All-Stars in 1949. He was on the Canadian tour with the Ligons in '49 and '51. Later he returned to Texas to play in organized ball in the Gulf Coast circuit with Brownsville, and also with the semi-pro Texas Jasper Steers.

Eugene Bremmer (Bremer)—Pitcher, 5'8", 160 lbs. Batted right, threw right

Bremmer, who had a solid and lengthy career in the Negro Leagues (including four all-star selections), showed up in the tiny South Saskatchewan community of Broadview in the midst of the Great Depression to star on the newly integrated Buffaloes baseball team. He was just a few years into his career. He may have drawn the attention of the Broadview team when he pitched in Winnipeg in 1935 in a series of exhibition games against Satchel Paige and the Bismarck Corwin-Churchills (which went on to capture the inaugural National Baseball Congress semi-pro title).

Around his stint in Broadview he also put in a little time with Negro League teams in the United States. In the fall of 1942, sports pages carried news that Bremmer and two other Negro League stars—third baseman Parnell Woods and outfielder Sam Jethroe—were to get tryouts with the Cleveland Indians in 1943. However, just days after the announcement, Bremmer was in a serious accident in which two of his Cleveland Buckeyes' teammates were killed. Bremmer suffered a fractured skull when a truck rammed the rear of the car in which the players were riding. The Cleveland tryout never took place.

He continued to pitch in the Negro Leagues until 1948 and then had a couple of brief trials in organized pro ball in the late 40s and early 50s. He died in 1971 in Cleveland, Ohio at the age of 54.

Chester Arthur "Chet" Brewer—Pitcher, 6'4", 180 lbs. Batted both, threw right

Often overshadowed by Satchel Paige, Brewer carved out an outstanding career of his own over nearly thirty years on diamonds in the United States, Canada, the Dominican Republic, Mexico, Japan, the Philippines, Panama, Puerto Rico, Haiti, Cuba, and China.

He was among the best pitchers in the Negro League particularly in his stints with the Kansas City Monarchs. Near the end of his career, which began in 1925, he joined the St. Jean Braves of the Quebec Provincial League in 1949 (at that time an outlaw circuit). He left the

Chet Brewer was an outstanding pitcher, especially in his career with the Kansas City Monarchs, which began in 1925 and included a dozen seasons. He was in his mid–40s when he pitched in Western Canada in the 1950s (photograph courtesy the National Baseball Hall of Fame Library, Cooperstown, N.Y.).

Braves near the end of June to join the Michigan City Cubs of the Michigan-Indiana League where he finished with a 9–4 record with 78 strikeouts. Brewer traveled west in 1951 to suit up with the Sceptre and Indian Head teams in Saskatchewan. In 1952 he became one of the first black managers in organized ball when he pitched and directed the Porterville (California) Padres of the Class-C Southwest International League (at age 45 he won six games with an ERA of 3.38). That season he managed the league's all-star team against Modesto. In 1953 he put the finishing touches on his career (much of it spent on the West Coast where he headed teams in the California Winter League for seven campaigns) with a season as the playing-manager of the Carman Cardinals of the ManDak League. He pitched in just three league games and one exhibition, but still managed to impress. Brewer died in 1990 at age 83.

1949 St. Jean Braves—Won 4, Lost 2
1951 Sceptre Nixons—Statistics not available
1951 Indian Head Rockets—Won 4, Lost 0, 7 G, 5 GS, 4 CG
1953 Carman Cardinals—Won 0, Lost 0, 3 G, 2 GS

Left: The oil painting of Chet Brewer is by artist Jacqueline Jolles of upstate New York, who, through meeting former Negro leaguer Armando Vasquez, began developing a deep appreciation of the former Negro League stars.

Jolles was born in Portland, Oregon, and studied painting/fine art at Antioch College in Yellow Springs, Ohio, and New York Studio School, in New York City, where she found her profound affinity to the portrait and figurative art of Rembrandt, Giacometti, Soutine and others.

Her love of baseball inspired her recent paintings of players with a special interest in the history of the "Negro" baseball League. And to her great joy she had legendary figures such as Monte Irvin, James "Red" Moore, and Armando Vasquez sit for live portrait sessions. The Negro league portraits were part of a solo exhibition in 2007 at the Atlantic City Art Center sponsored by the John Henry Pop Lloyd Committee in Atlantic City, New Jersey. Jolles has also exhibited in New York, San Francisco, and Maryland.

Canadian Highlights: June 26, 1933, Brewer dazzled the crowd at Wesley Park in Winnipeg pitching the Kansas City Monarchs past St. Paul Northern Pacific 6–1.

> A lanky right-hander with huge hands, Brewer had everything a good pitcher should have. His change of pace was baffling, his speed dazzling, and his hook bewildering to the Saints. Thirty men faced him and three hits were all that he allowed, while ten fell prey to his delivery [*Winnipeg Tribune*, June 27, 1933].

June 6, 1935, Satchel Paige and Chet Brewer faced off in a classic duel at Osborne Stadium in Winnipeg as Bismarck took on the Kansas City Monarchs in an exhibition game. The two great right-handers battled to a 0–0 tie. Paige allowed 7 hits and fanned 17 while Brewer gave up just 5 hits and compiled 13 strikeouts.

May 30, 1951, at the Swift Current Tournament, Brewer pitched a six-hit victory over Indian Head. June 13, again pitching for Sceptre, he relieved in the sixth inning and proceeded to mow down the next eleven Medicine Hat batters for the victory. July 14, now with Indian Head, Brewer allowed just three hits and had 14 strikeouts as the Rockets clobbered Estevan 21–0. Brewer tossed a four-hit shutout August 3 to lead Indian Head to first prize money at the Tisdale Lions Club Tournament. Rockets beat North Battleford 6–0 in the final. August 15, Brewer pitched a perfect 9th inning in the opening Saskatchewan semi-pro playoff game then fired a three-hitter in the second game as Indian Head walloped Dauphin 11–1 and 23–1 to capture the title.

Brewer pitched in just three league games for Carman in 1953, but in one of them, May 20th, he combined with Willie Hutchinson on a five-hit, 6–0 shutout of Minot.

Former teammate George Mahaffy recalled, "Chet Brewer was 42 or 44 at the time and he had a little money because he came up in a big, green Buick and he brought two Cuban ballplayers with him—Pedro Osorio and Bobby Prescott. Brewer got 450 dollars a month at a time when a room in a hotel was worth a dollar a night. Chet was the highest paid we ever had."

Sherwood "Woody" Brewer—Infield/Outfield, 5'8", 175 lbs. Batted right, threw right

The combative Brewer carved out a 16-year baseball career including stops with three legendary Negro teams—the Harlem Globetrotters, Indianapolis Clowns and Kansas City Monarchs. Following a stint in the Army during World War II, he began his career with the Globetrotters in 1946, then playing as the Seattle Steelheads, in an attempt to bring Negro League ball to the West Coast. He played Negro ball through 1951.

In 1952, at age 29, Brewer spent his first summer in organized professional baseball in the Class-D, Sooner State League. He returned to Negro ball for the 1953 and 1954 seasons with the Kansas City Monarchs (in '53 his keystone partner was shortstop Ernie Banks, elected to the Baseball Hall of Fame after a sterling career with the Chicago Cubs). Brewer was back in pro ball in 1955 and 1956 with San Angelo, Texas of the Class-C Longhorn and Class-B, Southwestern Leagues. He began the 1957 season with Winona Chiefs of the Southern Minnesota League before traveling north to Saskatoon, Saskatchewan, to join the city's entry in the Western Canada League. He was on the go again the following season moving to the Yankton Terriers of the Basin League in South Dakota.

Back in Canada in 1959, Brewer was the sparkplug of the Medicine Hat Superiors of the Southern Alberta League. He wrapped up his career back with Kansas City, as playing-manager, in 1960 and 1961.

His intensity was displayed in several outbursts over the years. In 1953, Brewer was arrested by police in Salina, Kansas after a fight in the downtown area with an airman from the local Air Force base. The airman suffered a broken nose. In June 1955, he was at the center of a 25-minute free-for-all when he and Negro teammate Ben Lott were involved in a donnybrook after unflattering comments from their Big Spring, Texas, opponents. A month later, he was suspended for three games and fined $100 after a fight during a game at San Angelo, Texas. In 1956, Brewer got into a fight with his manager in the dugout during a game at

Hobbs, New Mexico. As police escorted the pair out of the stadium, they began battling for a second time. In Medicine Hat, in July, 1959 (during a game in which future major leaguer Ray Washburn fired a no-hitter) Brewer touched off a half-hour riot following allegations of racial taunts. In August, he was ejected from a game and suspended for the rest of the season after heated words and a pushing incident with chief umpire Jim Prior.

Brewer died in 2003 in Chicago. He was 79.

1957 Saskatoon Gems—.263, 9 HR, 32 RBI
1959 Medicine Hat Superiors—.303

Canadian Highlights: June 28, 1957, Brewer had 3 hits in a victory over Lloydminster. In a July 1st doubleheader, Brewer had a homer and two singles in the opening game and drove in three runs with a homer and single in the nightcap as Saskatoon split with North Battleford. July 13, he had four hits as Saskatoon trounced Edmonton 14–7. July 21, Brewer had five hits as the Gems and Lloydminster divided a twin-bill.

June 17, 1959, Brewer had a double and two singles to help Medicine Hat edge Lethbridge 9–8. July 5, he belted a pair of homers as the Superiors took a twin-bill from Calgary. July 8, Brewer took over the lead in the batting race with a .358 average. August 10, back in the lineup after serving a three-game suspension, Brewer clubbed a bases-loaded double to clinch a win for Medicine Hat. It was his second double of the game.

July 30, 1960, Brewer had three hits as Kansas City Monarchs shaded Saskatoon 4–3 at the Lethbridge Rotary Tournament.

John Britton—Third Base, 5'8", 160 lbs. Batted left, threw right

Britton started his career in 1940 with the Minnesota Gophers traveling team. In 1942, he played for the Minneapolis–St. Paul Bombers and then performed in the Negro League from 1943 to 1949 with the Birmingham Black Barons. In 1950 it was up to Canada and the Winnipeg Buffaloes in the newly formed Man-Dak League. The following summer he moved over to the Elmwood Giants. After the Man-Dak League he continued his career in Japan with the Hankyu Braves for two seasons, batting over .300 both years. In 1954 Britton closed out his career barnstorming with Satchel Paige and the Harlem Globetrotters.

1950 Winnipeg Buffaloes—.328 1 HR, 26 RBI
1951 Elmwood Giants—.310 3 HR, 40 RBI

Canadian Highlights: May 27, 1950, Britton had three safeties, including a home run in leading the Buffaloes to a 6–5 victory over Brandon. June 3, he had three hits, one a double, and also stole a base in a 4–0 blanking of Carman.

In 1951, Britton picked a good day (July 4) to celebrate as he came up with Carman down a run and with two on in the bottom of the ninth inning. He singled to drive in both runners for the 7–6 win. July 9, he led Elmwood to a 9–1 victory over the strong Winnipeg Buffaloes team. He hit a home run, double and drove in three.

Ken Broady—Pitcher. Threw right

Broady was a mainstay for the Ligon All-Stars for at least four years, 1947–48 and 1950–51. During the '47 barnstorming tour, Broady also pitched for a Manitoba team, the Portage La Prairie club, during a tournament in Winnipeg. At the time he was described as, "a fugitive from a touring colored aggregation from south of the line." *(Winnipeg Tribune Aug 4, 1947)*

Dick Brookins—Third Base.

Brookins created quite a stir in the Western Canada Baseball League of 1910. First, because of his play, "Brookins, the Indian, has been sensational in fielding, batting and base running so far." *(The Lethbridge Daily Herald, May 3, 1910)*. Soon, however, only his color seemed to matter. The third baseman, who had played three years of organized ball in the United States, was banned from the league after allegations arose that he was partly Negro. His team, the Regina Bone Pilers, had to forfeit several games when opponents declined to play with Brookins in the lineup.

> Nearly all the clubs in the Western Canada circuit have entered a protest against Dick

Brookins of the Regina club on the ground that the blood of African chieftains courses through his veins. Winnipeg is one of the cities which has objected, while Medicine Hat and Calgary have also registered a big kick. They claim a dusky player has no place in organized baseball. Brookins is playing a strong game for Regina and his withdrawal would be a serious loss. He was signed up with Vancouver last year, but after reporting was turned loose without a trial. Brookins, while here, claimed he was an Indian. He is a cracking good third baseman, and it is only the strain in his blood that keeps him out of good company. He was slated for a trial in the American Association, but was let out without it after he had reported [*Manitoba Free Press*, May 16, 1910].

Brookins played in 20 games before the ban, batting .223.

Barney Brown—Pitcher/Outfield, 5'11", 155 lbs. Batted left, threw left

In a Negro League career which stretched from 1931 to 1949, Brown was among the premiere hurlers for the Cuban Stars, New York Black Yankees and Philadelphia Stars. He was an all-star five times. In addition, he was a dominant mound force in Mexico, before

Veteran left-hander Barney Brown (left) and infielder Jim Valentine of the 1952 Brandon Greys hanging out in downtown Brandon before heading to the ballpark (photograph courtesy Lois Bentley).

winding up his 25-year pitching career in Canada where he performed in the ManDak, Western Canada and Intercounty leagues. Brown, who also played the outfield, added winter ball flings in Cuba, Puerto Rico and the Dominican Republic to his lengthy resume.

He made his initial trip north in 1952 to pitch for the Brandon Greys and returned the following season. In the summer of 1954, he pitched for Brantford in Southern Ontario's Intercounty League. Brown came back to the prairies for his final two baseball seasons when he joined the Lloydminster Meridians of the Western Canada League. In 1955, at age forty seven, he was among the top pitchers in the league even though he didn't make his Meridians' debut until the first week of July. Brown made eleven starts and completed them all while finishing with a 2.90 ERA.

In his career, Brown who hit two home runs during the 1934 season, appears not to have hit another in his next 22 years of play. Brown died in October of 1985 in Philadelphia. He was 77.

> Barney Brown was one of the great pitchers in the Negro League along with Satchel Paige. He was great. When we had him in Lloydminster he'd throw two pitches that would hit the front of the plate, couldn't even get it to the catcher. Then he'd come up there and strike the side out. And, he was an old man. When Barney Brown came to Lloydminster, he was almost fifty years old. He was like Satchel Paige. He just didn't get the breaks. That guy was something else. And he was a little guy too. But he had so much on the ball I tell you. He had guys swinging at the ball before it got to the plate. I played with him in the Negro League. Man, he was amazing, I couldn't believe it. That man thrilled the crowd so much in Lloydminster, they'd never seen nothing like it [Teammate Curly Williams on Brown, telephone interview, 2001].

1952 Brandon Greys—Won 4, Lost 1
1953 Brandon Greys—Won 9, Lost 4, 15 G, 11 GS, 9 CG
1954 Brantford Red Sox—Won 7, Lost 3
1955 Minot Mallards—Won 0, Lost 3, 9.00 ERA
1955 Lloydminster Meridians—Won 5, Lost 5, 10 G, 10 GS, 10 CG, 2.90 ERA
1956 Lloydminster Meridians—Won 4, Lost 6, 11 G, 11 GS, 3 CG, 6.31 ERA

Canadian Highlights: In his first three starts with Brandon in 1952, Brown was 3–0 with three complete games, twenty four strikeouts and just two earned runs in twenty seven innings.

He kicked off the 1953 season with five straight wins for the Greys, one of them a two-hitter (May 21).

July 3, 1955, in his Lloydminster debut Brown gave up a run in the first inning then pitched shutout ball in winning 5–1. August 24, Brown pitched all eleven innings in a 2–2 tie, giving up just five hits.

July 12, 1956, the 48 year old Brown tossed a two-hitter as Lloydminster beat Moose Jaw 8–1.

Ben Brown—Shortstop

The 23-year-old middle infielder was among a group of players from the Philadelphia area recruited to play for Rosetown in the inaugural year of the re-born Western Canada Baseball League. He played in all of Rosetown's sixty games.

1954 Rosetown Phillies—.266, 4 D, 7 T, 7 HR, 35 RBI

Canadian Highlights: May 25, 1954, Brown clubbed a homer and a triple and knocked in three, but Rosetown fell 18–15 to North Battleford. June 6, Brown, in what must have been a career worst performance, was charged with seven errors as Rosetown lost to Indian Head 13–6 in a game which produced 17 errors. He did have a home run on offense. June 13, Brown had three hits, one of them a triple, as the Phillies topped Moose Jaw 11–6. July 3, Brown had a homer and two singles in a 9–8 loss to North Battleford.

Boyd Brown—Pitcher. Threw right

He was listed at 23 years of age when he joined the Rosetown Phillies for the 1954 season.

Canadian Highlights: July 13, 1954, Brown allowed just seven hits over 11 innings as Rosetown edged Lloydminster 3–1. The only run against Brown scored on an error. July 17, Brown tossed a five-hitter and drove in the winning run in the bottom of the 9th in a 2–1 win over Indian Head. August 17, Brown not only fired a fine six-hitter, but belted a double and two singles as the Phillies trounced North Battleford 10–2

Don Brown—Outfield/Pitcher, 6'0", 175 lbs. Batted left, threw left

His first stop in organized ball was in 1954 with the Joplin Cardinals. Brown moved up to the Winnipeg Goldeyes in 1955 and stayed for three seasons with the Northern League club. In addition to his outfield duties in 1955, he did some pitching for the Goldeyes. He spent eight years in pro ball, all but one in the St. Louis system before retiring in 1962. During his career he advanced as high a Triple-A.

- 1955 Winnipeg Goldeyes—.288, 1 HR, 25 RBI, Won 2, Lost 3, 5.76 ERA
- 1956 Winnipeg Goldeyes—.244, 1 HR, 25 RBI
- 1957 Winnipeg Goldeyes—.301, 3 HR, 51 RBI

Canadian Highlights: In 1957, Brown led the Northern League in runs scored, 98, hits, 152, and was selected to the all-star team.

Eddie Brown—Second Base

Brown, who toured Western Canada with Ligon's Colored All-Stars in 1948, returned to the prairies to join the famous Bentley brothers of hockey fame on the Delisle team 1949–1951.

- 1949 Delisle—Statistics not available
- 1950 Delisle—.167
- 1951 Prince Albert/Delisle—Statistics not available

Canadian Highlights: June 23, 1948, Brown had four hits to lead Ligon's All-Stars to a 4–0 win over Winnipeg Reos to advance to the final of the Brandon Tournament.

July 17, 1949, the second sacker had a homer in each game as Delisle and North Battleford divided a twin-bill. August 19, Brown had a triple, double and single in a 9–4 win over Saskatoon Legion. September 7, he had three hits as Delisle captured the provincial title downing Moose Jaw Purity Canucks 8–3.

Ray Brown—Pitcher/Outfield, 6'1", 195 lbs. Batted both, threw right

Brown had a 16-year career in Negro ball, mainly with the Homestead Grays, before winding up his career in Mexico and Canada. In 2006, Brown received the ultimate baseball honor winning induction into the National Baseball Hall of Fame at Cooperstown.

At age 42, he joined Sherbrooke, Quebec late in the 1950 season and returned the following year to help the Athletics to the Provincial League title. After the Sherbrooke stadium burned down and the team disbanded, Brown moved on to play for the Thetford Mines Miners, of the Quebec Senior League, for the 1952 season. In 1953 he was playing manager for the Lachine Indians of the Laurentian League and led them to the championship. It was Brown's third championship team, in three different leagues, in as many seasons. And, there was one last curtain call. He was convinced to return to Thetford Mines, now in the Provincial League, to help with a late season push for a playoff spot. He had a win in his only decision. That was the end of his career. For a number of years after he quit the diamond, he chose to reside in Canada. Brown died in 1965 in Dayton, Ohio. He was 56.

- 1950 Sherbrooke—Won 1, Lost 5, .250, 2 HR, 7 RBI
- 1951 Sherbrooke—Won 11, Lost 10, 3.31 ERA, .193, 4 HR, 13 RBI
- 1952 Thetford Mines—Won 16, Lost 5
- 1953 Lachine—Won 13, Lost 5
- 1953 Thetford Mines—Won 1, Lost 0

Canadian Highlights: In 1950, after a slow regular season, he pitched in 9 of the team's 13 playoff starts and also helped on offense batting .353.

In 1952, Brown recorded 4 playoff victories and, in 1953, Brown won nine straight games for Lachine.

Tom "T.J." Brown—Shortstop/Second Base, 5'6", 170 lbs. Batted right, threw right

Brown came out of East Moline, Illinois where he lettered in football as his school didn't have a baseball team. He made his professional baseball debut in 1938 in Tampico, Mexico and then played in the Negro League from 1939 to 1950 mainly with the Memphis Red Sox, Indianapolis Clowns and Cleveland Buckeyes. Brown was selected to the 1942 East-West All-Star Game. His career was interrupted in 1945 and 1946 for military duty. In 1951, he joined the Carman Cardinals in the ManDak League and in mid season was traded to the Elmwood Giants. It would be his only season in Canada. He ended his career with two seasons, 1952 and 1953, in Class-D organized ball with the Danville Dans in the Mississippi-Ohio Valley League.

1951 Carman/Elmwood—.212, 0 HR, 13 RBI

Canadian Highlights: May 29, 1951, Brown drove in three runs with a triple and two singles in a 10–9 win over Winnipeg. A bases-loaded triple on June 28 helped Carman to a 13–3 win over Minot.

Willard "Home Run" Brown—

Outfield, 5'11", 200 lbs. Batted right, threw right

In 2006, Brown's baseball exploits were highlighted with his selection, posthumously, to the National Baseball Hall Of Fame at Cooperstown.

In a career which included 15 seasons in the Negro Leagues, and a quarter-century over-all, Brown played in eight East-West All-Star games and became known as "Home Run" Brown. How did Brown achieve such distinction in a league with had produced such sluggers as Josh Gibson and Mule Suttles? The moniker was given by Gibson himself after the big catcher witnessed another of Brown's long-ball performances.

The Louisiana native helped the Kansas City Monarchs to dominance in the Negro American League over more than a dozen years beginning in 1935, interrupted by two years in the Army during the Second World War. In 1947, in his early 30s, he won a major league trial with the St. Louis Browns but was released after just 21 games. He returned to the Monarchs with two outstanding seasons, hitting .374 and .371 while making his mark in winter ball with the Santurce Crabs in Puerto Rico. Twice he won the triple crown in the winter league. In the 1947–48 season, he hit .432, with 27 home runs and knocked in 86 in just 60 games. He also starred in Mexico and Canada. In 1954, Brown beat up on pitching in the Double-A, Texas League to tune of .314, 35 homers, 120 RBI. After five seasons in the minors, Brown suited up Minot Mallards in the final year of the ManDak in 1957. The next year was back with the Kansas City Monarchs for one last campaign. He died in Houston in 1996. He was 81.

> Of all the Negro baseball stars I think Willard Brown, center fielder for the Kansas City Monarchs, is the best. He can hit a longer ball than any man I've ever seen. He hits more home runs than Josh Gibson, the great colored catcher. He has a wonderful throwing arm and is murder on the base paths. But he's just one of those guys who does a job day in and day out without a flash of color [Goose Tatum quoted in the *Wisconsin State Journal*, July 9, 1945, p.17].

1950 Ottawa Nationals—.352, 7 D, 1 T, 1 HR, 18 RBI
1957 Minot Mallards—.307, 9 D, 9 T, 9 HR, 29 RBI

Canadian Highlights: July 30, 1957, Brown paced Minot to a 7–5 second game victory by hitting two home runs and a single. August 2, in an 8–6 loss to the Brandon Greys, Brown was the top Minot hitter with a home run, double and single.

Clarence Bruce—

Infield, 6'1", 170 lbs. Batted right, threw right

The light-hitting infielder played in Farnham, Quebec in the Provincial League in 1949 and 1950 after two seasons of Negro League play with the Homestead Grays.

1949 Farnham Pirates—Statistics not available
1950 Farnham Pirates—.222, 1 D, 0 T, 0 HR, 6 RBI

Jack Bruton—Infield/Pitcher. Threw right

Bruton (sometimes identified as Burton) had a career in Negro ball going back to 1936. His last stop in the Negro circuit was with the Cleveland Buckeyes in 1950 when he played part of the season with the Minot Mallards in the ManDak League. In 1951, he split time between Estevan Maple Leafs of the Western Canada League and Minot. In 1953, he was back in Canada with the Regina Caps.

> 1951 Estevan Maple Leafs—.275 (Incomplete), Won 2, Lost 4, 8 G, 6 GS, 5 CG
> 1953 Regina Caps—Statistics not available

Canadian Highlights: May 21, 1951, Bruton drove in five runs with four hits as Minot dropped an exhibition match to Estevan.

May 18, 1953, Bruton pitched a shutout as Regina blanked Saskatoon Gems 3–0 in the first game of a twin-bill.

Nip Bruton—Pitcher. Threw right

The younger Bruton had visited the Canadian prairies as a member of the San Francisco Cubs in 1950. Nip, Jack's brother, pitched in 10 games, including four starts for the Minot Mallards of the ManDak League in 1951. Another brother, Bill, played in the major leagues for the Milwaukee Braves.

Canadian Highlights: August 4, 1951, Bruton gave up two runs in the first inning then blanked the Greys at Brandon the rest of the way, allowing just three hits over the distance, as Minot trounced the host club 12–2.

Allen "Lefty" Bryant—Pitcher, 5'11", 160 lbs. Batted left, threw left

Bryant pitched in the Negro Leagues from 1937 to 1947, with play interrupted by service in the Army during the Second World War. He spent much of his career with the Kansas City Monarchs and helped form one of the most feared pitching rotations in baseball history. In early 2005, ESPN.com selected the quartet of Satchel Paige, Hilton Smith, Chet Brewer and Bryant as the 8th best, single-season mound staff of all time (Maddux, Glavine, Smoltz et al of the 1998 Braves ranked #1).

The little lefthander had one frustrating season in organized professional baseball in 1958 when he went 1–8 with the Class-C Leavenworth Braves of the Western Association. The Braves set a baseball record losing their first 22 games, then topped that later in the season dropping 23 straight matches. Overall, the Braves won 25 and lost 112.

Lefty Bryant sought refuge in North Dakota in 1949 when he signed on with the Minot Merchants. He traveled a little farther north in 1950 to join the Estevan Maple Leafs of Saskatchewan's Southern League. He returned to Estevan in 1951 when the team played in the Western Canada League. In 1952, he first lined up with Minot of ManDak League and in midseason was traded to the Winnipeg Giants. Bryant died in 1992 in Kansas City a few days before his 74th birthday.

> 1950 Estevan Maple Leafs—Won 4, Lost 0, 4 G, 4 GS, 4 CG
> 1951 Estevan Maple Leafs—Won 5, Lost 5, 13 G, 12 GS, 8 CG
> 1952 Minot Mallards—Won 0, Lost 1
> 1952 Winnipeg Giants—Won 3, Lost 1

Canadian Highlights: July 19, 1950, Bryant pitched a five-hit, 7–1 victory over the Moose Jaw Canucks. August 8, Bryant fired a four-hit shutout as Estevan Maple Leafs downed Weyburn Beavers 7–0 in semi-final action at the Moose Jaw Exhibition Tournament. Bryant also helped at the plate knocking in three runs with a double and single.

June 27, 1952, Bryant, just traded from Minot to Winnipeg, pitched a four-hitter in beating the Brandon Greys. July 17, Bryant held Brandon to four hits as Winnipeg Giants walloped Brandon 8–1 in the opening game of the invitational tournament at Brandon.

Don Buford—Outfield, 5'7", 160 lbs. Batted both, threw right

The 22-year-old Buford answered an SOS from Lloydminster–North Battleford Combines in 1959 and turned an eye opening season into a contract with the Chicago White Sox and a ten year playing career in Major League Baseball and four years in Japan.

While more than a dozen of his teammates at the University of Southern California (where he also starred as a running back on the football team) won season opening jobs in Western Canada in '59, the under-rated Buford was still available when the Combines came calling in early July. In spite of missing a quarter of the season, Buford led the league in triples and stolen bases while batting a solid .284 and drawing oohs and ahhs with his defense and speed.

Buford played on the 1958 College World Series champion Trojans and won a World Series ring with the Baltimore Orioles in 1970. In 2001, he was inducted into the USC Athletic Hall of Fame and, in 2008, was chosen for the International League's Hall of Fame.

Over a period of nearly thirty years, after ending his playing career, Buford continued in baseball, mainly at the minor league level, as a coach and manager. He had major league coaching stints with San Francisco, Baltimore and Washington.

His son, Damon, followed him to the major leagues playing for five teams over nine seasons.

1959 Lloydminster/N. Battleford—.284, 10 D, 11 T, 3 HR, 29 RBI, 19 SB

Canadian Highlights: Buford was praised for his "breath taking" catches and fancy base-running July 30, 1959, after scoring the winning run in the fourteenth inning in a 7–6 victory over Saskatoon. Trapped in a "hot box" between home and third base, he outran a relay throw to notch the deciding run. In the bottom of the inning he saved the victory by making a sensational grab of a towering drive to the deepest part of center field.

Picked up by the Edmonton Eskimos for the decisive round of the playoffs, Buford cracked a homer and two singles in the final game to give Edmonton the league title.

Earl Bumpus—Pitcher/Outfield, 6'1", 215 lbs. Batted left, threw left

The lefthander's experience in the Negro League ran from 1944 to 1948 with the Kansas City Monarchs, Birmingham Black Barons and Chicago American Giants. When he came to Canada and the Carman Cardinals of the Man-Dak League in 1951, the club's year book placed Bumpus in semi-pro ball in 1950 with the Evansville, Indiana, Dodgers. He was reported to have been the playing manager finishing with a 10–4 pitching record. Bumpus died in 1985 in Kentucky. He was 71.

1951 Carman Cardinals—Won 0, Lost 0

Buddy Burbage—Third Base/Catcher/Outfield, 5'6", 160 lbs. Batted left, threw right

Burbage, with a Negro League career which extended back to 1929, came to Western Canada in 1953 to play for Grandview of the Manitoba-Saskatchewan League. A year later, Burbage, then in his late 40s, was a regular with the 1954 Rosetown Phillies of the Western Canada League. Burbage, who played until age 47, died in 1989 in Philadelphia.

1953 Grandview—Statistics not available
1954 Rosetown Phillies—.263, 5 D, 2 T, 1 HR, 18 RBI, 8 SB

Canadian Highlights: July 3, 1954, Burbage knocked in three runs with a homer and single but Rosetown lost 9–8 to North Battleford. July 11, Burbage had a double and two singles in a loss to Moose Jaw. July 19, Burbage had four hits as Rosetown clobbered Indian Head 13–1.

Ernest Burke—Pitcher/Third Base, 6'1", 180 lbs. Batted left, threw right

Burke, born in Maryland, came to Canada during his pre-teen years following the death of his parents. He was raised by a French-Canadian family in Iberville, Quebec, before returning to the United States to enlist in the Marines during the Second World War. His baseball career was put on hold until after his military service. In 1947 and 1948, Burke was in the Negro Leagues in the uniform of the Baltimore Elite Giants. The following summer he moved into organized ball in the Colonial League with Kingston (Ontario) then joined St. Jean in the Quebec Provincial League for the 1950 and 1951 seasons. Burke had success both as an everyday player and on the mound. He closed out his career in 1954 in the Pioneer League. Burke died in early 2004 of complications following kidney surgery.

1949 Kingston/Poughkeepsie—.253, 8 D, 2 T, 1 HR, 16 RBI

1950 St. Jean Braves—Won 15, Lost 3, 4.34 ERA, .308, 11 D, 1 T, 2 HR, 22 RBI

1951 St. Jean Braves—Won 8, Lost 8, 4.92 ERA, .258, 4 D, 1 T, 4 HR, 17 RBI

Harry Butts—Pitcher. Batted right, threw left

Three years experience in the Negro League with the Indianapolis Clowns preceded Butts' decision midway through the 1951 season to head north to Manitoba to join the Brandon Greys. In 1952, after a short time with Vancouver of the Western International League he returned to the Greys. He finished out his career in 1953 in the Piedmont League.

1951 Brandon Greys—Won 5, Lost 0, 7 G, 6 GS, 5 CG

1952 Vancouver Capilanos—Won 0, Lost 2, 6.75 ERA

1952 Brandon Greys—Won 5, Lost 9, 111 IP, 73 BB, 96 SO

Canadian Highlights: In July of 1951, Butts notched five straight, complete-game victories in a span of 19 days. July 1, he scattered eight hits in a 7–2 win over Minot. July 5, Butts held Minot to five hits in another 7–2 triumph. July 9, he beat Carman 4–2 with a seven-hitter and July 14 it was a seven-hitter in a 13–3 win over Brandon. July 19, Butts again went the distance in a 5–3 win over Winnipeg.

Thomas "Pee Wee" Butts—Shortstop, 5'7", 145 lbs. Batted right, threw right

Butts was regarded as one of the top shortstops in the Negro League, a six-time all-star during his tenure from 1938 to 1950 and 1954.

He came to Canada in 1951 to play with his friend Willie Wells who was the manager of the Winnipeg Buffaloes. When Wells moved over to the Brandon Greys in 1952, Butts followed. He concluded his pro career in 1955 with stints in the Class-A, Western League and Class-B, Big State League along with a return visit to the Negro loop with the Memphis Red Sox. He died in 1973 in Atlanta.

1951 Winnipeg Buffaloes—.286, 1 HR, 26 RBI

1952 Brandon Greys—.215, 0 HR, 8 RBI

Canadian Highlights: In an article on July 2, 1951, in the Winnipeg Free Press, it was reported that the St. Louis Browns were going to sign Butts and Charlie White of the Buffaloes. However, only White received a contact. August 9, Butts had three hits in leading Winnipeg to an 11–4 win over Brandon. September 3, in a playoff doubleheader, Butts had two hits in the opener and three in the nightcap as the Buffaloes split with Minot.

Lorenzo Cabrera—First Base, 6'1", 210 lbs. Batted left, threw left

The lefty first baseman played for the New York Cubans from 1947 to 1950 along with a decade of winter ball back home in Cuba usually producing batting marks above .300 with moderate power. In 1951 he played thirty-one games with Ottawa in the International League, then was sold to Oakland in the Pacific Coast League. In 1954, he was with Bryan Indians in the Class-B, Big State League, hitting .345 with 31 doubles, 12 triples and 12 home runs. He hit .308 in the Big State League in 1955 before closing out his career in 1956.

1951 Ottawa Giants—.236, 5 D, 2 T, 0 HR, 7 RBI

Luis Cabrera—Pitcher, 5'10", 175 lbs. Batted right, threw right

Cabrera played the 1948 season with the Indianapolis Clowns and, in 1949, pitched in the Colonial League. He came to Canada for two seasons, 1950 and 1951, to pitch for St. Jean in the Quebec Provincial League.

1950 St. Jean Braves—Won 7, Lost 6, 4.37 ERA

1951 St. Jean Braves—Won 2, Lost 8, 4.97 ERA

Rafael "Rafe" Cabrera—Pitcher/Infield/Outfield. Batted right, threw right

A versatile player, Cabrera was in the Negro League from 1944 to 1948 with the Indianapolis Clowns and New York Cubans. He started the 1948 season with New York before traveling to Manitoba, Canada, to join the Brandon Greys. He played two seasons for Brandon in the Manitoba Senior League and stayed with

Rafael "Rafe" Cabrera played for five seasons in Western Canada after Negro ball experience with Indianapolis Clowns and New York Cubans (photograph courtesy Lil Lowe).

the club when the Greys joined the ManDak League in 1950. Cabrera was a potent offensive force for the Greys during their 108 game, 1949 season leading the team in homers, with 13, runs, 129, and runs batted in, 89. In 1950, he was the runner-up to Butch Davis in the batting race, hitting .374. His farewell season was 1953 which he split between Brandon and the Winnipeg Royals.

    1948 Brandon Greys—.287
    1949 Brandon Greys—.317, 25 D, 14 T, 13 HR, 23 SB, 89 RBI, Won 2, Lost 0
    1950 Brandon Greys—.374, 6 HR, 33 RBI
    1951 Brandon Greys—.207, 3 HR, 36 RBI
    1953 Brandon/Winnipeg—.222, 4 HR, 27 RBI

    The 1949 statistics include league, tournament, and exhibition games.

Canadian Highlights: July 3, 1948, Cabrera had three hits, two of them triples, as Brandon trounced Winnipeg Reos 18–5. July 28, he was the Brandon star with three hits, including a triple, and fine defensive play in a 9–0 romp over Elmwood. Cabrera, who had five putouts and eight assists from his second base post, also was instrumental in three double plays.

June 18, 1949, Cabrera drove in four runs with a homer and two singles in a 13–1 victory over Winnipeg Vets. It was his 5th homer in eight days. June 25, he knocked in six runs with two triples, a double and single as Brandon clobbered Carman 13–3. Hit by injuries from a highway accident, Greys sent Cabrera to the mound in an exhibition game against Neepawa July 18. The right-hander responded with a complete game, eight-hitter in an 11–4 win. August 27, his grand slam home run featured Brandon's 12–5 win over Regina at the Minot Tournament. It was Cabrera's second basesloaded homer in a week.

In the 1950 season opener on May 24, Cabrera knocked in three runs as Brandon toppled Minot 12–1. Over a little more than a month of the 1950 season, Cabrera had three, four-hit games and five, three-hit games, including a double-header in which he had six hits and a mammoth home run.

> ... it was shortstop Rafe Cabrera's four-ply smash which really set tongues wagging. He sent one of Ted Abel's pitches clear over the football exit gate in deep left-center field and passers-by said it landed smack in the middle of Tenth Avenue and bounced into the Milne coal yard.... His sock easily covered 450 feet through the air [*Regina Leader-Post* June 3, 1950].

May 22, 1951, Cabrera clubbed three hits, a homer and double included, to lead Brandon to a 5–2 win over Carman. June 11, he had another three-hit day as Brandon shutout Winnipeg 4–0. In 1951 playoff action, he had three hits September 5 as the Greys beat Carman 10–3 and another three safeties September 6 as he scored the winning run in a 3–2 decision over Carman. September 11, he had a homer and single as Brandon took a two-game lead in the ManDak final against Winnipeg.

Marion "Sugar" Cain—Pitcher, 5'11", 196 lbs. Batted right, threw right

With his arm and his bat, Cain was one of the most dominant players of the ManDak League from 1951 to 1957. He had first gained notice in Canada in 1948 when he toured with his San Francisco Cubs. His Negro League play went back to 1936 in Philadelphia before he moved west in the mid 1940s to play in the California Negro leagues. Cain joined Minot Mallards in 1951 for the first of seven seasons in the Manitoba-Dakota League.

With the collapse of the ManDak loop after the 1957 season, Cain returned to Negro ball as playing manager of the Kansas City Monarchs. He included some barnstorming with major leaguers in the fall and winter. The talented right-hander was one of the top performers with the Willie Mays All-Stars and later with the Don Newcombe and Hank Aaron All-Stars. He also pitched in Mexico and was back with Minot when the city entered the Northern League.

In 1959, Cain led the Kansas City Monarchs to top money in the Lethbridge, Alberta, Rotary Tournament. He was the winning pitcher in the championship game. The 1960 season appears to have been his final fling.

> 1951 Minot Mallards—Won 7, Lost 8, 17 G, 14 GS, 12 CG, .268
> 1952 Minot Mallards—Won 7, Lost 3, 10 G, 9 GS, 8 CG, .279
> 1953 Minot Mallards—Won 12, Lost 5, 17 G, 17 GS, 15 CG, .357
> 1954 Minot Mallards—Won 11, Lost 1, 13 G, 13 GS, 11 CG, 106 IP, 34 BB, 98 SO, .451, 2 HR
> 1955 Minot Mallards—Won 8, Lost 4, .254
> 1956 Minot Mallards—Won 10, Lost 5, 15 G, 15 GS, 15 CG, 2.29 ERA, .325
> 1957 Minot Mallards—Won 7, Lost 5, 3.94 ERA, .318

Canadian Highlights: July 6 and July 14, 1952, Cain fired back-to-back shutouts in league play. In between he tossed a four-hitter to lead Minot to top money in the Foam Lake Tournament.

June 24, 1953, Cain blanked Saskatoon 1–0 on a five-hitter in an interlocking game at Saskatoon. July 10, it was a two-hit shutout for Cain in a 7–0 win over North Battleford in interlocking play.

June 14, 1956, Cain fired a seven-hit shutout in Minot's win over North Battleford.

Walter Calhoun—Pitcher

Calhoun was a member of the mound staff of the 1950 Indian Head Rockets.

Canadian Highlights: July 6, 1950, Calhoun pitched a four-hit shutout as Indian Head beat Sceptre 7–0 in the first game of a doubleheader. He bashed a triple in the second game.

Charles Calvert—Pitcher/Infield

Quebec was a regular stop for Chappie Johnson's Colored All-Stars during the late 1920s and early 1930s and they became so popular and well received that Johnson sponsored an all-black team in a Montreal area circuit. It led to the early integration of teams in the province. In 1935 Calvert was one of the local black athletes playing in independent leagues in Quebec.

Winters Calvin—Outfield

Winters' California buddies Nat Bates, Pumpsie Green and Willie Reed had played with Medicine Hat Mohawks in 1951 and when they joined Indian Head Rockets in 1952 he was encouraged to join them. Along with the others, Calvin was a star high school and junior college player in the Oakland area.

Canadian Highlights: August 13, 1952, Calvin belted a four-bagger in a losing cause for the Rockets against the Florida Cubans.

Henry "Red" Cameron—Catcher

Cameron was a backstop for the Indian Head Rockets in 1950 and 1951.

> 1950 Indian Head Rockets—Statistics not available
> 1951 Indian Head Rockets—.387 (incomplete)

Canadian Highlights: August 21, 1951, in playoff action, Cameron had a double and two singles in a Rockets' loss.

Roy "Campy" Campanella—Catcher, 5'9", 190 lbs. Batted right, threw right

Campy was still in the minor leagues with the Montreal Royals when Paul Richards, then playing-manager of Buffalo (and a former major league catcher), had no hesitation in naming Campanella is the best catcher in the

From a Negro League catcher at age fifteen, Campanella reached the majors eleven years later, in 1948, and starred for nine seasons. He was an all-star eight straight seasons, winning the National League's Most Valuable Player Award three times (photograph courtesy the National Baseball Hall of Fame Library, Cooperstown, N.Y.).

business. *(The Sporting News, January 7, 1948, p.11)*

The stocky backstop had finished 1947 as the best defensive catcher in the International League leading the circuit in games, putouts, and assists. Of 60 steal attempts against him, Campanella nailed 39. He was a near unanimous choice as an all-star.

By the time he reached Brooklyn, the 26-year-old Campanella already had 11 years of professional experience—eight years in the Negro Leagues, a year in Mexico and two in the Dodger system. He was just fifteen when he first put on the catching gear for the Baltimore Elite Giants. It wasn't until 1946, however, after Jackie Robinson had integrated the minor leagues, that Campy got his shot. He did not disappoint. Campanella, an all-star in the Negro League, was a major league all-star eight straight seasons. Campy and Don Newcombe formed the first black battery in major league history. One of the legendary "Boys of Summer," he was the National League's Most Valuable Player three times. His best season may have been in 1953 when he batted .312 with 41 home runs and 142 runs batted in. He played in the World Series five times.

Just four months after the Dodgers had played their last inning at Ebbets Field in Brooklyn (and were well into planning for the 1958 season in Los Angeles), Campanella suffered serious injuries in an automobile accident. He was paralyzed from the neck down. In 1969 he was inducted into the Hall of Fame at Cooperstown. He died in 1993.

1947 Montreal Royals—.273, 25 D, 3 T, 13 HR, 75 RBI

Frank Campos—Outfield, 5'11", 180 lbs. Batted left, threw left

The Havana born outfielder, who began his pro career with five straight seasons in Class-B (three years with the same team), jumped to the majors with Washington for 71 games over three seasons, 1951 to 1953. He had a .279 career average. Campos was in the Toronto lineup for 21 games in 1953. He died in 2006 at age 81.

> 1953 Toronto Maple Leafs—.239, 0 D, 0 T, 3 HR, 6 RBI

Sebastian Antonio "Tony" Campos—Second Base, 5'11", 175 lbs. Batted right, threw right

Born in Havana, Cuba, Campos entered organized ball in 1947, playing for St. Petersburg in the Florida International League. It was one of eleven years in baseball including stops in the United States, Cuba, Mexico, Venezuela, the Dominican Republic, Nicaragua, Colombia and Canada.

In 1952, he journeyed north after signing with Drummondville of the Quebec Provincial League. Campos played in the ManDak League in 1954 with the Williston Oilers and batted .289 with 6 home runs and 39 runs batted in. He played winter ball in Cuba for the Almendares teams that won the 1954 and 1955 pennants and for Cienfuegos which won the Cuban title and the Caribbean Series in 1956. His brother Frank, an outfielder, was with the Washington Senators for parts of three seasons in the early 1950s. Tony Campos died December 29, 2002 in Cuba. He was 77.

> 1952 Drummondville—.240, 20 D, 5 T, 1 HR, 26 RBI

Canadian Highlights: June 4, 1954, Campos had a triple and single as Williston fell to the Greys in Brandon, 4–1. July 15, he knocked in two runs with a triple and single as the Oilers downed Brandon 7–1. July 30, another two-run triple by Campos helped Williston beat Carman 9–3.

Avelino Canizares—Shortstop, 5'7", 140 lbs. Batted right, threw right

Canizares, a Cuban, played the 1945 season with the Cleveland Buckeyes, but spent most of his playing time in the Mexican League. In 1950 he was with Sherbrooke in the Quebec Provincial League. He continued playing ball until 1964, at the age of 45.

Antonio Sebastian "Tony" Campos, Cuban born, played for eleven seasons in, at least, eight different countries—Cuba, United States, Mexico, Venezuela, the Dominican Republic, Nicaragua, Colombia and Canada (photograph from the Mah Collection, courtesy Tony Campos, Jr.).

> 1950 Sherbrooke Athletics—.294, 18 D, 0 T, 0 HR, 37 RBI

Pedro Cardenal—Outfield, 5'10", 170 lbs. Batted right, threw right

A fleet-footed outfielder, Cardenal got his start in 1953 in the Sooner State League where he hit .293 and led the league in triples, with 19. In 1954, he joined the Duluth Dukes in the Northern League and returned to the circuit in 1955 and 1956 as a member of the Winnipeg Goldeyes. He bounced around the Cardinals' minor league system until 1958. From 1959 to 1964 he finished his career in the Mexican League.

> 1955 Winnipeg Goldeyes—.289, 15 D, 10 T, 9 HR, 57 RBI
> 1956 Winnipeg Goldeyes—.315, 17 D, 9 T, 8 HR, 96 RBI

Canadian Highlights: July 1, 1956, he had 3 hits and 4 RBI as the Goldeyes beat the Fargo-Moorhead Twins 9–5 in the first game of a twin-bill. He banged out 2 more hits in the second game as the Goldeyes swept winning 4–2. July 18, Cardenal was the star of the all-star game with three hits, two of them doubles, and two runs batted in as the all-stars beat Eau Claire Braves 7–1. His teammates selected Cardenal as the Goldeyes' Most Valuable Player.

Sylvester "Pee Wee" Carlisle (Carlyle) — Second Base

Carlisle came out of Wiley College in Marshall, Texas to play in the Negro League with the Kansas City Monarchs in the mid 1940s. He went on to suit up with the Cuban Stars, Cincinnati Crescents, Harlem Globetrotters and Duluth Travelers. The second sacker came to Canada in 1952 for a brief stint with the Carman Cardinals in the ManDak League before returning to the road to barnstorm with the Globetrotters. He was a light hitter, but strong defensively.

1952 Carman Cardinals —.211, 0 HR, 0 RBI

Wayne "Pappy" Carr — Manager

After a pitching career in the Negro Leagues in the 1920s, Carr turned to managing and piloted teams, Negro and integrated, into the 1950s. He toured Western Canada in 1949 with the San Francisco Sea Lions and directed the Estevan Maple Leafs of the Southern League in 1950. The following season he was back across the border managing the Duluth Travelers.

Lindsay Carswell — Outfield

The speedy center fielder had experience with the Jacksonville Eagles of Southern Negro ball before three stints in Western Canada. He played with the barnstorming Indian Head Rockets in 1950 and the 1951 Rockets of the Western Canada League, and then, in 1953, the Regina Caps of the Saskatchewan League. In 1952 Carswell had a brief fling in the pro ranks with Porterville of the Southwest International League.

Canadian Highlights: August 10, 1951, Carswell, just back from injury, had two hits and scored three times in the Rockets' 7–1 win over Moose Jaw. August 16, Carswell had three hits as Indian Head clobbered Swift Current 17–4.

June 23, 1953, his three-run, inside-the-park, homer highlighted a six-run inning as Regina Caps downed Moose Jaw 10–4. July 27, Carswell, who played brilliantly in center field, had three hits as the Caps downed Saskatoon Gems.

Ernest "Spoon" Carter — Pitcher, 6'0", 185 lbs. Batted left, threw right

Carter had a successful 18-year career in the Negro League stretching from 1932 to 1949. His tenure included time with two of the best Negro League teams, the Pittsburgh Crawfords and Homestead Grays.

He closed out his playing days in Canada in 1950 when he took to the mound in the inaugural season of the Manitoba-Dakota (ManDak) League with the Winnipeg Buffaloes. At age 47, Carter managed to carve out a 4–2 won-lost mark in 12 games as the Buffaloes captured the league title. He died in 1974 at age 71.

1950 Winnipeg Buffaloes — Won 4, Lost 2, 12 G, 5 GS, 2 CG

Canadian Highlights: June 14, 1950, Carter pitched Winnipeg into the final of the Brandon Tournament in a 6–2 win over Regina. July 27, Carter had three hits and went the route for the "W" in the Buffaloes' 8–2 victory over Carman. August 22, the right-hander fired five innings of one-hit relief to capture the win in a 14-inning triumph over Minot.

Bill "Ready" Cash — Catcher, 6'1", 190 lbs, Batted right, threw right

Cash was a fixture in the Negro Leagues for eight years, 1943 to 1950, as catcher for the Philadelphia Stars.

He first came to Canada in 1951 to play for Granby in the Quebec Provincial League, then back in the good graces of organized baseball. He attracted the attention of the Chicago White Sox and played in their minor league system in 1952. Cash returned to Canada in 1953 to begin the season with the Brandon Greys of the ManDak League. However, Cash picked up the scent of more cash and after just six weeks in Brandon he accepted a more lucrative offer with a team in the Dominican Republic. He returned to the Dominican circuit in 1954 before coming back to the ManDak League, this time with the Bismarck Barons, in 1955. He had a superb season hitting .357 with 15 home runs and 61 runs batted in.

    1951 Granby Phillies—.296, 21 D, 2 T, 16 HR, 54 RBI
    1953 Brandon Greys—.363, 6 HR, 23 RBI

Canadian Highlights: May 22, 1953, Cash had a homer, triple and double in an 18–5 win over the Winnipeg Royals. June 9 saw Cash hit a double that drove in the winning run in the ninth inning that gave Brandon a 4–3 win over Winnipeg. Cash had a big day at the plate, on June 17, as Brandon beat the Royals 13–3. He led the Greys with a two-run homer, a double and two singles.

Irwin "Chuck" Castille—Shortstop/Third Base

Castille had a lone season of Negro League action, in 1951 with the Birmingham Black Barons, before coming north. In June of 1952, he joined the Brandon Greys in the ManDak League for just one summer. The next year he was back in the Negro League.

    1952 Brandon Greys—.309, 1 HR, 22 RBI.

Canadian Highlight—July 29, playing against the Winnipeg Giants, Castillo had a triple, two doubles and a single in five trips to the plate

Jose "Bobby" Cesar—Shortstop, 5'11", 165 lbs. Batted right, threw right

A slick shortstop with pop, the 19-year-old import from Cuba was among the leading hitters and run producers in the Western Canada League in 1957. The Regina Braves' star led the circuit with 11 triples, was among the leaders in runs batted in and finished seventh in the batting race.

He arrived with a half-dozen Cuban players on the recommendation of the Havana Sugar Kings (an affiliate of the Cincinnati Reds) of the Triple-A, International League. Cesar had the misfortune of joining the Los Angeles Dodgers organization at the time shortstop Maury Wills was establishing himself as an all-star and the stolen base king of the major leagues.

Cesar played in Triple-A in each of his last three pro seasons and suited up in winter ball with the Havana Reds. His first full pro season was his best as he clobbered Class-D pitching in the Arizona-Mexico League for a .342 average, 35 doubles, 15 triples and 15 home runs.

    1957 Regina Braves—.336, 18 D, 11 T, 1 HR, 58 RBI
    1960 Montreal Royals—.333, 1 HR, 3 RBI

Canadian Highlights: June 17, 1957, Cesar had a triple and single in a 7–4 win over Moose Jaw. July 12, Cesar drove in four runs with a double and two singles as Regina dumped North Battleford 14–7. July 29, Cesar had three hits to lead Regina to an 8–7 win over Edmonton. August 4, Cesar's 9th inning single broke up Gene Graves' no-hit bid. The next night, Cesar drove in the winning run in the bottom of the 9th as the Braves beat Edmonton ace Dale Zeigler. August 8, Cesar drove in a pair with a triple and single in a 9–7 win over Saskatoon. August 12, Cesar had three hits in a win over North Battleford. August 14, Cesar knocked in four runs with a triple and double as Regina topped Moose Jaw 8–2 in the first game of the double-header. He had a double and single in the nightcap. September 5, Cesar drove in two runs with a pair of doubles, but Regina dropped a 7–6 playoff decision to Moose Jaw.

"Shortstop Bobby Cesar, whose sparkling defensive play alone rates him as all-star timber, belted a double and two singles to chase four more Brave runs across the plate" [*Regina Leader Post*, July 13, 1957].

"Bobby Cesar is quickly gaining the reputation of being the best shortstop ever to show here" [*Regina Leader Post*, July 17, 1957].

"...oddity of the night was the fact that Bobby Cesar didn't come up with at least one fantastic play at short" [*Regina Leader Post*, July 19, 1957].

Mario Chacon—Pitcher

The Cuban hurler pitched in Mexico in 1949

and came to the Brandon Greys of the Man-Dak League in 1950. He saw little action.

1950 Brandon Greys—Won 0, Lost 0

Dave Chadwick—Pitcher. Threw right

Chadwick, age twenty, pitched and played a little outfield for the Regina Caps of the 1951 Western Canada Baseball League. It was reported that he had signed a tryout with the Pittsburgh Pirates for 1952.

1951 Regina Caps—Won 5, Lost 3, 15 G, 8 GS, 5 CG, .244

Canadian Highlights: July 6, 1951, Chadwick fired a three-hitter as Regina downed Medicine Hat 5–1. July 20, Regina won a semi-final berth at the Indian Head Tournament as Chadwick out pitched Indian Head's Jesse Blackman and Chet Brewer in the Caps' 7–2 win. An error, which plated two runs, cost Chadwick the shutout. July 28, Regina took a 6–3 decision from Swift Current as Chadwick relieved in the first inning and allowed just one hit the rest of the way as the Caps won 6–3. August 6, Chadwick pitched Regina into the semi-finals at the Edmonton Tournament going all the way in a 4–3, 10 inning, win over the Central Alberta All-Stars. August 10, playing the outfield, Chadwick clouted a two-run homer to help Regina top Estevan 4–1.

Homer Chandler—Pitcher/Outfield

Chandler, from Fulton, Kentucky, came to Canada in 1949 to join the Elmwood Giants in the Manitoba Senior Baseball League. After an uncertain first few weeks (there were rumors in the paper of his release) Chandler settled in to be a workhorse for the Giants making 22 starts and winning 11 games. Showing prowess with the bat, he also played the outfield and hit a respectable .256.

1949 Elmwood Giants—Won 11, Lost 7, 22 G, 20 GS, 11 CG *

All games, league, exhibition, tournament

Canadian Highlights: June 1, 1949, while pitching in the ninth inning he beaned Winnipegs' Tommy Ketchur. With Ketchur knocked unconscious, Chandler was so shaken that he pulled himself out of the game. Ketchur ended up in the hospital and was out of the lineup for nearly a month. June 6, Chandler fired a four-hitter with 10 strikeouts and drove in three runs with a double and single in the Giants win over the Winnipegs. July 29, Chandler had a no-hitter, albeit just four innings, in a tournament win over St. Boniface. August 2, he blanked the Vets on seven hits in a 3–0 win for Elmwood.

Ed Charles—Third Base, 5'10", 170 lbs. Batted right, threw right

Charles was another who used the Quebec Provincial League as a stepping stone to the major leagues. He joined the loop in 1952 and played well in his only season. He played minor league ball up until December, 1961, when he was dealt to the Kansas City A's. In 1962 he played the first of his eight major league seasons, which included a stint with the Mets and finished with a .263 major league career average.

1952 Quebec Braves—.317, 23 D, 11 T, 3 HR, 88 RBI

Johnny Charles—Center Field, 5'7", 160 lbs. Batted right

The Milwaukee Braves' prospect played in the Quebec Provincial League in 1953 and 1954.

1953 Quebec Braves—.321, 18 D, 11 T, 1, 55 RBI
1954 Quebec Braves—.180, 5 T, 6 RBI

Thad Christopher—Catcher/Outfield, 6'1", 185 lbs. Batted left, threw right

Christopher played for a dozen Negro teams from 1935 to 1945. Among others, he suited up with the Newark Eagles, Pittsburgh Crawfords, New York Black Yankees, Ethiopian Clowns and Homestead Grays. In 1948, in Canada with the Brandon Greys, he finished second in batting in the Manitoba Senior League with a .333 mark (behind future hockey Hall of Famer Terry Sawchuk). He returned to the Negro League in 1949, but was back in Brandon for a brief spell in 1950 when the Greys joined the ManDak League. He ended his career with the Brooklyn Cuban Giants barnstorming team. He passed away in 1973 in California at age 60.

1948 Brandon Greys—.333
1950 Brandon Greys—Statistics not available

Randy Cisco—Second Base

Cisco was among the players recruited from the Washington-Philadelphia area to form the 1954 Rosetown Phillies.

Canadian Highlights: May 19, 1954, Cisco, in the leadoff spot, had four hits to lead Rosetown in a 7–6 win over Saskatoon.

Ignacio Cisnero—Pitcher

The Cuban moundsman pitched as a starter and reliever for the Florida Cubans in 1952 and Saskatoon Gems in 1953. He was a main figure in the famous Rosetown Riot of 1952 in which Cisnero, with a bat in hand, chased North Battleford's Curtis Tate through the baseball diamond to a parking lot, over a gravel highway and across a farmer's field after the Beavers' player had felled one of the Cubans with a bat during a tournament game in Rosetown. It was necessary to bring in the Royal Canadian Mounted Police to end the brouhaha.

James "Buzz" Clarkson—Outfield, 5'11" 195 lbs. Batted right, threw left

Clarkson's Negro League career, mainly as a shortstop, ran from 1937 to 1947 and 1949 to 1950. An accomplished hitter, with power, he batted over .300 most seasons. In 1948, in Canada with the St. Jean Braves, Clarkson had one of his best seasons with a .408 average and 31 home runs. From 1951 to 1956 he played in organized ball reaching the majors in 1952 for 14 games with the Boston Braves. In one of his best years, Clarkson belted 42 home runs and drove in 135 in 1954 as he hit .324 in the Double-A, Texas League. He died in 1989.

1948 St. Jean Braves—.408, 14 D, 1 T, 31 HR

Canadian Highlights: Clarkson tied for the league lead (with Joe Atkins) with 31 home runs in 1948.

Jimmy Claxton—Pitcher. Batted left, threw left

Claxton, born in Canada, broke the color line in 1916 posing as a Native American in pitching in two games, both on the same day, with the Oakland Oaks of the Pacific Coast League. Identified as the "Indian southpaw," he started the first game of a double-header and lasted only into the third inning. He relieved in the 9th inning of the second game. He pitched a total of 2⅓ innings allowing four hits and two earned runs. He went on to play in Negro and semi-pro competition and claimed to have pitched in all but two of the 48 contiguous states of the United States. Claxton was the first black player to appear on a baseball card. He was in the 1916 series of Zeenuts' cards as his brief stay with Oakland just happened to coincide with the arrival of the candy company's photographer. He died in 1970, at age 77, in Tacoma.

Roberto (Walker) Clemente—Outfield, 5'11", 175 lbs. Batted right, threw right

The young Puerto Rican was one of the Dodgers' few mistakes of the era. And, what a mistake! Clemente was signed by Brooklyn in 1954 and assigned to Montreal. The 19-year-old batted just .257 and the team failed to include him on their list of protected players and he was quickly snapped up by the Pittsburgh Pirates with the first pick in the 1954, Rule 5 draft. The Pirates paid all of $4,000 for the future Hall of Famer. After an 18-year career marked by twelve all-star appearances, twelve Gold Glove Awards, four batting titles and an MVP Award, he won a spot in the Hall of Fame at Cooperstown.

He was killed in a plane crash in 1972 when trying to deliver aid to earthquake victims in Nicaragua. Each year, Major League Baseball presents the Roberto Clemente Award in honor of a player of outstanding baseball skills who makes an impact with devoted work in the community. In 2003, Clemente was awarded, posthumously, the American Presidential Medal of Freedom. The award, marking distinguished service, is the highest civilian honor in the United States.

1954 Montreal Royals—.257, 5 D, 3 T, 2 HR, 12 RBI

Luther "Shanty" Clifford—Catcher/Outfield, 6'0", 200 lbs. Batted right, threw right

Clifford had a three year stay in the Negro League, 1948 to 1950, as the circuit began to wind down after the integration of the major leagues. He saw time with the Homestead Grays and Kansas City Monarchs. In 1951, Clifford sampled the Canadian scene playing with the Brantford Red Sox in the Intercounty Baseball League in southern Ontario. The following summer, he came to Western Canada and joined the Brandon Greys in the ManDak League. After a return to Negro ball for 1953, Clifford went back to Brantford in 1954 and spent another five seasons in the Intercounty circuit. He won the batting title in 1956 with a .397 mark.

> 1951 Brantford Red Sox—Statistics not available
> 1952 Brandon Greys—.330, 3 HR, 23 RBI
> 1955 Brantford Red Sox—.340, 10 HR, 40 RBI
> 1956 Brantford Red Sox—.397
> 1957 Brantford—Statistics not available
> 1958 Galt Terriers—.366, Led the league with 31 RBI

Canadian Highlights: July 26, 1952, Clifford pounded out four hits in a 14–10 Brandon win over Winnipeg. July 29, Clifford knocked in three runs with a double and single as the Greys whipped Winnipeg 13–1. August 5, Clifford poked a pair of homers, good for four runs batted in, in a loss to Carman. August 14, Clifford had four hits as Brandon shaded Minot 12–11.

July 2, 1955, Clifford had four hits, three runs batted in and a stolen base in a losing cause to Kitchener. July 18, Clifford registered another four hit day in Brantford's 8–3 win over Galt. July 19, his two-run homer was the big blow as Brantford topped London 5–4. July 30, Clifford notched three hits, including a homer, in a 5–3 win over Galt. August 2, a two-run blast, his second in as many games against Galt, was key as Brantford blanked Galt 3–0. August 28, Clifford drove in five runs with two homers and a single as the Red Sox trounced Oshawa 14–1.

Bob Clipper—Shortstop/Catcher

The versatile athlete, who played both shortstop and second base, ended up as the catcher for the Prince Albert squad of the Northern Saskatchewan League in 1951. He had joined Prince Albert after a brief spin with Kamsack of the Manitoba-Saskatchewan League.

Lillord Cobb—Pitcher/Outfield. Threw left

The lefthander came out of Negro ball in the Detroit area to win a tryout with the Tigers, but failed to get a contract. He came to Canada in 1949 to pitch and play the outfield for the Carman Cardinals of the Manitoba Senior League. Cobb also played the 1950 and 1951 seasons with Carman when they were in the ManDak circuit. He attended Lawrence Technological University in Detroit and graduated with a Bachelor of Science degree in Mechanical Engineering. It has been reported that in the 1960s he patented a design that was among the innovations which helped Apollo 11 reach the moon.

Cobb had five sons—Matthew, Marvin, Michael, Marcus and Marty. Marvin was a baseball and football star at the University of Southern California. He turned pro in football, as a defensive back with the Cincinnati Bengals of the National Football League. Lillord Cobb died in 2006 at age 81.

> 1949 Carman Cardinals—Won 3, Lost 8, 13 G, 10 GS, 7 CG, .269
> 1950 Carman Cardinals—Won 5, Lost 4, 9 G, 9 GS, 8 CG, .238, 2 HR, 14 RBI
> 1951 Carman Cardinals—Won 1, Lost 1

Canadian Highlights: August 23, 1949 Cobb pitched a two-hitter in the fourth game of the playoffs against the Brandon Greys. He fanned nine batters. It was his second two-hitter in three days.

July 18, 1950, he pitched a five-hit, 8–0 win over Brandon and struck out seven. August 4, Cobb pitched all 13 innings, but lost 1–0 to Brandon. August 31, Cobb pitched and batted Carman to a 6–3 playoff victory over the Greys. He hit a home run and single to drive in two runs.

Howard Coffee—Pitcher

Coffee came to Canada in 1950 and played with Grandview, Manitoba, in the Northern Manitoba Senior League. In 1951, he joined the Negro League and played until 1954 with the Philadelphia Stars and Indianapolis Clowns

Jose Colas—Outfield. Batted right, threw right

Colas, born in Cuba, played in the Negro League for the Memphis Red Sox from 1947 to 1952. Early in the '52 season he joined the Brandon Greys of the ManDak League. He played in organized ball in 1954 in the Mississippi-Ohio League

> 1952 Brandon Greys—.245, 3 HR, 21 RBI

Canadian Highlights: Brandon lost 9–3 to Minot on July 24, but Colas was the game's defensive star making ten putouts in center field, some of the spectacular variety. August 14, Colas hit a towering two-run homer in the bottom of the 11th inning to give Brandon a 12–11 victory over Minot

Emery Coleman—Pitcher. Threw right

The 17-year-old joined the Regina Caps for the 1953 season and, after a stint with the Jacksonville (Florida) Eagles, returned the following summer to suit up with Moose Jaw.

> 1953 Regina—Statistics not available
> 1954 Moose Jaw—Won 1, Lost 4, 8 G, 8 GS, 4 CG

Canadian Highlights: June 2, 1953, Coleman went the distance as the Caps downed the Southern League All-Stars 11–3.

August 12, 1954, Coleman's three-run triple was the crucial blow as Moose Jaw topped Lloydminster 7–5. The right-hander allowed seven hits in gaining the win.

Johnny "Lefty" Coleman—Pitcher. Threw left

Coleman came to the Indian Head Rockets in 1951 after a season in the Negro League with the Baltimore Elite Giants. He then joined North Battleford Beavers for two seasons, 1952 and 1953. He returned to the Negro League in 1954 to pitch for the Birmingham Black Barons.

> 1951 Indian Head Rockets—Won 5, Lost 2, 8 G, 7 GS, 5 CG
> 1952 North Battleford Beavers—Won 7, Lost 3, 84 IP, 28 BB, 75 SO
> 1953 North Battleford Beavers—Won 9, Lost 4, 34 BB, 68 SO

Canadian Highlights: July 18, 1951, Coleman fired a five-hit shutout as the Rockets dumped Moose Jaw Canucks 5–0 in the opening round of the Indian Head Tournament. August 3, Coleman pitched Indian Head into the final of the Tisdale Tournament with a three-hitter as the Rockets downed Delisle in a semi-final match.

June 11, 1952, Coleman fired a five-hitter, with 12 strikeouts and no walks, as North Battleford advanced at the Lloydminster Tournament with an 11–2 win over Great Falls, Montana. August 14, Coleman was brilliant in a two-hit shutout of Moose Jaw in playoff action. He fanned eight and walked one. August 26, Coleman pitched a four-hit shutout as the Beavers staved off elimination in the final series with a 2–0 win over Saskatoon.

May 18, 1953, Coleman tossed a three-hitter to lead North Battleford to a 9–0 whitewash of Moose Jaw. June 1, Coleman was all the Beavers needed in an 8–0 blanking of Regina. He scattered eight hits in his mound work with seven strikeouts and one walk. At the plate he had a three-run double. June 16, Coleman tossed a six-hitter with 14 strikeouts and poked a three-run homer as North Battleford dumped Westlock 10–1 at the Lloydminster Tournament.

Major Coleman—Pitcher. Threw right

Coleman was recruited from the Philadelphia area to help form the "all-colored" Rosetown Phillies entry in the Western Canada Baseball League in 1954, the lone season for the club.

> 1954 Rosetown—Won 2, Lost 3, 6 G, 6 GS, 3 CG

Canadian Highlights: July 16, 1954, in his debut with the Phillies, Coleman scattered nine hits and fanned nine in notching a 6–4 complete game victory over North Battleford. His teammates made five errors to account for most of the damage against him. August 8, Coleman allowed just four hits and fanned twelve, but lost 1–0. August 12, Coleman again suffered a tough loss in throwing a three-hitter in a 3–2 defeat to Saskatoon. August 17, Coleman allowed just two hits over 8 shutout innings as Rosetown blanked North Battleford 4–0.

Hubert "Pee Wee" Collins—Shortstop/Second Base, 5'6". Threw right

The little middle infielder was a regular with the 1950 Indian Head Rockets and the 1951 Regina Caps, leading the league in stolen bases in 1951 with 20.

> 1950 Indian Head Rockets—Statistics not available
> 1951 Regina Caps—.269, 20 SB (incomplete)

Canadian Highlights: July 28, 1950, Collins belted a two-run triple and double to push Indian Head to a 6–2 win over Estevan at the Swift Current Tournament.

June 2, 1951, Collins reached base five times, on two hits, two walks and a fielder's choice and added three stolen bases in a loss to Estevan.

Buford "Tex" Conley—Pitcher/Outfield

Conley pitched for the 1950 Estevan Maple Leafs of the Southern (Saskatchewan) League and returned in 1952 to play for Roblin, Manitoba, of the Manitoba-Saskatchewan League. He was back in 1953 with the Bowsman, Manitoba, Maroons (they had been called the Arrows, but their new uniforms—slightly used—had the name Maroons emblazoned across the front, so the team did the practical thing and renamed the team). He had come to Canada after a brief trial in Class-D pro ball.

Canadian Highlights: August 6, 1950, Conley pitched a seven-hitter as Estevan shaded the touring Muskogee Cardinals 4–3. In playoff action, August 19, Conley had three hits to lead Estevan to an 8–4 win over Notre Dame in a semi-final series. August 25, Conley again punched out three hits as Estevan won their semi-final with a 7–3 win. September 6, Conley had a two-run homer as Estevan won the Southern League title downing Moose Jaw 13–4.

Howard "Butch" Conley—Second Base. Threw right

Conley came to Carman, Manitoba in 1952 to play for the Cardinals. He had barnstorming experience with the Brooklyn Cuban Giants the previous year.

> 1952 Carman Cardinals—.185, 0 HR, 7 RBI

Sandalio "Sandy" Consuegra—Pitcher, 5'11", 165 lbs. Batted right, threw right

Consuegra, born in Potrerillos, Cuba, in 1920, began his career in 1949 with the Havana Cubans in the Florida International League. Havana was the first Cuban team to play in the American minor leagues, a farm team of the Washington Senators.

In 1950, after eleven games with the Cubans, he was promoted to the major league club. He continued to pitch at the big league level until 1957, spending time with the Senators, Chicago White Sox, Baltimore Orioles and New York Giants. He started the 1957 campaign with the Orioles, but spent most of the season with the Vancouver Mounties and ended up being claimed by the Giants.

He had an outstanding season in 1954 with the White Sox and finished the season with a 16–3 record, the best winning percentage in the American League. He also pitched in the all-star game that season. He ended his eight year major league career with a 51–32 record and 3.37 ERA.

In 1957, pitching in relief for the Mounties, he had an outstanding season. He pitched briefly in 1958 with the Triple-A, Havana Sugar Kings and with Monterrey in the Mexican League. He closed out his career in 1961, after two games with Charlotte in the South Atlantic League. He died in 2005 in Miami, Florida, at the age of 85.

> 1957 Vancouver Mounties—Won 7, Lost 1, 1.99

Tom Cooper—Catcher/First base/Outfield, 5'11", 175 lbs. Batted both, threw right

Cooper played for the Kansas City Monarchs from 1947 to 1952. In 1953, he was in organized ball with Schenectady in the Eastern League. In 1954, he played in Canada with Three Rivers, then a Philadelphia Phillies farm team, in the Quebec Provincial League.

1954 Three Rivers Phillies—.227, 0 HR, 7 RBI

Sherman Cottingham—Pitcher, 6'1", 180 lbs. Batted left, threw right

Cottingham had an initial taste of the Canadian prairies in 1963 when he toured with the Satchel Paige All-Stars. Fans of the era may not have recognized his name as he often was identified as Satchel Paige Jr. when he came in to finish up the mound duties for the barnstorming team.

One of the stops on the tour was in North Battleford, Saskatchewan, where the manager of the local club approached Cottingham about playing there the following season.

The Louisiana native had attracted interest from Paige when he pitched against the All-Stars in a game in Mississippi. Cottingham had been renting himself out to various teams to help pay his way through college.

> I had my own uniform, with my name on the back, and I had one guy who would catch me and I would bid myself out to whoever wanted my services. So I didn't play for any particular team. Somebody would call me like in Shreveport, Louisiana, and say come on over we want you to pitch this game and we have a big pot, winner take all. And I would go ... all over and I would charge a fee to pitch a game [2008 Interview].

In 1964, Cottingham accepted the North Battleford offer and during his summer break from school teaching duties pitched for the local club, the Beavers. He was outstanding, leading the league with 10 wins and batting over .300. He returned in 1965 and had 9 wins, second best in the loop. He was one of two imports allowed on the Northern Saskatchewan League team (the other was catcher Ira McKnight).

After his 1965 season, he was forced to remain close to home in Louisiana to work on his master's degree as he had been promoted to school principal. He continued to pitch in the south up to the early 1970s when he moved to Michigan.

His stint with North Battleford was the first time he had played on an integrated team or against a white or integrated team.

1964 N. Battleford Beavers—Won 10, Lost 2, .309, 3 HR, 14 RBI
1965 N. Battleford Beavers—Won 9, Lost 4, 3.12 ERA

Canadian Highlights: August 21, 1964, Cottingham fired a no-hitter as North Battleford topped Kindersley 5–0 in playoff action. In the 1965 playoffs, August 27, he fired a four-hit shutout in an 8–0 win over Unity for his second win of the series.

John Cowan—Infield, 5'11", 165 lbs. Batted right, threw right

Although a light hitter, Cowan carved out an impressive career in the Negro League 1933 to 1949. Among others, he suited up with the Birmingham Black Barons, Cleveland Buckeyes and Memphis Red Sox. In 1950, he left the Negro League and headed to Canada to join the Elmwood Giants in the ManDak League. Cowan died in 1993.

1950 Elmwood Giants—.249, 0 HR, 18 RBI

Canadian Highlights: On June 7, Cowan had three hits and led the Giants to a 12–6 victory

Satchel Paige Jr. or Sherman Cottingham? Often, when he toured with the Satchel Paige All-Stars in the early 1960s he was introduced as Satchel's son, but that was really Sherman Cottingham finishing up on the hill for the baseball legend. During one barnstorming stop, Cottingham was approached about joining a Canadian team and he ended up playing two seasons in Saskatchewan (photograph courtesy of Sherman Cottingham).

over Carman. On June 10, Cowan had another three-hit effort in a Giants victory over Minot Mallards.

Edward Lee Crowder—Pitcher/Outfield, 5'11", 168 lbs. Threw right

Crowder, from Omaha, Nebraska, played in Saskatchewan for the independent Swift Current Indians and the Saskatoon Legion of the Northern Saskatchewan League in 1950.

Canadian Highlights: In his debut, May 13, he fired three-hit, shutout ball for seven innings as Swift Current downed Shaunavon 8–3. May 26, the right-hander held Sceptre to four hits as Swift Current took top money at the Sceptre Tournament. June 10, Crowder, playing the outfield, thrilled the crowd with four, running, one-hand catches. June 28, Crowder fired a two-hitter and drove in both runs as the Indians stopped Lake Valley 2–1.

Marty "Matty" Crue—Outfield/Pitcher

Crue played in the Negro League from 1942 to 1950 for the New York Cubans and Homestead Grays. Early into the 1950 season he headed to Canada to join the Elmwood Giants of the ManDak League. Although he pitched when he played in the Negro League, he played only the outfield for the Giants in his short stay. In 1951 he was back in the Negro League with the New Orleans Eagles.

1950 Elmwood Giants—.267, 0 HR, 8 RBI

Canadian Highlights: May 31, Crue had three hits and drove in two Elmwood runs in a 12–6 Elmwood loss to Minot.

Bennie Crumpton—Outfield/First Base, 6'0", 180 lbs. Batted left

Crumpton started his career in 1954 with the Peoria Chiefs in the Illinois-Indiana-Iowa League. In 1955, he played briefly for Peoria and in May joined the Winnipeg Goldeyes. He played most of May, but could not get untracked in the hitting department. In June, he joined the Grand Forks Chiefs, where his bat came alive and he demonstrated some power. In 1956, he started the season with Williamsport in A-ball and again after a slow start was sent back to Grand Forks where he hit .336 and finished second in the batting race to Orlando Cepeda. He closed out his career in 1957 after playing briefly for Lincoln in the Western League.

1955 Winnipeg/Grand Forks—.302, 16 D, 2 T, 22 HR, 63 RBI

Canadian Highlights: He struggled most of May, but on June 9, 1955, he hit three singles as the Goldeyes beat Eau Claire Braves 8–6.

Aug 18, 1956, playing for Grand Forks, Crumpton belted a grand slam homer against the Goldeyes at Winnipeg Stadium.

Bob Cunningham—Pitcher

Cunningham started the 1950 season with the Cleveland Buckeyes in the Negro League. Shortly into the season he headed to Canada to join the Elmwood Giants in the ManDak League.

1950 Elmwood Giants—Won 4, Lost 5, 16 G, 11 GS, 4 CG

Canadian Highlights: May 31, Cunningham pitched shutout ball into the 8th inning, but an ankle injury on a fielding play sent him to the clubhouse. The Giants' relievers promptly gave up 12 runs as Elmwood lost 12–6. June 4, he went the distance in an 8–3 win over Carman. Cunningham won four straight in June before losing his last five decisions.

Nate Dancy—Second Base, 5'11", 190 lbs. Batted right, threw right

The Californian was the second baseman on the West squad in the 1960 East-West All-Star game, the last of the celebrated Negro League classics. Dancy was the leadoff hitter for the Kansas City Monarchs in 1960 and made a Canadian tour with the club to the Lacombe (Alberta) Tournament in late July. Although the Monarchs were ousted in the opening round, three players caught the attention of the owner of the Saskatoon Commodores of the Western Canada League. Dancy, catcher Ira McKnight and pitcher Tommy Taylor were enticed to leave the Monarchs to play in Saskatoon with the Commodores.

Lloyd "Ducky" Davenport—Outfield, 5'4", 150 lbs. Batted left, threw left

The diminutive outfielder played in the Negro League from 1939 to 1950 and played in five Negro League all-star games. During his career he also played in Mexico and Cuba. He was short in stature, but big on talent. He came to Canada in 1951 and joined the Brandon Greys in the ManDak League. On June 9, he was traded to the Elmwood Giants for Joe Mitchell.

1951 Brandon Greys/Elmwood Giants—
.278, 1 HR, 20 RBI

Canadian Highlights: On May 25, Davenport had a double and two singles in Brandon's 10–3 victory over Elmwood. July 31, saw Davenport hit three singles and a double to lead the Giants to a 12–3 win over the Winnipeg Buffaloes.

Edward "Peanuts" "Nyasses" Davis—Pitcher, 5'11", 150 lbs. Batted right, threw right

One of the great showmen of the golden era of the Negro Leagues, the pitcher-comedian began his career with the Ethiopian Clowns in the late 1930s. He stayed with the Clowns (through their days as the Cincinnati Clowns, Cincinnati-Indianapolis Clowns and Indianapolis Clowns) for 12 seasons making several appearances in Winnipeg in the early 40s. Davis was enticed to join the Indian Head Rockets in 1951.

> Davis provided the comic relief needed to keep the fans interested in the game. 'Peanuts' would go into an exaggerated wind-up, twirling his glove and kicking his leg into the bleachers, then throw the ball. If the ump never called the pitch a strike Davis would rant and rave on the mound, making chicken-like squawks. Davis, however, is an outstanding pitcher even with his parodies. He has played with Jackie Robinson's All-Stars and chucked against two of baseball's all-time greats — Bob Feller and Satchel Paige [*Medicine Hat News*, June 15, 1951].

1951 Indian Head Rockets—Won 4, Lost 4, 14 G, 9 GS, 7 CG

Canadian Highlights: June 14, Davis allowed just one hit in four scoreless innings as Indian Head Rockets blanked Medicine Hat Mohawks 6–0 in the opener of a three-game series. July 21, Davis held Moose Jaw to seven hits in leading Indian Head Rockets to their 18th straight league victory, 11–2 over the Canucks.

> We had a pitcher named Peanuts Nyasses Davis, a knuckleball pitcher, and you couldn't even play catch with him unless you had a mask on. The ball'd hit you in the mouth. He could throw it with control and throw it hard! [Raydell Maddix in *The Negro Leagues Revisited*].

Johnny Howard Davis—Outfield, 6'2", 217 lbs. Batted right, threw right

The big outfielder was a star on the Newark and Houston Eagles of the 1940s, selected three times for the Negro League's East-West All-Star game. While his hitting drew the most notice, his "sensational" play in the outfield and on the mound also gained attention.

> Davis made a circus catch of a liner by Armour in the sixth inning.... In the eighth inning, when B. Williams and Elam had shown spells of wildness on the mound and filled the bases, manager Suttles called Davis in from center-field to pitch. He struck out Parker and E. Williams to retire the side [*Baltimore Afro-American*, May 29, 1943, p.25].

> Davis, who relieved Raymond Brown in the first inning, drove in five runs with a homer and single, while getting credit for the win [*The Sporting News*, September 15, 1948, p.30].

Davis played in the Negro League from 1941 to 1950. Like many Negro Leaguers, he came to Canada when opportunities began to diminish in the United States with the collapse of the Negro Leagues. In 1951, he was a major force for Drummondville Cubs of the Quebec Provincial League hitting .347 with 31 home runs. The next year he moved up to Triple-A with San Diego in the Pacific Coast League. The Chicago White Sox showed interest, but Davis broke his ankle and, at age 35, it pretty well ruined his major league opportunity. He played two more seasons in organized ball topping the

Florida International League in home runs, with 35, and RBI, 136, in 1953 then closing out his career in 1954 with Montgomery in the South Atlantic League.

Davis was a star in fall and winter ball as well, MVP in Puerto Rico in 1947–48 when, in addition to his batting feats, Davis fired a no-hitter for Mayaguez in downing Aguadilla 1–0. During the 1949–50 campaign, he had an opportunity to manage the club. In 1946, he was a key member of the Satchel Paige All-Stars in a post-season series against the Bob Feller All-Stars. In Kansas City, Davis belted a three-run homer in the 9th inning off Spud Chandler to give the Paige Stars a 3–2 win. He died in 1982 at Fort Lauderdale, Florida.

> 1951 Drummondville Cubs—.347, 28 D, 1 T, 31 HR, 116 RBI

Canadian Highlights: In the Provincial League, Davis finished second in the league in batting, home runs and RBI.

Robert Lomax "Butch" Davis—
Outfield, 6'0", 220 lbs. Batted left, threw right

Davis was the batting star the first two years of the new ManDak League. He came to Winnipeg in 1950 after playing in the Negro League from 1947 to 1949 with the Baltimore Elite Giants. The big outfielder hit .456 and .406 to capture batting titles in both 1950 and 1951 (he also led in stolen bases in 1950 with 18). Midway through the 1951 season he was signed by the St Louis Browns and played in Double-A at Albany and Scranton. In 1952, he reached Triple-A before leaving the pro ranks. He returned to the ManDak League with Minot in 1955 and was the runner up to Roy Weatherly for the batting title.

> 1950 Winnipeg Buffaloes—.456, 14 D, 4 HR, 38 RBI, 18 SB
> 1951 Winnipeg Buffaloes—.406, 9 T, 7 HR, 53 RBI
> 1955 Minot Mallards—.369, 21 D, 3 T, 6 HR, 37 RBI

Canadian Highlights: June 10, 1950, Davis belted a triple, double and single and drove in three runs as Winnipeg topped Brandon 9–5. June 12, he had three hits in an 11–5 victory over Minot and on June 21 he hit a double and two singles as the Buffs dumped Elmwood 6–3. July 1, it was Winnipeg 7, Elmwood 3 as Davis collected four hits. July 12, saw Davis hit a home run, double and single and drive in five runs in a Buffaloes' victory over Brandon. In 1950 the Winnipeg Tribune picked Davis to the ManDak All-Star team.

He was almost as good in 1951. June 19, Davis drove in three runs with a homer and double in a 12–4 romp over Brandon. He followed that on June 26, hitting a triple, double and single as Winnipeg edged Brandon 6–5. July 10, with St. Louis Browns' scout Fred Collins looking on, Davis clubbed a home run and two doubles in a 7–4 win over Elmwood. July 13, he had another big game hitting a triple and three singles against Minot. July 28, he had four hits in a thirteen inning win over Carman and July 30, in one of his last games before signing with the Browns he had five hits, one a homer, in six at bats.

Tommy Davis—Outfield, 6'2", 205 lbs.
Batted right, threw right

Signed by the Dodgers at age 17, Davis was in the majors by the time he was 20. He was an all-star and MVP candidate in 1962 (.346, 27 HR) and 1963 (.326, 16 HR). In early 1965, Davis suffered a gruesome ankle injury and missed the rest of the campaign. He bounced back in a limited role in 1966, but soon began a nomadic existence playing for 11 different teams, over the next 11 years. The travels included return engagements with four of the clubs. Over his 18 seasons in the majors, Davis carried a .294 average.

> 1958 Montreal Royals—.308, 0 D, 1 T, 1 HR, 7 RBI

Leon Day—Pitcher/Infield/Outfield,
5'9", 170 lbs. Batted right, threw right

Day was an outstanding Negro League player who, in 1995, was honored with selection to the Baseball Hall of Fame at Cooperstown. His Negro League career stretched from 1934 to 1949, mainly with the Newark Eagles. He was a versatile player who played many positions with skill. In June of 1950, he joined the Winnipeg Buffaloes of the ManDak League and, in a sensational finish to the season, pitched all 17 innings as the Buffaloes edged Brandon 1–0 to capture the league championship. Late in the 1951 season he left the Buffaloes and signed with the Toronto Maple Leafs in organized baseball. He pitched in 14 games with Toronto compiling a 1.57 ERA. He fashioned a 13–9 record with a 3.41 ERA in 45 games with Scranton in 1952. He also exhibited his talent at the plate, batting .314. The June 25th edition of The Sporting News noted that the right-hander was gaining recognition as the "Satchel Paige of the Eastern League." Day was back in Canada in 1953 with Edmonton of the Western International League and, in 1954, with Carman and Brandon in the ManDak circuit.

Teammate Frazier Robinson stated that Leon Day could do it all and that he was the most complete ballplayer he ever saw. *(Robinson in Catching Dreams by Paul Bauer)* Day died in 1995 at the age of 78.

> 1950 Winnipeg Buffaloes—Won 4, Lost 2, 6 G, 5 GS, 5 CG, .324, 0 HR, 14 RBI
> 1951 Winnipeg Buffaloes—Won 4, Lost 1, 6 G, 5 GS, 4 CG, .339, 3 HR, 20 RBI
> 1951 Toronto Maple Leafs—Won 1, Lost 1, 14 G, 1 GS, 1.58 ERA
> 1953 Edmonton Eskimos—Won 5, Lost 5, 23 G, 10 GS, 4.84 ERA
> 1954 Carman/Brandon—Won 0, Lost 2, .314, 5 D, 3 T, 1 HR, 17 RBI

Canadian Highlights: August 8, 1950, Day fired a three-hitter in a 4–1 victory over Carman. August 14, he had another three-hit performance in blanking Minot 9–0. He fanned eleven and walked only one. August 29, in the first game of the semi-final playoff against Minot, Day pitched a five-hitter, striking out eight, in a 3–2 win. September 14, in a splendid display Day pitched all seventeen innings in a 1–0 victory over Brandon that gave the Buffaloes the first ManDak League championship.

In 1951 on May 19, Day had three hits and drove in three runs while playing center field as the Buffaloes beat Brandon in their home opener. June 19, he pitched a five-hitter and had three hits in a victory over Brandon. The Winnipeg Free Press, on July 11, 1951, reported Day received $800 and Butch Davis $1000 for signing with the St. Louis Browns and both would be playing in St. Louis farm system.

August 29, 1954, Day had three hits in a losing cause as Williston dumped the Greys 14–8.

Dick "Lefty" Dean—Pitcher. Threw left

Dean joined the Elmwood Giants of the Manitoba Senior League in 1948 after experience with the San Francisco Sea Lions and the Harlem Globetrotters. He made just five starts in the regular season for the Giants finishing with a 1–2 won-lost record.

Canadian Highlights: July 7, 1948, Dean and Steve Wylie of Brandon hooked up in a game that ended tied 2–2. He would have gained the victory had it not been for fielding errors behind him.

Lionel Decuir—Catcher, 5'11", 165 lbs. Batted right, threw right

Decuir was one of three black players who played in Saskatchewan with the Broadview Buffaloes in the late 1930s. He later moved on to the Negro League with the Kansas City Monarchs.

Wesley "Doc" Dennis—First Base/Outfield, 6'0", 170 lbs. Batted right. threw right

Dennis had a brief stay with the Indian Head Rockets in 1950 after Negro League play with the Baltimore Elite Giants and Philadelphia Stars, going back to 1942. He toured with the Nashville Stars in 1949 and 1950 before being recruited by the Rockets. Dennis returned to the Negro League after his Canadian stopover and starred for the Birmingham Black Barons through the 1955 season. In a 1953 exhibition against the Roy Campanella All-Stars, with Don Newcombe pitching, Dennis had four hits. Dennis died in 2001 in Nashville.

Canadian Highlights: July 28, 1950, Dennis whacked a homer over the right-center field fence to account for the only run as Nashville All-Stars dropped a 3–1 decision in the Swift Current Tournament.

Carl Dent—Second Base/Shortstop

Stationed with the U.S. Army in Japan, Dent was a baseball and basketball star during his military service in the late 1940s. He was brought to Canada in 1950 by the Brandon Greys of the ManDak League. Shortly into the season he left the Greys for Roblin, Manitoba of the Northern Senior League. The flashy second baseman returned to the United States to play two Negro League seasons with the Philadelphia Stars, in 1951 and 1952.

Canadian Highlights: In an exhibition game on June 2, 1950, Dent drove in three runs with a triple and two singles as Brandon topped the Regina Caps.

Bill Dials—Pitcher, 6'2", 204 lbs. Batted right, threw right

Dials spent one summer in Western Canada pitching for the independent Swift Current Indians and Saskatoon Legion of the Northern Saskatchewan League.

Canadian Highlights: June 3, 1950, Dials held Sceptre to seven hits as the teams battled to a 2–2 draw in 10 innings. June 11, Dials' pitching led the Indians to a 10–1 triumph over Assiniboia. June 16, he pitched Swift Current to a 9–1 win over Eston.

Ezequiel Diaz—Shortstop

The Cuban shortstop had made a Canadian stop in 1952 as a member of the Florida Cubans, a barnstorming team. Through the experience he made contact with other organizations on the prairies and he signed on the next year with the Saskatoon Gems of the Saskatchewan Baseball League. He returned for a second season in '54.

> 1953 Saskatoon Gems—Statistics not available
> 1954 Saskatoon Gems—.272, 8 D, 5 T, 0 HR, 22 RBI

Canadian Highlights: May 24, 1953, Diaz doubled in the winning run in the 10th inning to give the Gems a 3–1 victory over North Battleford. July 11, Diaz had three hits and scored three times as the Gems topped Regina 9–3.

June 18, 1954, Diaz pounded out a double and three singles in an 8–2 win over Lloydminster. July 27, he had three hits in an 11–5 win over Moose Jaw.

Vincente Diaz—First Base

A Cuban import who played in his home country in 1953, Diaz was a member of the Lloydminster Meridians in 1954.

Canadian Highlights: June 23, 1954, Diaz went three for three as the Meridians topped Rosetown in the opening round of the North Battleford Tournament.

Ira Donaldson—Pitcher. Threw right

Donaldson appeared in a dozen games, mainly in relief, for the Regina Caps of the Saskatchewan League in 1953.

Canadian Highlights: May 15, 1953, in his debut Donaldson allowed just one hit over 3⅔ relief innings in a loss to Moose Jaw.

John Wesley Donaldson—Pitcher/Outfield, 6'0", 185 lbs. Batted left, threw left

Donaldson was one of the major stars of Negro ball even in the early years before the formation of the Negro Leagues. The left-hander played from 1913 to 1934 with a variety of teams, including the integrated All-Nations club, Gilkerson's Union Giants, Indianapolis ABCs, Lincoln Giants and Kansas City Monarchs. He also pitched for a number of semi-pro and independent teams and had his own team, the John Donaldson All-Stars.

In 1925, he was one of the first stars of the Negro League to lineup with a Canadian nine. Among other teams, he played with Radville, Saskatchewan. July 22, 1925 at Moose Jaw, Saskatchewan, in the Kiwanis Tournament, Donaldson threw a perfect game with 19 strikeouts to beat the host club.

> The color line drawn so tightly around major league baseball has barred from major league fields three of the greatest pitchers the game ever has produced. One of the trio, John Donaldson, pitching semi-pro ball in Kansas City, recently pitched thirty innings without allowing a hit or run—a record without parallel.
>
> 'If Donaldson were a white man, or if the unwritten law of baseball didn't bar ne-

groes from the major league, I would give $50,000 for him—and think I was getting a bargain,' said John McGraw of the Giants, after seeing Donaldson pitch several games in Cuba [*The Janesville Daily Gazette*, June 18, 1915].

Donaldson is far and away the most sensational colored slant producer ever in the diamond sport and he would, without a question, have been recorded in baseball history as the equal of the supernatural Rube Wadell if he had been of the white race [*Manitoba Free Press*, July 10, 1928].

Donaldson died in 1970 in Chicago. He was 78.

Jesse Douglas—Catcher/Infield, 5'10", 160 lbs. Batted both, threw right

While still a teenager (and already with Negro League experience), Douglas received a grand opportunity in 1939 hitting the road with the Satchel Paige All-Stars. That set the stage for a dozen years of Negro League play with Kansas City Monarchs, Birmingham Black Barons and Chicago American Giants, among others.

He performed both in the infield and outfield in the Negro circuit with success, adding catching duties during his time in Canada. 1951 was his first season north of the border in the ManDak League. He began '51 with the Elmwood Giants (even sitting in as playing manager for a time) before getting a chance in organized ball with Colorado Springs. He chose to return to the semi-pro ManDak loop in 1952 and stuck around through the 1953 and 1954 seasons. Douglas rounded out his career with two more campaigns in organized ball.

1951 Elmwood Giants—.239, 4 RBI
1952 Winnipeg Giants—.268, 9 D, 3 T, 2 HR, 25 RBI
1953 Winnipeg/Brandon—.252, 14 D, 2 T, 2 HR, 25 RBI
1954 Carman Cardinals—.286. 16 D, 1 T, 1 HR, 44 RBI

Canadian Highlights: July 14, 1952, Douglas replaced Double Duty Radcliffe as manager of the Winnipeg Giants. Curly Haas the General Manager of the Giants thought Douglas would get a better production from the Giants' veteran players. Under Douglas' leadership the Giants made the playoffs, but lost in the first round. July 19, Douglas singled in the fourth inning, stole second, and scored on a fly ball. In the eighth he blasted a towering home run to tie the game which the Giants won.

September 1, 1953, in an 11–3 playoff victory over Carman, Douglas had three hits. September 11, he followed that with a double and two singles in a 10–4 victory over Minot.

July 8, 1954, Douglas punched out two doubles, a triple and four RBI in an 18–12 slugfest over Williston. August 9, 1954, he was selected to play in the ManDak League All-Star game against the leading Minot Mallards. The all-stars were victors 14—4 and Douglas went 3 for 6 and knocked in 3 runs.

Sammy Drake—Third Base, 5'11", 175 lbs. Batted both, threw right

Sammy and his older brother Solly (below) were the first African-American brothers to play in the major leagues. Drake started playing ball in his home town of Little Rock, Arkansas. He was just nineteen when he came to Canada in 1954 to put on the uniform of the Carman Cardinals of the ManDak League. After just one season of ManDak ball he won a pro contract with the Chicago Cubs. He advanced to the major leagues with the Cubs and later the New York Mets. He retired after the 1965 season.

1954 Carman Cardinals—.304, 11 D, 4 T, 1 HR, 30 RBI

Canadian Highlights: June 2, 1954, Drake had three hits in a 13–0 romp over Williston. He had a double and two singles. June 14, Drake had two singles, scored twice and stole two bases as Carman edged Brandon 5–4. August 3, Drake hit a double and two singles in an 11–10 loss to Minot. August 9, Drake played in the all-star game and starred with three hits.

Solly Drake—Outfield, 6'0", 170 lbs. Batted both, threw right

Solly Drake began his career in Canada in 1948 when he was just eighteen years of age. He had been playing for a touring team, the Twin City Colored Giants, in an exhibition series at Winnipeg. After a game in which he belted a

Sammy Drake, the younger of the Drake brothers, won a pro contract at age 20 after a summer with the Carman Cardinals of the ManDak League. The third baseman played parts of three seasons in the majors (photograph courtesy the National Baseball Hall of Fame Library, Cooperstown, N.Y.).

Theological Seminary. In 2007, he was honored for twenty-five years of service as pastor of Ebenezer Missionary Baptist Church in Los Angeles.

> Solly Drake, who had several trials with the Chicago Cubs, is a marvel out there in the middle garden. He has great speed afoot, and can use it to advantage as he gets the jump on the ball as well as any ball hawk [*The Progress-Index*, June 9, 1958, p.7].

1948 Elmwood Giants—.160
1949 Elmwood Giants—.260
1950 Elmwood Giants—.300, 2 HR, 21 RBI

Canadian Highlights: July 19, 1949, Drake blasted a three-run homer in the second inning and a solo shot in the 8th to give Elmwood a 9–8 exhibition win over the Brooklyn Cuban Giants.

June 1, 1950, he drove in three runs with a triple and double as Elmwood ran up the score on the Winnipeg Buffaloes, 13–5. June 4, he hit a home run and double to pace an Elmwood

pair of home runs for Twin City, Drake was signed by Elmwood of the Manitoba Senior League. He stayed with the Elmwood Giants for three seasons, including 1950 when the club entered the ManDak League. A few months after the 1950 season, he was signed by the Chicago Cubs and ended up playing 141 games in the major leagues with the Cubs, Los Angeles Dodgers and Philadelphia Phillies.

After his playing career ended, Drake earned a Bachelor Of Arts degree from Philander Smith College and a Masters degree from Fuller

Solly and Sammy Drake were the first African-American brothers to play in the major leagues. Solly, an outfielder, suited up for parts of two seasons in the majors (photograph courtesy the National Baseball Hall of Fame Library, Cooperstown, N.Y.).

victory over Carman and on the 14th of June he doubled and had two singles as the Giants shaded Minot 5–4. August 18, saw Drake get four hits and three RBI as Elmwood clobbered Brandon 13–5. Drake, who drew raves for his defensive play, was selected to the ManDak League All-Star team in 1950.

Charlie Drummond—Pitcher, 6'0", 190 lbs. Batted right, threw right

Drummond, who barnstormed in Canada in the 1960s with the Philadelphia Stars, had earlier pitched in parts of three seasons in Canada, two with Vancouver of the Pacific Coast League. He was a workhorse in the California League in 1957 when he pitched in 40 games, 259 innings, and finished with 13 wins and 3.61 ERA. He had 251 strikeouts. Drummond died in 2004 at age 74.

  1955 Thetford Mines Miners—Won 0, Lost 1
  1956 Vancouver Mounties—Won 6, Lost 4, 4.11
  1957 Vancouver Mounties—Won 0, Lost 1

Claro Duany—Outfield, 6'2", 215 lbs. Batted left, threw left

The Cuban-born Duany left the New York Cubans to play for Sherbrooke, Quebec, in 1948. He had been selected for the Negro League's 1947 East-West All-Star game. Duany played in the Cuban winter league for more than a decade and had some outstanding seasons in Puerto Rico where he was known as the "Puerto Rican Babe Ruth." He was a star in the Quebec Provincial League for three seasons, 1948 and 1949 when it was still an outlaw circuit and 1951 when the league was back in organized ball. The big outfielder expanded his horizons to Mexico in 1950 and part of 1951 and ended his career in the Florida International League in 1952. He was 79 when he died in 1997.

  1948 Sherbrooke Athletics—.365, 17 D, 0 T, 27 HR, 90 RBI
  1949 Sherbrooke Athletics—.290, 18 D, 0 T, 22 HR, 99 RBI
  1951 Sherbrooke Athletics—.337, 23 D, 1 T, 23 HR, 84 RBI

Canadian Highlights: Duany's 99 RBI in 1949, led the league.

Mel Duncan—Pitcher, 5'9", 155 lbs. Threw right, batted right

The little right-hander pitched for the Kansas City Monarchs over four seasons, 1949 to 1951, and part of the 1955 season. He was with the Detroit Stars when he fired a no-hitter against the Memphis Red Sox on June 28, 1955 at Pine Bluff, Arkansas. A month later he joined the Minot Mallards of the ManDak League. He returned for the 1956 season of ManDak play and also pitched in Ontario's Intercounty League with the Galt Terriers and with Lethbridge White Sox of the Southern Alberta League. While not on the mound, Duncan often played the outfield.

  1953 Kitchener Panthers—Won 12, Lost 4
  1955 Minot Mallards—Won 2, Lost 1, 4.50 ERA, .324
  1956 Minot Mallards—Won 3, Lost 1, 7.76 ERA
  1958 Lethbridge White Sox—Won 5, Lost 3 (incomplete), .215

Canadian Highlights: August 9, 1955, Duncan belted a homer and two singles as Minot downed Bismarck 10–4. September 1, Duncan's 8th inning homer gave Minot a 4–3 win over Dickinson and a 2–0 game lead in the final playoff series.

May 31, 1958, Duncan allowed just three hits as Lethbridge whipped Granum 12–1. July 5, he held Calgary to six hits and bashed a key double as the teams fought to a 3–3 tie in a game called because of darkness. August 12, Duncan allowed three hits and a run in the first inning then blanked Calgary the rest of the way in a 16–1 victory. August 23, Duncan's two-run homer helped Lethbridge Warriors to a 6–0 win over Granum. August 27, Duncan blanked Vauxhall on five hits as the Warriors won 2–0.

Luscious "Luke" Easter—First base/Outfield, 6'4", 240 lbs. Batted left, threw right

Easter had an initial trip to Manitoba in July 1945, as part of a tour by the Detroit Motor City Giants, as a second baseman no less.

Two strong seasons with the Homestead Grays in Negro ball won Big Luke a major league trial with Cleveland in 1949. First assigned to San Diego in the Pacific Coast League, Easter had an outstanding start to the 1949 campaign. In 80 games he hit .363 with 25 home runs and 92 runs batted in. He was in the Cleveland lineup on August 11, 1949 at age 34. After a disappointing end to the '49 season, Easter averaged 29 homers and 102 RBI over the next three. In 1952 he was selected as the American League Player of the Year by The Sporting News.

By 1954 he was back in the minors, splitting time between Triple-A clubs in San Diego and Ottawa. He had another ten years playing in Triple-A (in one four-year period he averaged 36 homers and 111 RBI), retiring at age 49 at the end of the 1964 schedule.

Easter was robbed and murdered on March 29, 1979 outside a suburban bank while working for the Aircraft Workers Union in Cleveland.

In the spring of 2008, Easter was named to the International League's Hall of Fame.

1954 Ottawa Athletics—66 G, .348, 10 D, 0 T, 15 HR, 48 RBI

Canadian Highlights: July 13, 1945, Easter had two doubles, a single and a walk to lead Motor City Giants past Philadelphia Hilldales 7–6 in action at Winnipeg.

May 20, 1954, Easter hit the longest home run in the history of Ottawa's Landsdowne Park, a drive over the center field fence traveling more than 435 feet. In his first ten games with the Canadian club, Easter had hits in eight games for a .351 mark and he drove in 11. June 6, after two days off to rest his aching knees, Easter returned to the lineup with five hits, one of them a towering homer to down Richmond. July 3, the slugger drove in four runs with a homer and two doubles in a 16–6 win over Montreal.

Howard Easterling—Third Base, 5'10", 175 lbs. Batted both, threw right

Easterling had a distinguished career in the Negro League, 1936 to 1949. The five-time all-star played most of his fourteen-year Negro League career with the legendary Homestead Grays. At age 41, and near the end of his playing time, he came to Canada, in 1953, for a brief stint with the Brandon Greys of the Man-Dak League. In his final season, 1954, Easterling batted .294 in Mexican baseball.

Easterling died at age 83 in 1993.

1953 Brandon Greys—.267, 1 HR, 5 RBI

Canadian Highlights: May 21, 1953, Easterling drove in one of Brandon's runs in a 3–1 win over Minot. On May 27, he hit a home run in a Brandon win over the Royals.

Bob Enalls—Outfield

Recruited to play for the 1951 Regina Caps, Enalls was optioned to a Regina farm club at Dauphin of the Manitoba-Saskatchewan League where he hit .331.

Canadian Highlights: August 22, Enalls had two hits in a 7–5 playoff victory over Yorkton. Dauphin would be declared the league champion, when Yorkton failed to put a team on the field for the remainder of the series.

Frank Evans—Outfield

Evans had a three-year stint in Canada which spanned nearly thirty years! He came north in 1951, from two years with the Negro League's Cleveland Buckeyes, for a few games with the Brandon Greys. He was back in Canada in 1978 and 1979 as the club house attendant for the Triple-A, Vancouver Canadians in the Pacific Coast League.

Sergio Fabre—Pitcher. Threw right

The Cuban right-hander had two outstanding seasons, 1954–55, in Western Canada with a combined 18–1 mark, mainly as a reliever. On three occasions he won both games of doubleheaders. In 1955 he also played the outfield, batting over .300. He pitched for Canada at the Global World Series in 1955.

1954 Indian Head Rockets—Won 10, Lost 0, 13 G, 7 GS, 6 CG
1955 SaskatoonGems—Won 8, Lost 1, 19 G, 2.95 ERA, .314, 0 HR, 7 RBI

Canadian Highlights: July 22, 1954, Fabre had a double and two singles to back up his complete game pitching as Indian Head trounced Moose Jaw 15–6. The Rockets didn't provide much help in the field for Fabre making eight errors. August 13, Fabre hurled a three-hitter for his 6th straight win as Indian Head downed Saskatoon 7–1. August 17, Fabre picked up two wins, one in the completion of an earlier draw to go to 8–0 on the season. He allowed just five hits in the complete game victory. August 20, Fabre again registered two wins, his 9th and 10th without a loss, as Indian Head notched a pair of wins over Moose Jaw, 5–4 in the completion of a tie game, and 7–4 in the regular contest. August 29, Fabre hurled a six-hit shutout to give Indian Head a 4–0 playoff win over Saskatoon.

August 18, 1955, Fabre again picked up wins in both ends of a double-header as Saskatoon dumped North Battleford twice.

Ralph Fennell — Pitcher

From Detroit, Fennell pitched in Southern Saskatchewan in the early 1950s. A brief story in the Yorkton Enterprise (1953) said he had played in Willowbrook (a few miles west of Yorkton) in 1951 and "was a tremendous favorite and probably the best ball player ever to show there. He will be Yorkton's Jackie Robinson, as he is the first Negro ball player ever signed by Yorkton teams." *(May 23, 1953)*

Humberto "Chico" Fernandez —

Shortstop, 6'0", 165 lbs. Batted right, threw right

The Cuban shortstop was signed by the Brooklyn Dodgers as a teenager and made his pro debut in 1951 in the Class-C Pioneer League. He spent four straight seasons with Montreal Royals before winning a trial with the Dodgers in 1956. He turned it into a nine year career in the majors, mainly with the Phillies and Tigers. In his best major league season, Fernandez hit .249 with 20 home runs for Detroit.

- 1953 Montreal Royals—.247, 21 D, 2 T, 2 HR, 34 RBI
- 1954 Montreal Royals—.282, 44 D, 3 T, 5 HR, 52 RBI
- 1955 Montreal Royals—.301, 34 D, 7 T, 4 HR, 62 RBI
- 1956 Montreal Royals—.277, 17 D, 2 T, 1 HR, 32 RBI

Canadian Highlights: May 9, 1954, he had four hits in a loss to Toronto. July 17, Fernandez had another four-hit day as Montreal topped Rochester 6–2.

> Chico Fernandez is the greatest shortstop ever developed in the International League, and the most improved player over one season that I have ever seen [International League President Frank Shaughnessy quoted in *The Sporting News*, September 8, 1954, p.25].

May 4, 1955, Fernandez led the Royals with three hits, a triple included, as Montreal beat Syracuse 5–3. On defense, he participated in three double plays. June, 1955, newspapers reported the Dodgers had been offered $125,000 for Fernandez and a similar amount for second baseman Charlie Neal.

Rodolfo "Rudy" Fernandez — Pitcher, 6'1", 190 lbs. Batted right, threw right

The right-hander had Negro League experience from 1932 to 1946 in addition to playing time in Cuba, Venezuela, Puerto Rico, Nicaragua and the Dominican. In 1951, he pitched for Eston, Saskatchewan. He died in 2000 in New York.

Amancio Ferro — Pitcher. Threw left

Ferro came to Canada from Cuba as an eighteen-year-old in 1951 to join the Brandon Greys in the ManDak League. Winless during the regular schedule, he won two key games in the playoffs. The next season he was in organized ball fashioning a 14–9 record with the Hannibal Stags of the Class-D, Mississippi-Ohio Valley League. He compiled a 6–0, 1.95 record in the league in 1953. Ferro played one more season, 1954, before bowing out of pro ball.

- 1951 Brandon Greys—Won 0, Lost 6, 10 G, 5 GS, 2 CG

Canadian Highlights: Ferro did not have much success pitching during the regular season. August 11, he lost to the California Mohawks 4–1 in spite of allowing just three hits and striking out 15. September 7, he blanked Carman Cardinals 1–0 in the deciding game of their semi-final series. September 12, he beat the Winnipeg Buffaloes 5–4. His opponent was Leon Day, who was just back from the Toronto Maple Leafs.

Wilmer Fields—Pitcher/Outfield, 6'3", 220 lbs. Batted right, threw right

For a player who began his career as a pitcher, Fields' accomplishments as a hitter were outstanding. He played in the Negro League from 1940 to 1950 (mainly with the Homestead Grays), losing three seasons to military service during the Second World War. He had an extensive background in winter ball including a spot on the Puerto Rican team in the inaugural Caribbean Series in 1949.

He first came to Canada in 1951 to play for the semi-pro Brantford Red Sox of the Intercounty Baseball League in southern Ontario. After compiling a 9–1 mark on the hill and leading the league in hits, home runs and runs batted in, he was selected as the league's Most Valuable Player.

Fields attracted the attention of the nearby Toronto Maple Leafs of the Triple-A, International League, but he lost much of the 1952 season with Toronto to injury as a broken wrist kept him on the sidelines for six weeks. He began the 1953 season in Spring Training with Toronto before jumping the club to play in the Dominican Summer League (in a July 12, 1954 item in the Toronto Star, Fields said he was offered $2,250 a month, plus expenses to play in the Dominican). Soon he was back in Canada with Brandon, Manitoba, in the ManDak League. While his stay was short—a little over a month—Fields made quite an impression. When he left the league in late August, the Winnipeg Free Press *(August 20, 1953)* noted he had been one of the best players to ever play in the ManDak League. He suited up in southern Ontario in 1954 with Brantford and 1955 with Oshawa Merchants. Fields often reflected upon the reception he received in Brantford.

> It was like a home away from home. The people accepted my family with so much enthusiasm that our stay there was the finest we ever experienced anywhere but at our home [Fields quoted by David Menary in *Terrier Town: Summer of '49*].

Wilmer Fields was a star performer, both on the mound and at the plate, for the Homestead Grays over an eight-year stretch from 1940 to 1950 (losing three seasons to military service during the war). Later, he spent five summers in Canada, playing so well he was called "Wilmer the Great" (photograph courtesy of the National Baseball Hall of Fame Library, Cooperstown, N.Y.).

In 1956, he led Fort Wayne Dairymen to the National Baseball Congress semi-pro title at Wichita batting .500 and driving in 12 runs in 8 games. He was selected to the "All-World" team at the Global World Series in Milwaukee as the Dairymen, representing the United States, won the championship. The following year, Fields was chosen as the MVP of the National Baseball Congress Tournament as he led the defending champions into the final of the tourney. In what appears to have been his last season, he played in South Dakota's Basin League in 1958 with the Yankton Terrys and finished up in Mexico. He died in 2004, at age 81.

In 2006, Fields was honored, posthumously, at a special conference in Dartmouth, Nova Scotia, as an inaugural selection to the Black Hockey and Sports Hall of Fame.

- 1951 Brantford Red Sox—Won 9, Lost 1, .381, 10 HR, 47 RBI, Named Most Valuable Player
- 1952 Toronto Maple Leafs—.291, 2 HR, 13 RBI
- 1953 Brandon Greys—.356, 4 HR, 35 RBI
- 1954 Brantford Red Sox—Won 8, Lost 2, .379, 24 D, 14 HR
- 1955 Oshawa Merchants—Won 6, Lost 1, .425, 12 HR, 55 RBI

Canadian Highlights: Fields was the Intercounty League's Most Valuable Player in 1951 after leading the circuit in pitching (9–1), hits, home runs and runs batted in. He led the league in hits each year he played in Ontario. He was the batting champion in both 1954 and 1955, either leading or tying for the lead in homers. His 24 doubles in 1954 remained a league record through the 2008 season.

May 12, 1951, he drove in four runs with three hits, one a homer, as Brantford topped Kitchener 12–7.

July 22, 1953, Fields drove in three runs as Brandon beat Carman 13–7. July 24, Fields drove in six runs with a grand slam homer and single as the Greys trounced Winnipeg Royals 13–5. July 30, he punched out two doubles and a single, driving in three runs, in an 11–1 victory over Moose Jaw. August 2, Fields had a homer in Brandon's win over Carman and the following day had two doubles in a 5–3 win over Minot. August 16, he bashed a pair of four-baggers against Carman.

July 2, 1955, Fields belted a homer and triple, drove in three runs, and scored twice to lead Oshawa Merchants to a 5–3 win over Galt to retain their lead atop the Intercounty League standings. July 7, Fields knocked in four runs to lead Oshawa by Brantford, 10–2. July 21, Fields drove in three runs with two doubles and a single as Oshawa demolished Brantford 20–7. July 24, Fields had three hits, one a towering homer, in a 6–1 win over Kitchener. August 3, he fired a three-hit shutout to down Galt 2–0. The following day he had three hits, one a bases-loaded double, in a 14–5 victory over London. August 8, Fields was the winning pitcher and had three hits in a 5–1 win over St. Thomas. August 21, Fields bashed a grand slam homer and a three-run shot and scored three times in a 12–7 victory over Galt. August 26, Fields had a homer, double and single as Oshawa blanked St. Thomas 4–0.

Rayford "Ray" Finch—Pitcher. Threw left

Finch played in the Negro League in 1949 and 1950 with the Cleveland Buckeyes before leaving for Canada to join the Elmwood Giants in the ManDak League. He pitched for three seasons with the Giants, a workhorse for the first two summers when he led the league in appearances. He was in 22 games, 10 of them starts in 1950 and 26 games with 18 starts and 17 complete games in 1951. He appeared hurt in 1952 when he appeared in comparatively few matches. Finch closed out his career in 1953 when he pitched briefly with Danville in the Mississippi-Valley League and had a 1–2 record.

- 1950 Elmwood Giant—Won 2, Lost 6, 22 G, 10 GS, 4 CG
- 1951 Elmwood Giants—Won 10, Lost 12, 26 G, 18 GS, 17 CG
- 1952 Winnipeg Giants—Won 0, Lost 3

Canadian Highlights: June 12, 1950, umpire Mark Van Buren called six balks against Finch in a game against Brandon. August 10, Finch was suspended along with Brandon's Ramon Rodriquez and Rafe Cabrera following a bean ball incident.

July 12, 1951, Finch pitched a one-hitter over ten innings to give Elmwood a 1–0 win over the Greys and top money at the Brandon Invitational Tournament.

Ed Finney—Shortstop/Second Base, 5'8", 188 lbs. Batted right, threw right

Finney played in three of the major Canadian leagues. He had a three-year stay in the Negro League, 1948 to 1950, with the Baltimore Elite Giants. He came to Canada in 1951 and joined the Brandon Greys in the ManDak League. He made a brief appearance in the Quebec Provincial League in 1951 and in 1953 he played for the Brantford Red Sox of the Intercounty League in Ontario.

1951 Brandon Greys—.239, 1 HR, 9 RBI
1953 Brantford Red Sox—Statistics not available

Canadian Highlights: May 26, 1951 Finney broke his leg sliding into second base in a 9–6 loss to the Winnipeg Buffaloes. It would be late in the season before he would return.

John Ford—Catcher

Ford was a catcher for the Regina Caps of the Saskatchewan League in 1953.

Willie Fordham—Pitcher. Threw left

Fordham pitched in Canada with the Oshawa Merchants of the Intercounty League and also with Belleville (Ontario). He had a little experience during college, hurling on weekends for the Philadelphia Meteors. He won a professional contract in 1952 and he pitched for the Class-B, Harrisburg Senators, in the Phillies' system, and finished with a 3–3 record. After the league folded, he stayed in Harrisburg to pitch in the Eastern Negro League with his hometown Giants.

July 16, 1994, the City of Harrisburg held Wilbur Lewis Fordham Day to salute his contributions to the area.

Mike Fornieles—Pitcher, 5'11", 155 lbs. Batted right, threw right

The 155-pound Cuban right-hander was signed by the Washington Senators in 1950 at age 18. He won 17 games in his first season of pro ball and had 14 wins in his second season when he advanced all the way to the major league club winning a pair of games with a 1.37 ERA. It was the beginning of a 12-year major league career, half spent with the Red Sox. During the 1955 season he was assigned to Toronto for a half-dozen games. Fornieles died in 1998 at the age of 66.

1955 Toronto Maple Leafs—Won 5, Lost 0, 2.36

Canadian Highlights: August 18, 1955, Fornieles held Richmond to four hits, allowing just an unearned run in a 7–1 Toronto victory. August 25, Fornieles tossed a complete-game seven-hitter as Toronto again beat Richmond, this time 6–1.

Carlos Forten—Pitcher. Threw right

The Cuban import was with the barnstorming Florida Cubans in 1952 when the Cubans were the hit of the prairies with tournament victories at Lacombe, Lethbridge, Camrose and Indian Head and a share of top money at Lloydminster. They were the runners-up at the Kamsack and Rosetown tournaments. He pitched in the ManDak League in 1953 with Brandon Greys and Winnipeg Royals.

1952 Florida Cubans—Statistics not available
1953 Brandon/Winnipeg—Won 3 Lost 5, 19 G, 8 GS, 2 CG, .375

Canadian Highlights: June 5, 1952, Forten fired a seven-hit shutout as the Florida Cubans upset the Indian Head Rockets 8–0. June 22, he scattered eight hits as the Cubans topped Leduc Oilers 9–2 to take top money at the Camrose Tournament. August 9, he blanked Trail Smoke Eaters on five-hits to take a 2–0 win and top prize at the Lethbridge Rotary Tournament. Forten beat 17-year-old Ted Bowsfield who went on to a major league career.

July 29, 1953, Forten pitching in his first game for Winnipeg, held Moose Jaw to seven hits and fanned 12 without a base on balls as Winnipeg Royals prevailed 4–2. August 11, Forten allowed just five hits, but lost a heartbreaker to Minot 1–0.

Luis Fouste—Pitcher. Batted left, threw left

The Cuban lefty pitched mainly in relief for the Regina Braves in his lone season in Canada, 1957.

> 1957 Regina—Won 2, Lost 2, 14 G, 3.34 ERA

Canadian Highlights: June 14, 1957, Fouste tossed three shutout innings in relief to preserve a win for Regina over Saskatoon. June 16, the Cuban lefty fired four shutout innings as he combined with starter Gene Walker on a four-hitter in another win over Saskatoon. June 26, Fouste had the first complete game of the season for Regina as he scattered eight hits in an 11–2 win over Lloydminster.

John W. "Bud" Fowler—Pitcher/Second Base, 5'7", 155 lbs. Batted right, threw right

Fowler (born John W. Jackson) is thought to have been the first professional black baseball player (until blacks were banned from organized ball, around the turn of the century, Fowler would often be the lone colored player). He began his career as a pitcher, later becoming an all-around star, especially as a second baseman. Fowler played for more than two decades, in the United States and Canada.

In 1881, the Guelph Maple Leafs signed Fowler but members of the club refused to play with the colored pitcher in the lineup. Recruited by Petrolia, another Ontario team, the Imperials took the field but sent a loud message to Fowler by making 19 errors behind him.

He died in 1913 in Frankfurt, New York, a few weeks shy of his 55th birthday.

Sam Fowlkes—Pitcher. Threw right

The Louisiana native pitched in the Negro League for the Chicago American Giants in 1948 and with the Kansas City Monarchs and Cleveland Buckeyes in 1950. During a Canadian tour with the Monarchs in 1950 he was the winning pitcher for the Monarchs in a win against the House of David in Regina. Fowlkes appears to have liked his trip to Saskatchewan as he joined the Bentley brothers' Delisle Gems in 1951. Later he had three years in organized ball in Texas and New Mexico.

Fowlkes was the workhorse of the Delisle team in '51 appearing in 12 games, topping the league in wins, with seven.

> 1951 Delisle Gems—Won 7, Lost 3, 12 G, 9 GS, 6 CG

Canadian Highlights: June 17, Fowlkes held the powerful North Battleford Beavers to four hits in posting a 4–0 shutout. He had another four-hitter on June 22 in a win over Prince Albert. July 22, his three-hit shutout resulted in a 1–0 win over Colonsay. His mound opponent, John Carlson, fired a one-hitter in taking the loss.

Hipple "Hippo" Galloway—Outfield/Second Base

While growing up in Dunnville, Ontario, Galloway was a member of various integrated sports teams. He drew notice as a member of the Woodstock, Ontario, hockey team in 1899 and later that year also played baseball with Woodstock's Canadian League team. However, after players on rival teams refused to play against him, Galloway was released and he left Canada to play in the United States for the Cuban Giants. He was one of the last blacks in organized ball until Jackie Robinson was in the Montreal Royals' lineup in 1946 (a few players, such as Dick Brookins, 1906–1910, and Jimmy Claxton, 1916, had made appearances, but claimed to be Native Americans).

Juan Rene Garcia—Shortstop

Garcia manned the middle infield for the Indian Head Rockets in 1954.

> 1954 Indian Head—.279, 13 D, 4 T, 4 HR, 28 RBI, 13 SB

Canadian Highlights: June 20, 1954, Garcia bashed a triple, double and single for the Rockets in a loss to Rosetown. June 27, Garcia had a double and two singles as the Rockets dumped Rosetown 11–2. July 12, he belted a homer and triple in the Rockets' 9–2 win over North Battleford. July 22, a double and three singles from Garcia resulted in three runs batted in as Indian Head dumped Moose Jaw 15–6. July 26, Garcia, with a double and two singles, led the Rockets' attack in a 4–3 win over Lloydminster. August 17, Garcia had a three-run homer in the first game and a homer and single in the second to pace Indian Head to a twin-bill sweep of Lloydminster.

Oswaldo Garcia—Right Field

Garcia came from Havana, Cuba in 1954 to travel to the "Great White North" and baseball with the Lloydminster Meridians of the newly formed Saskatchewan League.

 1954 Lloydminster Meridians—.144, 0 HR, 27 RBI.

Canadian Highlights: July 8, 1954, Garcia belted a double and two singles to help Lloydminster tie Indian Head 8–8.

Rolando Garcia—Pitcher. Threw right

The right-hander from Cuba pitched for the 1952 Indian Head Rockets and 1954 Saskatoon Gems.

Silvio Garcia—Shortstop/Third Base
6'0", 195 lbs. Batted right, threw right

Along with Jackie Robinson, the Brooklyn Dodgers considered Garcia as a candidate to be that specially selected player to integrate major league baseball. According to Cuban baseball historian Edel Casas, Dodger president Branch Rickey met with Garcia in Havana in 1945, but the all-star shortstop was already 31 and thought to be on the downside of his career.

Garcia started out in Cuba in 1937 and was an instant star. He played in the Negro League and Mexico from 1940 to 1948. During the 1949 season he joined Sherbrooke in the Quebec Provincial League and for three seasons was regarded as one of the league's star players and a fan favorite. He hit .283 in his final season, 1952, with the Havana Cubans of the Florida International League. In 1975 Garcia was selected to the Cuban Baseball Hall Of Fame. He died in 1978.

 1949 Sherbrooke Athletics—.315, 30 D, 0 T, 4 HR, 76 RBI
 1950 Sherbrooke Athletics—.365, 29 D, 4 T, 21 HR, 116 RBI
 1951 Sherbrooke Athletics—.346, 34 D, 1 T, 12 HR, 82 RBI

Canadian Highlights: In 1949 he led the Quebec Provincial League with 126 hits. Garcia was the first player to win the league's Triple Crown, with a .365 average, 21 homers and 116 RBI in 1950 and he again led the league with 150 hits.

Charles Gary—Third Base/Outfield,
5'9", 170 lbs. Batted left, threw right

Gary was a top ten hitter in the Saskatchewan League in 1953, his lone season in Canada. He batted .322 for the Regina Caps. He had ventured north to Saskatchewan after Negro League play from 1948 to 1950 with the Homestead Grays.

 1953 Regina Caps—.322

Canadian Highlights: May 15, 1953, Gary was on base five straight times (four hits and a walk) in the league opener at Regina. May 31, saw Gary have three hits in a 4–0 shutout of North Battleford. June 12, he had three hits in a 9–5 inter-league game against the Carman Cardinals. He had another three hit game on June 23, and drove in three runs, in a victory over Moose Jaw. July 7, Gary had five hits, knocked in four and scored twice as Regina clobbered Saskatoon 24–7. July 31, Gary had two hits and knocked in a pair in a 7–5 loss to Saskatoon. August 15, he had 3 hits in a 6–4 Regina win over Saskatoon.

Hiram "Mike" Gaston—Pitcher, 5'10", 165 lbs. Batted left, threw left

Gaston pitched in the St. Louis system from 1955 to 1958. He got his start in Class B for the Peoria Chiefs in 1955. In 1956, he was back in Peoria and also appeared in four games with Omaha (1–1) at the Triple-A level. The 1957 season saw him split time between Decatur of the Midwest League and the Winnipeg Goldeyes of the Northern League. He was back in Winnipeg 1958 and pitched with some success. In 1959, Gaston lined up with Nuevo Laredo in the Mexican League and briefly in the Western Canada League with the Saskatoon Commodores. In 1962, he appeared with the St. Lazare Athletics in the Manitoba Senior Baseball League.

1957 Winnipeg Goldeyes—Won 4, Lost 5, 5.61 ERA
1958 Winnipeg Goldeyes—Won 8, Lost 4, 3.36 ERA
1959 Saskatoon Commodores—Won 0, Lost 1
1962 St. Lazare Athletics—Won 1, Lost 0

Canadian Highlights: When his baseball career ended he was one of only a few import players who settled down in Winnipeg, Canada. Gaston became a high school teacher.

Sammy Gee—Shortstop/Outfield, 5'8", 170 lbs. Batted right, threw right

In 1947, Gee came out of Miller High School in Detroit to begin his baseball career in Canada. As a teenager, he joined the Three Rivers Royals, a Brooklyn farm club, in the Canadian-American League. He tried organized ball again in 1948 and after his release joined the New York Cubans in the Negro League. He hit just .184 in his pro debut season, but compiled a .321 mark the following year with Olean in the PONY League. The Michigan native also played baseball and basketball for the Harlem Globetrotters.

1947 Three Rivers Royals—.184, 0 HR, 5 RBI

Eric George—Pitcher. Threw right

One of a small number of players from Panama who appeared in the Western Canada League. He suited up with the Indian Head Rockets in 1954 before pitching a few games in organized ball in 1955 for the San Angelo Colts in the Longhorn League.

Canadian Highlights: May 31, 1954, the slender George fired a four-hitter as Indian Head shaded Saskatoon 4–3.

Alphonso Gerrard—Outfield, 5'10", 180 lbs. Batted right, threw left

Gerrard put in five seasons in the Negro League, 1945 to 1949, with the New York Black Yankees, Indianapolis Clowns and Chicago American Giants. In his first taste of organized ball he played in the Colonial and Canadian-American Leagues. In 1951, he moved on to the Quebec Provincial League with Three Rivers and the following season with Three Rivers and Granby. He wrapped up his professional play in 1953 in Puerto Rico.

1951 Three Rivers Royals—.337, 8 D, 6 T, 1 HR, 55 RBI
1952 Granby Phillies—.303, 13 D, 3 T, 0 HR, 46 RBI

Walter Lee "Dirk" "Bubblegum" Gibbons—Pitcher, 5'10", 190 lbs. Batted left, threw right

Gibbons had a sensational debut season in Canada with Brandon Greys, then of the Manitoba Senior League. Just twenty years of age, he became an instant star and a very popular player in compiling an over-all 19–5 won-lost record in 28 games, 23 of them starting assignments. He also played the outfield and was no slouch at the plate hitting .272.

The right-hander had pitched for the Indianapolis Clowns in 1948 and at the beginning of the 1949 season.

He returned to Brandon in 1950 when the Greys had joined the new ManDak (Manitoba-Dakota) League. Again, Gibbons was a mainstay winning eight of twelve decisions. He completed eleven of his twelve starting assignments. Baseball took a back seat to military duty in Korea 1951–1952, but he returned to the ManDak League in 1953. Brandon, which held his rights, was over stocked with pitchers and let Gibbons sign with the Winnipeg Royals. It was a good move for the Royals as the right-hander had another good season as only Sugar Cain of Minot had more wins. The Royals disbanded in 1954 and Gibbons returned to the Greys. When Brandon ceased operations in 1955, Gibbons moved on to the Minot Mallards, also a ManDak franchise. He played for Minot until the league disbanded in 1957. Gibbons was inducted into the Manitoba Baseball Hall Of Fame in June, 2006.

1949 Brandon Greys—Won 19, Lost 5, 28 G, 23 GS, 20 CG, 198 IP, 229 SO *
1950 Brandon Greys—Won 8, Lost 4, 12 G, 12 GS, 11 CG
1953 Winnipeg Royals—Won 10, Lost 6, G 19, GS 16, CG 8
1954 Brandon Greys—Won 11, Lost 7, 155 IP, 47 BB, 70 SO

1955 Minot Mallards—Won 5, Lost 7, 5.44 ERA

1956 Minot Mallards—Won 6, Lost 7, 20 G, 13 GS, 6 CG 6, 4.95 ERA

1957 Minot Mallards—Won 3, Lost 9, 4.33 ERA

1949 statistics include all games — league, tournament, exhibition, playoffs

Canadian Highlights: May 24, 1949, Gibbons pitched a five-hit, 5–0 shutout beating Elmwood. He again topped the Elmwood Giants June 4, this time 8–1, for his third straight victory. He had fourteen strikeouts. June 17, he fired a two-hitter and had eleven strikeouts in an 18–1 victory over the San Francisco Sea Lions. June 28, he hooked up in a pitching duel with Rufus Ligon of the Ligon Traveling All-Stars. Gibbons gave up only four hits and added sixteen strikeouts for the win. July 2, he beat the St. Louis Black Cardinals 12–0 on a one-hitter and struck out eighteen batters. July 8, he carried a no-hitter into the ninth inning before giving up one hit in blanking the Minot Mallards 5–0 for his 10th straight victory.

June 12, 1950, he fired a six-hitter and provided the offense with two triples and a pair of singles in a 4–2 triumph over Elmwood. June 23, Gibbons allowed just four hits in besting the Harlem Globetrotters, 5–1.

August 10, 1953, Gibbons tossed a three-hitter against his former club as Winnipeg Royals edged Brandon 3–1.

July 30, 1954, back with Brandon, Gibbons hurled an 8-hit shutout in a 7–0 win over Minot. August 30, he blanked Williston on six hits as the Greys topped the Oilers 6–0 in the seventh and deciding game of their semi-finals series. It was Gibbons third win in the playoffs.

Josh Gibson, Jr.—Second Base/Third Base, 5'10", 170 lbs. Batted right, threw right

The son of the Negro League's greatest slugger, the young Gibson played for two seasons in the Negro League with the Homestead Grays before a summer in the Quebec Provincial League. Sam Bankhead was a good friend of Josh Gibson Sr. and when he became manager

The summer of 1949 was a marvelous one for the Brandon Greys. The team played 108 games in 113 days losing just 18 times. Front row—Chuck Wilson, Winslow Means, Armando Vasquez, Jack Sinclair, Don Gardner (batboy), Frank Watkins, Steve Clark, Dirk Gibbons. Back row—Pop Summers (trainer), Rafe Cabrera, Ian Lowe (playing-manager), Gerry MacKay, Coney Williams, Ramon Rodriguez, Ross Pollock, Percy Fenwick (manager) (photograph courtesy Lil Lowe).

of Farnham, Quebec, in 1951, he brought Josh Jr. with him to Canada. The younger Gibson died in 2003.

    1951 Farnham Pirates—.230, 2 HR, 20 RBI

James "Junior" Gilliam—Second Base/Third Base, 5'10", 170 lbs. Batted both, threw right

Junior was the man to replace his idol as second baseman of the Dodgers. In 1953 Gilliam was Rookie of the Year in the National League as he batted .278 with 17 triples and 100 bases on balls. Jackie Robinson shifted to third base and the outfield to accommodate his young teammate. Gilliam had begun pro ball at age 16 in the Negro Southern League. In 1946, he joined the famous Baltimore Elite Giants and spent five years with the club, an all-star the last three seasons. Signed by the Dodgers and, like Robinson, sent to Montreal, he was an all-star in both his summers with the Royals, Most Valuable Player in 1952. Gilliam, whose 14-year Dodger career spanned both Brooklyn and Los Angeles years, played in seven World Series. Gilliam died in 1978 at Inglewood, California a few days before his 50th birthday.

    1951 Montreal Royals—.287, 22 D, 9 T, 7 HR, 73 RBI
    1952 Montreal Royals—.301, 39 D, 9 T, 9 HR, 112 RBI

Granville "Happy" Gladstone—Outfield, 5'11" 170 lbs. Batted right, threw right

Gladstone, born in Panama, was a member of the 1950 Indianapolis Clowns. In 1951, he played Triple-A with Portland in the Pacific Coast League and, in 1952 and 1953, was with Victoria, British Columbia, in the Western International League. He continued playing in organized ball, mainly in Triple-A, until 1959.

    1952 Victoria Tyees—.295, 40 D, 6 T, 15 HR, 126 RBI
    1953 Victoria Tyees—.348, 23 D, 2 T, 19 HR, 93 RBI

Hubert "Country" Glenn—Pitcher/Outfield, 6'5", 200 lbs. Threw right

Glen came to Canada after Negro League experience with the Philadelphia Stars, New York Black Yankees, Brooklyn Brown Dodgers and Indianapolis Clowns, from 1943 to 1949, and a half dozen seasons in industrial leagues. In 1950, he joined the San Francisco Cubs and was on a barnstorming tour which included a stop in the farming community of Claresholm, Alberta. Soon he would return.

The following season he was a sensation in leading Claresholm Meteors to the Foothills League championship. He won 17 games in 21 decisions with 207 strikeouts in 166 innings pitched. He was just as effective at the plate hitting .535 with 17 doubles, 4 triples and 9 homers in just 99 at bats. Glenn handled mound work for the Meteors for four seasons and also linked up with Carmangay Eagles for some tournament play. He died in 2007 at age 90 in Hickory, North Carolina.

    1951 Claresholm Meteors—Won 17, Lost 4, .535, 9 HR
    1952 Claresholm Meteors—Statistics not available
    1953 Claresholm Meteors—Won 16, Lost 7, .450, 13 HR
    1954 Claresholm Meteors—Statistics not available
    1954 Carmangay Eagles—Statistics not available

Canadian Highlights: In a July, 1951, game Glenn blasted four homers and two singles in seven at bats as the Meteors crushed Okotoks. In September, after losing the first semi-final match 2–1, he pitched five straight playoff victories, two in one day, to hand Claresholm the Foothills championship.

August 17, 1952, Glenn's bases loaded single in the ninth inning gave Claresholm a 5–4 win over Granum and a berth in the Foothills League final. He had earlier belted a two-run homer and topped it off with a route going performance on the mound.

Claresholm kicked off the 1953 Foothills-Wheatbelt season May 24th trouncing Granum 21–8 as Glenn had a pair of two-run homers and drove in six runs. July 15, Glenn's arm and bat carried Claresholm into the final game of the Champion Lions' Tournament. He tossed a three-hit shutout and had a double and three singles as the Meteors won 3–0 then pounded a pair of homers and threw three shutout innings in relief as Claresholm won the second game of the day, 11–7. July 27, Glenn hit for the cycle to carry Claresholm past Granum 16–2 and into the Foothills League final. August 7th, he bashed a triple and two singles as the Meteors took their second title in three years.

July 16, 1954, saw Glenn drive home five of seven Carmangay runs as the Eagles beat Vauxhall in the Taber, Alberta, Tournament

Stanley "Doc" Glenn—Catcher, 6'3", 197 lbs. Batted right, threw right

Glenn was still a high school student when he first played in the Negro League with the Philadelphia Stars in 1944. He continued with the Stars for seven seasons before dedicating four years to organized ball, including two summers in Canada with the Quebec Braves of the Provincial League. Glenn stayed in Canada in 1954 and 1955 to suit up with the semi-pro St. Thomas Elgins in the Intercounty Baseball League in Ontario. Glenn went on to become president of the Negro League Players Association and, in 2006, released a book, *Don't Let Anyone Take Your Joy Away: An inside look at Negro League baseball and its legacy*, based on his experiences in baseball.

> 1952 Quebec Braves—.248, 10 D, 1 T, 5 HR, 27 RBI
> 1953 Quebec Braves—.275, 20 D, 3 T, 16 HR, 90 RBI
> 1954 St. Thomas Elgins—Statistics not available
> 1955 St. Thomas Elgins—Statistics not available

Manuel Godinez—Pitcher/Outfield. Batted right, threw right

The Cuban right-hander toured with the Indianapolis Clowns from 1946 to 1949. In 1950, he headed north to Canada to play for the Brandon Greys in the ManDak League. He played only one season for Brandon and pitched with some success.

> 1950 Brandon Greys—Won 4, Lost 2, 9 G, 8 GS, 2 CG, .208, 0 HR, 16 RBI

Canadian Highlights: June 13, 1946, Godinez tossed a four-hitter and fanned ten as Havana La Palomas trounced the Chicago Brown Bombers 12–1 at Osborne Stadium in Winnipeg.

June 20, 1950, in a brilliant mound duel, Godinez suffered a 1–0 loss to Taylor Smith and the Winnipeg Buffaloes as each pitcher gave up just four hits. June 24, Godinez had three hits in an exhibition game loss to the traveling Harlem Globetrotters and on July 3 he had three hits and three RBI in a tournament win over Minot.

Ruben Gomez—Pitcher, 6'0", 175 lbs. Batted right, threw right

Gomez, from Puerto Rico, used the Quebec Provincial League to get noticed by organized baseball.

He had great success during his career in Puerto Rico, with a won-lost record of 174–119 and a 2.99 ERA. He came to Canada in 1950 and played in St. Jean, Quebec, where, after a 14–4 season, he caught the eye of the Washington Senators who signed him to a pro contract and sent him back to St. Jean for the 1951 season. Left unprotected by Washington, Gomez was drafted by the New York Yankees at the end of the 1951 season. Released by the Yankees and signed by the New York Giants, he was in the major leagues in 1953 for the first of ten seasons. He finished 13–11 in his rookie campaign and 17–9 the following summer when the Giants advanced to the World Series against Cleveland. He won his only start in the fall classic and became the first Puerto Rican player to win a World Series game.

> 1950 St. Jean Braves—Won 14, Lost 4, 26 G, 20 GS, 3.90 ERA
> 1951 St. Jean Braves—Won 12, Lost 6, 28 G, 18 GS, 4.41 ERA

Canadian Highlights: In 1950 he tied for the lead in strikeouts with 140. Gomez held the league record for shutouts in a season with five.

Hiram Gonzales—First Base/Outfield 5'9", 175. Batted left, threw left

Signed by the Washington Senators in 1947, Gonzalez kicked off his pro career at age twenty-two with the Havana Cubans of the Class-C, Florida International League. In a twelve-year career in organized ball, he spent seven years in the Florida loop before reaching Triple-A with the Havana Sugar Kings in 1957. His best season was his lone summer in Canada, 1951, with the Sherbrooke Athletics of the Provincial League, when he hit .319 with 12 home runs.

    1951 Sherbrooke Athletics—.319, 31 D, 4 T, 12 HR, 53 RBI

Wilfredo Gonzales—Pitcher. Threw left

Gonzales' Canadian career was among the shortest on record. He came to Brandon, Manitoba in June of 1950. He got his first start on June 14 and went just three innings in a loss to the Winnipeg Buffaloes. There was no record of Gonzalez appearing in any other games.

Julio Gotay—Third Base/Shortstop, 6'0", 180 lbs. Batted right, threw right

Gotay received a cool reception at the beginning of the 1958 Northern League season. Not from the fans. It was the weather. It was the first time the Puerto Rican native had seen snow. The good-humored infielder was seen "warming up" throwing snowballs.

He was an instant hit in Winnipeg in 1958 after a mediocre start to his pro career the previous summer in Class-D ball batting just .233 and .224 in his stops in the Appalachian and Florida State leagues. With the Goldeyes he finished with a .323 average and a league-leading 24 home runs. He was in the major leagues at age twenty-one and spent parts of ten seasons in the big leagues with St. Louis, Pittsburgh, California and Houston. Gotay played in 389 games and finished with a career batting average of .260. His final pro season was in 1971 in Triple-A with Tulsa.

    1958 Winnipeg Goldeyes—.323, 23 D, 5 T, 24 HR, 95 RBI

Canadian Highlights: Gotay led the league in home runs with 24, a Goldeyes' team record. He was voted to the Northern League All-Star team at third base. May 14, Gotay clubbed a two-run, ninth inning homer that gave the Goldeyes a 7–6 victory over Aberdeen. June 27, he had four hits in a 19–8 win over the Minot Mallards. July 16, Gotay blasted a pair of homers to lead the Goldeyes to a 5–1 win over Eau Claire Braves.

Cleveland Grant—Third Base.

Grant came out of Texas with Ligon's Colored All-Stars to barnstorm Western Canada in the years after the Second World War. Along with a starring role with the All-Stars, Grant suited up with teams in Saskatchewan's Southern League. He played with Regina and Moose Jaw from 1946 to 1948 before attracting the attention of Buck O'Neill of the Kansas City Monarchs. In the late 1940s, Grant played for the Monarchs and the Satchel Paige All-Stars.

After time in military service, Grant, who did not have an opportunity to attend high school, as his hometown (Hondo, Texas) did not have a high school for black students, went to college in San Antonio and Austin where he played both college baseball and basketball. He returned to the semi-pro ranks in the San Antonio area in 1953 and played another five seasons.

His son, Darryl Grant, turned to football and played for eleven seasons in the National Football League as a defensive tackle with Washington and Tampa Bay.

Morrell Graves—Second Base

Graves graduated from semi-pro ball with the Detroit Wolves to make the trip to Manitoba in 1950. Red House was the Detroit manager and when House was signed to manage the Carman Cardinals, Graves followed him to Carman playing only briefly before returning to Detroit.

    1950 Carman Cardinals—.200

Chappie Gray—Shortstop/Third Base

Gray was known as the "chanting shortstop" during his barnstorming tours because of his constant chatter on the field and in the dugout.

He played in West Coast Negro baseball with the Oakland Beavers, Oakland Larks and San Francisco Tigers from 1947 to 1949. He joined the Estevan Maple Leafs for the 1950 season.

Canadian Highlights: July 26, 1950, Gray was the offensive star with five hits, including a homer and a triple, as Estevan upset Minot Mallards 9–2 at the Tournament of Champions in Moose Jaw. Gray led the tournament with nine hits.

Pancho Gray—Pitcher

The veteran pitched for the Indian Head Rockets in 1950, and both Moose Jaw and Rosetown in 1954.

Canadian Highlights: July 21, 1950, Gray held the powerful California Mohawks to seven hits as the Rockets won the Indian Head Tournament with a 5–1 victory in the final

Cotshel Green—Pitcher. Threw right

The right-hander hurled for the 1950 edition of the Indian Head, Saskatchewan, Rockets.

Elijah "Pumpsie" Green—Third Base/Catcher/Outfield, 6'0", 175 lbs. Batted both, threw right

In the 8th inning of a July 21st, 1959 major league game in Chicago, Pumpsie Green entered the contest for the Boston Red Sox as a pinch runner. It was the first time an Afro-American had played for the Boston squad, the last of the major league teams to integrate. He became the seventh player with roots in Canadian ball to integrate a major league team. Green played in the majors over five seasons, four with Boston and one with the Mets.

He was just seventeen when he came out of the Oakland area in 1951 (along with buddies Nat Bates and Willie Reed) to suit up with the Medicine Hat Mohawks. He also played the following season in Canada as a member of the Indian Head Rockets (with Bates, Reed and another Oakland-area pal, Winters Calvin). He won considerable praise both for his offensive and defensive contributions (at third base, catcher and the outfield).

> 1951 Medicine Hat Mohawks—.227 (incomplete)
> 1952 Indian Head Rockets—Statistics not available

Canadian Highlights: June 27, 1951, Green belted a homer and double and scored three times in an 18–6 win by the Mohawks over Estevan. He knocked in two runs the following day as the Mohawks won again, 7–2. July 19, Green bashed two triples and three singles and notched the winning run to lead Medicine Hat to a 3–2 win over Estevan to advance in the Indian Head tournament. July 28, Green tripled, drove in a run and scored as the Mohawks shaded Indian Head 2–0 although getting just two hits. August 2, Green had two hits and scored a pair to lead the Mohawks past Swift Current 3–2. August 19, Green had three hits and scored two to pace Medicine Hat to a 6–1 win and top money in the Invitational Tournament at Medicine Hat.

> Pumpsie Green played standout ball for the Mohawks over the weekend. He hit two for four Saturday as he played third base, then picked up three for four Sunday in his catching role. The 17-year-old is fast becoming one of the west's top prospects for major league status [*Medicine Hat News* August 20, 1951].

July 21st, 1959, Elijah "Pumpsie" Green put on his Boston Red Sox jersey and took the field against Chicago at Comiskey Park. Twelve years after Jackie Robinson had broken the color barrier, the Red Sox, the last of the teams to integrate, finally followed suit (photograph courtesy the National Baseball Hall of Fame Library, Cooperstown, N.Y.).

Louis Green—Catcher, 5'8", 185 lbs. Batted right, threw right

Born in Shawneetown, Illinois, Green honed his skills with the Jacksonville, Florida, Stars and Jacksonville Eagles after a four and a half year hitch in the Army during the Second World War. Green was thirty years old when he came north with the Jacksonville club in 1950 when the Eagles played the summer season as the Indian Head Rockets. He moved to North Battleford in 1951. Green a strong defensive catcher, was the Beavers sparkplug for seven seasons. While he rarely hit for a high average, his ability to draw bases on balls turned him into an asset at the plate. In 1955, for example, he was second in walks, with 53, and produced an on-base percentage of .378 in spite of a .200 batting average.

> 1950 Indian Head Rockets—Statistics not available
> 1951 Indian Head Rockets—Statistics not available
> 1952 North Battleford Beavers—.288, 3 HR, 27 RBI
> 1953 North Battleford Beavers—Statistics not available
> 1954 North Battleford Beavers—.208, 0 HR, 19 RBI
> 1955 North Battleford Beavers—.200, 0 HR, 15 RBI
> 1956 North Battleford Beavers—.208, 0 HR, 10 RBI
> 1957 N.Battleford/Lloydminster—.081, 0 HR, 7 RBI

Canadian Highlights: August 3, 1950, Green punched out three hits as Indian Head downed North Battleford in the final of the Rosetown (Saskatchewan) Tournament. The club had earlier captured the prestigious Indian Head event.

August 9, 1953, he had four hits to help the Beavers whip Regina 16–0.

September 9, 1954, Green was in the spotlight as he singled to drive in the Beavers' first run and worked a bases-loaded walk to knock in the second marker as the Beavers downed Saskatoon 3–2 to capture the deciding game of the league championship.

July 16, 1956, the talkative backstop was ejected in the first inning of a game for "talking to the batter during a pitch." In 1956, Green was the catcher on the Canadian team at the Global World Series.

July 19, 1957, the likeable Green was saluted by the Beavers and the community in a special ceremony following his release by the club. Among the gifts was a wallet containing $348. He later rejoined the Beavers to finish the season and his career.

Shaeffer Green—Pitcher/Outfield, 6'1", 190 lbs.

Brought to the Regina Caps of the Southern League in 1949 as a pitcher, the 24-year-old Pittsburgh native had a much bigger impact as a hitter.

> 1949 Regina Caps—.353 (3rd), Won 2, Lost 1

Canadian Highlights: June 15, 1949, in a twin-bill against Ligon's All-Stars, Green had a triple, double and single in the first game and a triple and single in the second game. June 20, Green belted a pair of homers and a double to drive in four runs against the touring Muskogee Colored Cardinals. August 4, Shaeffer went 4 for 4, including a pair of home runs, and drove in five runs to pace Regina Caps to a 9–4 win over Minot Merchants. August 5, Shaeffer had another pair of four-baggers as Regina dumped Lake Valley 17–3 to advance at the Moose Jaw Tournament.

Shedrick Green—Outfield

Green was an outfielder for the Indian Head Rockets of the 1951 Western Canada Baseball League.

> 1951 Indian Head Rockets—.296 (incomplete)

Canadian Highlights: June 15, 1951, Green had three hits in a losing cause to Medicine Hat. July 14, Green's first inning, three-run homer set the pace as the Rockets crushed Estevan 21–0. July 18, Green had two hits and scored twice as the Rockets won their opening game at the Indian Head Tournament. July 22, Green had three hits as Indian Head stretched its winning streak to 18 games in an 11–2 win over Moose Jaw. August 13, Green punched out three hits in three trips as the Rockets dropped a 7–4 decision to Medicine Hat. August 16, Green had three hits in a 17–4 win over Swift Current.

James Elbert "Joe" Greene (Green)—Catcher, 6'0", 200 lbs. Batted right, threw right

A very skilled player, Greene was the catcher on the great Kansas City Monarchs of the 1940s. He had started his Negro League stint in 1932 with the Atlanta Black Crackers. In 1951, with his career and the Negro League in decline, he came north to the Elmwood Giants. He played just one season, but still displayed considerable catching and batting talent.

    1951 Elmwood Giants—.301, 2 HR, 16 RBI

Wilbur "Willie" Greene (Green)—Pitcher/Utility, 6'0", 175 lbs. Batted right. threw right

Barnstorming teams, the Oakland Beavers and San Francisco Cubs, brought Greene to Western Canada in the late 1940s. During the 1949 tour, which also took him to North Dakota, Greene left the club to join the Minot Merchants, a team which regularly played against squads from Canada. He moved to Estevan, Saskatchewan, for the 1950 and 1951 seasons before returning to Minot in 1952. He split the 1954 season between Carman and Minot of the ManDak League and Moose Jaw of the Western Canada League.

    1950 Estevan Maple Leafs—Statistics not available
    1951 Estevan Maple Leafs—.228, Won 1, Lost 2, 8 G, 3 GS, 1 CG
    1952 Minot Mallards—Won 2, Lost 1, .133, 0 HR, 8 RBI
    1954 Minot/Carman—Won 2, Lost 1, .182, 0 HR, 3 RBI

Canadian Highlights: July 27, 1950, at the Moose Jaw Tournament, Greene poked a homer as Estevan beat Minot and then picked up a win in relief as the Maple Leafs downed Moose Jaw. August 22, Greene fired a six-hit shutout as Estevan trounced Notre Dame 11–0 in the Southern League semi-finals.

May 21, 1951, Greene poked a double and two singles to lead Estevan past Minot 9–7.

May 30, 1952, Greene tossed a six-hitter in a 5–2 Minot win over Brandon. July 24, Greene's triple and double were key hits in Minot's 9–3 win over Brandon.

June 1, 1954, Greene had three hits for Moose Jaw in a loss to Saskatoon.

J.D. Greer—Pitcher

Greer was a pitcher during the early part of the 1953 season with the Regina Caps of the Saskatchewan League.

Bob "Schoolboy" Griffith—Pitcher, 6'5", 235 lbs. Threw right

Griffith's Negro League career, which began in 1933, spanned 15 years. In 1947 and 1948, he pitched for Rochester in the Southern Minnesota League and led the club to the state tournament. He had a league best 11–4 record in 1950.

Griffith's first season in Canada was 1951, when he pitched in Granby, Quebec (at the time in organized baseball), and had some success. In 1952, he was back in the Southern Minnesota League with the Waseca Braves and, in 1953, the imposing right-hander joined the Brandon Greys. Even though he was nearly 40 when he joined Brandon, his 21 appearances and 14 starts were among the league leaders. He was back with the Rochester Royals in 1954, and the following season Griffith pitched for Faribault, Minnesota and finished with a 10–3 record and a 3.78 ERA. Minnesota newspaper reports indicated that Griffith was a very popular player during his time in the league. He died in 1977 in Indianapolis at age 65.

> Griffith, rated by many as highly as Satchel Paige, who will pitch this afternoon, did everything except make the ball bat for him. The first five pitches were all delivered differently, and each succeeding one was more baffling to the batter than the one before [*Winnipeg Free Press*, August 21, 1937, p.24].

    1951 Granby Red Sox—Won 6, Lost 5, 15 G, 11 GS, 4.39 ERA
    1953 Brandon Greys—Won 8, Lost 6, 21 G, 14 GS, 6 CG

Canadian Highlights: August 20, 1937, Griffith fired a five-hitter with 15 strikeouts as the Cuidad Trujillos topped the Jesse Petty Wisconsin All-Stars 14–1 in an exhibition game at Winnipeg.

May 24, 1953, Griffith fired a four-hitter in a Brandon win over Carman. July 18, he beat Minot 8–5 and led the Greys at the plate with a double and two singles.

Acie "Skeet" Griggs—Infield, 6'0", 200 lbs. Batted right, threw right

The older brother of Bennie Griggs, "Skeet" suited up with Bennie on the 1954 Saskatoon Gems of the Saskatchewan Baseball League. He began his baseball career in the City League of Birmingham, Alabama, as a 14-year-old in 1938. He went on to play with the Negro League's Birmingham Black Barons, Atlanta Black Crackers, and New York Cubans in the late 1940s and early 50s after a tour with the U.S. Navy in the Second World War. After his baseball career he was a high school mathematics teacher and athletic coach for nearly forty years. He died in 2007 at the age of 82.

Canadian Highlights: May 17, 1954, Griggs had a pair of hits and continued to impress at second base as Saskatoon topped North Battleford 6–2. June 18, Griggs drove in a pair of runs with two hits and attracted notice with outstanding defensive work in the outfield. June 27, two doubles and a single by Griggs were key blows as Saskatoon topped North Battleford 8–5.

Benjamin L. "Bennie" Griggs—
Pitcher/Outfield, 5'11", 200 lbs. Batted right, threw right

Baseball was in the family. His brothers, Acie and Wiley, played for the Birmingham Black Barons and other clubs in the Negro Leagues. In the late 1940s, Bennie competed in industrial leagues around his home town of Birmingham, Alabama, and with the Chattanooga Choo Choos and New Orleans Creoles.

Griggs was still a teenager when he got his first taste of the Canadian prairies in 1948 pitching for the touring Birmingham All-Stars. He returned the next two seasons as a mainstay of the Delisle Gems, the team of the Bentley brothers of ice hockey fame. While a star on the mound (going 9–0 in regular league games), he also proved to be adept at the plate as he finished as the fourth best hitter in the Saskatchewan and District League in 1950 with a .352 batting average. In 1951, he was drafted into the U.S. Army and spent most of the next two years in Korea. Wounded in action, he was awarded a Purple Heart.

In 1953, Griggs was back in Canada to join the Saskatoon Gems of the Saskatchewan League and tied for the league lead in wins, with 9, and led all pitchers in strikeouts with 92. The right-hander anchored the Saskatoon staff for three seasons. In 1954, he had a won-lost mark of 10–5 in a league-leading 133 innings. He was 9–4, with a 3.72 ERA in 1955 and led the circuit with 16 starts and was just one inning behind the league leader.

In 1955 and 1956, Griggs was a prominent member of Canada's team at the Global World Series.

The mound workhorse joined North Battleford for the 1956 season, the first of five with the Beavers. He finished 7–7, in '56, and finished among the leaders in innings pitched and strikeouts. His 147 innings led the league in 1957, when he finished 10–9 with 120 strikeouts. Again, in 1958, he led the loop in innings, 120, and strikeouts, 93, while tying for the lead in wins, 9. He also helped out at the plate with a .289 average.

Griggs, now 30 (but showing his age as 25 on official documents for professional baseball purposes) took a fling at pro ball beginning in 1959. He had a superb summer in the Milwaukee farm system when he went 21–7 in 235 innings and was an all-star with the Wellsville Braves of the Class-D, New York-Penn League. It was his best season as he led the league in wins, complete games, 21, innings pitched, 235, and strikeouts, 175. He finished 8–10, 3.84 ERA, the following season in moving to Jacksonville of the Class-A, South Atlantic League. He split the 1961 season between Jacksonville and Cedar Rapids of the Class-B, Three I League.

Early in the '61 season, Griggs pitched perhaps his best single game as he tossed a no-hitter for $9\frac{2}{3}$ innings only to come away a 1–0 loser as the opposing pitcher singled in the winning run in the 12th frame.

Griggs began the 1962 campaign with

Yakima in the Class-B, Northwest League compiling a 2.33 ERA in 27 innings before returning to Canada and the North Battleford Beavers. He went on to lead the Northern Saskatchewan League in wins, finishing 9–3. His 10–3 record in 1963 was the best winning percentage in the loop and he was one of the top hitters, batting .348. While baseball may have been his game, golf was his love.

> He was a good golfer. We'd go over there to play baseball and they'd have to get him off the golf course to pitch. They say, man go get Bennie the game is getting ready to start. He'd rush from the course, put his uniform on and throw about two pitches and he'd be ready [Former teammate Curly Williams, Interview, 2001].

Griggs died in November, 2006 at age 78

- 1949 Delisle Gems—Won 4, Lost 0, 8 G, 7 GS, 4 CG
- 1950 Delisle Gems—Won 5, Lost 0, 6 G, 5 GS, 4 CG .352 (4th in the league)
- 1953 Saskatoon Gems—Won 9, Lost 7
- 1954 Saskatoon Gems—Won 10, Lost 5, 19 G, 13 GS, 12 CG, .284 AVE
- 1955 Saskatoon Gems—Won 9, Lost 4, 17 G, 16 GS (1st), 7 CG
- 1956 N.Battleford Beavers—Won 7, Lost 7, 21 G, 16 GS, 7 CG, 3.63 ERA
- 1957 N.Battleford Beavers—Won 10, Lost 9, 29 G, 16 GS, 8 CG, 4.53 ERA
- 1958 N.Battleford/Lloydminster—Won 9, Lost 3, 19 G, 13 GS, 11 CG, 5.09, .289, Lethbridge White Sox—Statistics not available
- 1962 North Battleford Beavers—Won 9, Lost 3, .276
- 1963 North Battleford Beavers—Won 10, Lost 3, .348

Canadian Highlights: June 8, 1949, Griggs fired a three-hitter to lead Delisle to victory over Kamloops in the final of the Lloydminster Tournament.

In 1950, at the Lloydminster tourney, Griggs pitched Delisle to a 6–1 victory in the Gems' opening round game on June 7th (also leading the offense with a homer) and combined with Murray Coben on a shutout the following day as Delisle again won top prize with a 10–0 victory in the final. August 9, the right-hander chalked up a one-hit shutout, with 13 strikeouts, against Prince Albert.

In 1953, Griggs, who tied for the league lead in wins during the regular season, was a major force in the playoffs with six starts, five complete games, including a pair of shutouts. He was even better on the tournament trail. His triumphs included a three-hit shutout over Ligon's All-Stars in the Saskatchewan Optimist Tournament on June 30th, a one-hit shutout of Weyburn at the Indian Head Tournament July 16th, and a one hit shutout of Indian Head Rockets at the Rosetown Tournament on July 29th.

In the 1954 playoffs, Griggs won three playoff starts, all complete games, allowing a total of ten hits. In one victory, September 3rd, he gave up two hits and a run in the opening frame, then pitched no-hit ball the rest of the way.

September 25th, 1955, he fired a four-hitter as Canada topped Mexico at the Global World Series.

August 21, 1957, Griggs tossed a four-hit shutout as North Battleford beat the Lloydminster Meridians 4–0.

August 22, 1958, Griggs pitched 7⅔ innings of shutout ball in relief to lead Lloydminster–North Battleford Combines to a 4–3 win over Edmonton and a berth in the Western Canada Baseball League finals.

June 10, 1962, Griggs registered a two-hit shutout as North Battleford notched a 2–0 win over Neilburg. June 24, the right-hander fashioned a four-hitter and belted a homer in the Beavers' 12–2 win. July 8, he had another two-hit shutout in a 1–0 win over Saskatoon. July 18, Griggs had his first no-hitter as North Battleford topped Unity in a rain shortened five inning affair. August 3, he had a three-hit 6–0 shutout over Neilburg. Griggs picked up three wins in the playoffs including the final on September 9th as the Beavers beat Kindersley 3–2.

July 14, 1963, saw Griggs fire a shutout and belt a homer to lead North Battleford to an 11–0 win over Biggar. September 1, Griggs, with ten wins in the regular season, captured his fourth playoff victory as North Battleford downed Kindersley to capture the North Saskatchewan Baseball League championship for the second straight season.

Napoleon "Nap" Gulley—Pitcher/Outfield, 6'1", 175 lbs. Batted left, threw left

Gulley played for six teams in the Negro League, beginning in 1941. In '49, he played briefly for the Farnham Black Sox and St. Jean Braves in the Provincial League in Quebec, an independent circuit at the time. The Oakland, California, native had earlier visited Winnipeg as a member of the Harlem Globetrotters when they took on the House of David in a 1945 series in Canada. He began play in organized ball, in 1950, in the Chicago Cubs' system with Visalia in the California League. He stayed with Visalia for three seasons and made the all-star team in 1952 when he hit .333 with 43 doubles and 8 home runs. In 1953, he was back in Canada with the Victoria Tyees, an independent team in the Western International League. In 1955, again he was an all-star in playing for Spokane in the Northwest League. His last season of professional ball was in 1956.

1949 Farnham/St. Jean—Won 0, Lost 3
1953 Victoria Tyees—.270, 4 HR, 23 RBI

Ed Hamman—Player/Owner/Entertainer

For over thirty-five years Hamman was involved either as a player at the minor league level or as an entertainer. Newspaper reports called him "the funniest man in baseball." Although he was white, he was a regular performer with black barnstorming teams. For five years he traveled with Abe Saperstein's famous Harlem Globetrotters basketball and baseball teams. Hamman did double duty as the team's business manager and entertainer. During his career he performed at stadiums in the Man-Dak League and Western Canada. He enjoyed interaction with the fans, especially giving children a chance to meet a clown. In 1953, the National Baseball Congress awarded Hamman a plaque for long and meritorious service to baseball. He died in 1989 in Florida.

George Handy—Second Base/Third Base, 5'6", 175 lbs. Batted left, threw right

The summer Jackie Robinson integrated organized baseball, Handy began his career in the Negro League. After three years with the Memphis Red Sox and a cameo with the Houston Eagles, he shifted to organized ball with Bridgeport in the Class-B, Colonial League. He had a fine season, hitting .346 with 22 home runs and returned for the 1950 season. However, early in the schedule, Handy jumped to St. Hyacinthe of the Quebec Provincial League for the first of two summers in Quebec.

1950 St. Hyacinthe Saints—.352, 11 D, 4 T, 5 HR, 60 RBI
1951 St. Hyacinthe Saints—.333, 17 D, 6 T, 13 HR, 72 RBI

Walter Hardy—Infield, 5'10", 160 lbs. Batted right, threw right

A "good field, no hit" middle infielder, Hardy had some Negro League time with the New York Black Yankees, New York Cubans and Kansas City Monarchs before he came to Canada to join St. Jean in the Quebec Provincial League. He played for three seasons with the Quebec team raising his average to .276 in his final season.

1950 St. Jean Braves—.200, 1 HR, 9 RBI
1951 St. Jean Canadians—.251, 6 HR, 30 RBI
1952 St. Jean Canadians—.276, 4 HR, 45 RBI

Wilmer Harris—Pitcher, 6'0", 175 lbs. Batted right, threw right

Harris pitched for the Philadelphia Stars in the Negro League from 1945 to 1950. In 1951, he traveled to the small community of Elgin, New Brunswick, to play semi-professional ball in Canada. Harris returned to Philadelphia for a final season with the Stars in 1952. He also hurled in winter ball in the Caribbean.

Bob Harvey—Outfield, 6'1", 220 lbs. Batted left, threw right

A two-sport star at Bowie State (Maryland) University, Harvey excelled at football winning a spot in the school's athletic Hall of Fame. His baseball career took some time to develop. It took him nearly five years of semi-pro ball to get an opportunity in the Negro League. Once aboard, the big outfielder was a solid contributor. He was a prominent member of the

Newark and Houston Eagles from 1944 to 1950, including the 1946 championship team, and had two all-star selections to his credit. With the Negro loop on its last legs, Harvey came to Canada in 1951 to participate in the ManDak League with the Elmwood Giants. He topped the league in homers, 9, in his only season. He retired after the '51 campaign. He died in 1992 in New Jersey.

1951 Elmwood Giants—.306, 9 HR, 43 RBI

Canadian Highlights: The Giants beat Carman 9–1 on June 20 and Harvey led the way with four singles for a perfect day at the plate. June 26, Harvey blasted a two-run homer in the eighth inning in a 4–2 Giants win over Carman. June 30, Harvey had a homer and single, scored twice and knocked in a pair as the Giants whipped the Buffaloes. July 16, he drove in four runs in a 15–1 victory over Winnipeg. July 21, he drove in the winning run in the eleventh inning to give the Giants a 2–1 win over Carman.

Jehosie "Jay" Heard—Pitcher, 5'7½", 145 lbs. Batted left, threw left

The little lefty had a background of seven years in the Negro League with Birmingham Black Barons, Houston Eagles and New Orleans Eagles when he entered organized ball in 1952 in the St. Louis Browns system. Professing to be just 26 (not 32), Heard had a sensational first season with Victoria, British Columbia, of the Western International League. He finished with 20 wins and led the loop in strikeouts with 216. His accomplishments included a no-hitter and a one-hitter.

> There is no more popular player on the Victoria club than the jaunty, self-assured Heard, who—no pun intended—has plenty of color and knows it [*Victoria Colonist,* June 22, 1952].

Down in Venezuela for winter ball, he led the league in ERA with a 3.03 mark and then advanced to Triple-A for the 1953 season and won 16 games for Portland on the way to a "cup of coffee" in the majors with Baltimore in 1954. He continued in the minors, mainly in Triple-A, until 1957. He died in 1999 in Birmingham, Alabama.

1952 Victoria Tyees—Won 20, Lost 12, 2.94 ERA

Canadian Highlights: May 30, he pitched in both games of a twin-bill tossing a seven inning, complete game in the opener and seven innings in relief in the second game. He allowed just a single run in each game. He lost both. July 31, Heard allowed just a 4th inning single in tossing a one-hitter as Victoria trounced Wenatchee 13–1. September 10, the diminutive hurler won his 20th in style, with a no-hitter. He gave up a run in the first inning on a walk and three errors. Heard was a force on offense as well with three hits and three runs and reached base a fourth time when hit on the head by a pitched ball.

Arlington Henderson—Catcher

Henderson was the regular catcher for the all-black Rosetown entry in the 1954 Saskatchewan Baseball League.

1954 Rosetown Phillies—.238, 2 HR, 33 RBI, 16 SB

Canadian Highlights: June 18, 1954, Henderson drove in three runs with a pair of hits in the Phillies' 7–6 loss to Indian Head. June 20, Henderson clouted a homer and triple as Phillies dumped Indian Head 9–4. July 2, Henderson belted a homer and single, driving in three runs, in a loss to Saskatoon. July 13, Henderson had three of Rosetown's six hits in a 3–1, 11-inning win over Lloydminster.

Al Henry—Outfield

Henry was an in-season addition to the sad sack (last place, five managers) Moose Jaw Maples of the 1953 Saskatchewan League. He had a fine season hitting .294.

1953 Moose Jaw Maples—.294

Canadian Highlights: July 6, 1953, Henry had three hits as Moose Jaw whipped Regina 12–3 in the first game of a double-header, then had two hits in the nightcap. August 7, Henry was 3 for 3, with a walk and two stolen bases, to help Moose Jaw down Regina 7–0.

Jose "Hippy" Hernandez—Playing-manger/Pitcher. Threw right

A playing-manager, Hernandez brought his Cuban colleagues to the prairies in the early 1950s. The original squad was the barnstorming Florida Cubans in 1952 which morphed into the Indian Head Rockets for 1953 and 1954 when they were hired on to represent the small Saskatchewan community.

> 1952 Florida Cubans—Statistics not available
> 1953 Indian Head Rockets—Statistics not available
> 1954 Indian Head Rockets—Won 5, Lost 2, 10 G, 7 GS, 4 CG

Canadian Highlights: June 11, 1953, Hernandez fired a four-hitter as Indian Head downed Carman of the ManDak League 6–1 in exhibition action. Hernandez bested Chet Brewer in the mound duel. July 16, Hernandez pitched the Rockets to top money at the Indian Head Tournament. He hurled a five-hitter as the Rockets downed Saskatoon 6–2 in the final. July 24, Hernandez powered the Rockets on the hill, with an eight-hitter, and at the plate, with three safeties, as the Rockets swamped Regina Royal Caps 14–4.

May 25, 1954, Hernandez belted a homer to support his own pitching effort in a 4–4 draw with Moose Jaw. June 17, Hernandez allowed just six hits and no earned runs and drove in all three Rockets' runs with a double and single in a 3–2, 10-inning win over North Battleford. July 25, he scattered eight hits in a 5–1 victory over Lloydminster.

Mario Herrera—Center Field. Batted right, threw right

The fleet center fielder made his Canadian debut with the Florida Cubans in 1952 when the Cubans were barnstorming across Western Canada. Herrera was enticed to join the Saskatoon Gems in 1953 and spent four seasons with the Western Canada League team.

> 1952 Florida Cubans—Statistics not available
> 1953 Saskatoon Gems—19 SB
> 1954 Saskatoon Gems—.255, 1 HR, 26 RBI, 24 SB
> 1955 Saskatoon Gems—.215, 0 HR, 21 RBI, 30 SB
> 1956 Saskatoon Gems—.247, 1 HR, 15 RBI, 10 SB

Canadian Highlights: From 1953 to 1955 Herrera led the league in stolen bases with 19, 24 and 30 steal seasons. He was the center fielder on the Canadian team at the Global World Series in Milwaukee in 1955.

June 6, 1953, Herrera drove in the winning run in the 10th inning in a 7–6 win over Moose Jaw. The next day, his homer helped in a 4–1 victory over North Battleford. June 19, Herrera had four hits in a 16–9 triumph over Moose Jaw. July 28, Herrera clubbed a homer and triple to lead Saskatoon to a 7–1 win over Indian Head at the Rosetown Tournament.

July 2, 1954, Herrera had three hits and four stolen bases as Saskatoon whipped Rosetown 8–5. July 8, Herrera drove in three markers with a double and two singles as Saskatoon dropped Rosetown 14–9. August 3, Herrera knocked in three runs with a triple and two singles and added a pair of stolen bases. August 24, in the opening game of the playoffs, Herrera had two hits, drove in a pair and stole two bases as Saskatoon topped Indian Head 6–0. September 5, Herrera had four hits and scored twice in the Gems' playoff loss to North Battleford. September 8, Herrera had two hits and scored a pair in the Gems 5–1 playoff victory.

August 8, 1955, Herrera's two-run triple helped Saskatoon to a 10-inning 7–6 win over Moose Jaw.

July 10, 1956, Herrera's three hits led Saskatoon to an 8–2 win over Moose Jaw. August 14, Herrera had a double and two singles in a 5–1 win over Regina. August 21, Herrera's two-run homer was key a win over Regina.

Roberto Herrera—Catcher, 6'3", 220 lbs. Batted right, threw right

The native of Havana, Cuba, signed with the St. Louis Cardinals in 1956, starting the season in the Class-D, Florida State League. Herrera played three seasons in the St. Louis farm system before joining the Winnipeg Goldeyes in 1959. He was a big hit with Winnipeg fans and was dubbed the "Cuban Rifleman" because of his strong throwing arm.

The Cardinals reported he had the strongest arm in their organization. He vaulted to Triple-A the next season and kicked around in seven organizations over the next nine years. He closed out his career in the Mexican League

    1959 Winnipeg Goldeyes—.303, 12 D, 5 T, 13 HR, 50 RBI

Canadian Highlights: June 5, Herrera clouted three hits, scored twice and drove in three runs to lead the Goldeyes past Fargo-Moorhead 11–1. June 27, the big catcher had a big offensive day, with two homers and a single, scored four times and knocked in four as the Goldeyes clubbed Aberdeen 16–4. At the end of the 1959 season, Herrera was selected to the Northern League All-Star team.

Robert "Big Daddy" Herron—

Outfield/Pitcher, Height 6'3", 220 lbs. Batted right, threw right

Herron was one of the most feared sluggers on the prairies over a seven year period beginning in 1949 when he left a barnstorming team from San Francisco to play for the tiny Saskatchewan community of Carlyle, where he supplemented his income by setting up a shoeshine stand in a local barber shop. (Herron also set up a stand in Saskatoon the following season, but he was charged with not having a business license and not having a Canadian work permit. He pleaded guilty, paid a fine and the shoeshine business came to an end).

Herron was back with Carlyle in 1950, but the team folded after just a couple of weeks and he moved on to Saskatoon where he also played the following season. North Battleford came calling in 1952 and Herron spent four summers with the Beavers, intertwined with two years of pro ball with Artesia, Texas of the Class-C, Longhorn League (in 1954, in Texas, he batted .346 with 19 home runs and 119 RBI and posted a 4–0 mark on the mound).

The imposing Texan had batting marks of .295, .341, .306 and .324 in his last four seasons in Canada. Twice he led the league in home runs, topping the circuit in runs batted in three times (finishing 2nd the other season), leading in total bases two years and finishing second the other two. His playoff performances were the stuff of legend. In the late 1950s, the Phys-Ed graduate joined the legendary Kansas City Monarchs. Herron hit .324 with Kansas City in 1959 with 24 home runs and he batted in 106. He even won five decisions on the hill.

He had a triumphant return to Canada when the Monarchs won top money in the 1959 Rotary Tournament in Lethbridge, Alberta. Herron died, at age 69, in 1994, in Wichita Falls, Texas.

    1949 Carlyle—Statistics not available
    1950 Saskatoon Cubs—Won 8, Lost 3, 13 G, 11 CS, 7 CG, .315
    1951 Saskatoon 55s—.375 (4th), Won 2, Lost 1, 4 G, 4 GS, 2 CG
    1952 N. Battleford Beavers—.295, 4 D, 4 T, 12 HR, 46 RBI
    1953 N. Battleford Beavers—.341, 17 D, 5 T, 12 HR, 60 RBI
    1956 N. Battleford Beavers—.306, 18 D, 2 T, 11 HR, 60 RBI
    1957 N. Battleford Beavers—.324, 21 D, 5 T, 14 HR, 64 RBI

Canadian Highlights: While much better known as a hitter, Herron had early success on the mound. In 1950, he led the Northern Saskatchewan League with an 8–3 record. In an exhibition tilt, he threw a one-hitter with sixteen strikeouts against the highly-rated California Mohawks. But, it was mainly the bat which won the headlines.

In a 1951 exhibition against the Ligon All-Stars, Herron had a homer, triple and two singles as the Saskatoon 55s whipped the visitors 14–1. He batted .375 in regular season play to place 4th in the loop.

May 16, 1952, the big right-hander fired a four-hit shutout as the Beavers blanked Moose Jaw 4–0. In the playoffs, he was the hero as North Battleford defeated Saskatoon to win the Saskatchewan Baseball League title. August 28, he drove in six runs with four hits, one of them a homer, to send the final series to a seventh and deciding game. August 31st he had another four hits, two of them home runs, and had five runs batted in as the Beavers won the championship game.

May 17, 1953, the big outfielder smashed two homers, one a grand slam, as North Battleford whipped Regina 15–7. August 9, Herron's grand slam homer was part of the fireworks as the Beavers walloped Regina 16–0. August 11, Herron drove in six runs with a homer and two singles as North Battleford edged Moose Jaw 15–13. August 22, Herron's three-run homer was the difference as the Beavers edged Moose Jaw 5–4 to even their semi-finals series. Two days later he belted a bases-loaded single in the 5th inning to send North Battleford to an 8–4 win and a berth in the final. August 30, his three-run blast provided the margin of victory as the Beavers got by Saskatoon 8–7 to tie the final at two games apiece. On September 1st, he homered to force a deciding game in the final.

July 6, 1956, Herron paced North Battleford with a pair of homers in a 5–4 win over Regina. Two days later, he hit another two home runs in a 9–6 triumph over Moose Jaw. July 12, Herron drove in five runs with a homer and two doubles in a 16–4 win over Regina. August 16, Herron had four hits and four runs batted in as the Beavers whipped Regina 12–2. September 3, Herron had a homer and a single as the Beavers downed the Meridians 9–1 to win the Western Canada League title and a trip to the Global World Series.

July 2, 1957, Herron's two-run homer in the bottom of the ninth gave North Battleford a 6–5 win over Saskatoon. July 20, he had four hits in a losing cause to Moose Jaw. August 4, Herron's grand slam homer was the key blow as North Battleford came from behind to whip Lloydminster 19–13.

July 31, 1959, Herron's homer in the 4th inning was the only run as Kansas City Monarchs blanked Medicine Hat 1–0 at the Lethbridge Tournament.

Elmer (Jim) Hester—Pitcher. Threw right

Hester, who toured with the Muskogee Cardinals, pitched for the Kamsack Cyclones in tournament events in 1949 and Estevan Maple Leafs of the Western Canada League in 1951.

> 1951 Estevan Maple Leafs—Won 0, Lost 1, 2 G, 2 GS, 0 CG

Carl Higginbotham—Pitcher, 6'1". Threw right

The right-hander was a 1951 import recruit by the Regina Caps of the Western Canada League. He saw limited action before an early-season release.

Benny Hill—Pitcher. Threw right

The veteran was the playing-manager of the Rosetown Phillies in 1954, recruited by Fred Banks, a Philadelphia promoter, to head the all-black squad in the inaugural season of the Saskatchewan League. Hill, from Norristown, Pennsylvania, was a fixture in circuits in the Philadelphia/Washington area playing with teams such as the Philadelphia Black Meteors and Hilldales.

> Hill is the first Negro player in the 14-year history of the East-Penn circuit and is the first Negro to wear an East Greenville uniform in 63 years of baseball in that small community [*Pottstown Mercury*, May 14, 1948].

He had a fine 1954 season finishing with a 7–2 record in 21 games pitched, and with a batting mark over .300.

> 1954 Rosetown Phillies—Won 7, Lost 2, 21 G, 7 GS, 4 CG, 94 IP, 32 BB, 81 SO, .309

Canadian Highlights: May 18, 1954, Hill went the distance to notch his first win as Rosetown dumped North Battleford 6–2. July 28, Hill fired a four-hit shutout as Rosetown defeated Colonsay 4–0 at the Rosetown Tournament. He had another outstanding effort the next day, allowing just one earned run, but fell 2–0 to Lloydminster.

Sam Hill—Outfield, 6'2", 178 lbs. Batted left, threw right

As a teenager, Hill began his pro career in the Negro League in 1947 and 1948 with the Chicago American Giants winning a slot in the '48 all-star game. With the Negro loops fading with the integration of organized ball, Hill hooked up with Rochester Royals in the semi-pro Southern Minny League in 1949 and traveled further north in 1950 to Winnipeg and the inaugural season of the ManDak League. The center fielder put in three seasons in the ManDak circuit, two with Winnipeg and another in

Carman before a return to Minnesota for the 1953 campaign.

Hill took a spin in organized ball in 1954 in the Pittsburgh farm system with Class-A, Williamsport hitting .272 with 12 homers. He bounced back to the Rochester Royals for 1955 and Bismarck of the ManDak League in 1956 before his final two summers in the minor leagues, mainly in the Northern League.

- 1950 Winnipeg Buffaloes—.209, 0 HR, 15 RBI
- 1951 Winnipeg Buffaloes—.290, 3 HR, 26 RBI
- 1952 Carman Cardinals—.288, 5 HR, 33 RBI
- 1956 Bismarck Barons—.335, 20 HR, 73 RBI

Canadian Highlights: July 18, 1951, Hill hit two doubles and a single in a 6–5 victory over Minot. Three days later he had another three hits in a 9–8 win over Minot. August 9, he was the big man at the plate with four hits including a home run and three RBI as Winnipeg trounced Brandon 11–4.

August 4, 1952, Hill starred in the field and hit two doubles and a single in a 2–1 Carman loss to Brandon. August 18, Hill slammed two home runs, a triple and single in the first game of the semi-final playoff against the Giants. In 1952, there was a report from Carman in which Minot's ace pitcher Sugar Cain named Sam Hill as the toughest batter in the league

Stamp J. Holly—Outfield

Holly had a brief stay with the Winnipeg Buffaloes of the ManDak League in 1950. He had Negro ball experience, 1945–46, with the Seattle Steelheads, Harlem Globetrotters and New Orleans Black Pelicans.

Leniel "Lennie" Hooker—Pitcher, 6'0", 160 lbs. Batted right, threw right

Hooker, a knuckleball pitcher, hurled in the Negro League from 1940 to 1948 with the Newark Eagles and Houston Eagles. In 1949 he toured with the barnstorming Brooklyn Cuban Giants before finding some job security in the Quebec Provincial League with Drummondville where he played for three seasons. He died in 1977 in New Jersey. He was 56.

- 1949 Drummondville/Farnham—Statistics not available
- 1950 Drummondville Cubs—Won 11, Lost 6, 2.53 ERA
- 1951 Drummondville Cubs—Won 10, Lost 9, 3.79 ERA

Billy Horne—Second Base/Shortstop, 5'10", 165 lbs. Batted right, threw right

Horne was a strong defensive middle infielder who played for eight seasons in the Negro League with four teams, including the Chicago American Giants and Cleveland Buckeyes. His "brilliant fielding" was noted in the Winnipeg Free Press in 1949 when Horne suited up with the New Orleans Creoles on a barnstorming tour of Western Canada. Halfway through the 1951 ManDak schedule, Horne answered an appeal from the Carman Cardinals to join their lineup. He hit just .207 in twenty-one games.

- 1951 Carman Cardinals—.207, 0 HR, 6 RBI

Canadian Highlights: August 3, Horne punched out three hits as Carman trounced Minot 11–4. August 14, he drove in two runs and scored the winner in a 5–4 victory over Elmwood.

Charles "Red" House—Manager/Third Base

House had a taste of Negro League ball, beginning in 1937, with the Detroit Stars and Homestead Grays. For the most part, he performed with teams in the Detroit area, including the Detroit Wolves. In 1950, he was recruited to manage the Carman Cardinals of the ManDak League. However, his stay was short lived as the club released him just two weeks into the season after his charges began with ten straight losses.

Canadian Highlights: May 25, 1950, House hit a triple and two singles in Carman's 7–2 loss to Brandon.

Elston Gene Howard—Catcher/Outfield, 6'2", 196 lbs. Batted right, threw right

While the Dodgers had integrated the major

leagues in 1947, the Yankees seemed in no hurry to follow. Seven seasons after Jackie Robinson's first game with Brooklyn, the Yankees remained lily-white.

In July, 1950, New York purchased Howard from the Kansas City Monarchs and by 1953 had a pair of black stars in Triple-A with the Kansas City Blues. Howard hit .286 with 10 home runs. Vic Power led the league with a .349 average and 16 homers. The Yankees cleared the way for Howard by trading Power after the '53 season. Howard was assigned to the independent Toronto Maple Leafs in 1954 where his .330, 22 homer, 109 RBI, MVP performance made it impossible for New York to ignore. He was in the majors the following summer for the first stage of a 14-year career. Howard, who won the American League's Most Valuable Player Award in 1963, was selected for the all-star game nine times. He had begun his pro ball journey in 1948 as a teenager in the Negro League with the Kansas City Monarchs. Howard died in 1980 in New York City.

> 1954 Toronto Maple Leafs—.330, 21 D, 16 T, 22 HR, 109 RBI

Canadian Highlights: May 24, Howard went 9 for 19 in a five-game weekend series to lift his league-leading average to .400.

> Howard went on an amazing batting streak starting July 11 in Havana. In the Leafs' next 13 games, excluding completion of two suspended contests, Howard made 22 hits in 45 times at bat. Ten of the first 11 safeties went for extra bases, including three homers, two triples and five doubles [*The Sporting News*, July 28, 1954, p.30].

Percy Howard—Catcher/Outfield

Howard, with a background in the Negro League and with barnstorming teams, didn't stay in one place too long. Among other Negro clubs, he played with the Cincinnati Crescents, Chicago American Giants, Indianapolis Clowns, Detroit Stars and Ligon's Colored All-Stars.

In 1949 Howard tried out organized ball in the Class-C, Western Association. Unfortunately, he signed up with one of the worst teams in minor league history. The Leavenworth Braves lost 22 straight games to begin the season and finished up with a 25–112 record. The following summer Howard suited up in Canada with the Winnipeg Buffaloes of the ManDak League, hitting just .194 in 31 games. In 1951, with a year away from the calamity at Leavenworth, Howard gave organized ball another try, this time in the Mississippi–Ohio Valley League. He hit just .244 and was soon back in semi-pro company.

He split the 1953 campaign between Ligon's All-Stars and Bowsman of the Manitoba-Saskatchewan League. Howard returned to the United States in 1954–55 to play in what little remained of the Negro Leagues.

> 1950 Winnipeg Buffaloes—.194, 0 HR, 8 RBI
> 1951 Winnipeg Buffaloes—Statistics not available
> 1953 Ligon's/Bowsman—Statistics not available

Canadian Highlights: June 26, 1953, Howard bashed a pair of home runs to lead Ligon's All-Stars to the championship at the Lacombe Tournament. His three-run homer on opening day was decisive as Ligon's won their initial start.

Art Hunt—Pitcher. Threw right

Hunt got a taste of Western Canada during his barnstorming tours with the Brooklyn Cuban Giants in 1949 and 1950. He left the Giants midway through the '50 season to join the Brandon Greys of the ManDak League. The right-hander was superb. He finished 9–0 during the regular season and added another three wins in the playoffs. Hunt returned to the Greys in 1951 before military service in Germany, 1952–1953, where he was the ace pitcher for one of the Army teams. Hunt played the 1954 season in organized ball with the Aberdeen Pheasants in the Northern League (10–18, 4.99 ERA).

> 1950 Brandon Greys—Won 9, Lost 0, 11 G, 8 GS, 6 CG
> 1951 Brandon Greys—Won 4, Lost 2, 9 G, 6 GS, 5 CG

Canadian Highlights: In 1950 and 1951, Hunt was as good as any pitcher in the ManDak League. In '50, he won nine straight games (eleven counting the playoffs). July 4, he had a no-hitter for six innings in a tournament win over Minot Mallards. He finished giving up six hits with eleven strikeouts. July 24, the Winnipeg Tribune described Hunt as putting on a brilliant mound display for twelve innings. He gave up five hits in a 2–1 victory over Minot. August 3, he beat Jim Newberry and the Buffaloes 2–1 and on August 11, Hunt came into the game in the eighth inning and put down fourteen straight batters in a twelve inning win over Elmwood. September 4, Hunt shut out Carman 7–0 to send Brandon into the playoff final against the Winnipeg Buffaloes. At the conclusion of the 1950 season, the Tribune newspaper picked Hunt to the all-star team.

In 1951 on June 11, Hunt pitched a six-hit 4–0 win over the league-leading Winnipeg Buffaloes and on July 3, he pitched a five-hitter in a 3–2 victory over Minot.

Marty Hurd — First Base, 5'10", 225 lbs.

Hurd joined the Calgary Dodgers of the Foothills-Wheatbelt League in Alberta in 1957 after a sterling season at the University of Arizona where he hit .473 to lead American college hitters. He was the first black baseball player at the school, ten years after Jackie Robinson donned a Brooklyn uniform. Hurd also suited up for the football team as a 225-pound guard and center. (In spite of his size, Hurd was surprisingly fast as evidenced by his 13 doubles and 11 triples in his '57 college season.)

> Hefty Marty Hurd lived up to his nickname 'Thundering' yesterday as he boomed a pair of tremendous triples and two singles in five times to the plate. One of Hurd's smashes was a soaring affair that caromed off the base of the center field fence, 430 feet from the batter's box. (*Tucson Daily Citizen*, March 26, 1958)

Hurd was a potent offensive force for Calgary during his four seasons in Alberta hitting .378, .341, .341 and .294. In 1957 he led the loop in runs and RBI. In 1959, Hurd topped the league in at bats and hits while tying for the lead in doubles, with 16.

1957 Calgary Dodgers—.378 (3rd), 40 R, (1st), 41 RBI (1st)
1958 Calgary Dodgers—.341
1959 Calgary Dodgers—.341 (T, 3rd)
1960 Calgary Buffaloes—.294, 6 HR, 31 RBI

Canadian Highlights: July 12, 1957, Hurd's three-run homer provided enough for victory as the Dodgers moved to the final of the Calgary Tournament by downing Kimberley 8–1. July 28, Calgary swept a pair as Hurd bashed a three-run homer in the first game and added a three-run shot and a solo homer in the second contest. August 16, Hurd bashed a pair of homers as Calgary shaded Vulcan 6–5 and had two homers on August 18th in the opening game of the playoffs. August 23, Hurd had four hits as Calgary advanced to the semi-finals of the Medicine Hat Tournament with an 8–0 win over Billings.

July 1, 1958, Hurd's three-run blast was enough as Calgary beat Red Deer 9–0 in the semi-final of the Calgary Elks' Tournament.

June 7, 1959, Hurd had a homer and six runs batted in as Calgary trounced Lethbridge 19–5. June 28, his three-run homer was the difference as Calgary topped Vauxhall 8–6. July 1, at the Calgary Tournament, Hurd belted a grand slam in Calgary's 14–4 triumph over Ponoka. July 12, Hurd had three hits, including a home run, in a 12–6 victory over Medicine Hat. July 21, in an exhibition game against the powerful Edmonton Eskimos of the Can-Am League, Hurd had four hits, including a pair of homers in a 14–13, 10-inning win. August 3, he knocked in four runs with three hits in a 13–7 win over Vauxhall. September 1, his grand slam in the 3rd inning sent Calgary on the way to an 18–8 thrashing of Vauxhall in playoff action.

July 18, 1960, Hurd bashed a three-run homer and single to pace Calgary Buffaloes to an 11–4 win over Lethbridge. He hit two more four-baggers the following day against the White Sox. July 27, Hurd's three-run homer sparked the Calgary offense in an 11–0 win over Barrhead in Tournament play.

Willie Hutchinson — Pitcher, 5'8", 152 lbs. Batted right, threw right

Hutchinson, from Dallas, Texas, had a decade of Negro League experience (with the Kansas City Monarchs and Memphis Red Sox) before he arrived in Carman, Manitoba in 1951 to pitch for the ManDak League team. Before he came to the Cardinals he put in one semi-pro season in Minnesota with the Rochester Royals. Wee Willie, as he was called, spent three years with the Cardinals in the ManDak League. He left the team mid-way through the 1953 season for his only stint in organized ball, pitching for the Danville Dans of the Mississippi–Ohio Valley League. However, he was back in Carman in late July. Hutchinson died in 1992 in Colorado at age 72.

- 1951 Carman Cardinals — Won 5, Lost 8, 16 G, 12 GS, 11 CG
- 1952 Carman Cardinals — Won 5, Lost 5, 99 IP, 28 BB, 52 SO
- 1953 Carman Cardinals — Won 3, Lost 6, 12 G, 9 GS, 5 CG

Canadian Highlights: June 12, 1951, Hutchinson fired a five-hit, 4–0 win over Minot. On August 11, he had another five-hitter in a 10–3 win again over Minot.

July 25, 1952, Hutchinson fanned eleven in a 4–2 win over Minot.

Cowan "Bubba" Hyde — Outfield,
5'8", 155 lbs. Batted right, threw right

Hyde was a veteran of Negro League play, going back to 1927, when he came to Canada to join the Elmwood Giants for the inaugural season of the Manitoba-Dakota (ManDak) League. He had given pro ball a try, in 1949, in the Class-B, Colonial League with the Bridgeport Bees hitting .327. Hyde was already 43 years old when he first suited up in Canada, in 1950, and yet he played for four seasons (and hit over .300 twice and even led the league in triples in his final campaign). He put in two years with Elmwood and one each with Winnipeg Giants and Brandon Greys, with a brief stint in Quebec in between. In 1997, Hyde was among the initial inductees into the Negro League Wall of Fame at Milwaukee's County Stadium. He died, at age 96, in 2003 in St. Louis.

- 1950 Elmwood Giants — .315, 0 HR, 5 RBI, 16 SB
- 1951 Elmwood Giants — .348, 2 HR, 10 RBI
- 1951 Farnham Pirates — .193, 0 HR, 5 RBI
- 1952 Winnipeg Giants — .256, 2 HR, 26 RBI, 9 SB
- 1953 Brandon Greys — .292, 16 D, 10 T (1st), 0 HR, 30 RBI, 9 SB

Canadian Highlights: July 15, 1950, Hyde hit a double and two singles in a 5–2 loss to Minot. July 24, he had three hits in a losing effort to the Winnipeg Buffaloes and on August 5, Hyde had three hits in an 11–10 win over the Buffs. He scored the winning run in the bottom of the ninth inning.

July 4, 1951, he had three hits in a 7–6 victory over Carman.

June 18, 1953, Hyde led the Greys with a triple and a single in a 6–3 win over Minot. July 5, he again led the Greys with a double and three singles in a 6–3 win over North Battleford. July 19, against Minot, Hyde had a triple and three singles in a losing cause. Hyde led the way for Brandon in a 6–0 win over Minot on August 7, when he tripled and hit two doubles to drive in three runs.

Antonio Iglesias — First Base

The Cuban import played just one season in Canada with the Indian Head Rockets in 1954.

Canadian Highlights: July 22, 1954, Iglesias belted a homer and single in the Rockets' 15–6 win over Moose Jaw. August 29, Iglesias poked a clean single up the middle with one out in the 9th inning to spoil a playoff no-hit bid by Saskatoon's Ted Wills, a future major leaguer. The Rockets' first baseman went to the Gems' dressing room after the game to apologize for ruining the no-hitter.

Lee Ingram — First Base

Ingram was the first baseman for the 1953 edition of Ligon's Colored All-Stars who settled down in Prince Albert, Saskatchewan, that summer and played for part of the season as the Prince Albert Imperials.

Canadian Highlights: June 28, 1953, Ingram bashed a grand slam homer and added two singles to lead Prince Albert to a 10–8 exhibition win over Saskatoon Gems. July 29, Ingram drove in three runs to lead the team to an 11–6 win over Edmonton Pontiacs.

Alvin Jackson—Pitcher, 5'11", 170 lbs. Batted left, threw left

The lefthander was just out of high school in Waco, Texas when he toured Western Canada with the Jasper Steers in 1954. He was just 18 when he pitched at the Indian Head Tournament. He fired a five-hitter, but lost a heart breaking 1–0 decision to Saskatoon. Overall, Jackson was reported to have had a record of 23-3 on the '54 tour of Canada. Jackson already had semi-pro experience with the Waco Tigers of the West Texas Colored League. After attending Wiley College and Paul Quinn College, he signed with Pittsburgh Pirates and went on to a ten year career in the major leagues. He posted a career record of 67–99 with a 3.98 ERA.

Daniel "Thumper" Jackson—Outfield

Jackson was the batting king of the South Dakota State League in 1952. He hit .450 for the Bridgewater Coyotes. It led to a trial in organized ball in 1953 and 1954 in the Northern and Pioneer Leagues. In '53, Jackson was the first Afro-American to be a regular with the Boise Yankees. After starting the 1957 season in the Western League in the United States, Jackson came to Saskatchewan to suit up with the Saskatoon Gems of the Western Canada League. He followed his Saskatoon stint with four years in Ontario's Intercounty League, including time as the playing manager of the Guelph Royals.

- 1957 Saskatoon Gems—.279, 10 D, 1 T, 4 HR, 20 RBI
- 1958 Kitchener/Galt—.366, 150, 5 T, 3 HR, 22 RBI
- 1959 Galt/Guelph—Led in RBI, 32
- 1960 Guelph Merchants—.370, 8 D, 3 T, 10 HR, 40 RBI
- 1961 Guelph Merchants—Led in hits, 49, tied for HRs, 8

Canadian Highlights: June 18, 1957, Jackson had three hits in a 3–0 loss to Edmonton. June 21, Jackson's solo homer in the bottom of the 8th inning proved to be the difference as Saskatoon edged Moose Jaw 6–5. June 25, Jackson's single scored Len Tucker with the winning run in the bottom of the 9th as Gems shaded Regina 9–8. July 9, Jackson drove in Len Breckner with the winning marker in the bottom of the 10th inning as Saskatoon came from behind to top Edmonton 10–9. August 9, Jackson had three hits in the Gems' 13–5 victory over Lloydminster.

Isaiah "Ike" Jackson—Catcher/First base/Outfield, 6'1", 215 lbs. Batted right, threw right

Jackson returned from military service in the Second World War to the ball diamonds of Fresno, California and the beginning of a career as a catcher. He had been an outstanding pitcher on Army teams, but an arm fracture forced a change in positions. With success in amateur ranks in Fresno (one of his teams played in two different leagues one season, winning one title, tying for first place in the other) Jackson attracted the attention of the Kansas City Monarchs. He spent two years with the legendary Negro League team.

In 1953, he moved into organized ball in the Class-D, Longhorn League and Class-C, Southwestern League with the Carlsbad Potashers and Midland Indians. He was named Rookie Of The Year in 1953, a season which included a stretch of eleven straight hits and a final mark of .383 with 26 homers and 123 RBI. But his numbers were dwarfed by the sensational season by Joe Bauman of the Roswell Rockets, who won the triple crown as he batted .400, belted 72 home runs and drove in 224 runs. Jackson did lead the league in doubles with 45. After two more sterling seasons in New Mexico and Texas, Jackson trekked to Regina in 1957 for his first tour in Canada. He played in Saskatoon in 1958. Jackson finished 4th in batting in the Western Canada League in 1957 with a .371 mark and led the loop in doubles with 23. Jackson died at age 40 in a veterans hospital in California.

- 1957 Regina Braves—.371, 23 D, 8 T, 5 HR, 53 RBI
- 1958 Saskatoon Commodores—.310, 11 D, 3 T, 3 HR, 23 RBI

Canadian Highlights: June 19, 1957, Jackson slammed a triple, double and two singles, knocked in a pair and even stole a base in a 10–7 loss to Moose Jaw. June 26, Jackson belted two doubles and a single to lead Regina past Lloydminster 11–2 and followed with a triple and two singles the next day in a 4–1 triumph over Edmonton. July 22, Jackson had six hits in six trips to the plate, three singles, a double, triple and homer, three runs scored and three RBI. In his next game he drove in five runs with a triple and three singles. July 31, Jackson knocked out three hits, including a two-run double in an 11–6 win over Lloydminster. August 12, he had three hits as Regina topped North Battleford 7–1 and another three hits, including a homer, the next day in an 8–5 loss to the Beavers. And, on the third day, Jackson drove in four runs with a triple and single in Regina's 10–6 win over Moose Jaw.

June 17, 1958, Jackson had three hits to lead Saskatoon to a 9–8 decision over Williston. June 20, Jackson slugged a pair of homers to pace Saskatoon past Edmonton 10–4. July 7, Jackson had four hits in a 7–1 win over Regina. It gave Jackson 13 hits in his last 21 trips to the plate. July 18, Jackson socked a three-run homer as Saskatoon topped Regina 7–5. August 6, Jackson had four hits as the Commodores edged Moose Jaw 2–1.

Reg Jackson—First Base

Jackson held down first base for the Rosetown Phillies in their sole season in the Saskatchewan Baseball League.

> 1954 Rosetown Phillies—.276, 11 D, 2 T, 2 HR, 33 RBI

Canadian Highlights: May 25, 1954, Jackson drove in five runs with a pair of doubles and a single as Rosetown dropped a slugfest to North Battleford 18–15.

Gene Jacobs—Outfield. Batted left

Jacobs was among the California kids who came north in 1951 to suit up as the Medicine Hat Mohawks (the successor to the barnstorming California Mohawks). The University of San Francisco outfielder also played for Sceptre, Saskatchewan. He went on to a four-year pro career, reaching as high as Triple-A. In his first professional season, with Porterville of the Southwest International League, Jacobs was among a dozen African-American players who had Canadian experience.

> 1951 Medicine Hat/Swift Current—.328 (incomplete)

Canadian Highlights: June 1, 1951, in center field and hitting cleanup, Jacobs had a triple and single, a stolen base and two runs batted in as the Mohawks topped Moose Jaw 5–4. June 15, Jacobs had two hits, two runs and drove in a pair in the Mohawks' 14–4 win over Indian Head. June 27, Jacobs knocked in five runs with three hits, two of them doubles, in an 18–6 win over Estevan. September 6, playing for Sceptre Nixons, Jacobs had three hits and scored three times as Sceptre won the Canadian semi-pro title with a 7–5 win over Indian Head. In the playoff series Jacobs had 12 hits in 21 at bats.

Willie Jefferson—Pitcher, 5'9", 165 lbs. Batted right, threw right

The little right-hander's career spanned nearly 25 years, from a 1928 beginning. He advanced to the Negro League in 1937 and played with the Cincinnati Tigers, Memphis Red Sox, Cleveland Buckeyes and Cincinnati Buckeyes along with two years in the Mexican League. Jefferson came to Canada in 1951 to pitch for the Elmwood Giants in the ManDak League. In 1953, he made a brief appearance with the Regina Caps in the Saskatchewan League.

> 1951 Elmwood Giants—Won 5, Lost 7, 17 G, 12 GS, 7 CG
> 1953 Regina Caps—Statistics not available

Canadian Highlights: On July 12, 1951, Jefferson pitched a one-hitter in the Brandon, Manitoba, Tournament as he beat Carman 3–0 and on July 17, he pitched a four-hitter as he beat Minot Mallards 6–1.

Daniel Jenkins—Pitcher, 6'1", 185 lbs. Threw left

Out of Durham, North Carolina, Jenkins played two seasons with the Indian Head Rockets, the barnstorming team of 1950 and league team of 1951.

> 1950 Indian Head Rockets—Statistics not available
> 1951 Indian Head Rockets—Won 1, Lost 0, 5 G, 5 GS, 0 CG

Canadian Highlights: June 25, 1950, Jenkins tossed a three-hitter to down Swift Current 3–1. July 28, a four-hitter by Jenkins led the Rockets to a 6–2 decision over Estevan at the Swift Current Tournament. August 3, Jenkins had a three-hitter with 11 strikeouts as Indian Head topped Delisle Gems 9–1 in the semifinals of the Rosetown Tournament.

Ferguson "Fergie" Jenkins—Pitcher, 6'5", 205 lbs. Batted right, threw right

The Chatham, Ontario, native, pitched for 19 seasons in the major leagues winning 284 games. He won at least 20 games for six consecutive seasons, beginning in 1967, and finished his career in ninth place on the all-time strikeout list with 3,192. Six times Jenkins finished in the top ten in voting for the Cy Young Award, winning the National League's Cy in 1971 when he won 24 games in completing 30 of 39 starts. That same year he hit six home runs, one short of the league record. In 1991 Jenkins was inducted into the Baseball Hall of Fame at Cooperstown.

Jenkins was a hockey and basketball star as a kid in Chatham (later he played basketball for the Harlem Globetrotters). He had begun his pro career in 1962 in the Class-D, Florida State League where he dazzled with a 7–2 record and an ERA of 0.97.

In 1984, with his big league career over, he joined the London Majors in the Intercounty Baseball League. At age 41, Jenkins led the circuit in wins, with 9, and tied for the most strikeouts. He wrapped up his outstanding career the following summer with the London club. In 2007, Jenkins received Canada's highest civilian honor, the Order of Canada.

James "Pee Wee" Jenkins—Pitcher, 5'8", 160 lbs. Batted right, threw right

Jenkins got his start in 1942 and 1943 in his home town of Farnville, Virginia from which he graduated to the Negro League, 1944 to 1950, mainly with the New York Cubans. Jenkins showed up in Canada in 1951 with Three Rivers in the Provincial League, then jumped to the Winnipeg Buffaloes in the ManDak League. When the Buffaloes ceased operations he made his way to the Brandon Greys for two seasons. While in the ManDak League he pitched with success. He closed out his career in 1954 with the Birmingham Black Barons. He died on April 21, 2002 in Farnville.

 1951 Winnipeg Buffaloes—Won 8, Lost 5, 17 G, 13 GS, 11 CG
 1952 Brandon Greys—Won 3, Lost 3, 57 IP, 33 BB, 24 SO
 1953 Brandon Greys—Won 5, Lost 2, 16 G, 7 GS, 2 CG

Canadian Highlights: May 22, 1951, Jenkins beat Jim Bolden and the Elmwood Giants 5–2 with a seven-hitter. July 13, Jenkins pitched a four-hit, 11–0 win over Minot Mallards and helped his team at the plate by hitting three singles. July 18, against Minot, he was the winning pitcher and hit a game-deciding home run in the ninth to give the Buffaloes a 6–5 victory.

August 4, 1952, in the last ManDak Tournament of the season in Winnipeg, he went the distance in a 2–1 victory over Carman and gave Brandon first prize money.

June 30, 1953, Jenkins ran his record to 3–0 with a 5–1 win over the Carman Cardinals.

Gentry Jessup—Pitcher, 6'0", 180 lbs. Batted right, threw right

Jessup was an outstanding Negro League pitcher who was selected for five consecutive East-West All-Star games.

Born in North Carolina, his career began in 1939 with a club called the Beckley Black Bingles, followed by his first action in the Negro League with the Birmingham Black Barons. The major portion of his career was spent with the Chicago American Giants for whom he pitched from 1941 to 1949. In one game, in 1946, Jessup and Peanuts Davis each went the distance in a 20-inning, 3–3 tie. He also pitched in Panama and Cuba and, during the 1946 off-season, with the Satchel Paige All-Stars in a barnstorming tour against the Bob Feller All-Stars. (Among those on the Paige All-Stars were Jessup, Quincy Trouppe C, Buck O'Neil 1B, Hank Thompson 2B, Howard Easterling 3B, Art Wilson SS, Monte Irvin LF, Willard Brown CF, Len Pearson RF, Hilton Smith P, Barney Brown P, Dan Bankhead P and Max Manning P.) He was named to the Cuban Baseball Hall of Fame in 1998.

Jessup came to Canada for the inaugural season of the ManDak League and was the Carman Cardinals' ace for three seasons. He also played the outfield. He obviously enjoyed his stays in Carman. He was quoted in the Carman yearbook as saying "coming back to Carman was like coming home." Jessup moved east after the 1952 season to suit up with the Galt Terriers of the Intercounty League. His 15 wins and 140 strikeouts led that circuit in 1953.

Apparently speed wasn't one of his assets.

> They called him Jeep because when he was summoned from the bullpen they would need to drive him in just so he'd get there before the game ended [David Menary, *Terrier Town: Summer of '49*].

Jessup died in 1998, at age 83.

- 1950 Carman Cardinals — Won 9, Lost 4, 16 G, 13 GS, 12 CG
- 1951 Carman Cardinals — Won 9, Lost 6, 16 G, 15 GS, 13 CG
- 1952 Carman Cardinals — Won 8, Lost 8, 125 IP, 47 BB, 64 SO
- 1953 Galt Terriers — Won 15, 140 SO
- 1955 Galt Terriers — Statistics not available

Canadian Highlights: July 5, 1950, Jessup belted a game-winning, three-run homer and went the distance on the hill as Carman shaded Winnipeg 4–3. The towering home run cleared the center field wall. July 26, Jessup fired a one-hitter in a 3–1 win over the Winnipeg Buffaloes. August 1, he pitched all ten innings in a 5–4 win over Elmwood. It was his sixth win in seven decisions. Jessup hurled a two-hitter and fanned ten in a 2–1 victory on August 17, and pitched another two-hitter on August 21, as Carman crushed Elmwood 12–1. Jessup also has three hits. At the conclusion of the 1950 season, the Tribune newspaper picked Jessup to the ManDak League All-Star team.

July 19, 1951, he beat Minot 1–0 on three hits and had six strikeouts.

In 1952, on May 24, he blanked Winnipeg 4–0 and on June 10, Jessup bested Sugar Cain in a pitchers' duel as Carman topped Minot 3–2. August 13, Jessup held Brandon to four hits in a 3–1 Carman victory.

July 6, 1955, Jessup won his 5th straight as Galt beat St. Thomas 8–2 on a seven-hitter with nine strikeouts. July 19, Jessup lost a bid for his 7th straight win as a fluke pinch hit drove in the only run as Galt lost 1–0 despite his five-hitter.

Sam "The Jet" Jethroe — Outfield, 6'1", 178 lbs. Batted both, threw right

The speedy Jethroe honed his skills in Negro ball with the Cincinnati Buckeyes and Cleveland Buckeyes, winning the batting title in 1944 and 1945 with marks of .353 and .393. He topped the Negro American League in stolen bases three straight years.

Jethroe was among three Negro players who were supposed to get tryouts with the Cleveland Indians in 1943, but nothing came of the promise. In 1945, Jethroe, Jackie Robinson and Marvin Williams worked out for the Red Sox at Fenway Park, but no contracts were forthcoming and the players later termed the event a farce. Early into the 1948 schedule, he signed with the Dodgers and was sent to the Montreal Royals where he played the 1948 and 1949 seasons. Although he had outstanding results with Montreal (including 17 homers and 89 steals in '49) he was traded to the Boston Braves. He broke in with the Braves on April 18, 1950 (at age 32) and was their first black player. Named the National League's Rookie of the Year, he led the league with 35 stolen bases. In 1953 he was back in the minor leagues for six seasons in Triple-A, five with the Toronto Maple Leafs (along with a two-game stint in the majors in 1954). He had some productive seasons with the Leafs, but never received another chance at the big league level. He died in 2001.

- 1948 Montreal Royals — .322, 19 D, 11 T, 1 HR, 25 RBI, 18 SB
- 1949 Montreal Royals — .326, 34 D, 19 T, 17 HR, 83 RBI, 89 SB
- 1954 Toronto Maple Leafs — .305, 36 D, 8 T, 21 HR, 84 RBI, 23 SB
- 1955 Toronto Maple Leafs — .262, 16 D, 4 T, 16 HR, 66 RBI
- 1956 Toronto Maple Leafs — .287, 25 D, 4 T, 19 HR, 68 RBI, 20 SB
- 1957 Toronto Maple Leafs — .277, 16 D, 6 T, 15 HR, 39 RBI, 24 SB

1958 Toronto Maple Leafs—.234, 11 D, 0 T, 2 HR, 18 RBI

Canadian Highlights: In 1949 Jethroe was selected to the International League All-Star team with Montreal and led the league with 207 hits, 154 runs and 89 stolen bases. In 1954, Jethroe was again selected to the all-star team with Toronto and led the league in runs, 113, and hits, 181. In 1956 with Toronto he led the league in runs with 105.

Felipe "Jimmy" Jimenez—Pitcher/Outfield, 5'11", 200 lbs. Batted right, threw right

Jimenez began his pro career in the Washington Senators organization in 1945. He continued in the professional ranks through 1953 including seasons in which he won 19 and 18 games and batted .315, .321 and .385. He joined the Carman Cardinals in 1954.

1954 Carman Cardinals—Won 0, Lost 5, .207, 0 HR, 6 RBI

Bob Johnson—First Base, 6'1", 180 lbs. Batted right, threw right

Previous to his Canadian experience, Johnson played his ball on Negro clubs in the Detroit area, one of them the Detroit Wolves. He was recruited in 1949 by the Carman Cardinals, then of the Manitoba Senior League and returned to Manitoba for the 1950 and 1951 seasons when the team was in the ManDak League. The Cardinals' 1951 yearbook noted that Johnson was a favorite player to youngsters in Carman. With his career over he became a church minister.

1949 Carman Cardinals—.337
1950 Carman Cardinals—.269, 1 HR, 26 RBI
1951 Carman Cardinals—.269, 2 HR, 32 RBI

Canadian Highlights: June 11, 1949, Johnson drove in four runs in a Carman victory over Brandon. In that game he had a home run and two singles.

June 16, 1950, he had three hits in a 5–2 win over Elmwood. July 18, Johnson had a home run, double and a single in a 4–0 loss to Brandon. August 11, 1951, Carman beat Minot 10–3 and Johnson led the way with three hits.

Clifford "Connie" Johnson—Pitcher, 6'4", 200 lbs. Batted right, threw right

Johnson's Negro League career spanned the period 1940 to 1950, interrupted by three years of military service during the Second World War. He spent most of his career with the fabled Kansas City Monarchs. Like many black players, Johnson used Quebec's Provincial League as an entry into organized baseball. In 1951, at age 28, he signed with St. Hyacinthe of the Provincial League following a strong winter league season in Panama and a pitching win over Cuba at the Caribbean Series. He finished 15–14, with a 3.24 ERA in Quebec and won a contract with the Chicago White Sox who assigned the right-hander to Colorado Springs of the Class-A, Western League. He won 18 games and was a unanimous choice for the all-star team.

He started the 1953 season in Triple-A, but soon won a major league berth with the White Sox. He was back in Triple-A with Toronto Maple Leafs in 1954 (when he finished with a 17–8 record and led the Leafs to the International League pennant). Johnson pitched in parts of five seasons in the major leagues with his best summer in 1957 with Baltimore Orioles when he won 14 games with an ERA of 3.20.

Johnson was back in Canada in 1959 and 1960 with Vancouver of the Pacific Coast League before winding up in Mexico in 1961. During his career he played winter ball in Panama, Puerto Rico and Cuba and barnstormed with the Roy Campanella, Willie Mays and Hank Aaron All-Stars. Johnson died in 2004 in Kansas City.

1951 St. Hyacinthe Saints—Won 15, Lost 14, 3.24 ERA
1954 Toronto Maple Leafs—Won 17, Lost 8, 3.72
1955 Toronto Maple Leafs—Won 12, Lost 2, 3.05
1959 Vancouver Mounties—Won 8, Lost 4, 3.16
1960 Vancouver Mounties—Won 0, Lost 1

Canadian Highlights: In 1951, he led the Provincial League in strikeouts with 172.

May 23, 1954, Johnson fired a three-hit shutout as Toronto downed Syracuse 2–0. June 22, he posted his fifth straight win with a three-hitter in a 3–1 victory over Buffalo.

Ernest Johnson — Outfield, 6'3", 180 lbs. Batted left, threw right

Johnson had three Negro League seasons, 1949, 1950 and 1953, with the Kansas City Monarchs. He came to the Quebec Provincial League in 1954 with the Thetford Mines Miners for his lone summer in Canadian ball. He then played five more seasons in organized ball, ending in 1959.

1954 Thetford Mines Miners — .288, 12 D, 2 T, 9 HR, 54 RBI

Frank Johnson — Pitcher, 6'1", 190 lbs. Batted left, threw right

Johnson was a 1958 mid-season pickup by the Moose Jaw Mallards. He had pro experience going back to 1955. His Canadian tour was not much to write home about (0–5, 7.97) although he did well as a hitter (.294). He had a nice pro season in 1959 finishing 9–1, 3.77 (in spite of issuing 91 walks in 117 innings) with Wellsville in the New York–Penn League.

Canadian Highlights: Johnson's July 27th start against Lloydminster–North Battleford was a prime example of "taking one for the team" as he went the distance getting pounded for 21 hits in a 13–2 loss to the Combines.

Harold Johnson — Shortstop/Second Base

From the Philadelphia area, Johnson was believed to be all of 19 years of age in 1953 when he arrived on the prairies with a barnstorming club, the Phillies, which played out of Medicine Hat, Alberta. When the club folded just weeks into the season, Johnson hooked up with the Saskatoon Gems of the Saskatchewan League. Late in the season he also played with Moose Jaw. He returned in 1954 with Rosetown of the Western Canada League and while he didn't hit for a high average, Johnson was a solid leadoff hitter (with his 56 walks he had an on-base-percentage of .423).

1953 Saskatoon Gems — .252
1954 Rosetown Phillies — .247, 7 D, 2 T, 4 HR, 20 RBI, 56 BB in 58 games

Canadian Highlights: July 6, 1954, Johnson drew rave reviews going two for two and handling ten chances flawlessly. August 2, Johnson poked a two-run homer and two singles to lead Rosetown against North Battleford. August 17, Johnson belted a homer and single, good for three RBI, as the Phillies trounced North Battleford.

Johnny Johnson — Pitcher/Outfield. Threw left

Johnson pitched and played the outfield for the 1948 edition of Ligon's All-Stars, a barnstorming team out of Texas and California.

Canadian Highlights: June 29, 1948, on loan to the Regina Caps, Johnson pitched in three games, a total of 27 innings, to lead the Saskatchewan club to top money in the Lanigan Tournament. After the Caps had given up three runs in the 3rd inning of their opening game, Johnson relieved and went the rest of the way in a 7–4, 12-inning victory. He tossed a 4–0 shutout in a semi-final match and then went the distance in the final as Regina won 8–3.

August 11, 1949, now touring with the New Orleans Creoles, Johnson tossed a seven-hitter against the Southern League All-Stars at Regina as the Creoles won 8–4.

Lou "Sweet Lou" Johnson — Outfield, 5'11", 170 lbs. Batted right, threw right

His bubbling personality and timely heroics made Lou Johnson one of the Dodgers all-time favorites. Not bad for a journeyman minor leaguer who played for at least 19 different teams in 7 major league farm systems in 16 leagues before getting an opportunity with Los Angeles in 1965.

His odyssey began in 1953 when he signed with the New York Yankees. That didn't work out too well as he hit just .194 in his first pro season. After limited success in Class-C ball in 1954, Johnson jumped to the Negro League and the Kansas City Monarchs in 1955. He did play a handful of games that season with St. Jean of the Provincial League. Later he spent three seasons with Toronto of the International League.

In 1965, when batting champion Tommy Davis went down with a fractured ankle, the Dodgers reluctantly called upon Johnson, who had jumped out to a quick start with Spokane of the Pacific Coast League. He was a catalyst as the Dodgers, riding the arms of Sandy Koufax and Don Drysdale, beat the Giants to win the National League pennant and then downed Minnesota to capture the World Series. Johnson's 4th inning homer in the 7th game was all the Dodgers would need as Koufax pitched a shutout.

Earlier in the season, in a scoreless game against the Cubs, Johnson walked in the 5th inning against Bob Hendley, advanced on a sacrifice bunt and stole third. He scored when the throw to third base sailed into the outfield. It was the only run in Koufax's perfect game. Johnson's double in the 7th inning deprived Hendley of a no-hitter.

> "He was a breath of fresh air," Koufax, who played with Johnson in 1965–66, said this week. "He lightened the ballclub and made sure that times were fun on the field" [*Daily News*, Los Angeles, June 10, 2005].

Over eight seasons in the majors he played for the Dodgers, Milwaukee Braves, Cleveland Indians and the California Angels. He finished his major league career in 1969.

- 1955 St. Jean Canadians—.300, 0 HR, 2 RBI
- 1961 Toronto Maple Leafs—.286, 22 D, 18 T, 13 HR, 64 RBI
- 1962 Toronto Maple Leafs—.317, 15 D, 10 T, 8 HR, 40 RBI
- 1963 Toronto/Syracuse—.296, 22 D, 9 T, 15 HR, 70 RBI

Ollie Johnson

Johnson, a black Canadian, played on teams in Oakville, Ontario (on the outskirts of Toronto) in 1916. Wanting better competition, Johnson headed to Buffalo and an all-black barnstorming team, the Cuban Giants.

Rufus Johnson—Outfield, 6'2", 185 lbs.
Batted right

Johnson was a 1953 mid-season addition to the Moose Jaw Maples (which, at one point had four managers within a one week span). He used the opportunity to showcase his skills for a chance in professional baseball. He advanced to a six-year career in pro ball. Johnson also performed in Canada on the basketball court as a member of the touring Iowa Colored Ghosts. He closed out his baseball career in 1960 in the Mexican League.

- 1953 Moose Jaw Maples—Statistics not available
- 1955 Quebec Braves—.260, 15 D, 6 T, 11 homers, 59 RBI

Canadian Highlights: July 6, 1953, Johnson drove in five runs with a triple and two singles as Moose Jaw shook off the sad-sack label with new blood in the lineup in a 12–5 win over Regina as part of a sweep of a double-header. July 22, in one few highlights for Moose Jaw, Johnson had a towering homer over the left field wall and two singles in a 3–1 loss to North Battleford. July 29, Johnson belted a homer, double and single against the Royals at Winnipeg. In playoff action, Johnson went 4 for 4 August 20 against North Battleford. August 22, North Battleford finally stopped Johnson who had come into the playoff match with 10 straight hits. He walked in his 11th appearance and then struck out to break the streak.

Tom Johnson—Pitcher

Johnson pitched briefly with the Indianapolis Clowns in 1950 and mid-way through the season jumped the Clowns and headed to Canada and the Brandon Greys. He pitched with little success and was released.

- 1950 Brandon Greys—Won 0, Lost 3, 7 G, 4 GS, 0 CG

Aaron Jones—Pitcher, 6'2", 220 lbs.
Batted right, threw left

As a teenager, Jones played for the Detroit Stars in 1954 and 1955 before a brief pro career (his best pro campaign was a 5–2, 3.66 season with Missoula in the Pioneer League). The big lefty came to Canada midway through the 1958 season and joined Medicine Hat, Alberta, in the Southern Alberta League. He was back in 1959 for a second tour.

1958 Medicine Hat—Won 3, Lost 1, 5 G, 4 GS, 3 CG
1959 Medicine Hat—Won 2, Lost 4, 11 G, 6 GS, 2 CG

Canadian Highlights: June 29, 1958, Jones fired a three-hitter as Medicine Hat topped Granum 7–2. July 8, he again beat Granum, this time allowing six hits in a 10–2 victory. August 2, at the Lethbridge Tournament, Jones pitched and batted Medicine Hat into the final round as he tossed a three-hitter, with 13 strikeouts, and belted a homer and single in a 4–1 win over Calgary.

August 5, 1959, Jones had three hits as the Superiors trounced Vauxhall 16–4. August 14, at the Medicine Hat Tournament, Jones fired a one-hitter in the 7-inning contest and fanned 18 as Medicine Hat whipped Kimberley 14–0.

Clarence Jones—Pitcher, 6'2", 195 lbs. Batted right, threw right

Jones had no Negro League experience when he came to Canada in 1951 and joined the Winnipeg Buffaloes in the ManDak League. He appeared in just six games, all blowout losses—11–4, 10–3, 15–1, 11–3, 23–10 and 11–3.

1951 Winnipeg Buffaloes—Won 0, Lost 1, 6 G, 1 GS, 1 CG

Collins Chesterfield Jones—Outfield/Utility, 5'11", 175 lbs. Batted both, threw right

A jail term, deserved or not, may have derailed a promising baseball and/or basketball career for Jones.

As a teenager the Michigan native excelled as a boxer (he was a Gold Gloves champion), on the basketball court and the baseball diamond. While still in his teens he was playing Negro ball with the Minneapolis–St. Paul Gophers and Cincinnati Clowns and, in 1944, had a spot on the Harlem Globetrotters baseball team in

The middle of the Lloydminster batting order in 1955 featured three former Negro League players. Left to right—Don Stewart, Collins Jones, Jim Valentine, Dick Barry, Curly Williams (photograph from the Mah collection, courtesy Chuck McGuigan).

the summer and the famous basketball squad in the winter. Jones was with the Globetrotters when the club made its 1945 tour of Western Canada. He was in the lineup in 1946 when track star and Olympic hero Jesse Owens brought major Negro League ball to the West Coast with a team in Seattle. Owens brought in the Globetrotters (calling them the Seattle Steelheads in an attempt to build up local support). The league folded in mid-season and Jones was back barnstorming with the 'Trotters and other teams such as the Cincinnati Crescents, Kansas City Stars, and Colored House of David.

In a curious case in December, 1948, Jones, who said he was 22, but was thought to be a few years older, was barnstorming with the Van Dyke colored House of David basketball team when he was charged with assault in connection with allegations of attempted rape. The incident occurred when team members went to the aid of a woman whose car had stalled in a snowdrift. He pleaded guilty and spent time in prison in Minnesota. Sentenced to serve a two-year sentence, he was released, however, in a little over a year and six years later was granted a pardon by the Governor of Minnesota.

Jones was well-liked in his Canadian stopovers :

> Moose Jaw's powerful outfielder, Collins Jones, is the league's leading hitter and is probably the most popular Negro performer to have played in the 'Friendly City.' Collins has become the idol of the city's youngsters as well as many of the adult spectators [*Moose Jaw Times-Herald*, July 21, 1954].

Upon his release from incarceration, Jones was back barnstorming with a team called the Broadway Clowns and he then made his way to Western Canada to play for Dauphin in the Manitoba-Saskatchewan League, and then on to Estevan, Moose Jaw and Lloydminster. In 1955 Lloydminster traded its best pitcher, lefty Max Weekly, to Moose Jaw to obtain Jones who had been cheated of the batting championship in 1954 (the league awarded the title to Ted Wills, a pitcher/outfielder, in spite of having fewer than the recognized standard of at bats). He did, however, lead the league in doubles (19) and runs batted in (46) to go along with his .331 average. 1955 was his last season in Canada. In 1957, he tried out with the Winona Chiefs of the West Minnesota League and played a little in Mexico. Jones died in 1991 in Minneapolis.

> 1950 Dauphin Redbirds—Statistics not available
> 1951 Estevan Maple Leafs—.243 (incomplete)
> 1952 Dauphin Redbirds—Statistics not available
> 1953 Dauphin Redbirds—Statistics not available
> 1954 Moose Jaw—.331 (2nd), 19 D (1st), 6 HR, 46 RBI (1st)
> 1955 Lloydminster—.285, 15 D, 3 HR, 45 RBI

Canadian Highlights: July 10, 1951, in the leadoff spot, Jones belted a double and two singles in a 3–2 loss to Medicine Hat. July 27, Jones had three hits in a losing effort to Medicine Hat, 8–7.

June 7, 1953, he belted a pair of homers to lead Dauphin past Bowsman 11–5.

June 5, 1954, Jones had a homer and two singles to lead the Moose Jaw offense in a loss to North Battleford. June 18, he poked a homer and two doubles as Moose Jaw dropped a 13–7 decision to North Battleford. June 21, he had four hits, including a triple and two doubles, as Moose Jaw shaded the Beavers 10–9. June 23, Jones' three-run homer was the big blow as Moose Jaw beat Saskatoon 9–8 in an opening round game at the North Battleford tournament. He had two home runs in tourney action the next day. July 2, the outfielder had four singles in a 13–1 win over Indian Head. July 18, the league's leading hitter, crushed a pair of homers, a double and single, knocking in four runs, as Moose Jaw dropped North Battleford 18–9. August 12, Jones had three hits, including a game-winning double in the 10th as Moose Jaw claimed a 4–3 win from Lloydminster. August 14–15, Jones had a five-hit weekend as Moose Jaw took a pair from North Battleford.

June 26, 1955, Jones made two spectacular running catches to help preserve Lloydminster's 4–0 win over Moose Jaw. July 15, Jones belted a grand slam home run and two doubles, good for six runs batted in, as Lloydminster whipped North Battleford 14–7. July 20, he had a triple and double to lead the Meridians to an 11–4 win over Regina. August 5, Jones had two doubles and a single in a 5–3 loss to Moose Jaw.

McHenry "Casey" Jones—Outfield

Jones finished in the top ten in batting in the Western Canada League in 1961 playing for the Edmonton Eskimos. His Edmonton manager, Clark Rex, discovered Jones playing winter ball in the Los Angeles area. Jones, patrolling center field for an all-black team from the Watts area, impressed Rex and was asked to join Edmonton for the summer.

> He was a very colorful player, about 6-foot-4, skinny as a rail and wore size 14 shoes. He could run like the wind, exceptionally fast. He wore white shoes and when he ran the white shoes really stood out. The fans loved it [Clark Rex, correspondence 2008].

Earlier, the fleet outfielder had experience in organized ball playing with Tucson in the Arizona-Mexico League in 1957.

1961 Edmonton Eskimos—.299

Canadian Highlights: July 10, 1961 Jones thrilled the home crowd with an inside-the-park homer to help the Eskimos to a 9–5 win over Saskatoon. July 17, he led Edmonton with two runs and drove in another in a 4–2 win over Medicine Hat. The following day he had three hits in a loss to the Meridians. July 30, at the Lethbridge Tournament Jones had a two-run homer as Edmonton won its first round game and then bashed a homer, a double and two singles to lead the charge as Edmonton crushed Lethbridge 10–1 to win a spot in the final. August 1, Jones had four hits in a 5–2 win over the Meridians.

Paul Jones—Pitcher, 6'3", 223 lbs. Batted right, threw right

Prior to his 1950 season with Elmwood Giants of the ManDak League, Jones had Negro League experience with the Louisville Buckeyes. After his first summer in Canada, he went to the Flint Arrows in the Class-A, Central League in 1951 and the following season to the Vancouver Capilanos in the Class-A, Western International League. In 1953, he joined the Lethbridge Cubs in the Big Six League in Alberta. Jones was back in organized ball in 1954 with Winston Salem Twins in the Class-B, Carolina League. In 1958, he returned to the Negro League with the Buckeyes.

1950 Elmwood Giants—Won 8, Lost 10, 20 G, 12 GS, 7 CG
1952 Vancouver Capilanos—Won 4, Lost 6, 3.45 ERA
1953 Lethbridge Cubs—Statistics not available

Canadian Highlights: June 1, 1950, Jones pitched a three-hit, 13–5, victory over the Winnipeg Buffaloes. The Buffs' runs were scored on three errors. July 26, he pitched a five-hitter and beat Brandon 9–2.

Frank Joyner—Pitcher, 5'10". Threw right

Joyner was on a barnstorming tour with the Brooklyn Cuban Giants in 1949 before settling in with the Philadelphia Colored Giants in 1950. In announcing his signing with the Regina Caps, the Leader-Post of Regina *(May 4, 1951)* reported he had won 17 games and lost just 3 in 1950. He had earlier played for the Raleigh Tigers of the Negro Southern League. In 1950, Joyner had a brief stay with the Caps before being assigned to the Dauphin Redbirds of the Manitoba-Saskatchewan League.

Canadian Highlights: May 19, 1951, Joyner went seven innings to best Negro League legend Chet Brewer as Regina upset Sceptre 6–5 in an exhibition match. On August 22, Joyner pitched a six-hitter and fanned eleven batters as Dauphin beat Yorkton, Saskatchewan, Cardinals 7–5.

Cecil Kaiser—Pitcher/Outfield/First Base, 5'6", 165 lbs. Batted left, threw left

In his early years, from 1939 to 1944, the little left-hander pitched for the Detroit Stars and Motor City Giants. He moved up to the Homestead Grays in 1945 and stayed in the Negro League until 1949. He added winter ball in Puerto Rico, Cuba, Mexico, Panama and the Dominican Republic. In the Negro League he was known as "Aspirin Tablet Man" or

"Minute Man." In 1951, he traveled north to Canada and pitched and played the outfield for Farnham in the Quebec Provincial League. He closed out his career in 1952 in the Florida International League.

1951 Farnham Pirates—Won 14, Lost 13, 3.96 ERA, .260, 4 HR, 25 RBI

John Irvin Kennedy—Shortstop/Second Base, 5'10", 175 lbs. Batted right, threw right

In 1949 John Kennedy :

a. was in the Army
b. had never played baseball
c. was in high school
d. was playing football in college
e. was playing baseball for the Richmond Giants
f. was playing baseball for the Durham Eagles

All of the above appeared in one story or another as Kennedy tried to fudge the truth about his age. In early 1957, he was about to get an opportunity to make the roster of the Philadelphia Phillies and it was much more advantageous to be listed at age 23 rather than his actual age of 30. Part of the lore was that Kennedy had never even played softball, let alone baseball, until the summer of 1950. Well, somehow he was recruited to play for the Winnipeg Buffaloes in the inaugural season of the ManDak League in 1950 and he returned the following summer. In 1951, he had a brief trial in the pro ranks with Albany, an independent club in the Eastern League. He turned down a chance to play in the St. Louis Browns organization in 1952 to join the Minot Mallards. It was his third season in the ManDak circuit.

Kennedy signed with the New York Giants in 1953 and played with St. Cloud of the Northern League before jumping to the Negro League for two seasons, one of them a superb summer with the Kansas City Monarchs. That all-star season with Kansas City in 1956 (.385, 17 homers) attracted the attention of the Phillies who signed him and invited him to their rookie camp the following spring. In between, Kennedy (along with Negro League star Wilmer Fields) starred for the Fort Wayne Dairymen as they captured the national semi-pro title at the National Baseball Congress tournament and went on to represent the United States at the Global World Series in Milwaukee. Kennedy hit .368 as the Americans topped seven other countries for the title. On April 22, 1957, Kennedy became the first black player in the history of the Philadelphia Phillies. He appeared in just five games. Kennedy died in 1998 at the age of 71.

1950 Winnipeg Buffaloes—.256, 0 HR, 22 RBI, 10 SB
1951 Winnipeg Buffaloes—.324, 16 D, 2 HR, 15 RBI,
1952 Minot Mallards—.286, 7 D, 8 T, 1 HR, 26 RBI, 14 SB

Canadian Highlights: July 12, 1950, Kennedy had three hits in a victory over Brandon Greys. July 26, Kennedy's 5th inning single was the only Winnipeg hit off Carman's Gentry Jessup.

June 1, 1951, the Winnipeg shortstop had three doubles to pace the Buffaloes to an 8–3 win over Minot. He had four hits on June 5th in the Buff's 12–5 triumph over Elmwood Giants and another four on July 3rd as Winnipeg trounced the Giants 16–4. He continued his assault on Elmwood pitching with a pair of homers on July 10 as Winnipeg won 7–4. September 3, Kennedy had three hits as Winnipeg won the opening game of its semi-final series with Minot.

June 1, 1952, Kennedy belted a homer and a pair of singles to lead Minot to a win over Carman and he had a triple and two singles June 22 as Mallards again topped the Cardinals. August 27, Kennedy drove in the only run as Minot won the opener of the ManDak final series 1–0 over Carman. The next day, he scored the winning run as Minot took a two-game lead in the series. September 2, his brilliant, back-hand stab of Sam Hill's liner ended a Carman rally and the game as Minot went up 3–1 in the final.

Clarence "Pijo" King—Outfield

King returned from Army service in the Second World War to suit up with the Birmingham Black Barons in the post–Robinson era. He played with the Barons for four seasons before heading north of the 49th parallel to join

Brandon Greys of the ManDak League. The fleet center fielder starred for the Greys over three seasons. In 1954, King joined Rochester of the South Minnesota League. Tragedy struck in September 1954, when King left the team following the news that his 10-month-old son had died in a Birmingham, Alabama, hospital. In the late 1950s he played with the Detroit Stars and Detroit Clowns.

1951 Brandon Greys—.274, 3 HR, 26 RBI, 18 SB (2nd)
1952 Brandon Greys—.315, 7 D, 3 T, 2 HR, 19 RBI,
1953 Brandon Greys—.292, 16 D, 6 T, 4 HR, 46 RBI, 12 SB

Canadian Highlights: June 11, 1951, King had three hits as Brandon blanked Winnipeg 4–0. June 27, King's third hit of the game, a two-run homer in the bottom of the 9th inning gave Brandon a 4–3 victory over Elmwood. July 5, he led Brandon with three hits as the Greys topped Minot 7–2. July 14, King had four hits as Brandon dumped Elmwood 13–3. September 5, in playoff action, King had a triple, double and single in a 10–3 win over Carman. September 11, King drove in four runs in a 17–8 playoff victory over Winnipeg.

July 19, 1952, King's triple and two singles paced the Greys in 4–3 win over Minot. July 26, King had four hits, including a homer to lead Brandon past Winnipeg 14–10.

May 22, 1953, the speedy outfielder had four hits as Brandon set a ManDak League record with 23 safeties in an 18–5 trouncing of Winnipeg. July 7, King had another four hits in an exhibition win over Indian Head, 10–9. July 9, he had three more and added two walks as Brandon dropped a 6–4 decision to North Battleford. July 22, King's three-run homer was a highlight as Brandon whipped Carman 13–7. July 24, he had another three-run homer in a 13–5 win over Winnipeg. July 28, King had three hits to push Brandon by the Winnipeg Royals, 8–4.

(Kings) Don King, Lionel King, Ralph King—Pitchers

All three Kings pitched for the 1953 Moose Jaw Maples. Don started the season with the club while Ralph and Lionel were mid-season additions. Ralph had begun the summer with the barnstorming Medicine Hat Phillies. Lionel returned in 1954 to play for Moose Jaw and Rosetown. In 1953, Moose Jaw manager Bill Peterson got an answer to lefty Don King's control problems. Peterson asked a soccer official to double-check the distance from the pitcher's rubber to home plate at Exhibition Park. The measuring tape showed 66 feet. It was supposed to be 60 feet, 6 inches. Said King, "No wonder my pitches have been falling into the dirt—it will be different from now on." (Regina Leader Post, May 25, 1953)

LIONEL KING
1954 Moose Jaw—Won 1, Lost 6, 20 G, 2 CG

Canadian Highlights: June 22, 1953, Ralph King, in his debut with the Maples, fired a seven-hit shutout as Moose Jaw blanked Saskatoon 2–0. July 15, Ralph fired a five-hitter to lead Moose Jaw to an 11–2 win over Regina Royal Caps at the Indian Head Tournament.

Jose Alberto "Coco" Laboy—Shortstop/Second Base, 5'10", 170 lbs. Batted right, threw right

As one of the original Expos, Laboy was one of the most popular of Montreal's new major leaguers. Part of the appeal was the catchy name (which had a bit of a French-Canadian flair). It wasn't as entertaining on the public address system as announcer Claude Mouton's elongated, four-syllable introduction of catcher John Boc-ca-BELL-la, but close. And, Laboy had a good rookie season hitting .258 with 18 home runs and 83 runs batted in.

The Puerto Rican middle-infielder had spent ten years in the minor leagues, one of them in Winnipeg, before getting an opportunity in the expansion draft of 1968. The Expos plucked him off the St. Louis roster.

Laboy had an outstanding season at Triple-A in 1968, with a .292 mark, 44 doubles, 15 home runs, and 100 RBI. He was the 54th pick (out of 60) in the National League's expansion draft held October 14, 1968.

While he led the Expos in doubles, with 26, in 1970, his average plummeted to .199. Laboy suffered a knee injury in winter ball at the start of the 1970–71 campaign and he got just 152 at bats in 1971 and fewer in 1972 following knee surgery. At the end of the 1973 season he was out of baseball.

> 1963 Winnipeg Goldeyes—.292, 15 D, 6 T, 21 HR, 77 RBI
> 1969 Montreal Expos—.258, 29 D, 1 T, 18 HR, 83 RBI
> 1970 Montreal Expos—.199, 26 D, 1 T, 5 HR, 53 RBI
> 1971 Montreal Expos—.252, 4 D, 0 T, 1 HR, 14 RBI
> 1972 Montreal Expos—.261, 2 D, 0 T, 3 HR, 14 RBI
> 1973 Quebec Carnavals—.109, 2 D, 0 T, 0 HR, 6 RBI
> 1973 Montreal Expos—.122, 1 D, 0 T, 1 HR, 2 RBI

Canadian Highlights: July 7, 1963, Laboy was named as the Northern League's all-star second baseman. August 3, he clouted a pair of homers, driving in three, in a 9–5 loss to Grand Forks.

In 1964, Laboy spent a little time in jail after a rhubarb in an August 20 game at Rocky Mount, North Carolina. In the 5th inning, one of Laboy's teammates was hit by a pitch. The Raleigh manager claimed it was intentional. When Laboy came to the plate, he bunted down the first base line and, as the pitcher came over to field the ball, he charged at him with bat in hand. Both benches emptied and a 15-minute melee ensued. Police were called to break up the battle which resulted in one player being sent to hospital. Laboy was taken to jail. Later he was released on $300 bond following two charges of assault with a deadly weapon. The next day he pleaded guilty and was handed a suspended sentence on payment of a fine and court costs of $20.25.

July 19, 1969, Laboy led the Montreal Expos to a 5–4 victory over the New York Mets. Laboy singled in the go-ahead run after earlier belting a homer. August 12, Laboy drove in five runs as Montreal swept a twi-nighter from the Reds, 8–3 and 5–2. November 29, Ted Sizemore was named National League "Rookie of the Year." Coco Laboy and Al Oliver tied for second.

September 12, 1972, saw Laboy lead the Expos to a 7–2 victory over the Cardinals. Laboy drove in four runs with a single, double and a home run.

Lee Landrum—Catcher

Landrum made his way to Canada with the barnstorming San Francisco Sea Lions who toured the prairies in 1948 and 1949. He had previous experience with the Denver White Elephants. When the Sea Lions disbanded in the summer of 1949, he joined several of his teammates on the Buchanan, Saskatchewan, All-Stars. In 1950 and 1951, he played for the Estevan Maple Leafs and, in 1952, it was the Indian Head Rockets. In 1953, Landrum joined Hubert Glenn on the Claresholm Meteors and finished up playing for the North Battleford Beavers in 1954.

> 1950 Estevan Maple Leafs—Statistics not available
> 1951 Estevan Maple Leafs—.264 (incomplete)
> 1952 Indian Head Rockets—Statistics not available
> 1953 Claresholm Meteors—Statistics not available
> 1954 N. Battleford Beavers—Statistics not available

Canadian Highlights: August 1, 1949, Landrum punched out three hits, including a pair of doubles, to pace the Buchanan All-Stars to a 7–2 victory over the Regina Caps.

June 15, 1950, Landrum cracked a two-run homer in a losing cause to Regina Caps. August 6, Landrum drove in the tying runs with a single then scored the winner as Estevan topped the touring Muskogee Cardinals 4–3.

July 3, 1953, at the Carmangay Tournament, Landrum had two hits in the first game and a two-run homer and single in a semi-final contest. The next day he had four hits to lead Claresholm to the top prize at the tournament with a 10–6 win over Granum. July 24, Landrum belted a homer and single as the Meteors won the Claresholm Tournament with a 7–5 win over Granum. July 27, Landrum belted a three-run homer and single to send Claresholm into the final of the Foothills-Wheatbelt League trouncing Granum 16–2. August 16, in all-star action, Landrum belted a three run homer to help the West All-Stars to a 15–3 win.

Horace Latham—Infield. Batted right

A versatile player, Latham was a shortstop on the Jacksonville, Florida, Eagles, the team which came to Canada in 1950 to represent the community of Indian Head, Saskatchewan. He was mainly a shortstop for Indian Head in 1951 (hitting .303 filling in for injured shortstop Clemente Varona) while performing primarily at second base and first base for Regina in 1953 when he batted .299 He also took a few turns on the hill. Latham played for the Indian Head Rockets for three seasons and one with Regina.

- 1950 Indian Head Rockets—Statistics not available
- 1951 Indian Head Rockets—.263 (incomplete)
- 1952 Indian Head Rockets—Statistics not available
- 1953 Regina Caps—.299

Canadian Highlights: August 8, 1950, Latham, taking a turn on the mound, scattered eight hits, with eight strikeouts and just one base on balls, as Indian Head beat the powerful Minot Mallards 6–3.

June 3, 1951, Latham belted three homers as Indian Head took a twin bill from Delisle 16–8 and 11–4. June 15, Latham's grand slam home run, one of three hits for the Indian Head second baseman, led the Rockets over Medicine Hat Mohawks 11–2. He drove in five runs and scored four times.

May 19, 1953, he knocked in three runs with four hits but the Caps lost to North Battleford 12–8. May 28, Latham had two homers, one a three-run shot, to lead Regina to a 7–6 win over North Battleford. June 29, Latham knocked in three runs with a pair of doubles in losing 6–5 to Saskatoon.

Alphonso Lattimore—Catcher

Lattimore, appears to have played in Quebec in the late 1920s as part of Chappie Johnson's all-black team in the Montreal area. The catcher went on to Negro ball with the Baltimore Black Sox, Brooklyn Royal Giants and Columbus Blue Birds.

Medino Lazaro—Pitcher

Lazaro was among the imports on the Drummondville Cubs in 1949 in the Quebec Provincial League. He pitched briefly and finished with a 0–1 record.

Toribio Leal—Pitcher, 5'6", 135 lbs. Threw left

The little lefty pitched for two seasons, 1951–1952, for the Indian Head, Saskatchewan, Rockets. He had pitched in Cuba and Mexico before his summers in Canada.

- 1951 Indian Head Rockets—Won 4, Lost 2, 9 G, 7 GS, 6 CG

Canadian Highlights: In his 1951 season, Leal was blessed with exceptional offensive support. June 16, Leal fanned 16 and allowed just an unearned run as Rockets swamped Lethbridge 18–1 at the Medicine Hat Tournament. July 4, Leal fired a two-hitter as the Rockets whipped Swift Current 13–1. July 11, Leal, who relieved starter Jesse Blackman in the second inning, pitched shutout ball the rest of the way to lead Indian Head over North Battleford to top money in the Foam Lake Tournament. August 8, Leal tossed six shutout innings and Indian Head trounced Estevan 14–0. August 15, Leal fired a five-hitter over eight innings as Indian Head took the opening game of the Saskatchewan semi-pro playoff 11–1 over Dauphin.

Roberto Ledo—Catcher

Ledo was among the many Cuban imports on the Florida Cubans of 1952 who set down roots for the summer in Saskatchewan. He was selected as all-star catcher at the 16-team Indian Head Tournament. After returning to Cuba, Ledo became a well-known manager. The colorful pilot directed the Orientales team which upset the powerful Industriales in 1967 in an historic final game in Havana. Industriales had won four consecutive titles. Ledo returned to Canada that season to manage the Cuban team at the 1967 Pan-American Games in Winnipeg.

Bob Levingston—Outfield, 6'2", 195. Batted right, threw right

Levingston was a two-sport star at the University of Southern California. A running back in football, he patrolled the outfield in baseball. An all-star at the 1960 College World Series, he was forced to sit out the 1961 season for failing

Roberto Ledo of the 1952 Florida Cubans became a celebrated coach and manager in Cuba (handling the Cuban team at the 1967 Pan American Games at Winnipeg). Roberto (Chico) Barbon was the first Cuban to play in the Japanese leagues. Back row (left to right)—Pedro Seoane 1B, Ledo C, Barbon LF, Julio Bonilla 2B, Orlando Arango P, Ezequiel Diaz SS, Mario Herrera CF, Gilberto Yzquierdo Mgr-C, Mario Penalver RF, Bus driver (name unknown). Front row (left to right)—Jose "Hippy" Hernandez P, Juan Dominguez P, Carlos Forten P, Ignacio Cisnero P, Dick Necker Batboy, Marcelino Arozarena Utility, Leopoldo Reyes 3B, Juan Prats (photograph courtesy Ken McCabe, Indian Head Sports Hall of Fame and Museum).

to meet academic requirements. He played with the Saskatoon Commodores of the Western Canada League in 1961 and, although he had to leave in mid-season to attend summer classes, was around long enough to win all-stars honors. Back playing for USC in 1962, he was selected to the All-Conference team. After a brief stint in pro ball, Levingston tried to return to football in 1964 in a tryout with the Oakland Raiders, but was cut before the beginning of the regular season.

1961 Saskatoon Commodores—.306

Canadian Highlights: June 15, 1961, Levingston punched out three hits and drove in three in Saskatoon's 12–5 win over Edmonton. June 25, Levington's two-run homer and triple paced the Commodores over Lloydminster. July 6, Levingston's two-run homer was key in a 9–4 win over Edmonton. July 17, he drove in all five runs with a homer and double in Saskatoon's 5–1 triumph over Lethbridge.

In left field, although there are some good ones at this position, Saskatoon's Bob Levingston, we think, has the class. Levingston's hitting over other contenders would carry considerable weight in the voting. He represents a lot of authority at the plate [*Saskatoon Star Phoenix*, July 11, 1961].

Herman "Lefty" Lewis—First Base/Outfield, 6'3", 180 lbs. Batted left, threw left

Lewis came out of the baseball rich Oakland area in 1950 to play for the Estevan Maple Leafs of the Southern League in Saskatchewan. He turned pro the following season and hit .308 with a league-leading 23 homers for Phoenix of the Southwest International League. He had a nine-year pro career, the final seven with Yakima of the Western International and Northwest leagues. He had some huge games against his Canadian competition. July 16, 1953, Lewis knocked in four runs with four hits in a 12–3 win over Vancouver. The next day he had three hits, including a game-winning triple in the 10th inning, and drove in three in a 10–9 triumph over Calgary. July 20, at Calgary, Lewis tied two league records in rapping out six hits, five of them singles, in a wild 19–12 victory over the Canadians.

George Ligon—Pitcher/Manager. Threw right

Ligon was born in 1910 in Austin, Texas, and began playing ball during his school days in Uvalde, west of San Antonio (the family later relocated to Hondo). A pitcher in his formative days, his playing career was put on hold during the Second World War when he saw service in the South Pacific.

He became an owner and manager when he decided to form his own team following some managerial experience in Mexico. The Ligon All-Stars, were a product of his enterprise.

They first hit the road in 1946. The following summer, the Ligons made a big splash in Western Canada winning top money in the inaugural Indian Head tournament.

> While an estimated 10,000 rooters jammed around the diamond until there wasn't space for even the circus Thin Man, George Ligon's colored All-Stars from California ... whacked out enough base hits to make Indian Head's enormously successful $2,000 baseball tournament a runaway show on Thursday, tacking a crushing 13–0 setback on Nick Metz and his Wilcox Cardinals.... Only in one game out of four did they yield any runs, making it rather decisive that they were the best ball club on the premises [*Regina Leader-Post*, August 8, 1947].

Ligon was none too shy in claiming success for his road show. In an article in the Galveston Daily News *(September 10, 1950)* it was claimed the All-Stars had won 120 of 151 games in 1947, finished 122-31 in 1948 and had a record of 113-20 as of early September, 1949.

In an 1982 interview with The Brawley (California) News, Ligon reflected upon his barnstorming days and said, "Canada ... that was the best."

Marvin Ligon—Outfield

Marvin played for his uncle, George Ligon, the owner of the Ligon All-Stars, for four seasons 1947 to 1950.

A Californian, Ligon faced some surprises in heading out to the various ball diamonds on the prairies.

> The war was just over ... making transition to trying to play baseball and we'd play on some weird fields. They just knocked down the wheat and we'd go out and play ball.

The contracts were pretty simple, "Get on the bus and ride 'til September."

Rufus Ligon—Pitcher. Threw left

Rufus and brother George had teamed up on Texas-based clubs in the 1930s before the two formed the barnstorming team which became a regular summer attraction in Western Canada in the late 40s through the mid 50s. The two Ligons were prominent members of the Texas Black Spiders which found a home in Iowa in 1937 and managed to capture the state's semi-pro baseball championship. In 1938, he was in Canada as part of an exhibition tour by the San Antonio Missions. Rufus went on to play in the Negro League with the Memphis Red Sox, 1944–46, before coming home to head up the pitching staff of the Ligon Colored All-Stars from 1947 through at least the 1950 season. In the late 1950s, he was back in Memphis to manage the Red Sox in the dying days of Negro league baseball.

George Lipscomb—Outfield

Lipscomb came north with the Jacksonville Eagles in 1950 when the team played in Saskatchewan as the Indian Head Rockets. He returned in 1954 to suit up for Moose Jaw Mallards.

1950 Indian Head Rockets—Statistics not available
1954 Moose Jaw Mallards—.278

Canadian Highlights: July 6, 1950 Lipscomb knocked out four hits to lead Indian Head to a 12–3 win over Sceptre.

July 16, 1954, Lipscomb had a double and three singles in his debut with Moose Jaw. July

18, he knocked in five runs with a homer and three singles to help Moose Jaw to an 18–9 win over North Battleford.

Cecil Littles — Infielder

Littles came up from St. Paul, Minnesota to play for the 1951 Estevan Maple Leafs.

> 1951 Estevan Maple Leafs — .308 (incomplete)

Johnny Lloyd — Outfield

Lloyd came from Louisiana with manager Wesley Barrow to join Elmwood Giants of the ManDak League in 1951. He was back in 1952 with the Baton Rouge Hardwoods at the Indian Head Tournament and then picked up by Regina of the Saskatchewan League. He returned to Regina in 1953. He played three seasons of organized ball, reaching Class-C. His best season was 1950, when he batted .311 in the Canadian-American League.

> 1951 Elmwood Giants — .375, 0 HR, 2 RBI
> 1952 Regina, Saskatchewan — Statistics not available
> 1953 Regina, Saskatchewan — .286

Canadian Highlights: May 26, 1951, Lloyd had three hits to help Elmwood shade Carman 8–7. May 30, Lloyd, who had a triple and single in the first game of a twin-bill, had a hit in the first inning of the second game, but injured his wrist sliding home.

July 21, 1952, newcomer Lloyd had three hits and scored three times in Regina's 14–0 triumph over Estevan. August 13, in the opening game of a semi-final series, Lloyd had a triple and two singles in an 8–1 win over Saskatoon.

June 27, 1953, Lloyd clouted three hits, including an inside-the-park homer, to pace Regina to an 8–3 win over North Battleford. August 5, Lloyd punched out two hits and scored twice to lead Regina over Saskatoon 4–2.

> Johnny Lloyd's circus catch in right center field was the best of them all, and the most outstanding fielding play of the baseball season in Regina ... Lloyd, who can run like a deer, came from nowhere in right field and stuck up his glove hand on the run and the ball stayed put [*The Leader-Post*, Regina, August 19, 1953].

Eddie Locke — Pitcher/Outfield, 5'11", 178 lbs. Batted left, threw right

In a career which spanned twenty-five years and more than a dozen teams, Locke had some outstanding seasons both as a pitcher and hitter. He played in the Negro League from 1943 to 1951 with the Cincinnati Clowns, Kansas City Monarchs, New York Black Yankees and Chicago American Giants. In 1950, he started in the Negro League, and then went into organized ball. In 1951, he again started in the Negro League, but moved on to play in the Mexican circuit.

From 1952 to 1959, he played minor league ball including a summer with Vancouver, British Columbia, of the Western International League. From 1953 to 1955, he fashioned seasons of 21–7, 24–15 and 20–7. During those three seasons he batted .368 with 17 home runs, .311 with 12 homers, and .355 with 11.

In that 1953 season, among his 21 wins were eight which came from four double-headers in which he pitched complete game victories in both ends of the twin-bills.

May 7, 1953, he surprised many at a pregame event at Lewiston, Idaho when he defeated Yakima, Washington, teammate Herman Lewis in a 75-year dash. Lewis had been hailed as the fastest player in the Western International League.

In 1956, Locke joined Monterrey of the Mexican League where he performed for four seasons, winning 18, 19 and 21 games in his last three campaigns. In 1967, after a seven year hiatus, the 44-year-old Locke returned to the mound with Monterrey and won ten games.

> 1956 Vancouver Capilanos — .265, 11 D, 9 T, 2 HR, 42 RBI, Won 11, Lost 13, 3.44 ERA

Lester Lockett — Outfield, 6'0", 195 lbs. Batted right, threw right

Lockett, who began his Negro League career in 1937, was a fixture in the circuit for a dozen years winning all-star status in 1943 (when he hit .408, but had fewer than a hundred at bats), 1945 and 1948. In 1949, he played for Panama in the inaugural Caribbean Series. A few months later he was on the 1950 Fort Wayne Capeharts as they won the American semi-pro title at the

National Baseball Congress Tournament at Wichita. He rounded out his career in Canada playing in the ManDak League with Winnipeg and Carman, with Kitchener in Ontario's Intercounty League and with Farnham in the Quebec Provincial League. Lockett is among the Negro Leaguers who've been honored at the Wall of Fame at County Stadium in Milwaukee.

> 1951 Farnham Pirates—.217, 5 D, 0 T, 1 HR, 21 RBI
> 1952 Kitchener Panthers—Statistics not available
> 1952 Winnipeg Giants—.390, 3 HR, 18 RBI
> 1953 Carman Cardinals—.332, 1 HR, 30 RBI
> 1954 Carman Cardinals—.248, 16 D, 1 T, 3 HR, 31 RBI

Canadian Highlights: July 26, 1952, Lockett had a homer and two singles, but it wasn't enough as Winnipeg dropped a 14–10 decision to Brandon. August 5, Lockett had three hits in a Giants victory over Minot. August 25, Lockett drove in three runs with three hits in a 9–8 playoff win over Carman.

May 27, 1953, Lockett had three hits in a Carman loss to Minot. He finished second in the batting race with a .332 mark.

Al "Buddy" Lombard—Pitcher/Shortstop

The versatile Buddy Lombard had come to Estevan Maple Leafs of the Western Canada League in 1951, after starting the season with Elmwood of the ManDak League. He both pitched and took a turn at shortstop. The Estevan experience followed a 1950 barnstorming tour with the New Orleans Creoles (the season the headliner for the Creoles was Toni Stone, the first woman to play in the Negro League).

> 1951 Estevan Maple Leafs—Won 1, Lost 3, 9 G, 5 GS, 2 CG, .175

Avery Long—Pitcher

Long was just 17 when he toured with Ligon's All-Stars in 1953. On June 25, at the Lacombe Tournament, Long fired a no-hitter as Ligon's dumped the Central Alberta All-Stars 6–0.

Carl Long—Outfield, 6'3", 192 lbs. Batted right

In 1952 and 1953, Long played for the Birmingham Black Barons and Philadelphia Stars in the Negro League winning a contract in organized ball with Pittsburgh in 1954. He was sent to the St. Jean Canadians, the Pirates minor league affiliate in the Quebec Provincial League. He had a fine season with 20 homers. Long played just three more seasons before an injury ended his career.

> 1954 St. Jean Canadians—.275, 18 D, 5 T, 20 HR, 80 RBI

Bernell "Chick" Longest—Second Base/Outfield, 6'0", 175 lbs. Batted left, threw right

Longest was a Negro Leaguer from 1942 to 1947 with the Chicago American Giants and the Chicago Brown Bombers. He came to Canada in 1951 to the Carman Cardinals in the ManDak League. He was a fixture with the club for four seasons before heading east to play in the Intercounty League in Southern Ontario with the Galt Terriers. Late in the 1955 season he joined Burlington, Vermont, in the Quebec Provincial League for a brief stint in pro ball.

> 1951 Carman Cardinals—.370, 8 HR, 28 RBI
> 1952 Carman Cardinals—.345, 10 D, 3 T, 8 HR, 41 RBI
> 1953 Carman Cardinals—.321, 12 D, 2 T, 6 HR, 40 RBI
> 1954 Carman Cardinals—.276, 13 D, 1 T, 4 HR, 37 RBI
> 1955 Galt Terriers—Statistics not available
> 1955 Burlington A's—.276, 1 HR, 20 RBI

Canadian Highlights: June 4, 1951, Longest drove in four runs with a two-run home run and a two-run double as Carman beat Minot 9–4. At the end of June, Longest was leading the league in batting with a .410 average. He was also leading in home runs, with seven. July 24, Longest had four hits in five at bats, but Carman came away with a loss.

June 4, 1952, he had two hits and drove in three runs in a 12–6 win. June 16, Longest led Carman to an 18–0 trouncing of Brandon with three doubles and two singles for a five hit game.

July 1, 1953, Longest hit a two-run homer in the bottom of the eleventh inning that gave Carman a 6–5 win over Minot.

July 27, 1954, he had three hits in helping Carman defeat Brandon 12–7 and on August 23, in a semi-final playoff game against Minot, he led the way with three hits.

July 16, 1955, Longest blasted a homer and two singles, drove in four runs, scored a pair and added a stolen base in 10–5 win for Galt over Oshawa in Intercounty action.

Wyman "Red" Longley—Utility. Batted right, threw right

The veteran utility man put in nearly twenty seasons of Negro ball, mainly with the Memphis Red Sox, in a career which stretched from 1932 to the early 1950s. Near the end of his playing days, for the 1950 season, Longley joined the Elmwood Giants of the ManDak League. He retired after one last season, 1951, back in the Negro League with the New Orleans Eagles.

1950 Elmwood Giants—.230, 0 HR, 10 RBI

Canadian Highlights: August 25, 1950, Longley had two hits as Elmwood beat the pennant winning Brandon Greys 4–2.

Hector Lopez—Infield/Outfield, 5'11", 182 lbs. Batted right, threw right

Lopez, who carved out a 12-year career in the major leagues, got his start in Canada in 1951 with St. Hyacinthe of the Quebec Provincial League. That winter, playing ball in Panama, Lopez won the batting title with a .336 mark and the Philadelphia A's purchased his contract for $1500. He was sent back to the Quebec squad for the 1952 season when he hit .325. After a stint in the Class-A, Eastern League in 1953, Lopez was in Ottawa, Ontario for Triple-A action with the Ottawa A's.

In 1955, he graduated to the majors with Kansas City (as the Philadelphia A's re-located to the Missouri city). He had a sparkling rookie season hitting .290 with 15 home runs. In his best year, 1959, Lopez hit 22 home runs and drove in 93 while batting .283.

In his tenure with New York, Lopez was often the third outfielder in the Yankees' pasture (a couple of guys, named Mantle and Maris, manned the other spots). Lopez played in five World Series, batting .286 in fifteen games. He was the second Panamanian-born player to advance to the majors (Humberto Robinson debuted 22 days before Lopez). He was the first black manager at the Triple-A level when he piloted the Buffalo Bisons of the International League.

1951 St. Hyacinthe Saints—.297, 11 D, 3 T, 2 HR, 31 RBI
1952 St. Hyacinthe A's—.329, 26 D, 7 T, 8 HR, 75 RBI
1954 Ottawa A's—.316, 17 D, 4 T, 8 HR, 53 RBI

Canadian Highlights: In 1952, he led the Provincial League in runs scored with 115.

Benjamin "Honey" Lott—Second Base/Third Base/Shortstop, 5'11", 170 lbs. Batted right, threw right

Benjamin "Honey" Lott was a power-hitting infielder (mainly at second base) for the New York Black Yankees and Indianapolis Clowns in the waning days of the Negro League and for four seasons in Canada in the ManDak and Western Canada Leagues (photograph from the Mah collection).

Lott (the nickname "Honey" appears to have come from his teammates in reference to a "sweet" right-handed swing) was an outstanding infielder who hit for both average and power. The Newark, New Jersey, native played in the waning days of the Negro Leagues with the New York Black Yankees and Indianapolis Clowns.

According to the La Crosse Tribune (July 20, 1950), Lott hit .342 in 1949 for the Black Yankees, knocking in 169 runs with 30 homers, 38 doubles and 9 triples and had a .351 mark mid-way through the 1950 season with 15 homers. Obviously, he was the Clowns' star attraction during the 1950 season as the team's advertisements touted Honey Lott, "Picked Outstanding Player of Negro American League." In late July, 1951, when Lott signed a pro contract with the Chicago White Sox, the Waterloo Daily Courier (July 25, 1951) reported he had hit .310 with 16 homers, 20 stolen bases and 61 runs batted in just 59 games with Indianapolis.

Lott began his stint in the White Sox system with Waterloo White Hawks of the Class-B, Three-I League, where he hit .304 before advancing to Class-A, Colorado Springs where he did even better, .345.

He spent 1952 playing in the Dominican Republic, before a brief stint in Double-A in 1953 with the Tulsa Oilers and then a trip north to suit up in Canada with Carman Cardinals of the ManDak League. He returned to Carman in 1954 and finished third in the batting race at .358, but left the following season for his final spin in organized pro ball in the Class-C, Longhorn League. It was back to the prairies in 1956 with the Lloydminster Meridians of the Western Canada League and 1957 with Brandon Greys in the final season of the ManDak League. Lott died in 1980 in Newark, New Jersey. He was 55.

1953 Carman Cardinals—.301, 9 D, 4 T, 1 HR, 21 RBI
1954 Carman Cardinals—.358, 17 D, 2 T, 7 HR, 53 RBI
1956 Lloydminster Meridians—.298, 11 D, 5 T, 10 HR, 38 RBI
1957 Lloydminster Meridians—.219, 0 HR, 6 RBI
1957 Brandon Greys—.273, 4 D, 3 T, 2 HR, 21 RBI

Canadian Highlights: June 12, 1953, Lott had a triple, two singles and two walks in five trips to the plate to lead Carman to a 9–5 win over Regina Caps in an interlocking game at Regina. August 9, he bashed a homer and triple in a 15–11 slugfest with Minot.

May 25, 1954, the second baseman knocked in three runs with three hits in a 5–4 win over Williston. July 8, Lott, who lasted just four innings because of an ankle injury suffered running the bases, led the offense with a grand slam homer, double and single, good for six runs batted in, as Carman whipped Williston Oilers 18–12. August 3, in another wild one, Lott belted a double and three singles in an 11–10 loss to Minot. August 23, he knocked in six markers in playoff action with a homer, two triples and a single as Carman topped Minot 12–5. He was also brilliant at second base, handling eleven chances without an error.

In 1956, with Lloydminster Meridians, Lott had four hits on June 13 as the Meridians downed Regina 6–3. The next day, he crushed a grand slam homer as Lloydminster trounced Edmonton 14–6. July 12, Lott had three hits in the opener of a twin-bill as Lloydminster downed Moose Jaw 8–1. He added two more safeties in the second game. July 30, he had a pair of homers in a 7–6 loss to Bismarck. In playoff action, August 27, Lott had two doubles and a single as the Meridians upset Edmonton 8–7 in the first game of a semi-final series. He put three hits in the books the next night as Meridians topped the Eskimos 7–2. Lott belted two homers in the best-of-three final series against North Battleford.

Lou Louden—Catcher, 5'10", 172 lbs.
Batted right, threw right

Louden spent five summers in Western Canada after having played in the Negro League from 1942 to 1950 with the New York Cubans. He came to Canada in 1951 and joined the Elmwood Giants in the ManDak League. He played for the Giants and Winnipeg Royals over three seasons, then joined the Brandon Greys in 1954. He returned to the Greys in 1957, the last season the ManDak League was in operation.

He died in 1989 in Newark, New Jersey.

1951 Elmwood Giants—.273, 2 HR, 22 RBI
1952 Winnipeg Giants—.328, 18 D, 1 T, 5 HR, 43 RBI
1953 Winnipeg Royals—.252, 8 D, 1 T, 2 HR, 32 RBI
1954 Brandon Greys—.278, 5 D, 1 T, 0 HR, 21 RBI
1957 Brandon Greys—.256, 5 D, 0 T, 3 HR, 24 RBI

Canadian Highlights: June 1, 1953, Louden hit an eighth inning single that drove in the winning run in a 4–3 victory over the Saskatoon Gems. August 21, Louden had three hits as Winnipeg defeated Carman 10–7.

June 22, 1954, Louden punched out three hits to pace Brandon to a 4–3 win over Minot. August 9, Louden was selected to the All-Star Game and got a hit as the 'Stars whipped Minot 14–4. Louden had three hits August 11 in a 10–3 win over Williston Oilers. August 14, he followed up with four hits in a wild 16–11 Brandon victory over Williston.

Jimmy Lovelace—Second Base

Lovelace was the second sacker for the 1950 Regina Caps of the Southern League in Saskatchewan.

Flash Maddox—Pitcher

Maddox was a California import for the 1950 Estevan Maple Leafs. He had pitched for the Oakland Larks and semi-pro teams in the Oakland area.

Willy Malone—Catcher/Outfield

Malone had no official Negro League experience, but had played ball in the Detroit area and in 1949, was with the Detroit Wolves. He came to Canada in 1950 with Red House and joined the Carman Cardinals. He played only briefly and was released.

Bob Manning—Pitcher

Manning was another player who came to the Carman Cardinals in 1950 with manager Red House. He had played in Detroit for the Wolves in 1949. He was released early in the season after pitching in just three games.

1950 Carman Cardinals—Won 0, Lost 1

Max Manning—Pitcher, 6'4", 185 lbs. Batted left, threw right

Manning, a side-arming power pitcher, had a productive career in the Negro League from 1938 to 1949 with the Newark Eagles and Houston Eagles. He spent 1941 to 1945 in military service. After the 1946 season he pitched for the Satchel Paige All-Stars against the Bob Feller All-Stars and in one game struck out fourteen batters. In 1951, at the end of his career, he joined Sherbrooke in the Quebec Provincial League and Brantford, Ontario, in the Inter County League. Manning died in 2003.

Everett Marcell(Marcel/Marcelle)—Pitcher/Outfield/Catcher, 6'3", 185 lbs. Batted right, threw right

Marcell, the son of Negro League third base star Oliver Marcelle, made his first foray into Western Canada in 1938 with the touring San Antonio Black Missions in their exhibition series against Grover Cleveland Alexander's Whiskered Wizards.

He followed his father into the Negro League playing from 1939 to 1944 and 1947 and 1948. In 1945 he played in the West Coast Negro League with the Seattle Steelheads (who were the Harlem Globetrotters with a new name in an attempt to establish a Negro circuit along the Pacific). Later that season, with the demise of the Steelheads, he toured with the 'Trotters in Western Canada. In 1946, he played for the Cincinnati Crescents barnstorming team, and in 1950, he joined Farnham in the Quebec Provincial League.

Marcell also had a pro career in basketball with the Harlem Globetrotters, Iowa Colored Ghosts and Los Angeles Red Devils (a teammate of Jackie Robinson). In football, he and Robinson played for the Los Angeles Bulldogs in the Pacific Coast Football League.

He died in 1990 at the age of 74.

1950 Farnham Pirates—.272, 10 D, 1 T, 7 HR, 42 RBI

Enrique "Ricky" Maroto—Pitcher, 5'6", 165 lbs. Batted left threw left

Maroto had a short stint with the Brandon Greys in 1952 before two seasons, 1954 and

1955, with the Negro League's Kansas City Monarchs. Twice he was signed by major league teams, first in 1956 by the St. Louis Cardinals then again in 1957 by the Washington Senators. Maroto played in organized ball from 1957 to 1961, when he closed out his career in Mexico.

Hiram Marshall—Catcher/Outfield/Third Base

Marshall played the 1946 season for a Negro team called the Boston Blues. He came north in 1952 to play for the independent Indian Head Rockets and the following season he joined the Regina Caps of the Saskatchewan League and captured the batting title with a .353 average.

> 1952 Indian Head Rockets—Statistics not available
> 1963 Regina Caps—.353

William "Jack" Marshall—Infield/Outfield, 5'11", 185 lbs. Batted right, threw right

Marshall played Negro league ball over a 19-year period, from 1926 to 1944, with a variety of teams including the Chicago American Giants, Kansas City Monarchs and Philadelphia Stars.

He was a regular on the Canadian prairies in the early 1930s as part of a traveling show he and promoter Rod Whitman of Lafleche, Saskatchewan, organized. They formed the Texas Colored Giants, the New York All-Stars and a minstrel and dance show. The entertainment package performed mainly in Western Canada. They offered $200 to any team of white players which could defeat them. They traveled thousands of miles in a caravan of three cars and three trucks. The team claimed it lost just 11 of 142 games in 1929 and 13 of 156 in 1930.

Sergio Martinez—Pitcher, 5'7", 160 lbs. Batted right, threw right

Martinez came to Canada after three years in organized ball pitching in the Florida International League from 1950 to 1952. He had a 15–9 record with a 2.95 ERA in 1951. The right-hander pitched for Saskatoon Gems and Regina Caps in 1953 and with North Battleford Beavers in 1955. The 1953 season was something of a Dr. Jekyll and Mr. Hyde summer for the Cuban import.

> 1953 Saskatoon/Regina—Statistics not available
> 1955 North Battleford—Won 2, Lost 4, 14 G, 7 GS, 2 CG, 4.15 ERA

Canadian Highlights: The 1953 season started well enough as Martinez shutout North Battleford on five hits as Saskatoon posted a 5–0 triumph on June 8. June 26, the right-hander tossed no-hit ball for 4⅓ innings in relief against the Beavers. The roof caved in July 7 & 8 as Saskatoon dropped a double-header to Regina, 12–5 and 24–7 and followed that with a 16–5 loss to Moose Jaw. Martinez was the losing pitcher in all three games. July 16 he bounced back with a five inning no-hitter as Saskatoon Gems trounced Lake Valley 10–0 at the Indian Head Tournament. The game was called after five frames by the "10-run Mercy Rule." His reward was a trade to Regina. July 27, he returned to Cairns Field, Saskatoon and blanked his former mates 10–0 with a three-hitter. June 19, Martinez pitched into the 12th inning with 13 strikeouts, but came away with a loss as his mates made four errors behind him.

Mac Massingale—Outfield

Massingale was listed in the lineup of the Kansas City Monarchs in 1945. He came to Canada in 1950 to try out with the Carman Cardinals of the ManDak League. He was released after just a few games.

> 1950 Carman Cardinals—Statistics not available

Jack Matchett—Pitcher, 6'1", 170 lbs. Batted right, threw right

Matchett was in the starting rotation (with the likes of Satchel Paige, Chet Brewer, Hilton Smith and Connie Johnson) for the fabled Kansas City Monarchs from 1940 to 1945 when the club won three straight pennants. He came north to Canada to continue his career in 1946 as an outfielder with the Saskatoon Legion of the Saskatoon Senior Baseball League in Saskatchewan. He became the club's playing manager in 1947.

Ray McCoy—Pitcher. Threw right

The younger brother of Carman pitcher Walter McCoy, Ray joined the Cardinals in 1953 and saw limited action, appearing in just three games. He pitched well when farmed out to Prince Albert, Saskatchewan. He had overcome polio as a child to become a high school and American Legion star in the late 1940s in San Diego.

1953 Carman Cardinals—Won 0, Lost 1

Walter McCoy—Pitcher, 5'11", 180 lbs. Batted right, threw right

McCoy was a solid starter in the Negro League for four seasons (1945 to 1948) with the Chicago American Giants before brief trials in organized ball in 1949 and 1950 with Visalia in the Class-A, California League and Sacramento of the Triple-A, Pacific Coast League.

In his initial season in the Negro League, he was the opposing pitcher as Ray Brown fired a perfect game against Chicago.

His foreign stops included the Dominican

In 2008, Walter McCoy was saluted by the San Diego Padres and Major League Baseball for his role in the Negro Leagues and in the community following his playing days. And, he continued to be active in baseball, passing along some tips to his grandson (photograph from the Mah Collection, courtesy Walter McCoy).

Republic, Venezuela and Mexico before heading north in 1952 to join the ManDak League. He pitched in Canada for four seasons with the Winnipeg Giants, Carman Cardinals, Oshawa Merchants (of the Intercounty League in Ontario) and Bismarck Barons. His younger brother Ray also pitched in the circuit.

Prior to his Negro League play, Pfc. McCoy was the pitching star and MVP for the Fort Huachuca U.S. Army club in Arizona. Among other efforts, he had a no-hitter and a one-hitter with 15 strikeouts (in a 7 inning affair).

> The fans were nicer than I ever encountered anywhere. They were so nice, they really treated the ballplayers like human beings, you know, as compared to here in the United States at that time [Walter McCoy, interview, 2008].

Walter McCoy came to Canada after Negro League experience in the 1940s with the Chicago American Giants (photograph from the Mah Collection, courtesy Walter McCoy).

1952 Winnipeg Giants—Won 4, Lost 4, 71 IP, 29 BB, 31 SO
1953 Carman Cardinals—Won 10, Lost 8, 21 G, 14 GS, 9 CG
1954 Carman Cardinals—Won 8, Lost 9, 126 IP, 57 BB, 70 SO
1955 Oshawa Merchants—Statistics not available
1955 Bismarck Barons—Won 3, Lost 6, 56 IP, 33 BB, 25 SO

Canadian Highlights: June 26, 1952, McCoy gave up a homer in the first inning then allowed just one more hit the rest of the way as Winnipeg downed Carman 8–1. August 22, McCoy allowed just six hits and fanned 11 in a 4–2 playoff win over Carman.

July 17, 1953, McCoy fired a five-hitter as Carman topped Brandon 3–1.

June 6, 1954, McCoy blanked Brandon 2–0. June 19, McCoy held Williston to seven hits and belted a homer in a 9–3 win for Carman. June 24, McCoy pitched a three-hitter, not allowing any earned runs, in a win over Brandon. July 1, McCoy hurled a four-hitter in a 4–0 shutout of Williston.

June 18, 1955, Walt McCoy hurled a four-hit shutout in his debut for Bismarck and the Barons downed Dickinson 2–0. June 26, McCoy held Dickinson to six hits in pitching a 9–2 win.

Fred McDaniels—Outfield/Infield, 5'11", 135 lbs. Batted left, threw right

McDaniels enjoyed a productive Negro League career which ran from the late 1930s to the early 1950s with the Memphis Red Sox, Kansas City Monarchs and New Orleans Eagles. In the late 1940s and early 1950s, he suited up for the Satchel Paige All-Stars. He had begun playing in 1938 for a touring team, the Texas Black Spiders. In 1952 and 1953, he played in the Quebec Provincial League and also played in Saskatchewan with the Ligon All-Stars.

Terris McDuffie—Pitcher/Outfield, 6'1", 200 lbs. Batted right, threw right

McDuffie, from New York City, played in the Negro League from 1930 to 1945 and was a familiar figure in baseball stadiums in Cuba, the Dominican Republic, Venezuela and Mexico. He was born in Mobile, Alabama, in 1910. On April 7, 1945, the Lima News reported that the Brooklyn Dodgers were going to give the 34 year old a tryout. The next day they reported that after the tryout Branch Rickey decided not to sign him. In 1948 and 1949, he played for St. Jean Braves in the Quebec Provincial League. He closed out his playing time in Canada in 1951 with the Sherbrooke Canadians in the Border League. In 1954, he played in organized ball for Dallas in the Texas League at the age of forty four. In 14 games he had an ERA of 3.04. He died in New York, at age 65, in 1968.

1948 St. Jean Braves—Won 19, Lost 8, .342, 5 HR, 20 RBI
1949 St. Jean Braves—Won 12, Lost 10, .267, 3 HR, 13 RBI
1951 Sherbrooke Athletics—Won 6, Lost 1, 4.86 ERA

Curtis McGowan—Pitcher, 6'1", 160 lbs. Batted right, threw right

McGowan made a few starts with Elmwood of the ManDak League in 1951 following a season with the Negro League Memphis Red Sox. After his release from Elmwood he joined the Drummondville Cubs in the Quebec Provincial League.

1951 Elmwood Giants—Won 0, Lost 1, 3 G, 1 GS, 1 CG
1951 Drummondville Cubs—Won 2, Lost 2, 14 G, 3 GS, 5.76 ERA

Henry McHenry—Pitcher, 6'0", 200 lbs. Batted right, threw right

McHenry's Negro League career spanned twenty years and a half-dozen teams, including the Kansas City Monarchs, New York Black Yankees, Philadelphia Stars and Indianapolis Clowns. In 1951, he pitched briefly with the Minot Mallards (North Dakota) in the ManDak League and Estevan Maple Leafs in the Western Canada League.

1951 Minot Mallards—Won 0, Lost 1
1951 Estevan Maple Leafs—Won 5, Lost 4, 12 G, 7 GS, 7 CG, .290

Canadian Highlights: July 11, 1951, McHenry provided sparkling relief pitching to capture both wins in a double-header sweep of Medicine Hat, 4–3 and 7–6. He took over in the 7th inning of the first game and in the second frame in the nightcap. August 8, McHenry held Indian Head to eight hits and he pitched around five errors as Estevan whipped the Rockers 10–2. August 15, McHenry had a no-hitter into the 9th inning, finishing with two-hitter, as Estevan topped Swift Current 2–1. Mound opponent Hal Price broke the spell with a double and scored on a single by Barney Fox. McHenry fanned six and walked none.

Vincent "Manny" McIntyre—Shortstop

McIntyre, better known for his skills in hockey, was the first black Canadian athlete to sign a pro baseball contract in the modern era. In 1946, just a few months after Jackie Robinson began play with the Montreal Royals, Brooklyn's top farm team, McIntyre signed to play for the independent Sherbrooke Canadians of the Class-C, Border League. The native of Fredericton, New Brunswick, was a star on ice, renown as one of the "Black Aces" (with Herb and Ossie Carnegie), on an all-black forward line. McIntyre had played semi-pro ball in Nova Scotia in 1944 helping Halifax Shipyards to the Halifax Defense League title. In 1949, he helped the Fredericton Capitals to the New Brunswick championship. In 1997, McIntyre was inducted into the New Brunswick Sports Hall Of Fame.

1946 Sherbrooke Canadians—.310, 1 HR, 17 RBI
1947 Sherbrooke/Drummondville—.223, 0 HR, 27 RBI

Gread McKinnis—Pitcher, 6'2", 170 lbs. Batted right, threw left

McKinnis pitched in the Negro League from 1941 to 1949, with five teams, winning all-star berths in 1940 and 1941. In 1950 McKinnis pitched in the Southern Minny League with the Rochester Royals. He came to Canada in 1951 to anchor the pitching staff of the Brandon Greys of the ManDak League. He turned to organized ball in 1952 pitching in the Florida International League and started there again in 1953 before returning to Brandon for more ManDak League action. McKinnis pitched in the Florida State League in 1955 and briefly for Minot in the ManDak League in 1956. He died, at 77, in 1991 in Chicago.

1951 Brandon Greys—Won 11, Lost 6, 19 G, 14 GS, 10 CG
1953 Brandon Greys—Won 7, Lost 5, 25 G, 11 GS, 3 CG

Canadian Highlights: May 30, 1951, newcomer McKinnis gave up two runs in the first inning and then pitched shutout ball as Brandon beat Winnipeg 5–2. August 6, McKinnis fired a five-hitter to top the Minot Mallards and their ace, Sugar Cain, 2–0. August 27, he won the pennant-clinching game, 6–2, over the Winnipeg Buffaloes.

July 30, 1953, Brandon clobbered Moose Jaw 11–1 in an interlocking game. McKinnis gave up seven hits and fanned fourteen. August 11, celebrating his 40th birthday, McKinnis had a shutout into the 9th inning and had two hits in Brandon's 5–2 win over Carman. September 7, the lefthander held Carman to one-hit as Brandon won the semi-final playoff series.

Ira McKnight—Catcher/Outfield, 5'10", 180 lbs. Batted right, threw right

McKnight had his first taste of Negro league ball in 1952, while still in high school, when he played with the Memphis Red Sox. He stayed at home for the next three summers and caught for teams in South Bend, Indiana, while attracting the attention of the Kansas City Monarchs. In 1956, his first season with the Monarchs, McKnight was chosen for the East-West All-Star Game. During a successful 1957 season he was signed by the New York Yankees. However, while with the Auburn Yankees of the New York-Penn League in 1958, he was injured after playing just eight games and released. McKnight rejoined the Monarchs.

In July, 1960, the legendary team was on tour playing in the Lacombe, Alberta, Tournament when Spero Leakos, the owner of the Saskatoon Commodores, enticed three Monarchs, including McKnight, to jump the team to play for his Saskatoon club. While he returned to Kansas City and toured with Satchel Paige over the next two seasons, he was back in

Canada in 1964 with the North Battleford Beavers. After a summer with Saskatoon in 1965, he became playing manager of another Saskatchewan club, the Melville Millionaires. He made a return to North Battleford in 1968 and was in Quebec in 1969 with Drummondville in the Provincial League for his final Canadian season. He wasn't quite through, however, returning to Chicago in 1970 to form his own club.

> 1960 Saskatoon Commodores—Statistics not available
> 1964 North Battleford Beavers—.385, 2 HR, 24 RBI, 18 SB
> 1965 Saskatoon Commodores—.316, 0 HR, 30 RBI, 24 SB
> 1966 Melville Millionaires—.359
> 1967 Melville Millionaires—Statistics not available
> 1968 North Battleford Beavers—.344, 1 HR, 16 RBI, 8 SB
> 1969 Drummondville Royals—.234, 9 D, 0 T, 0 HR, 22 RBI

Canadian Highlights: In 1964, McKnight finished third in the batting race while leading the Northern Saskatchewan League in runs, hits and stolen bases. The following season he was tops in runs, runs batted in and stolen bases. In 1968 McKnight was the league leader in runs and bases on balls.

Clyde McNeal—Infield, 6'0", 185 lbs. Batted right, threw right

McNeal came out of San Antonio to join the Chicago American Giants in 1944 for his first taste of Negro League action. He stayed with the club through 1950. After military service, McNeal signed with the Dodgers. Later, he played a few games in Triple-A with Montreal while spending most of his time in Class-B. In 1957, he joined the Bismarck Barons in the final season of the ManDak League.

> 1954 Montreal Royals—.125, 0 HR, 0 RBI
> 1957 Bismarck Barons—.304, 16 HR, 61 RBI

Winslow Means—Pitcher, 6'0". Threw left

After graduation from high school and a summer of semi-pro ball with the Black Stars of the Eastern Ohio League, the nineteen year old Means packed his bags for some barnstorming. He toured in 1947 with the Havana La Palomas and the following season with the fabled Harlem Globetrotters. In 1949, he was a key hurler for the Brandon Greys in a triumphant season in which the club won the Manitoba Senior League title and finished with an overall record of 87 wins, 18 losses and 3 ties.

Means, one of nine children, was married in the fall of 1949 and spent just a few weeks with Brandon in the spring of 1950. The left-hander stayed at home in Zanesville, Ohio, in 1951 and finished his career pitching for more than a decade with semi-pro teams in his home town.

> 1949 Brandon Greys—Won 18, Lost 4, 25 G, 20 GS, 17 CG *
> 1950 Brandon Greys—Won 1, Lost 0

*1949 statistics include all games—league, play-off, tournament, exhibition

Canadian Highlights: May 21, 1949, opening day, Means scattered seven hits and fanned fourteen in a 5–4 victory over Elmwood. June 25, he fanned eighteen as Brandon crushed Carman 13–3. July 1, Means pitched Brandon to top money in the Kinsmen Tournament blanking Minot Mallards 1–0. July 28, at Indian Head, Saskatchewan, Means fired a perfect game as Brandon won its opening round contest. August 13, he fired a one-hitter with ten strikeouts in a 6–0 shutout of the Winnipeg Vets. Means finished the 1949 season with an 18–4 mark in 25 games, 20 of them starts. He completed 16 and compiled 218 strikeouts.

Leonardo "Lazarus" Medina—Pitcher, 5'7", 160 lbs. Batted left, threw left

Medina spent most of his career in Panama, Puerto Rico and Venezuela although he pitched in the Negro League with the Cincinnati Clowns and Indianapolis Clowns from 1944 to 1946. In 1949, he came north to Canada and joined the Drummondville Cubs in the Quebec League. He pitched only briefly and returned to the United States.

> 1949 Drummondville Cubs—Won 0, Lost 1

Eli "Skip" Merritt — Pitcher. Threw left

The left-hander was recruited from the Philadelphia Colored Giants to pitch for the Regina Caps of the Western Canada League in 1951. Merritt was reported to have been the ace of the Giants' staff for the previous two seasons compiling a 23–2 record in 1949 and 20–2 in 1950. (The Leader-Post, Regina, May 4, 1951) In Regina, his bat drew almost as much attention as his arm.

> 1951 Regina Caps — Won 6, Lost 2, 15 G, 6 GS, 5 CG

Canadian Highlights: June 1, 1951, Merritt picked up a win with 7⅓ innings of three-hit relief, had three hits in four trips to the plate, and notched the winning marker as Regina rebounded to beat Estevan. June 14, he was in the spotlight as Regina came back from an early 3–0 deficit to down Estevan 8–7 to take top money in the Moose Jaw Tournament. Merritt came on in relief in the second inning and allowed just one earned run in 7⅓ innings and provided the offensive punch with a two-run homer in the 5th. June 21, Merritt went 11 innings in a 4–4 draw, called because of darkness. He had three hits, one of them a booming triple. July 26, Merritt held Indian Head to six hits to stop the Rockets' 22-game winning streak as the Caps won 5–3. He cracked a triple and scored the first run.

Sylvio Mesa — Outfield

The power-hitting Cuban outfielder was a mid-season addition to the 1954 Indian Head Rockets of the Saskatchewan Baseball League.

Canadian Highlights: In his debut with the Rockets, July 22, 1954, Mesa drove in four runs with a three-run homer and single as Indian Head topped Moose Jaw 15–6. He had two hits, including a triple the next day. August 2, Mesa cracked a pair of homers, driving in four runs, as the Rockets topped Moose Jaw 6–4. August 18, he scored the only run in the first game and belted a two-run homer in the second as the Rockets took a pair from Lloydminster. August 20, Mesa helped the Rockets to a pair of wins over Moose Jaw. In the completion of an earlier tie game, he tripled and scored the winner. In the regular contest he slammed a two-run homer.

George "Whitey" Michaels — Infield/Manager.

Michaels, a young veteran of barnstorming play in the Maritimes with the Boston Royal Giants, was a controversial choice as manager for the Dominion Hawks of the Colliery League in 1936. In a game at Sydney Mines, when he tried to take the field to replace his injured catcher, a group of noisy fans protested and prevented him from playing. The next three seasons, when the Colliery League was in organized baseball, black athletes were prohibited from playing.

Roland "Rollie" Miles — Second Base, 5'10", 178 lbs.

He's best remembered for his football exploits, but Miles first game to Canada to exhibit his skills on the baseball diamond. The 24-year-old speedster was the sparkplug for the Regina Caps of the Western Canada Baseball League in 1951, hitting .378. Miles had earlier impressed scouts at a Red Sox training camp.

He came north from St Augustine's College in North Carolina where he was a star in baseball, track and field and football (he was a Negro All-American on the gridiron). Enticed to try out for the Edmonton Eskimos football team, he quickly established himself as one of the top two-way stars in Canadian football. During his eleven year football career he was an all-star eight times — at running back, defensive back and linebacker. Miles, who died in 1995, at age 68, was inducted into the Canadian Football Hall Of Fame and was voted one of the top 50 players of the CFL's modern era.

> 1951 Regina Caps — .378, 14 SB (incomplete)
> 1952 Edmonton Pontiacs — Statistics not available

Canadian Highlights: June 11, 1951, Miles belted a homer and scored four times as Regina trounced Moose Jaw 10–6. June 13, Miles had a grand-slam homer and three singles to lead Regina over Moose Jaw 20–7 at the Mill City Tournament at Moose Jaw. June 15, Miles had three hits and scored three runs in a 12–9 win over Estevan. July 1, the second sacker socked a pair of homers as the Caps beat Indian Head

Rockets 9–2 in an exhibition match. July 5, Miles belted three hits in a 5–1 loss to Medicine Hat. On July 10, Miles drove in the only run with a triple as Regina shaded Moose Jaw 1–0. July 14, Miles blasted a homer and triple, scored three times and drove in a pair to lead Regina past Medicine Hat 10–9 in the first game of a twin-bill. He had a double and three singles in the second game. July 18, he punched out a triple, double and single to lead Regina to a 7–2 win over Dauphin (Manitoba) in the first day of action at the Indian Head Tournament. July 19, Miles ran wild in a 7–2 Caps win over the Rockets at the Indian Head Tournament. He stole second and third in both the 5th and 8th innings.

July 6, 1953, Miles had a homer and single for Edmonton Pontiacs in the final of the Camrose Tournament against Indian Head.

Zell Miles—Outfield

Miles was born in Eufaula, Alabama. He played for the Chicago American Giants in 1946. From 1947 to 1950 he barnstormed with the Harlem Globetrotters and also played with the Seattle Steelheads in the newly formed West Coast Negro League. He started the 1951 season with the Chicago American Giants. Then on July 18, he joined the Winnipeg Buffaloes in the ManDak League when they lost players to organized ball. He died in 1970 and is buried in Eufaula.

> 1951 Winnipeg Buffaloes—.286, 4 HR, 25 RBI

Canadian Highlights: July 27, Miles hit a home run, double and single in a 9–4 win over Minot. July 28, he had four hits in a thirteen inning 11–10 victory over Carman. August 4, Miles hit a home run and two singles as the Buffaloes beat Carman.

Harold Millon—Utility/Second Base

The Chicago American Giants had Millon in their Negro League lineup in both 1946 and 1947. He was up in Canada in 1948 to try out with the Winnipeg Blue Bombers football team. Then, in 1950, played a half-dozen games for the Carman Cardinals in the ManDak League.

Miguel Miranda—Catcher/Utility

Miranda played just one season in Canada, with the Indian Head Rockets of the Saskatchewan League in 1954.

Canadian Highlights: June 18, 1954, Miranda had three hits as the Rockets edged Rosetown 7–6. July 6, he paced the Rockets with a triple and two singles in a 12–7 win over Lloydminster. July 18, the Cuban catcher belted a two-run homer and a triple, but the Rockets fell, 9–7 to Rosetown. August 9, Miranda knocked in four runs with a double and two singles as Rockets beat the Beavers 10–7.

Joe Mitchell—Outfield

Mitchell got a taste of the prairies in 1949 and 1950 on a barnstorming tour with the Brooklyn Cuban Giants. He joined the Elmwood Giants of the ManDak League in 1951 and in mid–June was traded to the Brandon Greys. In 1952, he played with the Regina Caps and Brandon (both teams were being supplied with players by the same organizer and a few players suited up for both teams). Mitchell returned to Brandon in 1953.

> 1951 Elmwood/Brandon—.296, 4 HR, 43 RBI
> 1952 Regina Caps—Statistics not available
> 1952 Brandon Greys—.301, 11 D, 13 T, 0 HR, 28 RBI
> 1953 Brandon Greys—.268, 6 D, 5 T, 2 HR, 34 RBI

Canadian Highlights: May 26, 1951, Mitchell had three hits and scored the winning run in an 8–7 decision over Carman. July 22, Mitchell had two hits and drove in a pair in a 7–3 win over the Cardinals. The next day he drove in three runs in a 12–6 Brandon win over Winnipeg and a day later he had three hits, knocked in the tying run and scored the winner in a 10–8 victory over Carman. August 20, Mitchell had a double and two singles in a loss to Minot. September 14, Mitchell's homer in the 9th clinched the ManDak title for Brandon.

August 6, 1952, Mitchell poked a triple and three singles to help Brandon to an 11–6 win over Minot.

July 30, 1953, a three-run triple by Mitchell, one of three hits, was the key blow as Brandon whipped Moose Jaw 11–1. September 1, Mitchell's three hits helped Brandon to an 11–3 playoff win over Carman. September 5, Brandon won, 12–5, and took a 3–0 game lead in the semi-final series as Mitchell blasted a three-run homer. September 10, it was Brandon 9, Minot 4 in the opening game of the ManDak final series. Mitchell contributed two doubles and a single.

Ken Mitchell—Outfield

Mitchell, believed to be from the Vancouver, B.C. area, was a solid player for two seasons for Calgary (an opening day hero in his debut), in 1957 in the Foothills-Wheatbelt League and 1958 when the club played in the Southern Alberta League. He hit .322 and led the league in doubles (11) in 1957.

Canadian Highlights: June 2, 1957, Mitchell made the home fans happy on opening day with a two-out, three-run homer in the bottom of the 9th to give Calgary a 4–2 win over Granum. June 30, Mitchell had four hits to lead the Dodgers to a 6–5 win over Vulcan. August 4, Mitchell sparked a Calgary comeback with a grand slam homer as the Dodgers recovered from a 3–0 deficit to down Medicine Hat 8–7. August 20, Mitchell had a huge day with five hits, three of them homers, and seven runs batted in playoff action against Granum.

July 11, 1958, Mitchell punched out a pair of doubles and a single and knocked in the winning run in the 10th inning as Calgary got by Lethbridge 11–10. July 27, Mitchell drove in four runs with a homer and two singles as Calgary topped Lethbridge 14–10.

Juverno Joseph Monteiro—Outfield, 6'2", 185 lbs. Batted right, threw right

Monteiro, born in Portugal, was an outstanding hitter over five seasons in the Provincial League in Quebec. He was the batting champion in 1951 with Granby. He had four years in organized ball, including a .301, 25-homer season in the Piedmont League. In 1955 he was a leading offensive force for Minot of the ManDak League.

> 1948 Granby Red Sox—.358, 33 D, 13 T, 13 HR
> 1949 Granby Red Sox—Statistics not available
> 1950 Granby Red Sox—.284, 19 D, 2 T, 12 HR, 59 RBI
> 1951 Granby Red Sox—.353, 29 D, 3 T, 28 HR, 115 RBI
> 1955 Three Rivers Phillies—.264, 13 D, 0 T, 2 HR, 13 RBI
> 1955 Minot Mallards—.313, 14 HR, 51 RBI

Lee Moody—Infield/Outfield, 6'0", 190 lbs. Batted right, threw right

Moody played in the Negro League from 1944 to 1947 with the Kansas City Monarchs and Birmingham Black Barons. In 1950, he played with the Cairo Dodgers in the Kitty League and closed out his career in 1951 with Three Rivers in the Quebec Provincial League. Moody was 81 when he passed away in 1998 in Missouri.

> 1951 Three Rivers Yankees—.242, 0 HR, 16 RBI

Santiago Morciego—Pitcher, 5'10", 150 lbs. Batted right, threw right

Signed by the Philadelphia Phillies, the 16-year-old Cuban was reported to have attended the Phillies Spring Training camping in 1958. He had been assigned to Tampa of the Florida State League in 1957. The right-hander pitched in a dozen games for Regina of the Western Canada League in 1958.

> 1958 Regina Braves—Won 1, Lost 4, 12 G, 3 GS, 1 CG, 6.25 ERA

Canadian Highlights: June 20, 1958, in his debut, Morciego tossed four shutout innings in relief allowing just two hits and fanned three. July 28, Morciego fired three shutout innings in relief to pick up his lone victory. Earlier in the month, the teenager gave up 14 hits and 11 walks (with nary a strikeout) in seven innings to take a 14–2 defeat.

Barney Morris—Pitcher, 6'0", 170 lbs. Batted right, threw right

Morris was a hit in Canada near the beginning of his productive career. He was a member (along with Satchel Paige, Hilton Smith and Chet Brewer) of the pitching staff of the integrated Bismarck (North Dakota) Churchills who went on to capture the inaugural semi-pro National Baseball Congress title in 1935. The team played a series of exhibitions on the prairies in 1935 and 1936. Morris had a successful career in Negro league ball from 1932 to 1948. In 1949, he pitched with success for the Benton Harbor Buds in the semi-pro Michigan-Indiana League. He came to Canada in 1951 and tried, without much success, to resume his career with the Elmwood Giants in the ManDak League.

> 1951 Elmwood Giants—Won 0, Lost 0, 3 G, 1 GS, 0 CG

Canadian Highlights: June 21, 1935, Morris fired a three-hitter, with twelve strikeouts, and added a home run as Bismarck topped the Shreveport Acme Giants 8–0 in exhibition action at Winnipeg.

August 4, 1936, Morris fanned twenty in pitching Bismarck to an 8–3 win over Regina Nationals. August 7, 1936, Morris allowed just one earned run in hurling Bismarck to a win over Broadview (Saskatchewan) Red Sox.

Ed "Santa Fe" Morris—Pitcher, 6'3". Threw right

The California product pitched for Estevan Maple Leafs in 1950 and 1951. In March, 1951, he was reported to be the first Negro to be given a tryout with the Pittsburgh Pirates at their Spring Training site at San Bernardino, California. He had semi-pro experience in Southern California previous to his Canadian stint.

> 1950 Estevan Maple Leafs—Statistics not available
> 1951 Estevan Maple Leafs—Won 1, Lost 0

Canadian Highlights: July 22, 1951, Morris made his initial start for the Maple Leafs a winning one with an eight-hitter to stop Swift current to complete a three-game, weekend sweep.

Felton Morrison—Outfield

Morrison had exposure to the prairies in 1950 as he barnstormed in Canada with Sugar Cain's San Francisco Cubs. He would return in 1954 as a member of the Rosetown Phillies of the Saskatchewan Baseball League. Morrison was a tough man to walk or strikeout. In 58 games, he walked just 9 times and fanned 11.

> 1954 Rosetown Phillies—.269, 5 D, 6 T, 0 HR, 28 RBI

Canadian Highlights: May 20, 1954, Morrison had a triple, double and single for the Phillies in an 11–6 loss to Saskatoon. June 19, Morrison had a triple and two singles in a 10–9 loss to Moose Jaw. July 8, Morrison drove in four runs with three hits in a losing cause as Rosetown dropped a decision to Saskatoon. August 15, Morrison had three hits and knocked in a pair to lead Rosetown to a 6–4 win over Indian Head. August 24, Morrison had a homer and double for Rosetown in opening round playoff action.

Jim Morrow—Pitcher. Threw right

Morrow came north with the Jacksonville Eagles in 1950 as they formed the Indian Head Rockets. He pitched for the Rockets in 1950–1951 and part of 1952 before being acquired by Saskatoon Gems for whom he pitched until 1954. He was one of the top pitchers on the prairies, especially on the money trail, in tournament play. (Given Morrow's importance in out-of-league play, his total statistics—league, exhibition, tourneys, playoffs—are presented.)

> 1950 Indian Head—Won 7, Lost 1, 9 G, 6 GS, 6 CG
> 1951 Indian Head—Won 12, Lost 3, 19 G, 13 GS, 9 CG
> 1952 Indian Head—Statistics not available, Saskatoon—Won 2, Lost 1, 4 G, 4 GS, 2 CG
> 1953 Saskatoon—Won 14, Lost 4, 25 G, 17 GS, 13 CG,
> 1954 Saskatoon—Won 9, Lost 3, 23 G, 14 GS, 7 CG,

Canadian Highlights: June 28, 1950, Morrow, taking a turn in the outfield, had four hits to lead the Rockets over Lumsden 6–3. July 29, Morrow fired a six-hit shutout to advance Indian Head to the final of the Swift Current Tournament

July 25, 1951, Morrow fired a two-hit shutout and belted a homer and single in a 10–0 win for Indian Head over Moose Jaw. August 13, Morrow had a three-hit shutout as Indian Head downed Medicine Hat 2–0. August 17, Morrow fired a one-hit shutout as Indian Head downed Regina Caps 4–0.

June 17, 1952, Morrow set down Estevan Maple Leafs on four hits as Saskatoon Gems took the opening game of the Moose Jaw Tournament, 4–1. June 24, Morrow topped future major leaguer Truman Clevenger 1–0 in a 10-inning thriller at Saskatoon. He allowed just three hits and had 14 strikeouts in capturing his second win of the season.

June 6, Morrow held North Battleford to just three hits in posting a 4–1 victory. June 25, he had a no-hitter through seven innings, finishing with a three-hit outing, in a 5–1 win over Minot. He helped at the plate with three hits. July 1, the right-hander was tops on the hill and at the plate as Saskatoon advanced to the final of the Optimist Club Tournament with a 13–0 shutout of North Battleford. He allowed just five hits and his three-run homer proved enough for the victory. July 22, Morrow gave up just four hits as Saskatoon beat Indian Head 6–1 in the opening game of the National Baseball Congress Saskatchewan final.

June 21, 1954, Morrow held Indian Head to five hits as the Gems downed the Rockets 4–1. July 23, he fanned 13 as the Gems moved into the final of the Saskatoon Exhibition Tournament with a 7–1 win over Kamsack. August 15, Morrow tossed a five-hitter in downing Lloydminster 3–1. September 8, Morrow had a no-hitter into the 8th inning, ending with a three-hitter, as Saskatoon topped North Battleford 5–1 to even the final series at three games apiece.

Sydney Cy (Sy) Morton—Shortstop/Third Base, 5'9," 165 lbs. Batted right, threw right

Morton toured in Western Canada in 1950 when he barnstormed with the San Francisco Cubs and he was back in 1951 when he joined the Elmwood Giants and Winnipeg Buffaloes of the ManDak League. In 1953, he was with Grandview in the Manitoba Saskatchewan League and, in 1954, played for Rosetown Saskatchewan. Previous to his Canadian experience, Morton had played in the Negro League from 1940 to 1947.

1951 Elmwood/Winnipeg—.193, 0 HR, 5 RBI
1953 Grandview, Man-Sask—Statistics not available
1954 Rosetown Phillies—.277, 10 D, 8 T, 0 HR, 25 RBI

Canadian Highlights: July 30, 1951, Morton scored three times as Elmwood exploded for 23 runs in downing Winnipeg. August 16, Morton had three hits in a 4–3 win over Minot.

May 19, 1954, Morton belted a triple and two doubles and drove in a pair as Rosetown edged Saskatoon 7–6. July 17, Morton had a pair of triples as Rosetown edged Indian Head 2–1. July 29, Morton tripled and scored the winning run as Rosetown shaded Moose Jaw 4–3 to advance to the final of the Rosetown Tournament.

Eudie Napier—Catcher, 5'9", 190 lbs. Batted left, threw right

Napier played in the Negro League from 1941 to 1950 with the Homestead Grays and Pittsburgh Crawfords. He came north in 1949 for the first of two seasons with Farnham in the Quebec Provincial League. In 1952, he joined the Brantford Red Sox in the Intercounty Baseball League in Ontario. He died in 1983 at the age of 70.

1949 Farnham Black Sox—.266, 4 HR, 54 RBI
1951 Farnham Pirates—.285, 14 D, 1 T, 8 HR, 42 RBI
1952 Brantford Red Sox—Statistics not available

Canadian Highlights: Napier played in Winnipeg August 21–23, 1944, for the Pittsburgh Crawfords in a three game series against the Chicago Brown Bombers. He was back in Winnipeg in September of 1945, when the Crawfords played a series against the Honus Wagner All-Stars. Napier had three hits in the September 5 game as the Crawfords beat the All-Stars 3–2.

Pedro Naranjo—Pitcher, 5'10½", 180 lbs. Bats left, threw left

Naranjo saw limited action in the Negro League with the Indianapolis Clowns and also pitched in organized ball in 1952 with Decatur in the Mississippi-Ohio Valley League. He pitched with success that season going 13–10 with a 2.33 ERA. He came to Canada as an eighteen year old in 1950 and joined the Brandon Greys in the ManDak League. He would play two seasons for the Greys and close out his career in 1954 with the Detroit Stars.

>   1950 Brandon Greys—Won 3, Lost 1, 10 G, 4 GS, 2 CG
>   1951 Brandon Greys—Won 4, Lost 1, 7 G, 6 GS, 4 CG

Canadian Highlights: August 4, 1950, Naranjo pitched all thirteen innings in a four-hit, 1–0 shutout of Carman. He registered thirteen strikeouts. September 1, in the playoffs, he beat Carman 8–2 on a five-hitter and had three hits and three RBI to help his own cause. The win put Brandon into the league final against the Buffaloes.

August 6, 1951, he pitched a six-hit 2–0 win over Minot Mallards. September 4, in a semifinal game, he beat Carman 2–1 in ten innings.

Ray Nash—Catcher

Nash had no official Negro League experience when he came to Canada in 1950 to join the Dauphin Red Birds in the Northern Senior League. He would also play the next season with Dauphin when they were in the Manitoba-Saskatchewan League.

Canadian Highlights: July 4, 1950, Nash doubled in the winning run in the ninth inning that gave Dauphin a 4–3 victory over Neepawa. The Winnipeg Free Press reported that on August 2, in a game against Grandview, Nash, playing third base, made a number of fielding gems, stopping some hard smashes with uncanny ability.

Charles "Bomber" Neal—Outfield. Threw right

Neal was among the first of the black imports in the Halifax and District League in Nova Scotia playing for the Dartmouth Arrows in 1947.

Charlie Neal—Second Base, 5'10", 165 lbs. Batted right, threw right

Neal, from Texas, had experience as a teenager with the Atlanta Black Crackers. The middle infielder caught the eye of the Dodgers and was playing in the Brooklyn system by 1950. After six years in the minors, Neal graduated to the Dodgers and carved out an eight year career in the majors. He was a Dodger hero in the 1959 World Series following a season in which he was selected as an all-star and won a Gold Glove award for his defensive ability.

In 1962, Neal was an original Met as he played second, short and third for the team which lost 120 games in its debut season.

Neal died in 1996 at age 65.

>   1955 Montreal Royals—.274, 29 D, 14 T, 16 HR, 75 RBI

Emmett Neal—First Base

Neal, from the Oakland area, joined his baseball and college buddies Pumpsie Green, Nate Bates, Winters Calvin and Willie Reed on the Indian Head Rockets' roster in 1952. A year later, Army Private Neal was killed while serving with the Seventh Division in Korea.

Ted Neal—Pitcher, 5'9", 160 lbs. Batted right, threw right

Neal, who pitched in pro ball in 1956 and 1957, joined the Granum White Sox of the Southern Alberta League in 1958. He was rebounding after being injured in a car accident late in the 1957 season. (It was a little confusing for league fans as Granum had Ray Neal on its pitching staff and Tilbert Neal pitched for Calgary. In addition, both Ted and Tilbert had pitched for Tri-City of the Northwest League.) He returned to pro ball in 1960 pitching mainly in relief for Lewiston in the Northwest League (9–4, 3.87) and came north again in 1961 to pitch for the Edmonton Eskimos of the Western Canada League.

Henry Nears—Outfield

Nears was an outfielder with the 1950 edition of Ligon's All-Stars.

Canadian Highlight: June 20, 1950, Nears, with a triple and double, paced the Ligon All-Stars to a 7–5 win over Regina Caps.

Jim Nelson—Outfield

Nelson, from Minneapolis, played the early part of the 1958 season with the Lethbridge Warriors of the Southern Alberta League.

Canadian Highlight: June 6, Nelson led the Warriors with a triple and single in a 5-0 win over Vauxhall.

James Lee "Jimmy" Newberry—
Pitcher, 5'10", 170 lbs. Batted both, threw right

Newberry played in the Negro League from 1942 to 1950 with the Birmingham Black Barons before traveling to Canada to join the Winnipeg Buffaloes for the inaugural season of the Man-Dak League.

The native of Alabama spent two summers with Winnipeg before signing with the St. Louis Browns in 1952. The Browns, in the first transaction between a major league and a Japanese team, loaned Newberry and John Britton to the Hankyu Braves. Newberry was selected to the all-star team in Japan after finishing with an 11–10 record and a 3.21 ERA.

He returned to Canada's ManDak League in 1953 with the Carman Cardinals and led the league in appearances, pitching in 30 games. Then, over the next three years he played in organized ball and, in 1959, tried a comeback with the Lloydminster–North Battleford Combines in the Canadian-American League, but saw action in only one game.

- 1950 Winnipeg Buffaloes—Won 7, Lost 7, 18 G, 14 CS, 11 CG
- 1951 Winnipeg Buffaloes—Won 6, Lost 3, 12 G, 7 CS, 6 CG
- 1953 Carman Cardinals—Won 5, Lost 9, 30 G, 15 CS, 6 CG
- 1959 Lloydminster/N.Battleford—Statistics not available

Canadian Highlights: June 10, 1950, in his first start, he beat Brandon on an eight-hitter as he fanned eleven. June 17, Newberry tossed an eight-hit shutout as Winnipeg topped the Greys 8-0. August 24, Newberry won both ends of a double header, a four-hitter in the opener, a five-hit shutout in the second game. In the league finals on September 6, 7 and 8, Newberry was the pitching star as he won the first two games, then saved game three.

In the 1951 season opener, May 19, he hurled four no-hit innings in relief as Winnipeg beat Brandon. June 4, 1951, Newberry beat Carman 3-0. The game was completed in one hour and thirty seven minutes on a very cold day. June 22, he held Carman to five hits in a 5-1 win for Winnipeg.

Don "Newk" Newcombe—
Pitcher, 6'4", 220 lbs. Batted left, threw right

Not bad for a kid from New Jersey whose high school didn't have a baseball team—Rookie of the Year, Cy Young Award, Most Valuable Player. Newk is the only player in major league history to have captured all three of baseball's most coveted awards. And, he was an all-star in the Negro Leagues, the minor leagues and the major leagues. Three times the big right-hander was a 20-game winner. Not bad for a high school dropout who signed for a $1,500 bonus and $375 a month.

Newcombe caught a break at age 17 when Effa Manley of the Newark Eagles took a chance that his size (6-4, 220) would translate into a baseball player. It was 1944, and baseball, both black and white, had difficulty filling rosters with so many players away fighting the war. Newcombe took advantage of the opportunity. (In 1952 the Pittsburgh Courier published a poll on the all-time Negro League all-stars. Newcombe was selected to the second team.)

He caught the eye of the Dodgers in the fall of 1945 pitching for a Negro all-star team against a major league squad at Brooklyn's Ebbets Field. Newcombe and catcher Roy Campanella signed with Brooklyn and were assigned to Nashua of the Class-B, New England League where he had two outstanding seasons. But, the best was yet to come. A 17–6 season in Triple-A with Montreal in 1948 helped propel Newcombe into the Dodger rotation early the next season. It was the beginning of a 10-year major league career, shortened by injuries and alcoholism. He lost two years during his prime serving with the Army during the Korean War.

He provided fans with many sterling performances, including an attempt at a modern-era rarity, pitching a double-header. In September, 1950, Newcombe tossed a three-hit shutout against the Phillies in the first game and gave up just two runs in seven frames of the second before being removed for a pinch-hitter. It turned out, Newcombe was an excellent hitter and over his major league career batted

.271. In 1955, he hit .359 with seven home runs in 117 at bats. He finished his major league pitching career with a record of 149–90, and 3.56 ERA. In 1962, he closed out his career in Japan with the Chunichi Dragons as a first baseman/outfielder, batting .262 with 12 home runs.

In the 1970s, he rejoined the Dodgers and became the team's Director of Community Relations, heading up programs in drug and alcohol awareness and prevention.

>1948 Montreal Royals—Won 17, Lost 6, 3.14 ERA
>1949 Montreal Royals—Won 2, Lost 2, 2.65 ERA

Canadian Highlights: In Montreal, August 15, 1948, Newcombe pitched a no-hitter as the Royals beat Toronto Maple Leafs 8–0 in the seven-inning second game of a double-header. Leafs won the opener to snap the Royals 16-game winning streak. Five days later, Newcombe nearly duplicated the feat, allowing just a 4th inning single in a 3–0 win over Rochester.

Alex Newkirk—Pitcher, 5'10", 175 lbs.
Batted left, threw right

Newkirk pitched for the New York Black Yankees and New York Cubans from 1946 to 1949. In 1950, he joined the pennant winning St. Jean Braves of the Provincial League. He closed out his career in 1951 with the Granby Red Sox.

>1950 St. Jean Braves—Won 3, Lost 2, 3.53 ERA
>1951 Granby Red Sox—Won 7, Lost 12, 3.66 ERA

Esteban Orlando "Chico" O'Farrill—Shortstop. Threw right

The Cuban shortstop had a brief fling in Negro League ball with the Indianapolis Clowns, Philadelphia Stars and Baltimore Elite Giants from 1949 to 1951 before leaving for Western Canada and the Eston Ramblers of the Northern Saskatchewan Baseball League. He returned in 1953 to play for the independent Indian Head Rockets and in 1954–1955 as a member of the North Battleford Beavers of the Saskatchewan League.

In 1956, O'Farrill went to play in Nicaragua in the inaugural season of the country's professional league. He was a prominent player, coach and manager over the league's 12 seasons. He became an icon in the country as he stayed on as a coach and manager until 2004 when he retired (he did take a break from 1977 to 1987).

>1951 Eston Ramblers—.315
>1953 Indian Head Rockets—Statistics not available
>1954 North Battleford—.298, 11 D, 7 T, 5 HR, 35 RBI
>1955 North Battleford—.281, 18 D, 4 T, 1 HR, 28 RBI

Canadian Highlights: July 10, 1953, O'Farrill had a homer and single as Indian Head reached the final of the Kamsack Tournament shading Saskatoon 4–3, in 10 innings.

May 17, 1954, O'Farrill walloped a triple and two doubles in a losing cause for North Battleford. May 20, Chico's double in the 6th inning broke up Rick Herrera's no-hit bid as North Battleford topped Lloydminster 8–4. O'Farrill added another double in the 8th. June 20, O'Farrill's two-run homer was the difference as Beavers shaded Lloydminster 7–6. June 29, Chico had a homer and single as the Beavers shutout Lloydminster 6–0. August 2, O'Farrill knocked in four runs with a double and single to give the Beavers a 6–6 draw with Rosetown in a game called because of darkness. August 3, with a triple and three singles, O'Farrill led North Battleford's attack in an 8–1 win over Indian Head. August 24, his two-run homer in the 1st inning led North Battleford over Rosetown 7–2 in the opening game of their semi-final playoff series.

June 23, 1955, O'Farrill's three hits helped North Battleford to a 13–5 win over Lloydminster.

Ed Olivares—Third Base/Outfield, 5'11", 180 lbs. Batted right, threw right

Olivares was signed out of Puerto Rico by the Phillies in 1957 and spent the season with their Class-D, Tampa and Moultrie/Brunswick clubs. He was acquired by the Cardinals prior to the 1958 campaign and sent to their Class-D, Daytona Beach club. That summer he managed a "cup of coffee" with the Triple-A, Rochester Red Wings. He started the 1959 season at Double-A, Tulsa, and after 15 games was sent to the Winnipeg Goldeyes. In 1960 and 1961, he played at the Double-A and Triple-A levels and advanced to the major league roster for twenty-four games with the Cardinals. From 1963 to 1964 he played in the minor league systems of Houston and Minnesota and closed out his career in 1966 in the Detroit system.

> 1959 Winnipeg Goldeyes—.319, 13 D, 1 T, 16 HR, 73 RBI

Canadian Highlights: August 1, 1959, Olivares broke his leg, finishing him for the season. Nonetheless he tied for second on the Goldeyes in batting average, third in home runs and fourth in RBI.

John Henry Oliver—Pitcher

In 1949, Oliver was a member of the barnstorming San Francisco Sea Lions which ran into financial problems during its Canadian tour. Seven of the players, including Oliver, decided to jump the team and stay in the small Saskatchewan community of Buchanan and bolster the local squad.

Canadian Highlights: July 27, 1949, Oliver fired a five-hit shutout as Buchanan shaded Chamberlain 2–0 at the Indian Head Tournament. August 1, Oliver checked Regina Caps on 9 hits and had a double and single at the plate as Buchanan All-Stars dumped Regina 7–2.

Reinaldo Oliver—Catcher, 5'11", 185 lbs. Batted right, threw right

The Puerto Rican receiver spent five seasons in the St. Louis Cardinals system. Oliver started his career in organized ball in 1958 with the Class-D, Dothan Cardinals. In 1959, he was sent to the Winnipeg Goldeyes in the Northern League and, in 1960, spent the season in Class-B with the Winston-Salem Red Birds. In 1961, he split the season between Class-A and Triple-A. He was back with the Goldeyes in 1962 and it turned out to be his last season in organized ball.

> 1959 Winnipeg Goldeyes—.319, 13 D, 2 T, 3 HR, 39 RBI
>
> 1962 Winnipeg Goldeyes—.292, 11 D, 3 T, 4 HR, 29 RBI

Canadian Highlights: Oliver was selected to the 1962 Northern League All-Star team.

Pedro Osorio—Outfield, 6'0", 189 lbs. Batted right.

The native of Panama was at the center of a dispute early in the 1951 season. Brought from Panama, along with Bobby Prescott, to play for Sceptre, Saskatchewan, the two players jumped the team to join the Indian Head Rockets. Sceptre owner Red Nixon called it a "dirty deal" and complained that he had paid $916 in transportation costs for the pair, without compensation.

After his one season in Canada, Osorio carved out a solid career at the lower levels of the minors. He hit .312 in the Arizona-Texas League in 1953 and followed up with batting marks of .348 and .340 with Carlsbad of the Longhorn League 1954–55. In 1955 he had 20 home runs and 108 RBI.

In late August, 1955, Osorio was shot in the shoulder by a bar owner during a fight in the Saloon Bar in Carlsbad. Witnesses said there had been comments about Osorio's race before the fight broke out. The bar owner later pleaded guilty to a reduced charge of assault and battery. In 1957, he returned to play in Panama for the national team in the Caribbean Series.

> 1951 Indian Head Rockets—.328 (incomplete)

Canadian Highlights: June 19, 1951, Osorio's 4th inning homer proved to be the difference as Sceptre beat Indian Head 4–1 to take top money at the Medicine Hat Tournament. July 4, Osorio blasted a homer, double and two singles to lead Indian Head Rockets in demolishing Swift Current, 13–1. August 10, Osorio banged out three hits to help Indian Head top Moose Jaw, 7–1. August 22, Osorio clubbed a grand slam homer in the final frame to give Indian Head a 6–2 playoff win over Moose Jaw.

Alfonso "Buddy" Owens—Second Base/Third Base

Owens started the 1951 season in the Negro League with the Chicago America Giants, then jumped to Canada and joined the Winnipeg

Buffaloes in the ManDak League. In 1952, he started the season with Canton in the Mississippi–Ohio Valley League and after 21 games went back to the Negro League and the Chicago American Giants. In 1954, he played 21 games with the Winnipeg Goldeyes then joined the Brandon Greys in the ManDak League.

> 1951 Winnipeg Buffaloes—.244, 3 HR, 13 RBI
> 1954 Winnipeg Goldeyes—.217, 0 HR, 2 RBI
> 1954 Brandon Greys—.259, 6 D, 3 T, 3 HR, 18 RBI

Canadian Highlights: August 26, 1951, Woods was the hitting star with a home run, double and a single in the Buffaloes win over Carman. September 6, Woods hit a three-run home run in a 10–6 playoff victory over Minot.

Jake Page—Outfield

The speedy center fielder came to Estevan in 1951 from a baseball background in the San Francisco area. Page had played with the San Francisco Sea Lions and Berkeley Tigers in the Bay area.

> 1951 Estevan Maple Leafs—.388 (incomplete)

Ted Page—Right Field/First Base, 5'11", 175 lbs. Batted left, threw right

Page's tenure in Canada came in the late 1920s when he played in the Montreal area with an all-black team sponsored by Chappie Johnson's All-Stars. His Negro League career stretched from the early 1920s to 1937 and included stints with the Homestead Grays, Pittsburg Crawfords, and Philadelphia Stars.

Pedro Pages—Outfield. Batted both, threw right

Pages, an outfielder from Cuba, played in the Negro League in 1939 and 1947 for the New York Cubans and in between those years he played in Mexico. Pages was a player known for his speed. He came north to Canada in 1951 and spent one season with Sherbrooke in the Quebec Provincial League.

> 1951 Sherbrooke Athletics—.244, 15 D, 2 T, 2 HR, 34 RBI

Leroy Robert "Satchel" Paige—Pitcher, 6'4", 180 lbs. Batted right, threw right

Paige was one of the best pitchers—black or white—in baseball history. In 1971, he was the first Afro-American to be inducted into the Hall of Fame at Cooperstown.

His career spanned at least 40 years, from his 1927 season with the Birmingham Black Barons to his appearance with the Peninsula Grays of the Carolina League in 1966. Paige brought his teams, mainly barnstorming clubs, into Canada over five decades beginning in the late 1920s.

By the time he had an opportunity to play in the major leagues he was a few weeks shy of his 42nd birthday. Nonetheless, he went 6–1, 2.48 as a rookie, was a two-time all-star and pitched in 179 major league games over six seasons.

> I was born with control ... and I'm the easiest man in the world to catch. All a catcher has to do is show me his glove and I'll hit it every time. They can hold out two bats, one six inches above the other, at the plate, and I'll throw a ball between them from the pitcher's mound [*Toronto Star*, August 18, 1942, p.12].

> I got bloopers, loopers and droopers. I got a jumpball, a screwball, a wobbly ball, a whipsy-dipsy-do ball, a hurry-up ball, a nothin' ball and a bat dodger [*The Sporting News*, September 19, 1956, p.14].

Canadian Highlights: June 6, 1935, in a celebrated matchup with Chet Brewer, Paige fanned 17 in a 0–0 draw between Bismarck and Kansas City Monarchs at Winnipeg. July 17, he pitched Bismarck into the final of the Brandon, Manitoba, tournament with a 4–1 win over Acme Giants. August 5, Paige blanked Devil's Lake 9–0 in the final of the tournament at Portage La Prairie.

August 19, 1942, Paige came in for criticism in Toronto as fans wanted more than his usual three-inning stint. He faced just ten batters striking out four as the Kansas City Monarchs beat the House of David 6–1.

> His whip-like tosses, faultless in control, were heaved with a minimum of effort. The sheer power in that wing was demon-

strated when he donned the catcher's mitt to warm up pitcher Matchett in the fourth. Paige took a toss and without exertion threw a perfect "strike" to the second baseman [*Toronto Star*, August 20, 1942, p.16].

July 1, 1948, Paige cancelled a planned exhibition at Lethbridge, Alberta. It was learned a few days later that he had signed a major league contract with the Cleveland Indians.

May 27, 1950, Ol' Satch pitched three shutout innings in a start for Minot against Carman in ManDak League action. May 30, he allowed just one hit over three innings and fanned seven as Minot topped Brandon 4–3.

April 29, 1956, in his return to organized ball, Paige fired a four-hitter in his debut with Miami. He blanked defending champion Montreal Royals 3–0. June 24, against Toronto, the pitching legend relieved in the first inning with the bases loaded and one out and blanked the Leafs the rest of the way to register his 5th victory. He finished the season with an 11–4 record and 1.86 ERA. Not bad for a 50-year-old.

August 17, 1957, pitching for the Triple-A, Miami Marlins Paige allowed just one hit in 2⅔ scoreless innings to pick up his 8th win as Miami beat the Leafs in Toronto, 6–5 in ten innings.

In 1963, Paige, believed to be 57 years of age, made one of his last barnstorming tours of the prairies. In Brandon on July 21, he pitched the first two innings before handing over mound duties to "Satchel Paige Jr." It was really Sherman Cottingham who returned to Canada in 1964 and 1965 to pitch for the North Battleford Beavers.

Tom "Big Train" Parker—Pitcher, 6'1", 230 lbs. Batted right, threw right

Over a lengthy Negro League career, Parker had success both as a pitcher and hitter. He played Negro ball from 1929 to 1948 with a variety of teams most notably the Homestead Grays. His initial season with a Canadian club was in 1949 with Farnham in the Provincial League in Quebec. In 1951, Parker was with the Elmwood Giants and in 1952 with the Winnipeg Giants. He finished his career in 1953 with the Brandon Greys. Even at age 42, Parker pitched well in his final season winning six games and completing six of eleven starts. In 1951 he batted .429 with 4 home runs in just 42 at bats.

1949 Farnham Pirates—Won 4, Lost 5
1951 Elmwood Giants—Won 5, Lost 2, 10 G, 8 GS, 5 CG, .429, 4 HR, 11 RBI
1952 Winnipeg Giants—Won 5, Lost 3, 55 IP, 25 BB, 43 SO, .265, 1 HR, 7 RBI
1953 Brandon Greys—Won 6, Lost 4, 12 G, 11 GS, 6 CG, .286, 0 HR, 9 RBI

Canadian Highlights: July 2, 1951, Parker joined the Elmwood Giants for a tournament in Brandon, Manitoba. He made a good impression in firing a one-hitter and pitching shutout ball. July 9, he beat the Winnipeg Buffaloes 8–1 and blasted a three-run home run. July 21, Parker fanned ten in beating Carman 2–1. August 16, he beat the Minot Mallards 4–3 and hit a home run and single to help his own cause.

June 23, 1953, Parker pitched all twelve innings in a 1–0 win over the Winnipeg Royals. He gave up only four hits. August 7, he pitched a five-hit, 6–0 shutout over the Minot Mallards.

Jonathan Clyde Parris—Infield, 5'8", 170 lbs. Batted right, threw right

The Panamanian infielder had Negro League experience, 1946 to 1949, with the New York Black Yankees, Louisville Buckeyes and Philadelphia Stars. Parris arrived in Canada in 1951 to join the roster of St. Jean in the Quebec Provincial League. Later, he played five seasons in Montreal, 1955–1959, and one in Toronto, 1960, in the Triple-A, International League. He also spent many years in the Mexican League.

1951 St. Jean, Provincial—.294, 12 D, 0 T, 16 HR, 44 RBI
1955 Montreal, International—.289, 19 D, 4 T, 16 HR, 89 RBI
1956 Montreal, International—.321, 37 D, 0 T, 17 HR, 78 RBI
1957 Montreal, International—.238, 5 D, 0 T, 7 HR, 21 RBI
1958 Montreal, International—.300, 32 D, 6 T, 10 HR, 93 RBI
1959 Montreal, International—.299, 32 D, 0 T, 23 HR, 90 RBI

1960 Toronto, International—.208, 3 D, 0 T, 1 HR, 4 RBI

Canadian Highlights: April 19, 1955, his two-run triple handed Montreal a 2–1 win over Richmond. May 8, Parris belted an 18th inning homer to give the Royals a 5–3 victory at Columbus. August 19, Parris went 4-for-4 in an 8–2 victory over Columbus. August 31, three hits, a homer, double and single from Parris helped the Royals get by the Jets, 5–2.

June 17, 1956, Parris fattened his average during a six-game series with Columbus going 11 for 20 as part of a 16-game hitting streak. He led the International League in batting with a .321 average and was selected to the all-star team. It was his second batting crown in three years having won the Eastern loop title (and MVP award) in 1954.

April 30, 1958, Parris' two-run homer in the 9th provided Montreal with a 4–3 triumph over Miami. May 6, he knocked in four runs as Montreal trounced the Miami nine, 10–4. July 4, he exploded for five hits in a double-header sweep of Buffalo. Parris had three hits in the first game, including a double which drove in the winner in the 9th. He knocked in a pair in the nightcap with a homer and double.

June 24, 1959, he had a day for the scrap book with four hits, four RBI and five runs scored in a 19–5 trouncing of Richmond.

Roy Partlow—Pitcher/Outfield, 6'0", 180 lbs. Batted left, threw left

While Partlow had a solid Negro League career, beginning in 1934, probably he was best known as Jackie Robinson's black teammate on the Montreal Royals of 1946. However, it didn't last long as Partlow pitched in just ten games before being sent to Three Rivers of the Canadian-America League where he compiled a 10–1 record. He returned to Canada to play with the Red Sox of Granby in 1950 and 1951.

1946 Montreal Royals—Won 2, Lost 0, 10 G, 4 GS, 5.59, ERA
1946 Three Rivers Royals—Won 10, Lost 1, 14 G, 11 GS, 3.22, ERA
1950 Granby Red Sox—Won 7, Lost 2, 14 G, 10 GS, 1.96, ERA
1951 Granby Red Sox—Won 8, Lost 3, 16 G, 15 GS, 3.41, ERA

Lauro Pascual—Catcher, 6'0", 190 lbs. Batted right

Pascual was a Cuban player who was among the many imports attracted to the outlaw Mexican League during the late 1940s, a time when the circuit raided the majors for nearly two dozen regulars and sparked the first court challenge to baseball's reserve clause. As the arrangement in Mexico proved to be less than promised, most of the players, who had left organized ball, then jumped to the then independent Quebec Provincial League in 1948–1949 (including Sal Maglie, Max Lanier, Vic Power and Danny Gardella) and Pascual tagged along with them. (Happy Chandler, the commissioner of the majors, had ruled than the players would be banned from organized baseball for five years.) Pascual ended up with Sherbrooke in the Quebec League and displayed excellent catching skills.

1948 Sherbrooke Athletics—.232, 7 D, 1 T, 2 HR
1950 Sherbrooke Athletics—.237, 8 D, 3 T, 2 HR, 38 RBI
1951 Sherbrooke Athletics—.231, 7 D, 0 T, 0 HR, 20 RBI

Andrew "Pat" Patterson—Infield, 5'11", 185 lbs. Batted both, threw right

Patterson's lengthy Negro League career, from 1934 to 1949, included stops with eight teams. He was selected to four all-star squads. In August of 1950, he had a short spin in Canada playing with the Elmwood Giants in the ManDak League. He closed out his career in 1960 with the Detroit–New Orleans Stars. Patterson died in 1984 in Texas. He was 72.

1950 Elmwood Giants—.253, 1 HR, 6 RBI

Gabe Patterson—Outfield/Pitcher. Batted right, threw right

Patterson, who had his debut in the Negro League in 1941, was better known in Canada as a football player. The speedy halfback was an all-star in both 1947 and 1948, leading the league in scoring his first season and finishing just three points off the pace in '48.

In a game that packed thrills from whistle to gun, Patterson stood out as the speediest and trickiest backfielder seen in Calgary since Fritzie Hanson was at his best with Bombers and climaxed a brilliant all-around performance by starting a 110-yard touchdown dash that goes into the books as one of the best individual feats of western grids for many a year [*Winnipeg Free Press*, September 15, 1947].

After military service during the Second World War, Patterson returned to the Negro League with Pittsburgh Crawfords, New York Black Yankees, Philadelphia Stars and Homestead Grays. He combined his diamond exploits with football in Pittsburgh and then in Canada with the Regina Roughriders. In 1948 he took his baseball game to Quebec and the Provincial League. In 1951, he had a brief fling in organized ball in Class-C. He hit .337.

> 1948 Farnham Pirates—.365, 13 D, 1 T, 9 HR, 28 RBI

Dave Pearson—Pitcher. Threw right.

Pearson was a major force both on the mound and at the plate during the two seasons he spent as playing-manager of St. Lazare in the Manitoba Senior League. He hit .440 in 1964 to barely miss the batting title (Gord Lyall was best at .447). In 1965, he finished 6-0 on the hill with 60 strikeouts in 60 innings.

> 1964 St. Lazare Athletics—.440, 20 RBI, Won 4, Lost 6, 12 G, 11 GS, 7 CG
> 1965 St. Lazare Athletics—Won 6, Lost 0, .316, 27 RBI

Canadian Highlights: June 5, 1964, Pearson clouted a two-run homer and a pair of doubles in a win over Souris. July 16, he fired a 7-hit shutout, 1-0 over Brandon. August 11, the right-hander blanked Brandon on five hits and helped the offense with three safeties.

May 15, 1965, in the season opener, Pearson had four hits, a triple and double included, and pitched three shutout innings in relief as St. Lazare scored a 17-0 victory. June 21, Pearson tossed a five-hit shutout in a 3-0 triumph over Souris. July 8, it was a two-hit shutout as St. Lazare whipped Brandon 15-0. July 11, Pearson let his bat do the talking with a grand slam homer, double and single in an 11-7 win over Riverside. In playoff action August 12, he blanked Brandon with a four-hitter.

Frank Pearson—Pitcher, 5'6", 145 lbs. Threw right, batted right

The right-hander had a Negro League career over parts of seven seasons with Memphis Red Sox, New York Black Yankees, New York Cubans and Chicago American Giants. He toured Western Canada at least two summers, 1949 and 1953, with Ligon's All-Stars before returning for a final season with Memphis in 1954.

Canadian Highlights: June 26, 1953, in his second game of the day, Pearson fired a three-hitter as Ligon's All-Stars won top money at the Lacombe Tournament with a 9-2 win over Indian Head in the final. Pearson had earlier gone into the 6th inning as the All-Stars beat Delisle to advance to the final.

Leonard "Lennie" Pearson—First Base/Third Base/Outfield, 6'2", 200 lbs. Batted right, threw right

A five-time Negro League All-Star, Pearson played from 1937 to 1949 with the Newark Eagles, Baltimore Elite Giants and New York Cubans. In 1950, he moved into organized ball in the Boston Braves system playing with the Milwaukee Brewers in the American Association and batting .305. In 1953, he played in Drummondville. He died in 1980 in New Jersey at age 62.

> 1953 Drummondville Royals—.293, 13 D, 1 T, 16 HR, 58 RBI

Maurice "Baby Face" Peatros—First Base/Outfield, 5'11", 210 lbs. Batted left, threw left

Peatros played the 1947 season in the Negro League with the Homestead Grays before a summer in Quebec with Farnham Pirates of the Provincial League. From 1949 to 1952 he played in organized ball at the Class-C level. He returned to the Provincial League in 1953 to play with Drummondville Royals in what was his final season.

> 1948 Farnham, Provincial—Statistics not available
> 1953 Drummondville, Provincial—.290, 2 HR, 17 RBI

Charles "Mule" Peete—Outfield, 5'9½", 190 lbs. Batted left, threw right

Peete started the 1950 season with the Indianapolis Clowns, then jumped to Canada to join the Brandon Greys in the ManDak League. After two years of military service Peete went into organized ball and advanced to the Triple-A level for the 1955 and 1956 seasons. He batted .350 with 16 home runs at Omaha in '56 to win a spot with the St. Louis Cardinals. He made his major league debut with the Cards on July 17, 1956. November 27, he was on his way to Venezuela to play winter ball when he was killed in a plane crash.

>1950 Brandon Greys—.220, 2 HR, 14 RBI

Canadian Highlights: July 6, 1950, Peete had three hits in a 12–5 decision over Minot Mallards. He followed that effort with another three hit game, including a homer, on July 12.

Mario Penalver—Outfield

The Cuban outfielder played for three seasons on the prairies, 1952 with the Florida Cubans and 1953 and 1954 with the Indian Head Rockets. He placed second in doubles in 1954 with 15. In September 1954, Saskatchewan Baseball League president Buck Crawford announced Penalver had been suspended for a year for taking a swing at umpire Ace Corbin during a Rockets' loss to Saskatoon.

>1954 Indian Head Rockets—.241, 15 D, 2 HR, 28 RBI, 11 SB

Canadian Highlights: July 6, 1953, Penalver was the hero driving in the tying and winning runs in the 10th inning, one of three hits, as Indian Head downed Edmonton 5–4 in the final of the Camrose Tournament. June 6, Penalver belted a homer and added a pair of singles to pace Indian Head past Rosetown, 13–6. August 18, the center fielder punched out two doubles and a single, scored three times and drove in a pair to lead the Rockets over Lloydminster, 8–1.

Jim Pendleton—Shortstop/Outfield, 6'0", 190 lbs. Batted right, threw right

Pendleton had a fine 1948 season in the Negro League hitting .301 as the shortstop for the Chicago American Giants. Signed by the Dodgers, he started his organized ball career with St. Paul in the American Association where he stayed for three seasons. Pendleton was assigned to the Montreal Royals for 1952 and traded to the Milwaukee Braves the following year. For the next eight seasons he bounced between the major leagues and Triple-A before closing out his career in 1962 with the Houston Colt 45's. He had a lifetime major league batting average of .255. Pendleton died in 1996 in Texas. He was 72.

>1952 Montreal Royals—.291, 24 D, 14 T, 11 HR, 92 RBI

Canadian Highlights: After a strong season with the Royals, he was selected to the 1952 International League All-Star team at shortstop.

Conrado Perez—Second Base, 5'9", 170 lbs. Batted both, threw right

After five seasons in Mexico, Perez joined the Drummondville Cubs in 1949 and played in the Provincial League for three seasons. From 1952 to 1955 he played in organized ball.

>1949 Drummondville Cubs—.291, 12 HR, 44 RBI
>1950 Drummondville Cubs—.303, 19 D, 3 T, 10 HR, 62 RBI
>1951 Drummondville Cubs—.273, 19 D, 4 T, 21 HR, 87 RBI

Alonzo Perry—First Base/Pitcher, 6'3", 190 lbs. Batted both, threw right

An outstanding hitter and pitcher, Perry was often under-the-radar in the United States and Canada as many of his diamond exploits occurred in Mexico, Puerto Rico, Cuba and the Dominican Republic.

In his early Negro League career (1940, 1945 to 1950) he was known mainly as a pitcher, finishing 10–2 in 1948 and 12–4 in 1949 with the Birmingham Black Barons. As a first baseman-outfielder with the Barons in 1950, Perry began to exhibit his credentials at the plate with a .313 mark in 73 games along with 14 homers and 64 runs batted in. It won him a spot on the West All-Stars. He made two brief forays into organized ball, in 1949 and 1951 both at the Triple-A level.

He started the 1951 season in the United States with the San Francisco Seals of the Pacific Coast League, but just before the regular season began Perry was sent across the country to Syracuse of the International League. After just nine games with the Triple-A club, Perry turned north to join Brandon of Canada's ManDak League. He was outstanding, hitting .389, but after just five weeks he was on the move again as Licey of the Dominican Republic offered a better contract. He earned it, hitting .400 with 9 home runs in just 25 games. Perry spent four years with Licey twice leading the league in homers and runs batted in. In 1955 he shifted to Mexico and the start of a seven-year stretch with Mexico City and Monterrey. His lowest batting average over his Mexican tour was .318 and that came in 1962 when he topped the league in RBI with 105, the fourth time he had led the category. Perry had an amazing 1956 season when he led the Mexican League with a .392 average, 103 runs, 33 doubles, 13 triples, 28 home runs and 188 runs batted in.

Perry played a role in the signing, by the New York Giants, of one of baseball's greatest stars. In June of 1950, New York scout Eddie Montague had been dispatched to Birmingham to take a look at Perry, the Black Barons first baseman, but was more impressed with Perry's teammate and came away with a contract for center fielder Willie Mays.

He was just 59 when he died in Birmingham, Alabama in 1982.

> 1951 Brandon Greys—.389, 5 HR, 20 RBI

Canadian Highlights: May 30, in his first game with Brandon, Perry had three hits including a home run and double and added two walks and three RBI as the Greys downed Elmwood 8–6. In his next game he was even better. Perry had four hits, one an inside-the-park homer, to knock in another three markers as Brandon topped Winnipeg 5–2. June 15, Perry blasted the longest home run recorded at Kinsmen Memorial Stadium in Brandon. The ball cleared the center field fence and the street behind the stadium wall. It was one of four runs batted in for the big first sacker.

Lee Roy Pettus—Catcher/Outfield, 5'10", 165 lbs. Batted right

The young catcher from California spent two seasons with the Estevan Maple Leafs, the 1950 edition of the South Saskatchewan League and the 1951 squad which played in the Western Canada League. Pettus played professional ball in 1952 in the Southwest International League with Yuma Panthers.

> 1950 Estevan Maple Leafs—Statistics not available
> 1951 Estevan Maple Leafs—.291, 13 SB (incomplete)

Canadian Highlights: August 19, 1950, Pettus crushed a double and two singles for Estevan in an exhibition match against Minot Mallards.

June 2, 1951, Pettus had four hits in Estevan's 10–8 win over Regina. July 18, Pettus belted a homer, double and single as Estevan whipped Ligon's All-Stars 18–7 in the opening round of the Indian Head Tournament. August 15, Pettus' double drove in the winning run as Estevan shaded Swift Current 2–1 in the first game of a twin-bill. In the second game, Pettus scored on the front end of a double steal to give the Maple Leafs a 2–2 tie.

Frank Pickens—Pitcher. Threw right

Pickens visited Western Canada in 1950 as he barnstormed with the Louisiana Travelers before joining Minot of the ManDak League for a brief stint. He was back touring in 1952 as the Baton Rouge Hardwoods competed in the Indian Head Tournament. There he caught the notice of the Saskatoon Gems and pitched for the Saskatchewan club for the rest of the summer. He moved on to Regina for 1953 completing 10 of 13 starts and then gave organized pro ball a try for two seasons, fashioning a 20–10, 3.62 season with Midland Indians of the Class-C, Longhorn League in 1954. He returned to semi-pro ball in 1956 with the Jasper, Texas, Steers.

> 1952 Saskatoon Gems—Statistics not available
> 1953 Regina Caps—Won 5, Lost 5

Canadian Highlights: August 17, 1952, Pickens stopped Regina on three hits as Saskatoon posted a 1–0 shutout to square the playoff series at two games each. August 20, Pickens again shutout Regina, this time allowing six-hits in a 6–0 win as the Caps moved into the league final series against North Battleford.

May 31, 1953, Pickens held North Battleford to just five hits in tossing a 4–0 shutout with nine strikeouts. August 5, Pickens fired a three-hitter and allowed no earned runs in a 4–2 win over Saskatoon.

Leonard Pigg—Catcher, 5'9", 230–240 lbs. Batted right, threw right

The stocky catcher was a starter for the Havana La Palomas in 1946 on their tour of Canada. He then played in the Negro League from 1947 to 1949 with the Indianapolis Clowns and Cleveland Buckeyes and was the Negro American League batting champion with a .388 average in '49.

He returned to Manitoba in 1950 to play in Brandon and Roblin, Manitoba, before bouncing back to the Indianapolis Clowns in 1951. He was a star attraction for the Clowns, often used in newspaper advertisements.

> POUNDIN' PIGG—Leonard Pigg, Oklahoma born, and now residing at Seattle, Wash., who led the entire Negro American League in batting in 1949, and last season pounded the pill for a .410 mark at Roblin, Manitoba, Canada, is again whacking the ball solidly for the Indianapolis Clowns this season, with a .378 average, and doing most of the receiving in the Funmakers' drive to retain their first place position in the NAL. Pigg and his full 240 pounds, will be seen in action ... against the mighty Kansas City Monarchs baseball club [*The Cullman Banker*, August 16, 1951, p.3].

Pigg jumped back across the border in 1952 with Roblin and Carman and also played in Canada the following two seasons, in 1953 with Bowsman (Manitoba) Maroons and 1954 in Ontario with St. Thomas in the Intercounty League. He died in 1993 in Seattle a few weeks shy of his 74th birthday.

> 1950 Brandon Greys—.273, 0 HR, 5 RBI
> 1950 Roblin—Statistics not available
> 1952 Roblin/Carman—Statistics not available
> 1953 Bowsman Maroons—Statistics not available
> 1954 St. Thomas—Statistics not available

Canadian Highlights: May 24, 1950, Pigg had two hits, scored three and drove in a pair as Brandon clobbered Minot 12–1 in the Mallards' home opener.

July 19, 1950, The Free Press reported Pigg's catching and stick work led Roblin to a 5–3 victory over the Dauphin Red Birds. Pigg led the way with four hits.

Pigg clouted a grand slam home run on July 9, 1952, as Roblin beat Grandview 13–10.

Francisco "Chico" Pilato—Pitcher

Pilato was a pitcher with the 1954 Indian Head Rockets.

Canadian Highlights: July 26, 1954, Pilato notched his first win with a seven-hit, complete game against Lloydminster. August 11, Pilato allowed just six hits and two unearned runs in a 2–1 loss to Lloydminster. August 18, Pilato pitched both games of a double-header, firing a pair of five-hitters to win, 1–0 and 8–1. The first game went just five innings.

Felix Pine—Pitcher

Pine pitched for the Brooklyn Cuban Giants, a barnstorming team, in 1950. He came to Canada in 1953, fresh from service in the Army, and joined the Carman Cardinals in the ManDak League. In 1954, he returned to Negro ball with the Detroit Stars.

> 1953 Carman Cardinals—Won 1, Lost 2, 5 G, 5 GS, 1 CG

Canadian Highlights: Pine won his first game with the Cardinals on July 29, beating the Minot Mallards 9–4.

Alfred Pinkston—First Base/Outfield, 6'5", 224 lbs. Batted left, threw right

At 6'5", he was an imposing figure at the plate. After a season with New Orleans Creoles, Pinkston played the 1948 season with the Cleveland Buckeyes. He was back barnstorming with the Creoles in 1949–1950 before he joined Farnham in the Quebec Provincial League. He stayed in Canada for three seasons. In 1952, with St. Hyacinthe he won the Triple

Crown in the Provincial League hitting .360 with 30 homers and 121 runs batted in.

In 1959, at age 41, he kicked off a seven year career in Mexico during which he won the batting title four times. In 1960, Pinkston hit .397 and drove in 144 runs with 41 doubles, 11 triples and 26 home runs. Even at age 48, he batted .345 to cap his career. In 1975, he was the first American player to be inducted into the Mexican Baseball Hall Of Fame.

He died in 1981 in New Orleans, LA. He was 63.

- 1951 Farnham Pirates—.301, 32 D, 6 T, 15 HR, 72 RBI
- 1952 St. Hyacinthe A's—.360, 34 D, 4 T, 30 HR, 121 RBI
- 1953 Ottawa Athletics—.198, 6 D, 0 T, 1 HR, 9 RBI

Canadian Highlights: August 9, 1949, Pinkston crushed a three-run homer (veteran observers said it was one of the longest ever hit at Osborne Stadium in Winnipeg) to lead the Creoles to a 10–6 win over Elmwood Giants. August 11, Pinkston clubbed a long homer and added a single as the Creoles topped the Southern League All-Stars 8–4 at Regina.

In 1952 with St. Hyacinthe, Pinkston was the Quebec Provincial League's Triple Crown winner.

Dave Pope—Outfield, 5'10", 170 lbs. Batted left, threw right

Pope played for the legendary Homestead Grays in 1946 as a twenty-one year old. In 1948 and 1949, he came north to play with Farnham in the Quebec Provincial League and had two solid seasons, including a .365, 27 homer season, which led to a contract with the Cleveland Indians. In 1952, he had a "cup of coffee" with the major league club. He was traded to the Baltimore Orioles in 1955 and traded back to the Indians in 1956. After a short stint in 1956, he was back in the minor leagues and closed out his career in 1961 with the Toronto Maple Leafs in the International League. He was the brother of Willie Pope (below).

He died in 1999 at age 78.

- 1948 Farnham Black Sox—.365, 27 HR
- 1949 Farnham Black Sox—.293, 22 HR, 87 RBI
- 1959 Toronto Maple Leafs—.275, 30 D, 3 T, 16 HR, 69 RBI
- 1961 Toronto Maple Leafs—.240, 2 D, 0 T, 2 HR, 5 RBI

Canadian Highlights: May 10, 1959, Pope extended his hitting streak to 15 games with a grand slam homer as the Leafs bested Buffalo 12–10. He belted five homers, five doubles and a triple during the hit spree. Pope hit in 20 straight games before taking a collar.

Willie Pope—Pitcher/Outfield, 6'4", 240 lbs. Batted left, threw right

Previous to his three seasons in the Quebec Provincial League, Pope had Negro League experience with the Homestead Grays in 1947 and 1948. From 1952 to 1955, he continued to play in the minor leagues and pitched as high as Triple-A ball in the American Association.

- 1949 Farnham Black Sox—Won 11, Lost 15
- 1949 Farnham Black Sox—Won 12, Lost 11
- 1950 Farnham Pirates—Won 3, Lost 5, 2.38 ERA
- 1951 St. Hyacinthe Saints—Won 12, Lost 11, 3.32 ERA

Andy "Pullman" Porter—Pitcher, 6'4", 190 lbs. Batted right, threw right

Porter's Negro League career, with nine teams, lasted from 1932 to 1950 when he headed to Canada to join the Winnipeg Buffaloes of the ManDak League. He spent four summers in Canada. In 1951, he was with Eston, Saskatchewan, and the Saskatoon 55s. He suited up with both North Battleford and Carman in 1952 and closed out his career in 1953 with Carman.

- 1950 Winnipeg Buffaloes—Won 4, Lost 5, 11 G, 9 GS, 5 CG
- 1951 Eston Ramblers—Won 2, Lost 0, 2 G, 2 GS, 2 CG
- 1951 Saskatoon 55s—Statistics not available
- 1952 North Battleford—Statistics not available
- 1952 Carman Cardinals—Won 2, Lost 0
- 1953 Carman Cardinals—Won 4, Lost 4, 13 G, 12 GS, 4 CG

Canadian Highlights: June 19, 1950, Porter fired a three-hitter in beating the Minot Mallards 9–1. He followed that with a five-hit, 3–0 shutout on June 24 again against Minot.

June 8, 1951, the right-hander held Saskatoon to five hits in a 2–1 Eston triumph.

Bill Powell — Pitcher, 6'2½", 195 lbs. Batted left, threw right

Powell had five solid seasons in Negro League ball with the Birmingham Black Barons from 1946 to 1950. He was the winning pitcher in the East-West All-Star game in 1948 and also won a spot in the all-star game in 1950 when he finished 15–4, with an ERA of 3.00. His performance won him a contract in the Chicago White Sox system in 1951 where he won 14 games with Class-A, Colorado Springs and advanced to Triple-A. In 1953, he won 14 with Charleston in Triple-A and won a roster spot in Spring Training with the Cincinnati Reds in 1954. He continued to pitch in the Cincinnati, Baltimore and Philadelphia minor league systems through to 1959 when he traveled to Saskatchewan to play for Lloydminster of the Western Canada League. He ended his career in 1963. Powell died in 2004 in Birmingham, Alabama. He was 85.

> 1954 Toronto/Havana — Won 10, Lost 8, 4.23 ERA
> 1959 Lloydminster/N.Battleford — Won 2, Lost 7, G 21, GS 9, CG 3, 4.85 ERA

Victor "Vic" Power (Pellot) — Outfield/First Base, 6'0", 186 lbs. Batted right, threw right

Power, just a few months past his 21st birthday, was one of the younger players when he came to the Quebec Provincial League in 1949 to join the Drummondville Cubs, who at that time were an independent, semi-pro league. He was back again with Drummondville in 1950 when the team went into organized ball. Prior to the start of the 1951 season he was purchased by the New York Yankees.

In spite of three outstanding seasons at the Triple-A level (including the batting title in the American Association in 1954) he couldn't break into the Yankees' all-white lineup. (It wouldn't be until April, 1955 that the Yankees would field a black player.) In December, 1953, the Yanks dealt Power to the Philadelphia A's. The decision drew criticism from blacks and Puerto Ricans who claimed the decision was racially motivated. The Yankees' General Manager, George Weiss, denied the accusations saying the racial question had no bearing on the decision. Weiss had earlier described Power as "not being sufficiently gifted as a fielder to rate a trial with the Yanks." *(The Sporting News, December 30, 1953, p.20)*

He went on to a twelve year major league career with the A's, Indians, Twins, Phillies and Angels ending in 1965. He finished with a .284 average and seven Gold Glove Awards (for fielding excellence) and was selected to the all-star team seven times. Power, who stole only 45 bases in 12 seasons (while getting caught 35 times), tied a major league mark in 1958 when he stole home, twice, in the same game. He was the first Puerto Rican to play in the American League. He died in 2005.

> 1949 Drummondville Cubs — .345, 9 HR, 54 RBI
> 1950 Drummondville Cubs — .334, 14 HR, 105 RBI

Juan Prats — Outfield/Utility

The versatile Prats spent three summers in Canada with the Florida Cubans in 1952 and Indian Head Rockets in 1953 and 1954. He also had a brief stint in pro ball in 1952 and 15 games in the Provincial League in Quebec.

> 1952 Florida Cubans — Statistics not available
> 1952 St. Jean Canadians — .268, 0 HR, 0 RBI
> 1953 Indian Head Rockets — Statistics not available
> 1954 Indian Head Rockets — .212, 3 D, 3 T, 3 HR, 15 RBI, Won 1, Lost 2, 4 G, 3 GS, 3 CG

Canadian Highlights: July 17, 1952, Prats was selected as the all-star left fielder at the Indian Head Tournament.

May 25, 1954, hitting leadoff, Prats had three hits, one of them a triple, as Indian Head fought to a 4–4 tie with Moose Jaw. July 11, Prats, taking a turn on the mound, pitched a seven-hitter and punched out two hits in downing Lloydminster 3–2. In the second game, playing second base, he went three-of-three as the Rockets won 5–4. The following day, at both second base and center field, he had a homer and triple and drove in three runs in a 9–2 victory over North Battleford.

George Bertrand "Bobby" Prescott—
Third Base, 5'11", 180 lbs. Batted right, threw right

Prescott had just turned 20 when he made the trek from Panama to Saskatchewan to begin what would become a 20-year baseball career, including a stint in the major leagues with the Kansas City Athletics. Given that he played for at least 22 teams, it was no surprise that he switched uniforms just a month into his first season. Prescott and countryman Pedro Osorio were brought up to Canada by the team in Sceptre, Saskatchewan (at a cost of $916), but the pair quickly jumped to the Indian Head Rockets.

After his season on the prairies, Prescott signed with the Pittsburgh Pirates. A few years later, he was taken from the Pirates minor league system by the New York Giants. In 1961, the Giants traded him to Kansas City and within the year he was moved to the Dodgers. He did manage a ten-game, "cup of coffee" in the majors with KC.

Prescott had one of his best seasons in 1961 when in hit .301 with 32 home runs and 100 runs batted in with Honolulu of the Pacific Coast League. In the mid 1960s he was one of the most feared sluggers in the Mexican League. Over a five year period, beginning in 1964, he averaged 35 home runs and 109 runs batted in. The Panamanian star finished his career in 1970 in Mexico.

> 1951 Indian Head Rockets—.292 (incomplete)

Canadian Highlights: June 4, 1951, Prescott had four hits, including a two-run homer, driving in five runs to lead Sceptre over Edmonton Oilers, 11–2. July 5, now with Indian Head, Prescott crushed a pair of triples and a single to lead the Rockets by Swift Current 9–5. July 21, he had three hits in the first game and a homer in the second as Indian Head swept a pair from Moose Jaw, 11–2 and 8–6. August 3, Prescott had three hits, including a pair of doubles, to lead the offense as Indian Head topped North Battleford 6–0 in the final of the Tisdale Lions Club Tournament.

Al Preston—Pitcher/Outfield, 6'1", 170 lbs. Batted right, threw right

Preston played in the Negro League from 1943 to 1949 and 1952 with the New York Black Yankees, Chicago American Giants and Pittsburgh Crawfords. He had his first taste of organized ball, in 1947, with the Stamford Bombers in the Class-B, Colonial League. Stamford at the time had five Negro players, the most of any team in organized baseball. In 1950, Preston was a member of the Elmwood Giants entry in the newly formed ManDak League. In 1952, he was with the Chicago American Giants and in 1953 he was back in the ManDak circuit this time with Carman. He died in 1979 in New York City at age 53.

> 1950 Elmwood Giants—Won 2, Lost 2, 4 G, 4 GS, 2 CG
> 1953 Carman Cardinals—Won 4, Lost 5, 16 G, 11 GS, 2 CG

Canadian Highlights: July 3, 1950, in his first start for Elmwood, Preston scattered eight hits and helped his own cause by knocking in two runs as he beat the Winnipeg Buffaloes 8–4.

August 13, 1953, he evened his record at 4–4 with an 8–5 win over the Brandon Greys.

Joe Preston—Pitcher/Outfield

Preston was one of five Negro imports with the Elmwood Giants in 1949 (the others were Homer Chander, Bill Sanders, Arthur Ramsay and Dan Townsend). The 24-year-old was recruited from semi-pro ball in Pennsylvania.

Harold "Hal" Price—Pitcher, 6'1", 160 lbs. Batted left, threw left

The string bean southpaw came to Winnipeg with the touring Twin City Colored Giants in 1948 then decided to stay awhile. "Prince Hal" as he was fondly known in the local press, played for six seasons in Canada and was regarded as one of the best ever hurlers in Manitoba. He spent two summers with the Elmwood Giants (loaned to Brandon for a few tournament appearances), two with Sceptre/

Left-hander Hal Price, "Prince Hal" as he was known, spent six seasons pitching in Western Canada. In 1950, Price, playing for Sceptre, Saskatchewan, appears to be getting some pitching tips from manager Fergie Shields (photograph courtesy Great Sandhills Historical Society, Sceptre).

Swift Current in Saskatchewan and another two in Winnipeg, with the Giants and Royals. George Mahaffy, a Price teammate at Sceptre, remembered him well:

> We hired him away from the St. Louis Black All-Stars. He was recovering from a bullet wound in the leg and he was working in a car wash in St. Louis. He was at a tryout camp of the Chicago Cubs or White Sox and you know how ball players do, they got in a ruckus and somebody shot him. He went home and got traveling with this club and he stayed with us for two years and I tell you he was good [Interview, 2006].

Price had a brief trial in organized ball in 1952 in the Southwest International League with manager Chet Brewer at Porterville, but after a dozen games was back in Canada.

1948 Elmwood/Brandon — Won 4, Lost 7, G 12, GS 10, CG 10
1949 Elmwood/Brandon — Won 14, Lost 8, G 31, GS 18, CG 17 *
1950 Sceptre — Statistics not available
1951 Sceptre — Statistics not available
1951 Swift Current — Won 0, Lost 2, 3 G 2 GS, 2 CG
1952 Winnipeg Giants — Won 10, Lost 5, 153 IP, 70 BB, 130 SO
1953 Winnipeg Royals — Won 4, Lost 2, G 14, GS 10, CG 6

The 1949 numbers include all games — league, playoff, tournament, exhibition

Canadian Highlights: July 7, 1948, Price pitched a four-hitter to beat Brandon 5–4. Four Elmwood errors robbed him of a shutout. July 28, he was the hard-luck loser in a 2–0 loss to Brandon. Price allowed just three hits and fanned twelve.

May 25, 1949, Price had a no-hitter going into the 8th inning, but had to settle for a two-hit effort as Elmwood beat the Vets in Manitoba Senior League action. June 8, Price again came to the rescue for Elmwood, his 8th appearance in the Giants' first ten games. He snuffed out a 6th inning rally for the Vets and scored the winning run. June 20, he shut-out Brandon 6–0 on a one-hitter. Price won both games of a double header on July 22 against the Winnipegs by scores of 5–0 and 7–2. At the conclusion of the 1949 season, Price was picked to the Manitoba Senior League's All-Star team by the Free Press newspaper.

In 1951, at the completion of the Medicine Hat Tournament held on June 18, Price was named to the all-star team. He had fired a four-hitter, allowing just an unearned run as Sceptre downed Indian Head in the final. September 5, playing for the Western Canada Semi-Professional Championship, Price beat the Indian Head Rockets 7–1 with a three-hitter. He came back the next day and pitched all nine innings again beating Indian Head 7–5. The losing pitcher in that game was the great Chet Brewer.

June 24, 1952, Price threw a five-hitter and helped himself by hitting a two-run home run as the Giants beat Minot 8–3. July 16, he pitched all 13 innings in a 1–1 tie, called because of a curfew.

Creon Psome—Pitcher, 6'1", 180 lbs. Threw left

The 20-year-old student from the University of New York came to Moose Jaw in 1954 after earlier experience at Plattsburgh, New York and with the Halifax, Nova Scotia, Cardinals.

> 1953 Halifax Cardinals—Won 6, Lost 2
> 1954 Moose Jaw Mallards—Won 5, Lost 7, 13 G, 12 GS, 6 CG

Canadian Highlights: July 7, 1954, Psome fired a six-hitter to down Lloydminster 3–1. July 17, he allowed just five hits, but lost 3–2 to the Meridians. August 15, the lefty survived eight walks in four-hitting North Battleford in a 4–2 victory.

Isiah "Ike" Quarterman—Catcher, 5'11", 195 lbs. Batted right, threw right

Quarterman, a native of Florida, began his career as a teenager in his hometown of Jacksonville with the Redcaps. In 1950, when he was with the Jacksonville Eagles he came north when the team was hired to represent the Saskatchewan community of Indian Head in tournament and exhibition games.

Drafted into military service during the Korean War, Quarterman played on an Army team with future Hall of Famer Ernie Banks. Back in civilian life, the stocky catcher won a contract with the Braves (who moved from Boston to Milwaukee in 1953). He played with the Class-C, Quebec Braves for two seasons, hitting over .300 both summers. Quarterman settled in Albany, New York in the late 1950s and continued to play in the Albany Twilight League through to the mid 1960s. He was a deacon in the Baptist Church and a Staff Sergeant with the New York Army National Guard.

> 1950 Indian Head Rockets—Statistics not available
> 1953 Quebec Braves—.317, 15 D, 3 T, 3 HR, 43 RBI
> 1954 Quebec Braves—.306, 26 D, 0 T, 2 HR, 49 RBI

Canadian Highlights: June 26, 1950, he scored the tying run on the front end of a double steal as the Rockets fought to a 3–3 draw with Regina in a game called because of darkness. Quarterman paid the price, however, suffering a bruised hip as Regina catcher Gus Kyle, of hockey fame, sent Quarterman flying with a body check in trying to prevent the run from scoring. July 26, the backstop collected three hits in a loss to Swift Current at the Moose Jaw Tournament. August 2, he tripled home George Lipscomb in the bottom of the tenth to give Indian Head a 2–1 victory over Swift Current in opening day action at the Rosetown Tournament. August 16, Quarterman's two-run double was a crucial blow as the Rockets fought to a 6–6 draw with the host club at the Swift Current Tournament.

Patricio Quintana—Shortstop/Third Base, 5'11", 175 lbs. Batted right

The Cuban infielder managed a 14-year career in organized baseball, two years at the Triple-A level with the Havana Sugar Kings. His stops included a half-season with Vancouver of the Pacific Coast circuit. His best season came near the start of his career, in 1952, in the Class-C, Longhorn League, when he hit .322 with 24 home runs.

> 1958 Vancouver Mounties—.214, 9 D, 1 T, 2 HR

Theodore Roosevelt "Double Duty" Radcliffe—Pitcher/Catcher/Manager, 5'10", 190 lbs. Batted right, threw right

Famous sports writer Damon Runyon attached the nickname "Double Duty" to Radcliffe after watching him catch a Satchel Paige shutout in the first game of a doubleheader and then hurl a shutout of his own in the second game.

His versatility served him well in a Negro League career which spanned more than twenty years. Radcliffe appeared in six East-West All-Star games, three as a catcher, three as a pitcher.

In 1951, he came to Canada and joined the Elmwood Giants in the ManDak League as their playing manager, at age 49. In 15 games, he hit .340 and made five appearances on the mound, winning a pair. He was back in 1952, but was replaced in mid-season when Giants got off to a poor start. In 1999, Double Duty became the oldest player in a pro game when, at age 96, he threw a pitch in a Northern League game for the Schaumburg Flyers. He died in 2005 at the age of 103.

> 1951 Elmwood Giants—.340, 0 HR, 13 RBI, Won 2, Lost 0, 5 G, 1 GS, 1 CG
> 1952 Winnipeg Giants—Manager

Canadian Highlights: June 11, 1951, Radcliffe scattered eight hits in a 13–4 waltz over Minot. He fanned eight and walked only three. He helped himself at the plate by hitting two doubles and a single. August 11, he drove in four runs with three doubles and a single in a win over Winnipeg. Later he was handed a "substantial fine," believed to be $50, for an unwarranted attack on umpire Ted Early during the game.

June 11, 1952, just a month shy of his 50th birthday, Radcliffe gave Winnipeg fans a demonstration of how he won his nickname. He began the game catching starter Othello Strong, then, with two on and none out in the 4th inning, he took off his catching gear and moved to the mound. "Double Duty" went $4\frac{2}{3}$ innings, pitching well until a Winnipeg uprising in the 8th. He went 1 for 4 at the plate with one run batted in. Again he faced disciplinary action in 1952 when in a June 16 game with Minot he and the Mallards' Duke Bowman began throwing punches after a play at third. Both players were ejected and fined.

Art Ramsay—Outfield

Ramsay was one of five Negro players in the Elmwood Giants training camp in 1949. The Knoxville, Tennessee, native played the outfield for the 1951 Eston, Saskatchewan, Ramblers.

Jimmy Randolph—Third Base

The third sacker played two seasons in Canada, 1950 with the barnstorming Indian Head Rockets and 1951 with the Regina Caps of the Western Canada League.

> 1951 Regina Caps—.290 (incomplete)

Canadian Highlights: July 21, 1950, Randolph had four hits and drove in a pair as the Rockets won the Indian Head Tournament with a 5–1 win over California Mohawks in the final.

June 1, 1951, Randolph produced two hits, knocked in a pair, scored twice and stole a base in a wild 11–10 win over Estevan. The following night, he had three hits and drove in four markers. June 21, Randolph had three hits in a 4–4 draw with Swift Current in a game called after 11 innings because of darkness. July 11, he had three hits in Regina's 14–8 triumph over Moose Jaw. August 1, Randolph drove in three runs with a double and two singles to lead Regina to an 11–7 win over Medicine Hat in the opener of a double-header.

Hickey Redd—Third Base/Outfield

Redd hailed from Baton Rouge, Louisiana. He played in the Negro League in 1940 and

1941 with the Birmingham Black Barons and in 1946 with the Cincinnati Crescents. Redd moved on to the Harlem Globetrotters in 1948 and, in 1949, came to Canada and joined the Elmwood Giants in the Manitoba Senior League. He was back in 1950 to play for Elmwood in the new ManDak League. Following that summer he returned to the Negro League for the 1951 and 1952 seasons with the Chicago American Giants.

> 1949 Elmwood Giants—Statistics not available
> 1950 Elmwood Giants—.272, 0 HR, 7 RBI

Canadian Highlights: August 1, 1949, Redd had three hits as he led Elmwood to a 3–2 victory over A.N.A.F. Vets.

August 2, 1950, Redd was the top Elmwood batter getting three hits in a 12–3 loss to Brandon

Willie Reed—Second Base

Reed, from the Oakland area, came north to join neighborhood friends Pumpsie Green and Nat Bates with the 1951 Medicine Hat Mohawks and returned to the prairies the following season with the Indian Head Rockets.

> 1951 Medicine Hat Mohawks—.287, 13 SB (incomplete)
> 1952 Indian Head Rockets—Statistics not available

Canadian Highlights: June 15, 1951, Reed had two doubles and a single, scored three runs and stole a base as the Mohawks whipped Indian Head 14–4. June 27, in a twin bill sweep over Estevan, Reed had a triple, two runs batted in, three runs scored and two stolen bases in the 18–6 win in the opener and a double and single, two more runs driven in, and two stolen bases in the 5–0 triumph in the second game. June 29, Reed, hitting leadoff, had three hits and scored a pair as Medicine Hat fought to a 5–5 tie with Indian Head. July 25, he had two hits, two stolen bases and scored three runs as Mohawks clubbed Estevan 11–1.

Time and again, Reed won plaudits for his outstanding defensive play. He was selected as the all-star second baseman at the Medicine Hat and Indian Head tournaments in 1951 and 1952.

Leopoldo Reyes—Shortstop/Third Base/Outfield

The Cuban-born Reyes was a regular for four seasons in Western Canada with four teams, beginning with the Florida Cubans in 1952 when he was described as the property of the Pittsburgh Pirates. He was at the center of one of the much recalled stories from 1950s baseball, the "Rosetown Riot" of 1952. On July 31, Reyes was beaned with a baseball bat and sent to hospital in a fracas which broke out at the Rosetown Tournament and which required the intervention of the Royal Canadian Mounted Police. Early in the 1953 season he was acquired by the Saskatoon Gems for whom he played in 1954 before wrapping up his Canadian career with North Battleford in 1955.

> 1952 Florida Cubans—Statistics not available
> 1953 Indian Head/Saskatoon—.336
> 1954 Saskatoon Gems—.263, 11 D, 0 T, 1 HR, 24 RBI
> 1955 North Battleford Beavers—.271, 16 D, 1 T, 2 HR, 26 RBI

Canadian Highlights: July 17, 1952, Reyes was selected as the all-star third baseman at the 16-team Indian Head Tournament.

June 14, 1953, Saskatoon acquired Reyes from the Indian Head Rockets. June 25, his three hits paced Saskatoon to a 5–1 exhibition win over Minot. July 2, Reyes had three safeties as Saskatoon topped Moose Jaw, 7–4. July 11, Reyes punched out two doubles and a single, drove in a pair and scored once on a steal of home to pace the Gems, 9–3 over Regina. He finished 5th in batting with a .336 mark.

June 1, 1954, Reyes beat out three infield hits as Saskatoon beat Moose Jaw 10–7. June 4, Reyes had three singles in four trips to the plate in the Gems' 4–1 loss to Indian Head. June 17, Reyes belted a homer and single as the Gems tied Moose Jaw 7–7. July 4, Reyes had six hits in a twin-bill as Saskatoon split with North Battleford. July 19, Reyes drove in three runs with four hits, two of them doubles, as the Gems lost a 12-inning affair to Lloydminster in the opening game of the Saskatoon Exhibition Tournament. August 24, Reyes had three hits as Saskatoon blanked Indian Head 6–0 to win the semi-final series. September 7, Reyes punched out two doubles and two singles to lead the Gems to a 2–1 playoff victory over North Battleford. The next night, Reyes had three hits as the Gems won 5–1.

Harry "Lefty" Rhodes—Pitcher, 5'9", 169 lbs. Batted left, threw left

Rhodes pitched in the Negro League in 1942 and from 1946 to 1950 with the Chicago American Giants. In 1952, he accepted an offer from the Carman Cardinals in the ManDak League and had two successful seasons in Carman.

> 1952 Carman Cardinals—Won 3, Lost 3, 48 IP, 32 BB, 16 SO
> 1953 Carman Cardinals—Won 8, Lost 4, 26 G, 3 GS, 2 CG

Canadian Highlights: August 15, 1952, Rhodes pitched the first eight innings in a thirteen inning win over Brandon and helped the offense with three hits, including a pair of homers.

June 13, 1953, he pitched and batted Carman to a 9–2 victory over Moose Jaw in an interlocking game. Rhodes drove in three runs with a home run and triple.

John Richardson—Second Base

Richardson played the 1949 and 1950 seasons with the Homestead Grays. In 1951, he crossed the border to join the Brantford Red Sox in the Intercounty League in Canada. He played only a half season and returned to the United States.

Ted Richardson—Pitcher/Outfield, 5'6", 150 lbs. Batted left, threw left

The pint-sized lefty was just 17 when he began playing Negro League ball in 1951 with the Indianapolis Clowns. Over the next five years he spent the bulk of his time in the Negro circuit with the Clowns although he also suited up in the semi-pro ranks for parts of two seasons with St. Joseph, Michigan, Auscos.

In 1955, he helped pitch the Auscos to the Michigan semi-pro title and a fourth place finish at the national semi-pro tournament at Wichita. Attracting the attention of major league scouts, Richardson signed with the Detroit Tigers and pitched over three seasons in the Tigers' farm system (in 1957, Richardson

The little lefty, 5'6", 150 lbs, was an ace with the Indianapolis Clowns of the Negro League before a successful stint in pro ball and four years in Canada (photograph from the Mah collection).

and third baseman Bubba Morton were the first black players in the history of the Durham Bulls of the Carolina League). He was 10–9, with a 2.00 ERA in 1957 with Orlando in the Florida State League and 5–1, 1.94 in 1958 with Idaho Falls in the Pioneer League.

He left pro ball in 1959 to play for the Lloydminster, Saskatchewan, Meridians. Richardson's 9 wins in '59 were second best in the league and he tied for the top spot in 1960 with 11 victories. He was the runner-up in ERA with a 2.93 mark. His six straight wins in August helped the Meridians to their first league pennant.

Richardson died in May, 1974. He was just 45 years of age.

> 1959 Lloydminster/N.Battleford—Won 9, Lost 7, G 23, GS 18, 10 CG, 3.64 ERA
> 1960 Lloydminster Meridians—Won 11, Lost 5, G 21, GS 12, 10 CG, 2.93 (2nd)
> 1961 Lloydminster/Medicine Hat—Statistics not available
> 1962 Neilburg Monarchs—Statistics not available

Canadian Highlights: July 9, 1959, Richardson allowed just four hits as the Combines

Date: 5-20-59
Name: Theodore Richardson
Born in: Gainesville State: Florida
On: Dec. 15, 1933 Height: 5'6" Weight: 150
Playing Position: Pitcher Bat: Left Throw: Left
Date of Marriage and to whom: ....
Player's Nickname: Ted How did you acquire nickname? Short for First Name
Ancestry (check): English.... French.... German.... Hebrew.... Irish....
Italian.... Polish.... Slavic.... Other: Negro
Color of Hair: Black Color of eyes: Brown
Hobby or Hobbies: Billiards Name pronounced: ....
If a graduate of preparatory school, junior college or college, list name of institution, the years attended or when graduated and degree received: None

Address during off-season: 821 McFall St, Orlando, Fla.
Position during winter months: Masonry Work
Baseball Experience (list clubs and years, along with records): Indianapolis Clowns '53 & '4) Detroit Tigers Farm System, 1955 thru 1958) Jackie Robinson During off season with Clowns '53 & '54

If in military service—Date joined: Not in Service
Date Discharged: —— Rank: ——
Branch of service: ....
What do you consider your outstanding performance in baseball? Pitched two no hitters with the Jackie Robinson All Stars in Mexico

Note: Give full name, and be definite about "baseball experience".

Ted Richardson was listed at 21 years of age when he won a pro contract with Detroit in the fall of 1955. When he joined Lloydminster in 1959, he continued with that version of history on the player form he filled out for the club. Like many players he had shaved off a few years—in this case five years—in an effort to be more marketable (image from the Mah Collection).

downed Edmonton. July 27, he pitched a six-hitter and hit a homer as Lloydminster–North Battleford topped Regina 5–1. August 3, the little lefty held Williston to five hits and fanned fourteen in a 10–3 win. He helped the offense with a two-run homer. August 16, Richardson fired ten shutout frames, but came away with no decision as the Combines and Regina battled to a scoreless tie in 12 innings. August 20, he had a two-hitter in a 4–1 win over Williston. September 5, his five-hit shutout against Regina kept the Combines alive in playoff action.

July 7, 1960, in an uncharacteristic outing, Richardson allowed twenty hits, but staggered to the end in a 19–15 win for the Meridians over Saskatoon. August 12, he fired a two-hit shutout in Lloydminster's 1–0 win over Saskatoon. August 16, Richardson worked two scoreless innings in relief to win the first of a twinbill then tossed a three-hitter in the nightcap to collect his second win of the day in 2–1 and 3–2 triumphs over Calgary.

June 3, 1962, Richardson, pitching for Neilburg in the Northern Saskatchewan League, hurled a two-hit shutout over Unity.

T.W. Richardson—Pitcher

Richardson left the Birmingham Barons of the Negro League early in the 1952 season to pitch for Brandon Greys in Canada's ManDak League. He was a solid contributor for Brandon, taking five of seven decisions. It appears he returned to the Barons at the end of the Greys' season for the Negro League playoffs.

1952 Brandon Greys—Won 5, Lost 2, 12 G, 7 GS, 4 CG

Canadian Highlights: July 3, 1952, Richardson fired a three-hitter, allowing just one earned run, in a Brandon win over Winnipeg. August 12, fresh from a 3–1 victory over Carman on August 10, T.W. allowed just five hits as Brandon topped Winnipeg 5–1.

Bill Ricks—Pitcher, 6'1", 190 lbs. Batted right, threw right

Ricks was a pitching stalwart in his early years with the Philadelphia Stars. In 1944, he went 10–4 and led the league in strikeouts and, in 1945, won a spot on the East team for the East-West All-Star game. Midway through the 1949 season he left the Stars and signed with Fort Wayne General Electrics of the Michigan-Indiana League. In 1951, in his lone season in Canada, Ricks pitched for Granby in the Provincial League.

1951 Granby Red Sox—Won 8, Lost 8, 4.21 ERA

Marshall Riddle—Infield, 5'8". Batted right, threw right

Riddle played in Negro ball from 1937 to 1943, playing in the 1940 East-West All-Star game. Riddle next shows up in 1951 when he signed up with Three Rivers in the Quebec Provincial League.

1951 Three Rivers Royals—.238, 0 HR, 18 RBI

Modie Lee Risher—First Base/Catcher/Outfield. Batted right, threw right

Risher, a boyhood chum of Curly Williams, played Negro ball in South Carolina and Florida with the Lakeland Tigers, Charleston Black Sox and Jacksonville Eagles, among others. While Williams went on to the Negro League, Risher went to college and became an icon in his hometown of Charleston, SC for his work as an educator and coach. In 2007, Risher was inducted into the Charleston Baseball Hall of Fame. The previous year, the Charleston County Council voted to name the Burke High School Gymnasium in honor of Risher, a former three-sport star at Burke and, for decades, the school's football, baseball and basketball coach and athletic director. In 2004, he was inducted into the Charleston River Dogs Hall of Fame for his service to the African-American community. He played one season in Western Canada with the Lloydminster Meridians in 1957.

> Lloydminster? In my life that was the nicest year I ever had in baseball. Do you remember the McLeans? I never met anybody like them. I was in the store one day and Rod and his mother were there, you know Rod was just a young boy. He said, "Momma, look at that man, doesn't he

have a beautiful tan." And his mother was a little halfway embarrassed. The next thing I knew the father called me and they had me over for dinner that Sunday and from them on I used to be in their house all the time. The people in Lloydminster were so wonderful I will never forget them. Because they looked at you as a person, we didn't have any problems there and no where we went in Canada [Interview 2001].

1957 Lloydminster Meridians—.243, 2 HR, 21 RBI

John Ritchey—Catcher, 5'10", 170 lbs. Batted left, threw right

Ritchey had quite a debut in the Negro League. In 1947, his first and only season, he hit .378 to win the batting title. He left the Chicago American Giants after that summer as his performance opened a door to an opportunity in organized ball.

He was at San Diego State College (studying law and social services) when noticed by a scout for the Triple-A, San Diego Padres. He moved right into the Pacific Coast League, hitting .323 in his initial season in organized ball. He stayed in the PCL for three seasons before moving on to Vancouver in the Western International League in 1951. He had two solid seasons with the Capilanos before returning to action in Triple-A. With Vancouver, Ritchey led the league with a .346 batting average and was selected to the all-star team in 1951. In 1952, he batted .343 and again was an all-star.

He died in 2003 at the age of 80.

1946 Vancouver Capilanos—.346, 26 D, 5 T, 7 HR, 86 RBI
1947 Vancouver Capilanos—.343, 24 D, 8 T, 2 HR, 76 RBI

Bill Rivers—First Base

Rivers was believed to be a recent college graduate before he joined Regina Caps of the Saskatchewan League for 1953.

Canadian Highlights: May 17, 1953, Rivers had four hits in a losing effort to North Battleford. June 11, he drove in three runs with a double and single as Regina dumped Saskatoon 12–6. June 28, Rivers accounted for all of Regina's scoring with a two-run homer. August 22, Rivers' three-run homer in the first inning was the key blow as Regina topped Saskatoon 7–1.

Curt Roberts—Second Base, 5'8", 165 lbs. Batted right, threw right

After four years in the Negro League with the Kansas City Monarchs, Roberts began a 13-year stint in organized ball, reaching the major leagues with Pittsburgh in 1954 as the first Afro-American to play with the Pirates. He played in 171 games in the majors over three seasons, hitting just .223. He spent most of his time in Triple-A, putting up solid batting marks until his retirement in 1963. He was the MVP of the Montreal Royals in 1959.

Roberts was killed in 1969 when hit by a car while trying to change a tire on his own vehicle. He was just 40.

1959 Richmond/Montreal—.296, 34 D, 1 T, 11 HR, 56 RBI
1960 Montreal Royals—.308, 1 D, 0 T, 1 HR

May 31, 1959, Roberts belted a grand slam homer to lead Montreal by Buffalo 10–6. June 24, Roberts went 3-for-3, including an inside-the-park homer, and drove in six runs as Montreal destroyed Richmond 19–5. August 10, he was named to the International League All-Star Team.

Earl Robinson—Outfield, 6'1", 190 lbs. Batted right, threw right

Robinson was a baseball and basketball star at the University of California before a pro career in which he played in the major leagues with Los Angeles Dodgers and Baltimore Orioles. He played in 21 games with Montreal in 1958.

1958 Montreal Royals—.161, 1 D, 2 T, 0 HR, 4 RBI

Eloyd Robinson, Jr.—Third base/Shortstop/Second Base, 5'11", 180 lbs. Batted right, threw right

As an 18-year-old, Robinson was signed by the Brooklyn Dodgers in 1951, but things didn't work out and he ended up joining the independent Indian Head Rockets for the 1952 season. From that experience he won a contract in the St. Louis system. He was the third black player to be signed by the Cardinals (Western Canada star, Len Tucker, had been the first black player signed St Louis while Tom Alston another Indian Head player, was the first to reach the majors).

Robinson gave pro ball a whirl for three summers (a portion of one of them in Winnipeg) before returning to semi-pro ranks in 1956. He was back in Canada in 1958 with Saskatoon (adding some playoff action with Medicine Hat of the Southern Alberta League). He even offered to play for nothing if he didn't hit at least .300. (Winnipeg Free Press, May 27, 1958) He batted .320 in 1958 and .303 the following season.

  1952 Indian Head Rockets—Statistics not available
  1955 Winnipeg Goldeyes—.169, 0 HR, 7 RBI
  1958 Saskatoon Commodores—.320, 13 D, 3 T, 7 HR, 43 RBI
  1958 Medicine Hat Superiors—Statistics not available
  1959 Saskatoon Commodores—.303, 13 D, 2 T, 6 HR, 44 RBI

Canadian Highlights: July 3, 1958, Robinson drove in six runs with two homers, a double and single in an 11–7 Saskatoon win over Lloydminster–North Battleford Combines. July 7, Robinson had three hits and scored four times as Saskatoon beat Regina 7–1. After Saskatoon was bounced in the Western Canada playoffs, he joined Medicine Hat for Southern Alberta playoff action. He excelled. Robinson knocked in four runs with a homer and single in a 17–4 win over Vauxhall August 25 and followed up on August 28 with a two-run homer in a 6–3 win over Lethbridge. He had a homer September 6, three hits the next day, and a double and single on September 9 as the Superiors won the league title.

The Indian Head Rockets went back to barnstorming after the 1951 season when the team won 22 games in a row en route to the Western Canada League pennant. The 1952 club stuck to exhibitions and tournaments. Standing (left to right)—**John Jones UT, Emmett Neal 1B, Hiram Marshall UT, Nat Bates RHP, Eloyd Robinson SS, Horace Latham UT, Adair Ford C, Charlie McMillar P, Andy Porter RHP, Jim Williams (Manager). Front—Percy Trimont OF, Winters Calvin OF, Pumpsie Green 3B-C, Willie Reed 2B, Toribio Leal LHP, Orlando Garcia P, Joseph Brooks P-OF (photograph courtesy Ken McCabe, Indian Head Sports Hall of Fame and Museum).**

June 22, 1959, Robinson pounded four hits as Saskatoon topped Regina 4–0. June 27, Robinson belted three doubles in an 8–6 win over Edmonton. July 5, Robinson's three-run homer wasn't enough in an 8–5 loss to Edmonton. July 10, Robinson led Saskatoon with three hits in a 5–2 win over Williston. July 22, Robinson had a triple and two singles as Saskatoon blanked Regina 6–0. August 8, Robinson's grand slam homer was the telling blow as Saskatoon roared back from a 5–0 deficit to down the Combines 14–10. August 12, Robinson clubbed a two-run homer, triple and three singles as the Commodores whipped Williston 10–0. August 14, he belted a three-run homer in a 15–4 win over the Combines. August 17, Robinson bashed three doubles and a single in a loss to Regina. August 25, 1959, Robinson had another grand slam homer in a losing cause against Williston.

Frazier "Slow" Robinson—Catcher, 5'11", 178 lbs. Batted right, threw right

In the 1930s, Robinson got his start in the Texas-Oklahoma-Louisiana League with the Tulsa Blackballers, Abilene Eagles and Odessa ball clubs. In 1941, he played in the Baltimore area for the Sparrows Point Giants. Then it was on to the Negro League from 1942 to 1949 with the Baltimore Elite Giants and Kansas City Monarchs. He was a good defensive catcher and a fair hitter.

In 1950, he joined his friend and Winnipeg Buffaloes' manager Willie Wells in the ManDak League. Robinson played two seasons for the Buffaloes. In 1952, he closed out his career in the ManDak League with the Brandon Greys. Wells had become the Greys manager and Robinson's brother Norm was also on the Greys.

His career is well chronicled in his book *Catching Dreams: My Life in the Negro Baseball*

Winnipeg Buffaloes captured the championship in the inaugural season of the ManDak League. With a few cameo appearances by local players, the Buffs featured an all-black lineup, including two—Willie Wells Sr. and Leon Day—selected to the National Baseball Hall of Fame at Cooperstown and another, John Kennedy, who was the first black player in the history of the Philadelphia Phillies. Seated in front—Frazier Robinson C (left), Spoon Carter RHP (right). Standing (left to right)—Lyman Bostock 1B, Hutch Hutchinson Batboy, John Kennedy SS, Jim Newberry RHP, Sam Hill OF, Stanley Zedd (Owner), Andy Porter RHP, Jack Hector (team official), Taylor Smith RHP, Willie Wells Sr. MGR, Butch Davis OF, John Britton 3B, Joe Taylor C, Willie Wells Jr. INF, Percy Howard C/OF, Leon Day RHP (photograph courtesy the Archives of Manitoba).

Leagues. He died in 1997 in North Carolina. He was 87. His wife Winnie said her husband was a lifelong friend of Satchel Paige.

> 1950 Winnipeg Buffaloes—.278, 0 HR, 9 RBI
> 1951 Winnipeg Buffaloes—.318, 1 HR, 37 RBI
> 1952 Brandon Greys—.253, 0 HR, 13 RBI

Canadians Highlights: July 19, 1950, Robinson hit three doubles in a 5–4 win over Minot Mallards.

July 28, 1951, Robinson had three hits, including a home run, in a victory over Carman Cardinals

Humberto Robinson—Pitcher, 6'1", 155 lbs. Batted right, threw right

Robinson began his pro career in Canada in 1951 and 1952 with Farnham, Three Rivers, and Quebec City in the Quebec Provincial League. He won a contract with the Milwaukee Braves and advanced to the major league club in 1955 becoming the first Panamanian player to make the majors. From 1955 to 1960, he pitched in the major leagues with the Braves, Cleveland Indians and Philadelphia Phillies. Robinson also spent a season in Toronto with the Triple-A, Maple Leafs. He finished his major league career with an 8–13 won-lost record.

> 1951 Farnham Pirates—Won 17, Lost 13, 3.39 ERA
> 1952 Three Rivers/Quebec—Won 12, Lost 8, 2.96 ERA
> 1957 Toronto Maple Leafs—Won 18, Lost 7, 2.95 ERA

Jack (Jackie) Roosevelt Robinson—Second Base/First Base, 5'11½", 190 lbs. Batted right, threw right

Robinson, the first Afro-American in baseball's modern era, faced incredible pressures as a role model. Nonetheless, perhaps because of it, he excelled. He made a sensational debut. In his first game, Robinson drove in four runs with a three-run homer and three singles (two of the bunt variety) and stole two bases as the Montreal Royals scored a 14-1 opening day victory. On the season, he led the league in hitting with a .349 average, scored the most

April 10, 1947, during the 5th inning of a Spring Training game against Montreal, its Triple-A farm team, the Dodgers quietly circulated news of a roster move. The statement read, "The Brooklyn Dodgers today purchased the contract of Jackie Roosevelt Robinson from the Montreal Royals." It was signed by Dodger President, Branch Rickey. The following day, Robinson drove in three runs against the Yankees in his first game as a Dodger (photograph courtesy the National Baseball Hall of Fame Library, Cooperstown, N.Y.).

runs, 113, and was second in stolen bases, with 40.

As the league's top drawing card, Robinson led the Royals to the International League title and the Junior World Series championship in a matchup with Louisville of the American Association. Down two games to one, Montreal charged back at Delorimier Stadium to win three in a row to capture the Triple-A title.

> No team could have received a more riotous, yet whole-hearted, ovation at the finish of the series.... Never previously in the ball yard was there such a demonstration. The pennant celebrations in 1935 and in 1942 were mild in comparison.
>
> Dowager and debutante, millionaire and mechanic paid fitting tribute to a good ball club—the best in the wide sweep of the higher minor leagues. 'We want Robinson,

we want Robinson,' came the chant from the throng which refused to leave the place. First came [Manager Clive] Hopper, then came [winning pitcher Curt] Davis for a parade on the shoulders of the milling mob.

Then came Robinson, the colored comet, and before they sat him down tears slid down his cheeks. Jackie was deeply moved by the tribute [*The Sporting News*, October 16, 1946, p.17–18].

In 1947, Robinson was the National League's Rookie of the Year in a Hall of Fame Career which saw him selected to six all-star teams. He was the National League's Most Valuable Player in 1949. In 1962, Robinson was inducted into the Hall of Fame.

Robinson began to gain state-wide attention as an outstanding, four-sport athlete (football, baseball, basketball and track) at Pasadena Junior College. National recognition followed as he starred at UCLA, as national long jump champion, honorable mention as a football All-American, conference scoring leader and MVP in basketball and, a spot on the Bruins baseball team.

Ironically, baseball was his worst sport at college (he hit just .097). In one of the few times he received baseball notice in the press was when he was called in to pitch in a slugfest with the University of California Bears. As far as is known, Robinson's pitching career consisted of two wild pitches.

Robinson played pro football and basketball before joining the Army in 1942.

In 1945, Robinson played in his only season in the Negro League as shortstop for the Kansas City Monarchs, hitting .345.

> Jackie is considered the peer of all Negro shortstops and is a drawing card to rate with the immortal Satchel Paige [*Chester Times*, July 16, 1945, p.10].

Little did he know that he was Branch Rickey's choice to integrate major league baseball. Rickey had carefully cloaked his intention by establishing a new Negro League with the Brooklyn Brown Dodgers to play out of Ebbets Field. Even Dodger scouts were told they were evaluating Negro players for the Brown Dodgers. Rickey not only wanted a superior baseball talent, but a person of such character that he could withstand the hostility that was sure to come.

October 23, 1945, the ruse was over as Robinson's signing with Montreal was officially announced. His impact was unprecedented.

April 15, 1997, 50 years after his debut with Brooklyn, Major League Baseball announced that number 42, Jackie's uniform number, would be retired throughout both the major and minor leagues.

He died in 1972 at the age of 53.

> 1946 Montreal Royals—.349, 25 D, 8 T, 3 HR, 66 RBI, 113 R, 40 SB

Norm Robinson—Outfield. Batted right, threw right

In 1938, Robinson played for a Negro team in Texas called the Black Spiders. The following season he was on the road with the Satchel Paige All-Stars. In 1940, he won a spot in the Negro League and played until the early 1950s with the Baltimore Elite Giants and Birmingham Black Barons. Once the center fielder for the Barons, he made way for a young phenom by the name of Willie Mays. Robinson came to Canada in 1952 and joined his brother Frazier with the Brandon Greys in the ManDak League. In 1953, he closed out his career with the Carman Cardinals also in the ManDak League.

> 1952 Brandon Greys—.276, 9 D, 5 T, 1 HR, 27 RBI
> 1953 Carman Cardinals—.325, 9 D, 0 T, 1 HR, 35 RBI

Canadian Highlights: Robinson led Carman at the plate with four singles on June 7, 1953, as they beat Brandon Greys 5–3. July 3, Robinson had three hits in a Cardinals victory over the Winnipeg Royals.

Ray Robinson—Pitcher 6'2", 208 lbs. Batted right, threw right

Robinson played for the Newark Eagles, Cincinnati Buckeyes and Philadelphia Stars in a career that ran from 1938 to 1947. He joined Thetford Mines Miners for just two games in 1955, before leaving for Aberdeen in the Northern League. He closed out his career in 1956 in organized ball with Texas City in the Big State League

1955 Thetford Mines Miners—Won 0, Lost 1

Rogers Robinson—Outfield, 5'9", 160 lbs. Batted left, threw left

After a stint with the Class-D, Wytheville Cardinals in 1957, Robinson joined the Winnipeg Goldeyes Class-C team for the 1958 and 1959 seasons. He ended up spending eleven years in the Cardinals farm system, retiring in 1969 with Double-A, Arkansas. He reached Triple-A for brief appearances in 1961 and 1964.

1958 Winnipeg Goldeyes—.297, 22 D, 3 T, 10 HR, 60 RBI
1959 Winnipeg Goldeyes—.323, 27 D, 7 T, 15 HR, 83 RBI

Canadian Highlights: August 6, 1958, the Winnipeg Free Press reported Robinson had excelled in the fielding department in the Goldeyes' 6-3 loss to the Grand Forks Chiefs. He made two sensational catches and doubled off a runner at first base. Robinson also doubled and singled at the plate.

June 1, 1959, as the Goldeyes beat Grand Forks 13-2, Robinson led the attack with a home run, two-run triple and a single in five at bats.

O.B. Robison—Pitcher. Threw left

Robison joined the Winnipeg Buffaloes late in the 1951 season and pitched with some success. He had come to Winnipeg after pitching for the Hardwood Sports team out of Baton Rouge, Louisiana. He returned to the Sports in 1952 when the club came to Western Canada for the famous Indian Head Tournament. Robison was selected to the All-Star team after helping the club reach the tourney finals.

1951 Winnipeg Buffaloes—Won 4, Lost 2, 6 G, 6 GS, 3 CG

Canadian Highlights: August 11, 1951, Robison fired a six-hitter as Winnipeg clobbered Elmwood 16-2. August 16, Robison pitched a one hit 2-1, victory over Elmwood. September 1, in a semi-final playoff game, he fired a three-hitter as the Buffaloes walked all over the Minot Mallards, 11-0. September 7, he pitched Winnipeg to a berth in the league final with a 5-2 win over Minot.

Fernando "Freddy" Rodriguez—Pitcher, 6'0", 180 lbs. Batted right, threw right

The Cuban right-hander was a testament to determination. He pitched for 13 seasons before getting an opportunity in the major leagues. Rodriguez managed to suit up for 8 games in the majors, without a win. He began in Class-D in 1945 in the Appalachian League with Kingsport. Over the years he set down in Williamsport, Havana, Pensacola, Sherman-Denison, Big Spring, Abilene, Midland, Greenville, Minneapolis, Dallas, Buffalo, Chicago, Portland, Montreal, Philadelphia, St. Paul and Mexico City.

1959 Buffalo/Montreal—Won 3, Lost 7, 3.69, ERA

Hector Rodriquez—Third base/Shortstop, 5'8", 165 lbs. Batted Right, Threw Right

The Cuban infielder was 30 years old by the time the Dodgers purchased his contract from Almendares of the Cuban Winter League. Assigned to Montreal for the 1951 season, Rodriguez played seven summers in Canada at the Triple-A level in a career which spanned 15 years AFTER his play in Cuba, Mexico, Venezuela and one season (1944) in the Negro League with the New York Cubans. When he joined Montreal, General Manager Guy Moreau said Rodriguez knew only three words of English, "I got it."

He was named Rookie of the Year and an all-star in the International League in his first year in organized ball. He was third in voting for the Most Valuable Player award.

His reward was a trade to the White Sox with whom he put in his only season in the major leagues, hitting .265 in 1952. From 1954 to 1959, Rodriguez was a key member of the Toronto Maple Leafs of the International League. After two more Triple-A seasons, this time in the Pacific Coast League, he returned to Mexico to finish his career. He continued to play until 1966 and managed until 1976.

1951 Montreal Royals—.302, 28 D, 9 T, 7 HR, 95 RBI, 25 SB
1954 Toronto Maple Leafs—.307, 22 D, 3 T, 4 HR, 43 RBI

1955 Toronto Maple Leafs—.289, 31 D, 8 T, 9 HR, 57 RBI
1956 Toronto Maple Leafs—.273, 17 D, 3 T, 4 HR, 40 RBI
1957 Toronto Maple Leafs—.288, 19 D, 7 T, 2 HR, 62 RBI
1958 Toronto Maple Leafs—.228, 11 D, 2 T, 3 HR, 34 RBI
1959 Toronto Maple Leafs—.256, 16 D, 3 T, 6 HR, 30 RBI

Canadian Highlights: In the 1951 vote for Rookie of the Year, Rodriguez topped teammate Jim Gilliam by one vote.

September 10, 1954, he belted an inside-the-park grand slam homer as Toronto creamed Rochester 15–2. It was the only grand slam all season for the Leafs at home.

In 1957, Rodriguez was the runner-up to Mike Baxes of Buffalo for Most Valuable Player in the International League.

In his seven seasons in the International circuit, Rodriguez was on four pennant winners and finished a half-game out on another occasion.

Ramon Rodriquez—Catcher, 6'1", 210 lbs. Threw right

The Cuban receiver was just beginning his baseball career when he came to Manitoba in 1949 to play for the Brandon Greys. He was a rarity for a catcher, a speed demon on the base paths. He led the team in steals in 1949 with 54 in 100 games. Rodriguez was the Greys main backstop for three seasons. He went on to a six year minor league career, winding up in Mexico in 1960.

1949 Brandon Greys—.313, 33 D, 10 T, 3 HR, 87 RBI, 54 SB, Won 1, Lost 0 *
1950 Brandon Greys—.257, 1 HR, 31 RBI
1951 Brandon Greys—.269, 2 HR, 23 RBI

1949 statistics include all games—league, playoff, tournament, exhibition.

Canadian Highlights: June 4, 1949, Rodriquez hit a two-run triple in the fourteenth inning that gave Brandon a 7–5 victory over the Winnipegs. June 18, the speedy catcher stole home with the winning run in a 3–2 win over the Vets. August 24, he stole home in a 6–5 victory over Carman. September 7, in a rare pitching assignment, he hurled an 11–0 shutout over the St. Louis Black Cardinals and helped himself at the plate with three hits. At the end of the 1949 season, Rodriquez was picked as the league's all-star catcher, by the Winnipeg Free Press newspaper.

At the conclusion of the 1950 season he was again chosen to the all-star team this time by the Winnipeg Tribune newspaper.

On July 15, 1951, he doubled and hit a home run in a 7–4 loss to Minot.

Ruben Rodriquez—Pitcher. Batted right, threw right

The right-hander made two stops in Western Canada pitching for the Moose Jaw Mallards in 1957 and, in much improved fashion, for the Saskatoon Commodores in 1960.

1957 Moose Jaw Mallards—Won 3, Lost 1, 7 G, 5 GS, 2 CG, 8.10 ERA
1960 Saskatoon Commodores—Won 2, Lost 2, 4 G, 4 GS, 2 CG, 1.80 ERA

Canadian Highlights: July 17, 1957, after pitching to just two batters, Rodriguez was knocked unconscious when Ed Sada's line drive struck him on the side of the head. He was taken to hospital.

July 27, 1960, at the Lacombe Tournament, Rodriguez held Calgary to five hits and fanned eight in a 5–2 victory. Aug 19, he went ten innings to beat Calgary 2–1.

John Roseboro—Catcher, 6'0", 190 lbs. Batted left, threw right

Roseboro played in Montreal in parts of two seasons before a 14-year career in the major leagues, mainly with the Dodgers. He succeeded Roy Campanella, who had been critically injured in a car accident. Roseboro was an all-star catcher four times, was the starting catcher for the Dodgers in four World Series and won two Gold Glove awards.

He's probably best remembered for the "Marichal Incident" of August 22, 1965. In a game between the Dodgers and Giants at Candlestick Park, Juan Marichal had thrown brush-back pitches at Maury Wills and Ron Fairly. When Marichal came to bat, the Dodger pitcher Sandy Koufax did not retaliate, but Roseboro's throws back to the mound came close to Marichal's head. The Giants' pitcher turned and clubbed Roseboro with his bat, twice, opening a gash which required 14 stitches. Marichal was later suspended and fined.

Roseboro died in 2002 in Los Angeles. He was 69.

>1956 Montreal Royals—.273, 22 D, 2 T, 25 HR, 78 RBI
>1957 Montreal Royals—.273, 8 D, 1 T, 7 HR, 17 RBI

Canadian Highlights: August 2, 1956, Roseboro's three-run homer was the difference as Montreal rallied for a 7–6 win over Columbus Jets. August 10, Roseboro clouted a grand slam homer to lead Montreal by Rochester 7–4. It was his 7th homer in eight days. September 2, he belted a pair of homers and a single to plate four runs in a 14–4 triumph over Buffalo. The 23-year-old catcher was the league's hottest hitter during the last six weeks of the season. Hitting just .251 at the first of August, Roseboro batted .313 with 18 homers and 45 RBI in his last 39 games.

Wilfredo Salas—Pitcher. Batted right, threw right

Salas pitched in the Mexican League in 1946 and 1947. He started the 1948 season in the Negro League with the New York Cubans, but switched to the Quebec Provincial League and joined Sherbrooke. He played only one season and then spent 1949 to 1956 in the Mexican League.

>1948 Sherbrooke Athletics—Won 3, Lost 4

Billy Sanders (Saunders)—Catcher/Outfield

In 1949, Sanders was brought in by the Elmwood Giants for training camp, but ended up with the Carman Cardinals, also of the Manitoba Senior League. He was reported to be 23 years of age and having played with the Cleveland All-Stars. In 1952, he was an import player with the Grandview Maroons in the Manitoba-Saskatchewan League.

>1949 Carman Cardinals—.277
>1952 Grandview Maroons—Statistics not available

Canadian Highlights: August 6, 1949, Sanders banged out two hits to help Carman beat A.N.A.F. Vets 3–0.

Saunders hit a three-run homer in a Grandview loss to Roblin on June 7, 1952.

Carlos Santiago—Second Base/Shortstop, 5'11", 170 lbs. Batted right, threw right

Santiago, from Puerto Rico, was the first black Puerto Rican to play in organized baseball. He was in the Negro League with the New York Cubans in 1946 and in the minor leagues, 1948 to 1950. His single season in Canada was in 1950 with Farnham in the Quebec Provincial League. Santiago was inducted into the Puerto Rican Hall Of Fame in 1993.

>1950 Farnham Pirates—.195, 7 D, 0 T, 2 HR, 21 RBI

Oscar Sardinas—Outfield, 5'6", 170 lbs. Batted left, threw left

The little outfielder played in pro ball for eight years, one with the Montreal Royals in Triple-A where he had a solid 1956 season.

In 1957, while playing in Mexico for Monterrey, Sardinas tied a league record with six hits in six trips to the plate. Baseball legend Martin Dihigo had set the mark in 1937.

>1956 Montreal—.295, 15 D, 2 T, 7 HR, 51 RBI

Canadian Highlights: June 11, 1956, the Royals thumped Rochester 13–8 behind Oscar Sardinas who went 3 for 5 and knocked in 3 runs. In a series against Columbus, June 14 to 17, he went 11 for 25.

Pat Scantlebury—Pitcher/First Base, 6'1", 180 lbs. Batted left, threw left

The southpaw from Panama, had four strong seasons in the International League with Toronto to cap a lengthy career.

After Negro League play with the New York Cubans from 1944 to 1950, and time in Mexico, the Caribbean and semi-pro ball, Scantlebury lied about his age to win a contract in organized ball. He was 35, but said he was 28.

He had a superb season in 1953 with the

Texarkana Bears winning a league-leading 24 games and topping the circuit with 28 complete games. At the end of the season the Double-A, Dallas Eagles obtained his services for just $3,000. A team spokesman said there were three reasons for the low return, the pitcher's age, his hot-headedness and his habit of "keeping out of shape." *(The Paris News, Sept. 28, 1953, p.5)*

Nonetheless, Scantlebury continued to shine winning 20 games in 1954, eighteen with Dallas and two with the Triple-A, Havana Sugar Kings. More success with Havana in 1955 led to a spot with Cincinnati to begin the 1956 season in the major leagues. After six games he was back with Havana.

He wrapped up his career with a half dozen campaigns in the International League ending in 1961 at age 43. Scantlebury was a familiar figure in the fall on barnstorming teams such as the Roy Campanella All-Stars and the Luke Easter All-Stars.

He was well recognized in Japan after his performance in 1950 with the semi-pro champion Fort Wayne Capeharts.

> You could hear a murmur of approval run through the crowd when Scantlebury ... wound up for the first pitch and let one fly that really had smoke on it. Then, to show everybody he meant business, Scantlebury went into the same windup and tossed one that went about 12 feet in the air, performed a few fancy didoes and broke across the batter's belt buckle for a called strike [*Pacific Stars and Stripes*, September 11, 1950, p.3].

He died in 1991 at Glen Ridge, New Jersey.

1958 Toronto Maple Leafs—15–9, 3.87 ERA
1959 Toronto Maple Leafs—12–5, 3.07 ERA
1960 Toronto Maple Leafs—7–5, 2.63 ERA
1961 Toronto Maple Leafs—2–4, 3.43 ERA

May 14, 1958, Scantlebury tossed a seven-hitter against Montreal in a 6–1 win for Toronto. May 23, he was even better with a four-hit shutout, 6–0, over Richmond. August 1, the lefty picked up his 14th win in a 12–2 trouncing of Columbus. June 24, 1959, he won both ends of a double-header against Columbus with sparkling relief efforts, allowing just two hits in 6⅓ innings. July 4, Scantlebury held Buffalo without a hit in four innings of relief to pick up a win. July 18, he went the final two frames in an 11-inning win over Montreal to record his 6th straight victory. August 7, in a rare start, he gave up just four hits to beat Columbus 4–2. August 30, he fired a three-hitter to top Montreal 1–0.

September 21, 1960, in playoff action, Scantlebury did not allow a hit in 5⅔ innings of relief to help Toronto down Rochester 6–2.

Joe B. Scott—Outfield

His Negro League stay lasted from 1945 to 1949, mainly in a reserve role for the Memphis Red Sox. Scott then spent two seasons in Quebec in the Provincial League.

1950 Farnham Pirates—.312, 22 D, 2 T, 8 HR, 44 RBI
1951 Farnham/St. Hyacinthe—.264, 25 D, 2 T, 4 HR, 38 RBI

William "Willie" Scruggs—Pitcher

Scruggs pitched for five teams in the Negro League from 1949 to 1951 ending up with the New Orleans Eagles. The Brandon Greys of the ManDak League came calling in 1952 and Scruggs joined the club, but pitched in just four games, only one in regular league action.

1952 Brandon Greys—Won 0, Lost 1

Canadian Highlights: June 27, 1952, Scruggs allowed just five hits, but dropped a 4–2 decision to Minot. His Brandon mates made six errors.

Angel Scull—Outfield, 5'8", 165 lbs.
Batted right, threw right

The Cuban native, sometimes listed at 5'6", spent 18 years in professional baseball most in the Triple-A, International League. He played in all three major Canadian markets—Toronto, Montreal and Vancouver.

> In the 30 days after acquiring Angel Scull and Mike Goliat from Toronto ... Clay Bryant's Royals played .650 ball, won 21 of 32 games and pulled within a full game of

first place. "Scull restored out pitchers' confidence," Bryant said about the excellent defensive outfielder [*The Victoria Advocate*, July 24, 1959, p.8].

Scull died in 2005 at age 76.

> 1958 Toronto Maple Leafs—.283, 11 D, 4 T, 2 HR, 19 RBI
> 1959 Toronto/Montreal—.270, 27 D, 7 T, 4 HR, 49 RBI
> 1960 Montreal Royals—.291, 24 D, 7 T, 6 HR, 44 RBI
> 1962 Vancouver Mounties—.244, 0 D, 1 T, 0 HR, 8 RBI

April 3, 1958, in an exhibition against Spokane, Scull, who hit four home runs in all of 1957, belted a pair as Toronto crushed the Pacific Coast League team 18–9. A broken ankle shelved him for much of the season.

August 19, 1959, Scull punched out four hits (in just five innings) in Montreal's 9–8 win over Rochester.

June 22, 1960, the little center fielder had a two-run triple, single and two runs scored against Richmond. September 2, Scull's 5th inning homer gave Montreal a 4–3 win over Toronto.

Joe Searcie—Pitcher, 6'1", 190 lbs. Threw right

From semi-pro ball in Los Angeles, Searcie came to pitch for Regina Caps of the Southern Saskatchewan League in 1950 and with Moose Jaw in 1954.

> 1950 Regina Caps/Red Sox—Won 1, Lost 5, 7 G, 7 GS, 6 CG
> 1954 Moose Jaw Canucks—Won 2, Lost 2, 4 G, 4 GS, 4 CG

Canadian Highlights: June 14, 1950, Searcie fired a two-hit shutout as Regina whipped the Muskogee Cardinals 9–0 at the Brandon Invitational Tournament. May 24, 1954, Searcie held Indian Head to just four hits and one earned run as Moose Jaw won its season opener 6–2 over Moose Jaw.

Kelly Searcy—Pitcher, 5'10", 180 lbs. Batted left, threw left

Searcy had a good left arm and itchy feet. In a career which spanned just ten years he played for at least 20 different teams, in the United States, Canada, Mexico and Puerto Rico. He made his first appearance in Canada in 1950 with the touring Nashville All-Stars. It was the same season he pitched Negro League ball for both the Baltimore Elite Giants and Birmingham Black Barons.

In 1951, Searcy picked up the win for his performance in the East-West All-Star game and, in the fall, pitched for a Negro all-star team against the Roy Campanella All-Stars. 1952 was lost to military service in Korea.

He was an all-star again in 1953 upon his return to the Black Barons and in 1954 led the Negro American League with a 2.27 ERA as he finished with a 9–5 record and attracted the attention of the New York Giants. He signed and entered organized ball with Danville of the Class-A, Carolina League. It was a brief stint as he came back to Birmingham in 1955 and also suited up with the Mexico City Reds before answering a call from St. Joseph, Michigan, Auscos in their bid for the semi-pro title at the National Baseball Congress Tournament at Wichita. Searcy helped the team to a fourth place finish and was picked up by the Puerto Rican team for the Global World Series in Milwaukee.

The 1956 season began well for the southpaw, pitching for the Baltimore Orioles in Spring Training. However, he ended up pitching for five teams in '56, including Vancouver of the Pacific Coast League. He bounced around the next few seasons from Mexico, to Phoenix, Knoxville, Yankton (Basin League) and the Willie Mays' All-Stars before landing in Lloydminster and the Western Canada League for two career-ending seasons in 1959 and 1960.

> 1956 Vancouver Mounties—Won 0, Lost 3, 5.30 ERA
> 1959 Lloydminster Meridians—Won 6, Lost 5, 13 G, 12 GS, 4.72, ERA
> 1960 Lloydminster Meridians—Won 6, Lost 3, 15 G, 13 GS, 3.26, ERA

Canadian Highlights: July 8, 1959, Searcy took a hard-luck loss in his debut with Lloydminster allowing just six hits but losing 2–0 to Edmonton in a game delayed more than two hours by rain storms. July 26, Searcy fired another six-hitter, with no earned runs, getting a win this time, 10–4 over Williston. September 4, the lefty was handed another tough defeat, a 1–0 playoff loss to Edmonton.

July 5, 1960, Searcy won his fourth straight, 3–2 over Calgary. July 10, Searcy made it five in a row with a six-hitter in a 9–2 victory over Saskatoon. August 21, Searcy served up a five-hitter to lead Lloydminster past Saskatoon 2–1 to clinch first place in the Western Canada standings.

Pedro Seoane—Outfield/First Base

The Cuban import spend parts of three summers in Western Canada, first with the Florida Cubans in 1952, then the Indian Head Rockets in 1953–1954. Normally a first baseman or outfielder, Seoane took a few turns on the mound and behind the plate.

Canadian Highlights: June 5, 1952, Seoane had a four for four day as the Cubans whipped Indian Head 8–0.

June 4, 1954, Seoane belted a pair of homers and a double to lead Indian Head by Saskatoon 4–1. June 14, Seoane took to the mound and scattered six hits to beat Lloydminster 5–2. June 22, Seoane belted a homer and two singles, but the Rockets lost in extra innings. June 30, Seoane had three hits, including a homer, in a slugfest with Moose Jaw. July 1, Seoane had three hits, including a home run in a losing cause against Moose Jaw.

Dave Shaw—Outfield/Pitcher

Shaw was a core member of the potent Sceptre, Saskatchewan, barnstorming team in 1950.

Canadian Highlights: July 27, 1950, at the Moose Jaw Tournament, Shaw had a triple and three singles as Sceptre lost to Swift Current in the tourney final. August 3, Shaw lost a mound duel to Les Dean at the Rosetown Tournament as North Battleford won 3–1.

Jeff Shelton—Pitcher

In 1949, Shelton was an import player for the Galt Terriers in the Intercounty Baseball League. He was the first African-American player in Galt baseball, one of the first in the Intercounty circuit. The native of South Carolina had started his career with a local team, the Black Spinners in 1938. Shelton moved on to play in Cleveland and Buffalo before a stint in the Navy. In 1946, he returned to play for the Buffalo Harlem Giants, a team which made regular stops in Southern Ontario.

Freddie Sheppard—Pitcher/Outfield.
Batted right, threw right

Sheppard had Negro League experience in the mid 1940s with the Atlanta Black Crackers, Birmingham Black Barons and Chicago American Giants. In 1949, with the New Orleans Creoles and in 1950, as playing-manager of the Louisiana Travelers, he had a taste of the prairies on barnstorming tours. In fact, he left the Travelers in mid-season 1950 to join Minot, North Dakota, Mallards of the Man-Dak League. In 1951, the veteran of Negro League ball, spent the summer in southern Saskatchewan with the Estevan Maple Leafs, finishing 5th in the league with a .340 average.

1951 Estevan Maple Leafs—.340 (incomplete)

Canadian Highlights: August 9, 1950, a Sheppard homer helped Minot to the final of the Estevan Tournament.

June 2, 1951, he missed hitting for the cycle by a single as he belted a homer, triple and two doubles in a come-from-behind 10–8 win over Regina. June 15, Sheppard went 4 for 5 in a 12–9 Estevan loss to the Regina Caps. July 20, Sheppard had a homer, double, stolen base and two runs batted in, but it wasn't enough as Estevan went down 5–3 to Indian Head. July 7, Sheppard had a triple, double and single leading Estevan to an 11–3 victory over Moose Jaw.

Fate Simms—Pitcher/Catcher

A North Carolina product, Simms had an opportunity to visit Canada in 1949 as a member of the barnstorming St. Louis Black Cardinals. He came back in 1950 as the playing manager of the Dauphin Red Birds of the Northern Senior League in Manitoba. The following season he moved on to the Negro League and played for the Memphis Red Sox, Philadelphia Stars and Chicago American Giants.

Canadian Highlights: Normally a catcher, Simms took to the mound on July 4, 1950 and fanned eight in pitching Dauphin to a 4–3 win over Neepawa. August 9, he was on the mound again and clinched a playoff berth for the Dauphin Redbirds with a 6–2 victory over Gilbert Plains. He fired a seven-hitter and fanned eight.

Toby Simms—Shortstop

Simms was among dozens of players who first came north with the Ligon's All-Stars before settling down with prairie teams. Simms played with the Estevan Maple Leafs of the Western Canada League in 1951.

> 1951 Estevan Maple Leafs—.231 (incomplete)

Canadian Highlights: June 23, 1948, Simms had a double and single to pace the Ligon's attack in a 5–3 win over Brandon in the final the Brandon Tournament. June 28, Simms had a double and two singles and two runs batted in to help the Ligon All-Stars to a 12–1 win over Regina Red Sox

June 13, 1949, Simms had a homer and triple leading Ligon's All-Stars past Regina Caps 10–8 in the opener of a doubleheader. He added two hits in the second game. June 28, Simms drove in two runs with a double and single against Brandon. The next day he had a pair of triples against the Greys. August 21, Simms had three hits in a losing cause against Minot.

Gene Smith—Pitcher/Outfield 6'1", 185 lbs. Batted both, threw right

In his one season in Canada, Smith had more success as a hitter than a pitcher as he batted .325 with five home runs in 26 games. He had prior experience in the Negro League, from 1939 to 1950. After a semi-pro season with the Rochester Royals in Minnesota in 1950, he came north to Carman and the ManDak League.

> 1951 Carman Cardinals—Won 3, Lost 6, 10 G, 9 GS, 3 CG, .325, 5 HR, 16 RBI

Canadian Highlights: July 6, 1951, Smith beat the Winnipeg Buffaloes 7–3 on a five-hitter. July 24, he hit a home run and two singles in a Carman loss to the Brandon Greys.

John Ford Smith—Pitcher/Outfield, 6'1", 200 lbs. Batted both, threw right

In his Provincial League season with Drummondville, Quebec, in 1951, Smith tied for the league lead in wins, with 16. The right-hander came from a background in the Negro League where he played from 1939 to 1948 with the Chicago American Giants, Indianapolis Crawfords and Kansas City Monarchs. After he completed military duty he played the 1949 and 1950 seasons in organized ball with the Jersey City Giants in the International League. He closed out career in 1954 with El Paso.

> 1951 Drummondville Cubs—Won 16, Lost 8, 2.97 ERA

Lloyd Smith—Pitcher

Smith made the long trip from his home in Panama to play in Canada in 1954. He was a member of the Indian Head Rockets of the Saskatchewan League.

> 1954 Indian Head Rockets—Won 1, Lost 2, 4 G, 4 GS, 1 CG

Canadian Highlights: June 4, 1954, Smith fired a solid seven-hitter as Indian Head beat Saskatoon 4–1.

Taylor Smith—Pitcher. Threw right

Smith had two years of Negro League baseball as the circuit began to collapse with the integration of organized ball. He pitched in 1948 and 1949 with the Chicago American Giants and Birmingham Black Barons. In 1950, Taylor signed with Manitoba's Winnipeg Buffaloes for the first season of the ManDak League. He returned to the Buffs for the 1952 campaign. Taylor closed out his career in 1952 and 1953 back in the Negro League with the Birmingham Black Barons.

> 1950 Winnipeg Buffaloes—Won 7, Lost 7, 15 G, 15 GS, 12 CG
> 1951 Winnipeg Buffaloes—Won 3, Lost 10, 14 G, 13 GS, 3 CG

Canadian Highlights: May 24, 1950, Taylor pitched all 10 innings in a 4–2 opening day victory over Elmwood. He gave up five hits and struck out thirteen. Smith followed that on May 27, with a heart breaking 6–5 loss to

Brandon. Fourteen strikeouts gave Smith twenty-seven in his first two games. He lost the game on a dropped third strike. June 3, Smith pitched a five-hit, 4–0 shutout in beating the Carman Cardinals. June 20, he pitched another shutout in beating Brandon 1–0 allowing just four hits. August 4, he took a no-hitter into the eighth inning in beating Elmwood 6–2. He finished giving up four hits, striking out seven and walking two. August 12, the Buffaloes beat Carman 9–1 and Smith had another big game striking out seventeen Carman batters. At the conclusion of the 1950 season, the Tribune newspaper picked Smith to the Man-Dak League All-Star team.

Sylvester "Cy" (Sy) Snead—Pitcher/Utility, 5'10", 170 lbs. Batted right, threw right

Snead had a Negro League career that lasted from 1939 to 1946 with the Ethiopian Clowns, Kansas City Monarchs, Cincinnati Clowns and New York Black Yankees. He had first played in Western Canada in 1943 with the Ethiopian Clowns and returned in 1949, first with the Brandon Greys and then with the Elmwood Giants in the Manitoba Senior League. The Winnipeg Free Press reported Snead had been the manager of the Florida Gators.

The 1950 season saw the Giants move to the ManDak League and Snead stayed aboard. That season saw him take over as the Giants manager on July 23. In 1951, Snead moved on to the Quebec Provincial League and played 31 games for the Quebec team. He was reported to have played in South America in 1952 and closed out his career in 1953, back in Canada with Regina and Saskatoon of the Saskatchewan League. Snead died, at age 80, in 1995 in Florida.

- 1949 Brandon/Winnipeg—Won 6, Lost 1, G 9, GS 7, CG 5
- 1950 Elmwood Giants—Won 0, Lost 3, 5 G, 3 GS, 3 CG, .253, 1 HR, 15 RBI
- 1951 Drummondville/St. Hyacinthe—.174, 0 HR, 2 RBI
- 1953 Regina/Saskatoon—.259

Canadian Highlights: July 28, 1949, at the Indian Head Tournament Snead fired a three-hitter as Brandon trounced Notre Dame 17–3. August 4, Snead held Rolla to eight hits in a 14–1 exhibition victory. August 21, he fired a 6 hit, 4–2 win that moved Elmwood into the league final.

June 10, 1950, he had a triple and two singles in an 18–6 trouncing of Minot. June 23, Snead had three hits in an 8–7 win over Minot Mallards. July 3, Snead's two-run homer was decisive in an 8–4 decision over Winnipeg Buffaloes.

July 14, 1953, Snead contributed a triple and double, but Regina fell to Winnipeg 6–5.

Tom "Spring Legs" Snoddy—First Base

Snoddy, one of the designated funsters on the barnstorming Ligon All-Stars, was a regular on the prairies for at least three summers, 1948 to 1950 as the 'Stars barnstormed up to Western Canada from a base in Hondo, Texas.

> But the real highlight of the night was the extra curricular activities of Ligon First Sacker Spring Legs Snoddy. The rubbery first baseman made several outstanding stops during the evening and kept things going at the lively pace with his clowning antics [*The Galveston Daily News*, September 13, 1950].

Snoddy returned to Canada in 1954 with future major leaguer Alvin Jackson and the Texas Jasper Steers on their exhibition and tournament tour of the prairie provinces.

Tom Snowden—Pitcher. Threw left

Snowden was among a contingent from California's Coalinga College to play in Western Canada. The lanky left-hander, who also starred in basketball at Coalinga, spent the 1956 summer playing at Picture Butte, Alberta.

Canadian Highlights: June 23, 1956, Snowden held Granum to five hits as Picture Butte trounced the White Sox at the Vulcan Tournament. July 14, Snowden fired a four-hitter to lead the Indians to a 13–2 win over Granum at the Picture Butte Tournament. August 11, Snowden blanked Sceptre-Delisle 14–0 on a four-hitter at the Medicine Hat Tourney.

A multi-cultural mound staff in Picture Butte, Alberta, in 1956. Left to right—lefty Tom Snowden, right-handers Gary Harrison and John Chavez. A fourth starter, southpaw Willie Yahiro, not shown, was one of six Hawaiians on the team (photograph from the Mah Collection, courtesy Gary Harrison).

Herbert Souell—Second Base/Third Base, 5'10", 170 lbs. Batted both, threw right

Souell, a three-time Negro League all-star, had a solid career over more than a decade with the Kansas City Monarchs, Ethiopian Clowns, and Cincinnati Crescents. In 1951, he made a decision to travel north to Manitoba to suit up in the ManDak League with Carman. After a strong '51 summer, he was with Carman only briefly in 1952 as he entered organized ball for the first time. He returned to Carman in 1953. He was 65 when he passed away in 1978 in California.

> 1951 Carman Cardinals—.306, 7 HR, 39 RBI
> 1952 Carman Cardinals—Statistics not available
> 1953 Carman Cardinals—.302, 17 D, 3 T, 5 HR, 39 RBI

Canadian Highlights: May 21, 1951, Souell paced Carman to a 6–5 twelve inning win over the Brandon Greys. He was the big hitter with a home run, double and single. June 4, he had four singles in a 9–4 win over Minot. Souell had three hits, one a homer as Carman beat Winnipeg 7–3 on July 6. On August 1, he had three singles in a Carman win over Brandon.

On July 3, 1953, in a 12–8 Carman win over the Winnipeg Royals he had five hits and four runs batted in.

Al Spearman—Pitcher, 6'0", 185 lbs. Batted right, threw right

Spearman's career was just beginning as Jackie Robinson was settling in with the Brooklyn Dodgers. In 1948, Spearman pitched for the Wilson Stock Yards team in an Industrial League in Chicago. Two years later he was in the livery of the legendary Chicago American Giants. He left Chicago in 1951 for the Carman Cardinals of the ManDak League. He stayed in Canada the following season to pitch for the Winnipeg Giants before moving on to organized ball and considerable success including 18–3, 14–4, and 20–9 all-star seasons in the California League. He pitched as high as Triple-A and at one point had completed 48 of 50 starting assignments including a remarkable 33 in row.

> 1951 Carman Cardinals—Won 5, Lost 5, 13 G, 9 GS, 7 CG
> 1952 Winnipeg Giants—Won 1, Lost 3, 25 IP, 15 BB, 17 SO

Canadian Highlights: July 18, 1951, Spearman pitched all 14 innings and beat Lefty McKinnis and the Brandon Greys 4–3. Spearman fired a one-hitter on August 12, in beating Minot 4–1. Minot's run was scored on an error.

July 17, 1952, Spearman pitched a six-hitter to lead Winnipeg to the top prize money in the

Joe Spencer—Infield, 5'9", 150 lbs. Batted right, threw right

Spencer played in the Negro League from 1943 to 1948 for several teams, including the Homestead Grays, Newark Eagles and Baltimore Elite Giants. In addition, he slipped in some barnstorming in 1946 with the Cincinnati Crescents. The same year he was among the pioneers trying to establish a West Coast Negro League when he suited up with the Seattle Steelheads.

He started the 1949 season with the Harlem Globetrotters then jumped the club and signed with the Elmwood Giants, at the time in the Manitoba Senior League. Spencer was on the road again in 1950 traveling with the New Orleans Creoles. Then, in 1951, he was back for his second season in Canada with Elmwood, now in the ManDak League. He died in 2003 in Gretna, La.

 1949 Elmwood Giants—.254
 1951 Elmwood Giants—.239, 3 HR, 32 RBI

Canadian Highlights: July 22, 1949, Spencer had three RBI in each game in a double header victory of the Winnipegs. Elmwood won both games, 5–0 and 7–2.

May 26, 1951, Spencer hit a home run and a single in an 8–7 Giants' win over Carman Cardinals.

Ed Steele—Outfield, 5'10", 195 lbs. Batted left, threw right

Although he didn't begin playing Negro League ball until he was in his mid–20s, Steele fashioned an 11-year career with the Birmingham Black Barons, 1941 to 1951, and had a brief stint in the Pittsburgh Pirates organization with the Hollywood Stars and Denver Bears in 1952. He was 36 by the time he got an opportunity in organized ball and hit just .213 in Triple-A and .254 when sent down to Class-A ball. He came up to Canada and joined the Galt Terriers in the Intercounty League in 1953 and led the loop in homers, with 14. He played a second season in Canada and then closed out his career managing Detroit teams, through to 1959, in the final days of the Negro Leagues.

 1953 Galt Terriers—14 HR
 1954 Galt Terriers—Statistics not available

R.C. Stevens—First Base, 6'5", 219 lbs. Batted right, threw left

Stevens was drafted and signed by the Pittsburgh Pirates in 1952 and for the following season was assigned to the St. Jean Canadians in the Provincial League. He made his major league debut with the Pirates in 1958. He saw limited action at the major league level and ended his playing days in 1961 with Washington. Over his major league career he batted .210.

 1958 St. Jean Canadians—.313, 28 D, 5 T, 12 HR, 77 RBI
 1961 Toronto Maples Leafs—.243, 10 D, 0 T, 12 HR, 32 RBI
 1962 Toronto Maples Leafs—.241, 2 D, 1 T, 1 HR, 4 RBI
 1963 Toronto Maples Leafs—.115, 0 HR, 2 RBI

George Washington Stovey—Pitcher. Threw left

Stovey, believed to have been a Canadian * (although some sources indicate he was born in the United States) was among a small group of elite black athletes who played in integrated, pro baseball in the late 1800s but then would be among the first to be targets of growing racism which resulted in a ban on blacks in organized baseball.

> The Newark club will probably place a novelty in the field next season in the shape of a colored "battery." Stovey, the pitcher, and Walker, the catcher, are both colored men. Stovey played with the Jersey City club last season and showed he was a great pitcher. Several of the League managers contemplated signing him last season, but the prejudice against his color prevented. Had he not been of African descent he would have pitched for the New York club last fall [*The Sporting News*, December 18, 1886].

In 1887, the lefty hurler set an International League record with more than 30 wins (various sources put the number at 33, 34 or 35) and his reward was to get released as teams began to rid their squads of black players. In September, 1907, the Washington Post made note of the color line and some notable Negro players who had been excluded from the majors.

> The African athlete has found the color line in the big league a barrier that is insurmountable. While a few of them in the early days of the game managed to break in, they found life unpleasant and soon withdrew. Many of the Negro players in their own teams have shown skill fully equal to that of the best minor leaguers, and might have made good had they been given a show in the fastest company. One of the best of the black players was a catcher named Walker, formerly with the Syracuse Stars. Then there was Grant and Stovey. Today we have Foster, Williams and a number of others who would be major league stars if their color was not against them [*The Washington Post*, September 29, 1907].

Stovey's one-time battery mate, Fleetwood Walker, turned out to be the last black to play in the big leagues until Jackie Robinson suited up for Brooklyn in 1947.

Among the sources noting Stovey's Canadian background are James Riley (The Biographical Encyclopedia of The Negro Baseball Leagues), John Holway (Blackball Stars), MLB.com (Color line takes Stovey out of big leagues), and Bill Kirwin (Out of the shadows).

Othello Strong—Pitcher/Outfield, 6'3", 185 lbs. Batted both, threw right

The younger brother of two-sport star Ted Strong (Kansas City Monarchs, Harlem Globetrotters) Othello carved out his own success on both the baseball diamond and basketball court. In 1947, after three years in the Army, including a reported outstanding pitching mark with Fort Warren, he joined the Globetrotters baseball club and the Kansas City Stars basketball team, a farm club of the famous 'Trotters. With a second season with the Globetrotters under his belt he moved to the Chicago American Giants for parts of four seasons in the Negro League. He also suited up with Minot in 1949 and 1950 and Winnipeg in 1951 and 1952. In his lone season of pro ball, Strong was 3–2, 1.98 with the Class-D, Danville Dans.

Early in his career he had been tabbed as a future major leaguer. In a 1949 article in The Sporting News (January 12, 1949) Strong was among Negro players named as top young prospects.

1951 Winnipeg Buffaloes—Won 2, Lost 1, 4 G, 4 GS, 2 CG, .317, 4 HR, 16 RBI
1952 Winnipeg Giants—Won 1, Lost 2

Canadian Highlights: July 1, 1949, Strong lost a heart-breaker as he allowed just four hits and an unearned run, but Minot dropped a 1–0 decision to Brandon in the final of the Brandon Tournament. July 28, Strong fired a five-hitter to beat Brandon 4–2 to advance Minot to the final of the Indian Head Tournament.

August 4, 1951, Strong belted a double and four singles to lead Winnipeg Buffaloes to a 15–8 win over Carman. August 11, he drove in six runs with two homers, a triple and single as Winnipeg blasted Elmwood. September 7, Strong had three hits and knocked in three in a 5–2 Winnipeg victory over Minot.

June 12, 1952, Strong had six runs batted in with a pair of homers in a slugfest with Minot. July 16, Strong was suspended indefinitely after leaving the Winnipeg club. Two weeks later the Class-C, Albuquerque Dukes of the West Texas–New Mexico League announced they had signed Strong, but he failed to show.

Ted Strong—Shortstop/Third Base/Outfield, 6'3", 210 lbs. Batted both, threw right

A superb athlete, Strong was a two-sport star who played for two legendary teams—the Kansas City Monarchs in baseball and Harlem Globetrotters in basketball.

On the diamond, where he began his career in 1936, he was selected to five East-West All-Star games in his first six years in the league. He began his baseball career in Chicago and put in seasons with the Indianapolis A's and the ABC's before joining the Monarchs. He played for three seasons with Kansas City, and one in Mexico, in advance of three years of Navy service in the Pacific during World War II. After the war he played with the Monarchs and Indianapolis Clowns before joining Minot in 1949 and 1950. The latter season also found him playing with Swift Current, Saskatchewan. In 1951, he wound up his playing days with the Chicago American Giants, the team with which he began his career. On the court, he was a Globetrotter for 15 years serving as the team captain and a major drawing card. He died in 1978 in Chicago.

> Ted Strong, well over six feet tall and just inside of two hundred pounds is the newest sensation with the Harlem team and this man is destined to become one of the greatest players as well as an extremely pleasing showman. His giant maulers, said by many to be the largest in the professional basketball field, will stand him in good stead and already have aided him to become a sensation with his baseball handling of the basketball [*The Helena Daily Independent*, February 16, 1937, p.8].

1950 Swift Current Maple Leafs—Statistics not available
1950 Minot Mallards—.236, 0 HR, 7 RBI

Canadian Highlights: June 24, 1949, playing with the Harlem Globetrotters at Regina, Strong was cited for outstanding defensive plays at shortstop. He had two hits the next day in the Trotters' win over House of David. July 10, as a newcomer to Minot Merchants, Strong doubled to score the tying and winning runs in an 8–7, 11–inning win over Brandon. July 28, Strong's two-run homer was the difference as Minot downed Brandon 4–2 to advance to the final of the Indian Head Tournament. August 4, Strong had three hits in exhibition action against Regina Caps. August 8, Strong bashed a triple, double and two singles in a 7–5 loss to Brandon.

May 28, 1950, Strong scored three times and knocked in three runs with a triple, two doubles and a single, in demolishing Carman 21–6. July 27, Strong drove in five runs with a triple, double and single to lead Swift Current to top money at the Moose Jaw Tournament of Champions.

Armando Suarez—Pitcher, 6'1", 175 lbs. Batted left, threw left

The eighteen year old left-handed pitcher left Cuba in 1951 to join Brandon of the Man-Dak League, for his lone season in Canada. He was a solid performer for the Greys making thirteen starts, completing eight and winning seven out of twelve decisions during the regular season. After signing with the Dodgers he followed with six summers of organized ball and pitched as high as Triple-A. In his initial pro season in 1952 he won nineteen games in the Pioneer League.

1951 Brandon Greys—Won 7, Lost 5, 16 G, 13 GS, 8 CG

Canadian Highlights: Suarez made a strong impression as he won his first three games and saved a fourth in his first four contests. May 25, in his first game he had a shutout into the ninth inning before a of couple hits and an error spoiled the whitewash. The score ended 10–3 against Elmwood as he fanned ten and walked two. August 10, he beat the California Mohawks 1–0, giving up only three hits. The Mohawks were playing as Medicine Hat, Alberta, in the Western Canada League. September 14, in the ManDak League finals he beat the Winnipeg Buffaloes 5–3 to give Brandon the championship.

Arnaldo "Chico" Suarez—Shortstop, 5'8", 140 lbs. Batted right, threw right

The little Cuban started in the Cardinals system in 1958. The next season, at age twenty, he was sent to the Winnipeg Goldeyes for his lone season in Canada. It was a good one. He was seventh in the batting race, with a .316 mark, and led the circuit with 15 triples. He had 34 doubles, one behind the league-leader, Joe Pepitone. Moving up to Double-A during the 1950 season, he was out of pro ball at the end of the 1961 season.

1959 Winnipeg Goldeyes—.316, 34 D, 15 T, 2 HR, 69 RBI

Canadian Highlights: June 5, 1959, Suarez went three for six, including a double and drove in a pair as the Goldeyes beat Fargo-Moorhead 11–1. The following day the Winnipeg Free Press reported that "Little Chico Suarez, the stylish rookie ... plugs the shortstop hole so capably for the Goldeyes.... If he can continue his brilliant play, no one will be able to overlook him for All-Star honors." No one did.

Wilson Sullivan—Catcher

Sullivan had a brief stint as catcher for the Indian Head Rockets in 1954. His season came to an end when he injured his shoulder during a rundown play in early June.

Roland "Lefty" Summers—Pitcher, Threw left

The young lefthander from Philadelphia first pitched in Canada in 1952 as a member of the Minot Mallards of the ManDak League (in a start at Winnipeg, he was described as having "slow, tantalizing stuff"). He returned in 1954 with the Rosetown Phillies. Summers was reported to be 21 years of age when he played for Rosetown. In the 60s he pitched for the touring Philadelphia Stars.

> 1954 Rosetown—Won 6, Lost 5, 17 G, 12 GS, 6 CG, .289

Canadian Highlights: May 24, 1954, Summers fired a neat five-hitter, but ended up with a loss as Lloydminster shutout Rosetown 2–0. July 19, Summers held Indian Head to just three hits and had a shutout until the 9th in a 13–1 triumph over Indian Head. July 31, Summers had a shutout into the 9th inning before two errors led to a pair of runs against him in a 4–2 win over Moose Jaw. He helped at the plate with a run-scoring double and later singled and scored.

Roy Swanson—Catcher/Outfield

Swanson, who caught for the Atlanta Black Crackers, was first noticed in Western Canada when he toured with the Brooklyn Cuban Giants and New Orleans Creoles in 1949 and 1950. He left the 1950 barnstorming team to join up with the Estevan Maple Leafs of the Southern Saskatchewan League. In 1951, he was back in Canada with Elmwood Giants of the ManDak League.

> 1950 Estevan Maple Leafs—Statistics not available
> 1951 Elmwood Giants—.308, 1 HR, 21 RBI

Canadian Highlights: August 3, 1950, Swanson had two hits, one of them a three-run homer, as Estevan trounced Wilcox 10–1 at the Regina Exhibition Tournament.

May 23, 1951, Swanson led the Giants with three hits and two RBI as Elmwood lost to the Brandon Greys. May 25, he had four hits in a losing cause to Brandon and the next day singled in Joe Mitchell in the ninth with the winning run as they beat Carman 7–6.

Jose Milages Tartabull—Outfield, 5'11", 165 lbs. Batted left, threw left

The fleet outfielder was just 18 when he was part of a Cuban contingent on the 1957 Regina Braves. He took awhile before he could crack the regular lineup spending some time with Davidson, Saskatchewan, a Regina farm team.

His lack of power (just three extra base hits, two doubles and a triple, in 36 games,) was offset by his keen eye (.442 on base percentage) and speed (he was 4th in stolen bases in spite of playing in just over half the games).

Signed by the San Francisco Giants after the 1957 season, Tartabull was traded to Kansas City in 1961 and made his major league debut in 1962. He played in the majors for 9 seasons compiling a batting mark of .261. His son Danny played in the majors over 14 seasons. (Over his first 10 games in the majors, Danny hit as many home runs, two, as did his father in his 756 game career.)

Tartabull had a key role in the Red Sox "Impossible Dream" season of 1967. In the heat of the incredible pennant race his throw from right field to gun down Ken Berry at home plate preserved a dramatic win over the White Sox. The throw even became the subject of a novel *(Tartabull's Throw, by Henry Garfield).*

> 1957 Regina Braves—.301, 0 HR, 13 RBI, 12 SB

Canadian Highlights: July 22, 1957, Tartabull poked a pair of doubles and a single and scored three times from the leadoff spot as Regina crushed Lloydminster 17–1. August 11, Tartabull had three hits in a 6–2 loss to Saskatoon. August 29, he had three hits in playoff action against Moose Jaw. September 1, Tartabull had his biggest offensive day of the season as he clubbed a homer, triple and double to lead Regina to a 10–3 playoff victory over Moose Jaw.

Willie Tasby—Outfield, 5'11", 170 lbs. Batted right, threw right

The native of Shreveport, Louisiana, played in the major leagues for six seasons with Baltimore Orioles, Boston Red Sox, Washington Senators and Cleveland Indians. He finished with a career average of .250. His best season was in 1961 with the Senators when he belted 17 homers and drove in 63.

Tasby played all of three games with Vancouver in 1957. He quit the team, was suspended, but later suited up with another Baltimore affiliate, the Knoxville Smokies down in Class-A.

> 1957 Vancouver Mounties—.462, 2 D, 1 T, 0 HR, 4 RBI

Canadian Highlights: In pre-season action, March 26, 1956, Tasby paced the Mounties to 17–5 victory by hitting a home run and triple.

Tasby was the offensive star April 14, 1957 in the second game of a twin-bill against Los Angeles as he knocked in four runs with two doubles and two singles in a 5–1 victory.

Curtis Tate—Third base, 5'10", 185 lbs. Batted right, threw right

Tate arrived in Canada as a pitcher on a barnstorming team and stayed as a run producing third baseman for North Battleford Beavers. His stint with the touring Ligon All-Stars brought him to Saskatchewan where, in 1950, he jumped the team for an opportunity with the Beavers. For seven seasons, the Texas native was an integral performer. He also tried his hand in organized ball for one season, 1955, with Abilene in the Class-B, West Texas-New Mexico League where he finished with a solid .289 mark.

Tate died in 1970 in Texas. He was just 44 years of age.

> 1950 N.Battleford Beavers—.435
> 1951 N.Battleford Beavers—.395 (led in hits with 47)
> 1952 N.Battleford Beavers—.349, 8 D, 4 T, 3 HR, 41 RBI, 10 SB
> 1953 N.Battleford Beavers—.303, 43 RBI
> 1954 N.Battleford Beavers—.322, 12 D, 1 T, 5 HR, 39 RBI, 14 SB
> 1956 N.Battleford Beavers—.292, 11 D, 2 T, 5 HR, 43 RBI, 8 SB
> 1957 N.Battleford Beavers—.238, 13 D, 8 T, 5 HR, 51 RBI

Canadian Highlights: June 13, 1949, Tate went the distance on the mound as Ligon's All-Stars downed Regina Caps 10–6. He jumped the team a year later to join North Battleford.

His .395 batting mark in 1951 in the Northern Saskatchewan circuit was just a shade off the league lead as Reg Pendleton won at .397.

In 1952, he was runner-up in the batting race and was tied for second in RBI and stolen bases. He tied for the lead in triples in 1953 and tied for third in batting average in 1954.

May 25, 1954, Tate drove in ten runs with five hits, including a grand slam homer and double, scored three runs and stole a base to give North Battleford an 18–15 win over Rosetown.

August 2, 1956 with two out and a 3–2 count, Tate clubbed a grand slam homer in the 8th inning to hand the Beavers a 4–3 win over Regina. Tate helped the Beavers to four league championships, including the 1956 season when the Beavers represented Canada at the Global World Series at Detroit.

George Tatum—Pitcher

A native of Lake Charles, Louisiana, Tatum pitched in Canada with the Saskatoon Legion, of the Northern Saskatchewan League, in 1950.

> 1950 Saskatoon Legion—Won 1, Lost 2, 5 G, 3 GS, 1 GC

Canadian Highlights: May 19, 1950, Tatum's debut was his best effort of the season as he fired a three-hit shutout, fanning ten in the seven-inning contest.

Joe Cephus Taylor—Outfield, 6'1", 195 lbs. Batted right, threw right

Taylor ended up playing eight seasons in Canada with six different teams in four provinces. He started his career in 1949 with the Chicago American Giants as a catcher in the Negro League. He came to Canada in 1950 to join Willie Wells and the Winnipeg Buffaloes in the ManDak League. He was one of the younger players at 24 years of age and played in the outfield with Buffaloes. After the 1950 Season he went into organized ball and was an all-star in 1957 and 1959 with Seattle and Vancouver in the Pacific Coast League. He would play in the major leagues with the Philadelphia A's, Cincinnati Reds, St. Louis Cardinals and Baltimore Orioles. Taylor closed out his career with Baltimore in 1959 and ended with an over-all batting average of .249.

- 1950 Winnipeg Buffaloes—.237, 3 HR, 15 RBI
- 1951 Farnham Pirates—.360, 9 D, 1 T, 10 HR, 29 RBI
- 1952 St. Hyacinthe A's—.308, 35 D, 4 T, 25 HR, 112 RBI
- 1953 Ottawa A's—.313, 16 D, 3 T, 7 HR, 45 RBI
- 1954 Ottawa A's—.323, 24 D, 4 T, 23 HR, 79 RBI
- 1955 Columbus/Toronto—.286, 10 D, 1 T, 12 HR, 38 RBI
- 1959 Vancouver Mounties—.292, 25 D, 2 T, 23 HR, 77 RBI
- 1962 Hawaii/Vancouver—246, 15 D, 0 T, 13 HR, 37 RBI

Canadian Highlights: June 17, 1950, Taylor had two hits and knocked in a pair in a 9–0 win over Brandon. September 14, Taylor hit a single that drove in the winning run that gave the Buffaloes the league championship. The hit came in the seventeenth inning to win it for the Buffaloes.

Tommy Taylor—Pitcher, 6'1", 180 lbs. Batted left, threw right

Taylor started out in organized ball having signed with the Cincinnati Reds as a teenager. He pitched for parts of two seasons, 1957 and 1958, in Class-A ball. Released by the Reds after the 1958 season, he joined the Kansas City Monarchs and ended up pitching with the legendary Satchel Paige. While pitching at a tournament in Lethbridge in 1960 he was one of three Monarchs picked up by the Saskatoon Commodores of the Western Canada League. He joined Edmonton of the WCBL the following season and was acquired by Lethbridge of the Southern Alberta League for playoff action. He wrapped up his career with two seasons in Lloydminster when the team played in the Northern Saskatchewan League.

His son, Terry, had a ten year pro career including a handful of games with the Seattle Mariners in 1988.

- 1960 Saskatoon Commodores—W 2 L 1, 5 G, 4 GS, 2 CG, 3.96, ERA
- 1961 Edmonton Eskimos—Statistics not available
- 1962 Lloydminster GreenCaps—Won 9 (Tied 1st), .302
- 1963 Lloydminster GreenCaps—Won 10, Lost 3 *, .302, 0 HR, 7 RBI
- 1964 Melville Millionaires—Won 6, Lost 3, 15 G, 11 GS, 8 CG, .337

League and playoffs

Canadian Highlights: July 31, 1959, Taylor pitched a shutout in besting future major leaguer Thad Tillotson as Kansas City Monarchs shaded Medicine Hat 1–0 at the Lethbridge Tournament.

A year later, July 30, 1960, Taylor pitched the Kansas City Monarchs to a 4–3 win over Saskatoon at the Lethbridge Tourney. August 2, Taylor tossed a four-hitter for Saskatoon in a 5–1 win over Calgary. August 16, Taylor held Lethbridge to six hits and fanned eleven in a 2–1 win over Lethbridge. August 30, in the Western Canada League final series, Taylor fired a four-hitter and fanned 13 as Saskatoon took the opener.

July 30, 1961, Taylor fired a four-hit shutout with 14 strikeouts in an 8–0 win over Calgary in tournament action.

June 17, 1962, Taylor fired a three-hit shutout as the Lloydminster Green Caps downed Unity 3–0. Three days later he held Unity to four-hits in a 3–2 win. June 24, Taylor pitched a one-hitter, but six errors led to a 4–2 defeat.

May 26, 1963, Taylor had a no-hitter into the 6th inning as Lloydminster topped North Battleford 2–1. July 7, Taylor hurled a three-hitter and fanned 14 in a 4–1 win over Kindersley

Travis Taylor—Catcher

Taylor made at least a couple of tours of the prairies in the late 1940s as the backstop with the Muskogee Colored Cardinals. In 1950, he played for the Kamsack Cyclones of the Manitoba-Saskatchewan League.

Canadian Highlights: June 9, 1948, Taylor had four hits and drove in three as the Cards and Regina Caps split a double-header, each with a 6–5 victory. June 20, Taylor had a triple, double and single as Muskogee downed Regina Caps 12–9.

July 2, 1950, Taylor was the offensive star with four hits and two runs in a 9–4 victory over Dauphin.

Ron Teasley—Third Base/First Base, 5'11", 177 lbs. Batted right, threw right

Teasley, it turned out, was part of a ruse used by Branch Rickey, the Dodgers' general manager, to hide his search for black players for his major league team. Rickey established a new Negro League in 1945, with the Brooklyn Brown Dodgers as one of the clubs. It provided the real Dodgers an effective cover for the scouting of and discussions with black players, with Jackie Robinson the most prominent target. Teasley, a star at Wayne State University, signed up for the Toledo Cubs in the new league. Soon, however, Teasley and his colleagues realized the new loop was a sham. Rickey announced Robinson had signed, not for the new Negro league, but for major league baseball.

Teasley himself signed with the Dodgers in 1948, the eighth Afro-American to join the fabled system. Released halfway through the '48 season Teasley played Negro ball then came north in 1949 to hook up with the Carman

In 1949, Carman, Manitoba, featured an integrated team for the Manitoba Senior League season. Back row (left to right)—Lillord Cobb, Ron Teasley, Almer McKerlie, Johnny Caulfield, Nuts Anderson, Don Reid, Roger Shanner, Jack Schaefer. Front row (left to right)—Lefty Novak, Sonny Andrews, Jim McFadden, Gord Elliott, Walter Thomas, Clint McKerlie, Bob Johnson. Front—Ralph McIvor (Batboy) (photograph courtesy Ron Teasley).

Cardinals of the Manitoba Senior League. He returned in 1950 as the Cardinals moved into the new ManDak League.

While still playing ball, he completed his education at Wayne State University and received a degree in physical education. He was selected to the Wayne State University Hall Of Fame in 1986.

> 1949 Carman Cardinals—Statistics not available
> 1950 Carman Cardinals—.299, 3 HR, 19 RBI

Canadian Highlights: August 1, 1949, Teasley belted a two-run homer as Carman upset Brandon 9–6. August 19, he clouted two homers and a double to lead Carman to a 7–6 win in the first game of a twin-bill. He belted another four-bagger in the nightcap as Cards won 7–5. August 21, Teasley led a dramatic comeback by Carman as the Cardinals erased an eight-run deficit to top Brandon 9–8. Teasley, who had boomed a two-run homer in the 8th, singled across two runs in the 9th for the win.

June 6, 1950, the first sacker played a starring role in the all-star game (held to support the Manitoba flood relief effort). He led the Tribune All-Stars at the plate with two doubles and two RBI in an 8–4 victory over the Free Press All-Stars. June 7, Teasley led Carman at the plate in a 12–6 loss to the Elmwood Giants. He hit a pair of home runs and had four RBI.

Former diamond stars Chet Brewer (left) and Ron Teasley (right) years after hanging up their cleats (photograph courtesy Ron Teasley).

July 10, against Minot and July 27, against the Winnipeg Buffaloes, Teasley had three hits in each game. September 2, Carman forced a deciding game in their playoff series with Brandon, edging the Greys 4–3 and Teasley had three hits for Carman. The game was held up in the fifth inning as Carman disputed a decision to give Teasley a double rather than a homer on a blast over the head of Grey's right fielder Charles Peete. The umpires ruled the ball had hit the ground behind Peete and bounced over the fence and their decision stood.

Marvin Terrell—Outfield

Terrell came to Estevan in 1950 during a mid-season makeover of the Maple Leafs. He had visited Western Canada previously as a member of the touring New Orleans Creoles.

Fred Thomas—Outfield, 6'2", 195 lbs. Batted left

The Windsor, Ontario native was one of Canada's best athletes, a basketball, baseball and football star in mid 1940s to mid 1950s.

He returned from a stint with the Royal Canadian Air Force in the Second World War to take up studies and basketball at Assumption College in Windsor. During his air force training, Thomas played ball in the Halifax Defence League.

In 1945, at age 21, he led the Windsor basketball club to an upset of the barnstorming Harem Globetrotters. Thomas was a main factor as the Purple Raiders won the Canadian Senior Basketball title in 1949 and advanced to the final on three other occasions.

He also attracted the attention of the Cleveland Indians of the American Baseball League. He hit .351 in first half of the 1948 season with Farnham of the independent Quebec Provincial before Cleveland assigned the outfielder to Wilkes-Barre Barons of the Eastern League where he became the first black player in the history of the circuit. In 1949, he was back with Farnham for second season.

He juggled his baseball career and his Assumption College commitment with some pro basketball with the Kansas City Stars and New York Rens. In 1950, he traveled with the Stars when they provided the opposition on the

Globetrotters western tour. Thomas also found time to suit up with the Pride of Michigan and later, after college, would lead the Toronto Tri-Bells to the Canadian Senior Basketball title. In 1949, he played briefly with the Toronto Argonauts of the Canadian Football League. Injuries short-circuited his pro careers, but he continued to play semi-pro baseball and basketball in Canada.

In 1951, Thomas was the leading hitter in Ontario's Intercounty Baseball league with a .383 batting mark for the Kitchener Panthers. He combined with Negro League veteran Wilmer Fields to make Oshawa Merchants a powerhouse in the 1955 Intercounty season.

   1948 Farnham Pirates—.351, 23 D, 5 T, 4 HR
   1949 Farnham Pirates—Statistics not available
   1951 Kitchener Panthers—.383
   1952 Kitchener Panthers—Statistics not available
   1954 Galt Terriers—Statistics not available
   1955 Oshawa Merchants—9 HR, 42 RBI

Canadian Highlights: May 15, 1951, Thomas knocked in six runs with a triple and two singles as Kitchener demolished Galt 16–0. July 13, Thomas collected three hits, one a homer, and made two sparkling catches in center field to lead Kitchener over Waterloo 3–1.

May 21, 1955, he drove in three runs with a triple and double as Oshawa topped St. Thomas 8–0. July 1, Thomas' three-run home run was the difference as Oshawa downed Kitchener 8–6. July 11, he knocked in five runs with a homer, triple and double to lead Oshawa to a 10–1 trouncing of St. Thomas. July 14, Thomas clubbed a grand slam homer to lead the Oshawa comeback in a 6–5 win over Galt. July 24, he crushed a homer and two singles to pace the Merchants past Kitchener 6–1.

Valmy Thomas—Catcher, Outfield, 5'9", 165 lbs. Batted right, threw right

Thomas was born in Puerto Rico, but grew up in St. Croix in the Virgin Islands and as a youngster played his ball there. During his late teens and early 20s he was in the Navy in Puerto Rico and played winter ball in San Juan for the Senadores in 1949 and 1950. In 1950, he was signed by the Pittsburgh Pirates and sent to St. Jean, Quebec, under a working agreement with that club. At the end of that season he had a money dispute with the Pirates and left to play in the Dominican Republic. He played there from 1952 to 1954. Later, he was drafted by the New York Giants and sent back to St. Jean in 1955.

Two years later he advanced to the major leagues with the Giants and in 1958 moved with the club to San Francisco. On opening day 1958, Thomas and Ruben Gomez became the first Puerto Rican battery in major league history. Thomas is also recognized as the first Puerto Rican to play in the major leagues. Over his career he played for the Giants, Phillies, Orioles and Indians and finished his career with a .230 average

   1951 St. Jean Braves—.295, 9 D, 1 T, 9 HR, 48 RBI
   1955 St. Jean Canadians—.286, 18 D, 2 T, 9 HR, 63 RBI

Walter Thomas—Outfield, 5'10", 165 lbs. Batted left, threw right

Thomas had a long Negro League career from 1936 to 1947 with the Kansas City Monarchs, Detroit Stars, St. Louis Stars, Memphis Red Sox, Chicago American Giants and Birmingham Black Barons. In 1950, he joined the Carman Cardinals in the ManDak League and would play two seasons. He died in 1991 in Arkansas. He was 77.

   1950 Carman Cardinals—.245, 1 HR, 22 RBI
   1951 Carman Cardinals—.238, 0 HR, 16 RBI

Canadian Highlights: Thomas had three hits to lead Carman to a 6–1 win over Minot on June 13, 1950. August 25, he drove in four runs with a triple, double and single in Carman's 7–1 victory over Minot.

May 31, 1951, Thomas led a huge Carman comeback, rallying from a 10–2 deficit to win 14–11. He had four hits and knocked in three.

Johnny Thompson—Second Base

Thompson was one of few steadying forces on the sad-sack (14–45) Moose Jaw Maples of

1953. He hit .260 and played in the all-star game.

    1953 Moose Jaw Maples—.260

Canadian Highlights: June 9, 1953, Thompson had a triple and single, drove in two runs and scored three as Moose Jaw topped Regina 12–5. July 24, Thompson had a two-run homer in a Moose Jaw loss to Saskatoon. August 11, Thompson had three hits, but the Maples lost to North Battleford.

Tommy Thompson—Pitcher.

The Los Angeles, California, native pitched for the independent Swift Current, Saskatchewan, Indians in 1950.

Canadian Highlights: June 12, 1950, Thompson allowed six hits, none after the 4th inning, to lead Swift Current to a 3–1 win over Regina Caps. July 28, Thompson pitched the Indians into the second round of the Swift Current Tournament downing Shaunavon 6–2.

Carlos Thorne—Pitcher/Third Base,
6'1", 195 lbs. Batted right, threw right

Thorne signed with the Cardinals and reported to the Winnipeg Goldeyes in 1955 for his start in organized ball. He returned in 1956 and then bounced around the Cardinals system the next two seasons at the Class-A and Class-B levels. In 1959, he closed out his career in the Mexican League.

    1955 Winnipeg Goldeyes—Won 12, Lost 8, 3.54 ERA,
    1956 Winnipeg Goldeyes—Won 11, Lost 10, 4.89 ERA, .248, 2 HR, 20 RBI

Canadian Highlights: May 23, 1956, Thorne playing at third base, had a game that today would be shown on the late night TV "plays of the day." Thorne led the Goldeyes to an 11–5 win over the Duluth-Superior White Sox. He had a career day hitting a grand slam home run and followed that with a bases clearing double for a seven RBI day.

Robert Burns "Bob" Thurman—
Outfield/Pitcher, 6'1", 205 lbs. Batted left, threw left

Thurman had a late start in baseball, but still managed to ascend to a career in the major leagues, albeit well past his prime. His baseball skills were noticed while playing ball in the Army during the mid 1940s and his first Negro League play didn't come until 1946, at age 29, with the Homestead Grays.

He first attracted attention as a lefty pitcher, but it was his bat which carried him through a 15-year career, which included parts of five seasons with the Cincinnati Reds. Thurman left organized ball in 1953 to play for the Brantford Red Sox of the Intercounty League in Ontario. Two years later, at age 38, he won a spot with Cincinnati. In 1957 he hit 16 home runs in just 190 at bats for the Reds. Thurman played baseball year-round. He competed in Puerto Rico for a dozen seasons and is a member of the country's Baseball Hall of Fame. Upon retiring as a player, Thurman worked as a scout. He died in 1998 at age 81.

    1953 Brantford Red Sox—Statistics not available

Frank "Spike" Tillman—Shortstop

The 17-year-old infielder played with the 1950 edition of the Indian Head Rockets.

Canadian Highlights: June 26, 1950, Tillman had three hits in the Rockets' 3–3 tie with Regina

Jorge Torres—Second Base

The Cuban infielder played in Mexico in 1947 for the Pasquel brothers in their ill-fated league. When Roland Gladu became the playing manager of the Sherbrooke team he remembered Torres from his Mexican days and in 1948 invited him to come to Canada.

    1948 Sherbrooke A's—.305, 5 HR, 57 RBI

Walter Towns—Utility

The Los Angeles youngster was on the roster of the Vancouver Capilanos in 1952. He was being groomed as a catcher after having first played as a second baseman in high school then a pitcher in a trial in pro ball. Towns tried out in the Pioneer League in 1951 and returned to semi-pro ball in Los Angeles after being released.

Dan Townsend—Shortstop

Townsend was in the Elmwood Giants preseason camp in May of 1949. The Giants reported that Townsend was 24 years old and had played for the Cleveland Buckeyes.

Bob Trice—Pitcher, 6'2", 190 lbs. Batted right, threw right

Trice played the 1948 and 1949 seasons with the famous Homestead Grays before traveling to Quebec to suit up with Farnham of the Provincial League, which was entering organized ball. He spent the 1950 and 1951 seasons with Farnham and 1952 with St, Hyacinthe. In 1953, he was promoted to Triple-A with Ottawa and then with the Philadelphia A's. He played parts of three seasons with Philadelphia and Kansas City and ended with a 9–9 major league record. In 1953, he was the first African-American player on the A's. He died in 1988 in Wierton, West Virginia.

>1950 Farnham Pirates—Won 5, Lost 3
>1951 Farnham Pirates—Won 7, Lost 12, 5.15 ERA, .237, 2 HR
>1952 St. Hyacinthe A's—Won 16, Lost 3, 3.49 ERA, .297, 13 D, 5 T, 1 HR
>1953 Ottawa Athletics—Won 21, Lost 3, 3.10 ERA, .255, 4 HR
>1954 Ottawa Athletics—Won 4, Lost 8, 3.23 ERA, .298, 4 HR

Canadian Highlights: His sixteen wins for St. Hyacinthe tied him for the most victories in 1952. In 1953, with Ottawa, he was named to the all-star team and named Pitcher Of The Year in the International League

Percy Trimont—Catcher/Pitcher/Outfield. Batted both, threw right

Trimont starred for four seasons in Western Canada beginning in 1952 with the Indian Head Rockets. He was the main offensive force for the 1953 Regina Caps and the Saskatoon Gems of 1954–1955. A speed-power combination, Trimont led the Saskatchewan Baseball League in homers, triples and walks in 1954. The next year, he was among the leaders in stolen bases and again topped the circuit in bases on balls.

>1952 Indian Head Rockets—Statistics not available
>1953 Regina Caps—.338, 7 HR
>1954 Saskatoon Gems—.303, 9 D, 9 T, 11 HR, 39 RBI, 60 BB
>1955 Saskatoon Gems—.281, 4 HR, 39 RBI, 11 SB, 56 BB

Canadian Highlights: August 13, 1952, Trimont clubbed a pair of homers, two doubles and a single in five trips, but Indian Head dropped a 16–11 decision to the Florida Cubans.

May 17, 1953, Trimont had four hits, including a homer in Regina's loss to Moose Jaw. He had a three-run homer in a win the previous day. June 11, Trimont was the big gun for Regina with a three-run homer, triple and single as Caps thumped Saskatoon 12–6. July 1, at the Saskatoon Optimist Tournament, Trimont had five hits, including a two-run homer in a 12–5 win over Kamsack.

May 17, 1954, his three-run homer in the first inning was all the Gems needed in a 6–2 win over North Battleford. May 24, Trimont clubbed a towering homer over the center field wall and added a pair of singles as Saskatoon dropped a 5–2 decision to North Battleford. June 2, he drove in six runs with a homer, three triples and a single in a 12–1 triumph over Lloydminster. July 3, it was a triple, double and single, but Saskatoon still lost to Lloydminster 3–1. July 18, he bashed a homer, triple and single, driving in three runs in a 5–1 victory over Lloydminster. July 20, he drove in three runs with a homer, double and single against Moose Jaw.

June 19, 1955, Trimont's three-run homer and two-run single were the key blows as Saskatoon beat Lloydminster 8–6. July 23, he belted a pair of homers as the Gems beat North Battleford 7–5. September 8, Trimont had four hits, but the Gems lost a 6–5 playoff match to Edmonton. He had three hits the next night as the Gems won 9–7.

Quincy Trouppe—Catcher/Outfield, 6'3", 219 lbs. Batted both, threw right

The big receiver made his initial foray into Canada in 1935 with Satchel Paige and the Bismarck club which was tuning up for the inaugural national semi-pro tournament in Wichita. Trouppe caught Paige in the celebrated June 6th matchup in Winnipeg between Paige and Chet Brewer. The game ended in a 0–0 tie as Satchel fanned 17. Trouppe played in the Negro League, with the integrated Bismarck team, in Mexico and Canada from 1930 to 1951. He was a Negro League All-Star five times. At age 39, he turned to organized ball in 1952 advancing to the Cleveland Indians for a half-dozen games in the major leagues. Trouppe died in 1993 in Missouri.

1949 Drummondville Cubs—.277, 8 HR, 37 RBI

Leonard W. Tucker—Outfield, First Base, 6'2", 205 lbs. Batted right, threw left

The College of Sequoias and Fresno State University baseball and basketball star was the first black player to be signed by the St. Louis Cardinals.

He first came to play in Canada in 1952 with the Kamsack Cyclones of the Manitoba-Saskatchewan League. All he did, according to the Fresno Bee *(August 15, 1952)*, was hit .480 and lead the circuit in home runs, triples, doubles and stolen bases.

After a minor league career (which included some amazing numbers) he returned to Saskatchewan in 1957 to lead the Western Canada League in home runs and RBI while finishing second in the batting race (at .394). Tucker, playing for Saskatoon, had an on-base percentage of .506 and slugging mark of .778. He likely set a league record with hits in 23 consecutive games. He was back on the prairies in 1961 for a late-season and playoff appearance with the Lethbridge White Sox.

His 1956 season with Pampa, Texas, of the Southwestern League, is one for the books—565 at bats, 181 runs, 228 hits, 40 doubles, 13 triples, 51 homers, 181 runs batted in, 47 steals, .404 average. The closest he came to a major league roster spot came in 1958 in Spring Training with Washington.

1951 Kamsack Cyclones—.480
1957 Saskatoon Gems—.394, 18 HR, 69 RBI, 17 SB
1961 Lethbridge White Sox—Statistics not available

Canadian Highlights: July 3, 1952, Tucker belted a homer and a three-run double to lead Kamsack to a 5-4 win over the Florida Cubans. June 24, 1957, the newcomer to Saskatoon belted a two-run homer and single in a 4–3 win over Moose Jaw. The next day he had three hits, including a homer and scored the winning run in a 9–8 decision over Regina. June 28, Tucker drove in four runs, scored four and stole a pair of bases as the Gems trounced Lloydminster 17–7. July 1, in a twin-bill split with North Battleford, Tucker had two homers, a double and three singles. July 7, he drove in six runs with two homers and a double as the Gems downed Lloydminster 14–11. July 13, in a double-header sweep of Edmonton, Tucker had a bases-clearing double in the opener and a three-run homer in the second game. July 15, Tucker ran his hit streak to 21 games with a homer and double to pace Saskatoon over Regina 7–1.

August 17, 1961, Lethbridge scored a stunning upset in the opening game of the Western Canada Baseball League's final series as newcomer Len Tucker singled, stole second and scored the game's only run on an infield out in the 15th inning to give the Sox a 1–0 win over the Commodores at Saskatoon. August 19, in the third game of the series, Tucker scored the winning run in the 9th inning as Lethbridge won 2–1. He had scored the first run, scoring all the way from first base on a single. August 23, Tucker had a triple, double and single as Lethbridge won the title with a 4–2 win over Saskatoon. (The Commodores, who fielded five players who would go on to the major leagues, ran away with the league pennant finishing 21½ games ahead of Lethbridge.)

Bob Turner—Catcher. Batted right, threw right

Turner was a backup catcher with the Kansas City Monarchs in 1946 and the Houston Eagles in 1950 and had brief tours in organized ball in the late 1940s and early 1950s. He was the regular catcher for the Regina Caps of the Western Canada League in 1951 before the team ran into financial trouble and he left to join Minot of the ManDak League. After a season back in organized ball, with Chet Brewer's Class-C, Porterville Comets, Turner came to Carman for the 1953 ManDak season.

1951 Regina Caps—.275 (Incomplete)
1951 Minot Mallards—.182, 0 HR, 3 RBI
1953 Carman Cardinals—.204, 1 HR, 33 RBI

Walt Tyler—Outfield/Pitcher, 5'11", 198 lbs. Batted left

Tyler was a Rodney Dangerfield of minor league baseball. A consistent hitter and run-producer (and sometimes moundsman), he just did not receive the respect he thought due, given his on-field skills. In every full-season of play, Tyler put up top hitting marks—.366, .329, .387, .405, .344, .392, .370, .310 and .321, but, for the most part, spent his career in the lower rungs of the minor leagues. Off-field issues may have been a reason. In 1954, in Moose Jaw (after he had played and managed the team the year previous) Tyler got off to a hot start hitting .387 over the first few weeks then suddenly was released. A report from a meeting of league officials noted there was an agreement to keep him out of the circuit.

> The case of former Moose Jaw player, Walt Tyler, who was released Saturday by the Mallards, came in for discussion. After being released the player had sought a place with three other clubs, Saskatoon, Indian Head and Rosetown, it was disclosed. It was agreed by all Saskatchewan League clubs that they would not sign Tyler, but that he would be free to go to any other league [*Saskatoon Star-Phoenix*, June 14, 1954].

Tyler, who had hit .329 in 1953 and was hitting nearly .400 in the beginning weeks of the 1954 season, had come to Canada after starring with Chet Brewer's team in the Southwest International League in 1952 when he hit .366 and drove in 82 runs.

After his release from Moose Jaw, he departed for Mexicali in the Arizona-Texas League and hit .405 over the rest of the season and followed that with a .344 season in 1955 and a league-leading .392 in 1956. After a .370 summer with Tucson in 1957, Tyler moved on to the Double-A, Mexican League and was a top swatter there for two seasons.

1953 Medicine Hat Phillies—Statistics not available
1953 Moose Jaw Maples—.329
1954 Moose Jaw Mallards—.387

Canadian Highlights: May 14, 1953, Tyler, with the Medicine Hat Phillies, drove in four runs with three hits as the touring club downed Lethbridge 8–2. May 24, Tyler, who hurled the last three innings of the first game, tossed shutout ball as the Phillies downed Regina 1–0 in a five-inning affair in the nightcap. The first game went 15 innings. June 20, Tyler took over the reins of the Moose Jaw Maples, the team's fourth manager in a week. July 20, Tyler belted a pair of homers, one a grand slam, but Moose Jaw lost, 11–8, to North Battleford. July 25, Tyler allowed just five hits in downing Indian Head 4–3. July 28, Tyler drove in five runs with a pair of homers and a single at Carman as Moose Jaw lost to the Cards 11–6. August 14, Tyler had four hits and knocked in four as Moose Jaw fought to a draw with Regina in a game called because of darkness.

May 24, 1954, Tyler paced Moose Jaw with 3 hits in a 6–2 win over Indian Head.

Henry "Big Train" Underwood—Catcher

Underwood was the regular backstop for the Ligon All-Stars during their early barnstorming tours of Western Canada. He was with the squad in both the 1947 and 1948 tours.

Rene Valdes/Valdez (Gutierrez)—Pitcher, 6'3", 175 lbs. Batted right, threw right

The 6-foot-3 Cuban right-hander was a double-digit winner for ten straight years in the minor leagues from 1952 to 1961. In his best season he won 22 games in Triple-A with Portland Beavers of the Pacific Coast League. Valdez had a "cup of coffee" with Brooklyn in 1957. He was a steady performer for the Montreal Royals for four seasons before concluding his pro career with three years in Mexico.

1957 Montreal Royals—Won 11, Lost 13, 2.87, ERA
1958 Montreal Royals—Won 15, Lost 14, 4.03, ERA
1959 Montreal Royals—Won 11, Lost 8, 3.64, ERA

1960 Montreal Royals—Won 11, Lost 17, 3.92, ERA

Canadian Highlights: May 26, 1957, in his first game with the Royals, Valdes hurled a three-hitter only to lose 3–1 to Toronto. June 11, he was even better, with a two-hitter, in a 2–0 shutout of the Cubans. June 16, the right-hander, nicknamed "The Whip," tossed his second straight shutout in a 3–0 blanking of Miami.

July 1, 1959. Valdes fired a two-hit shutout in besting Columbus 2–0. July 14, he held Buffalo to six hits in a 2–1 triumph, his 4th in a row. August 6, he fired a six-hitter against Columbus, but lost 1–0 to Al Jackson.

James A. "Jimmy" Valentine—Second Base/Third Base/Shortstop, 5'8", 170 lbs. Batted right, threw right

After two years military service in the Navy, Valentine suited up in Negro League ball with the Memphis Red Sox in 1951 and most of 1952, when he also had a brief stint with Brandon Greys. He returned to Brandon for the 1953 season, spent 1954 with Memphis and the Louisville Black Colonels. After starting the 1955 season with the Detroit Stars, he joined the Lloydminster Meridians of the Western Canada League for two summers, 1955–1956. Back with Memphis for two years, he returned for a few games in 1959 with Lloydminster and with Medicine Hat of the Southern Alberta League.

1952 Brandon Greys—Statistics not available
1953 Brandon Greys—.306, 12 D, 1 T, 1 HR, 25 RBI
1955 Lloydminster Meridians—.307, 8 D, 2 T, 1 HR, 37 RBI
1956 Lloydminster Meridians—.249, 11 D, 0 T, 0 HR, 31 RBI
1959 Lloydminster/Medicine Hat—Statistics not available

Canadian Highlights: May 19, 1953 Valentine punched out a triple and two singles in a losing cause against Carman. May 22, Valentine got three hits as Brandon beat the Winnipeg Royals 18–5 in a slugfest. June 6, Valentine produced two doubles and a single in a loss to

The 1956 Lloydminster, Saskatchewan, Meridians featured four former Negro Leaguers, a Cuban import, a sprinkling of ex-pros, a few collegiate stars, and, a bat boy who, more than fifty years later, would co-author a book on Black and Caribbean players in Canada. Back row (left to right)—John Karpinski, Ben Lott, Gary Ball, Bill Bailey, Jim Hansen, Keith Gustin, Ed Kalski, Curly Williams, Stan Karpinski. Front row (left to right)—Dick Satalich, Jim Valentine, Eddie Morris, Roberto Zayas, Harvey Mah (batboy), Barney Brown (photograph from the Mah collection).

Carman. In mid-June, he spent a short time with the Winnipeg Royals before returning to Brandon. July 23, in his first game back with Brandon, he had three hits including a home run as Brandon beat the Winnipeg Royals 9–2. July 28, Valentine had another three-hit game in an 8–4 win over the Winnipeg Royals.

June 28, 1955, Valentine had three hits helping Lloydminster shade Regina 5–4. July 20, Valentine's bases-loaded triple in the 9th was the crucial hit as Lloydminster scored eight in the final frame to again beat Regina. He followed with three hits the next day in a loss to Moose Jaw. Lloydminster beat North Battleford 9–5 on August 21, and Valentine led the way with three hits.

June 10, 1956, Valentine drove in four runs as Lloydminster beat Edmonton 6–5. In a double-header, July 2, Valentine's two-run single in the 9th drove in the tying and winning runs in the opener and he knocked in six runs in the second game as Lloydminster beat the Eskimos 13–7. July 12, Barney Brown tossed a two-hitter and Valentine drove in three runs in an 8–1 win over Moose Jaw.

Russ Valentine—Pitcher. Threw right

Valentine was from Maryland and, in 1950, played with the Brooklyn Cuban Giants when they barnstormed across Western Canada. In 1951 he joined the Brandon Greys in the ManDak League. Released in mid-season, Valentine played with the Kamsack Cyclones of the Manitoba-Saskatchewan League before being resigned by the Greys.

1951 Brandon Greys—Won 1, Lost 1, 7 G, 4 GS, 0 CG

Jose Valladares—Second Base, 5'6", 150 lbs. Batted right, threw right

The Cuban middle infielder came north to play for the Indian Head Rockets in 1954, and just a month into the season was sold to the Saskatoon Gems where he finished out the season and returned for the following two summers. Although he had little power, he was among the top batsmen in the league during his tenure on the prairies. In 1956, Valladares led the league in runs, with 58, and stolen bases, 17. He had a pro career from 1957 to 1961 following his time in Western Canada.

1954 Indian Head/Saskatoon—.285, 1 HR, 25 RBI, 21 SB
1955 Saskatoon Gems—.302, 0 HR, 31 RBI, 14 SB
1956 Saskatoon Gems—.313, 0 HR, 31 RBI, 17 SB (1ST)

Canadian Highlights: June 4, 1954, Valladares had a triple and double as the Rockets topped Saskatoon 4–1. June 6, Valladares hit a double, two singles, scored twice and stole a base in a win over Rosetown. June 14, Valladares had 7 putouts, 3 assists and participated in 3 double-plays in a 5–2 victory over Lloydminster. June 27, his three-run homer led Indian Head by Rosetown 11–2.

July 16, 1955, he had three hits and scored four times as the Gems trounced Lloydminster 16–4. August 7, Valladares belted three hits as Saskatoon downed Edmonton 15–10. August 22, Valladares when 0 for 0 but scored four times as he got on base five times on walks.

July 19, 1956, Valladares went 5 for 5 to lead the Gems to an 8–3 win over Edmonton.

Mark Van Buren—Umpire

The colorful and controversial arbiter was believed to have played in the Negro League in the 1930s before switching to a role as an umpire. He worked his new craft in the Negro loop and with barnstorming teams, such as the Jackie Robinson All-Stars. In 1950, officials of the new ManDak League hired him to give the league umpires some experience and assistance. He was based in Brandon and would umpire over two seasons in the league. In an interview with the Free Press, Van Buren, commenting on the play in the ManDak League, said, "The ManDak League play was just as good as in the Negro League."

Canadian Highlights: June 12, 1950, Van Buren called six balks on Elmwood Giants pitcher Ray Finch. The Giants lost the game 4–2. September 14, in the final playoff game, Van Buren threw Buffaloes manager Willie Wells out of the game after a close play in the tenth inning with the score tied 0–0. Van Buren threatened to forfeit the game and a police escort was called, but Wells left the field voluntarily.

May 31, 1951, he tossed Minot Mallards manager Otto Huber from the game in the third inning. As Minot had no extra players, the game was about to be ended. However, after an apology from Huber, Van Buren allowed the Minot playing-manager to stay in the game and finish the contest.

Guillermo Vargas—Outfield, 5'11", 140 lbs. Batted right, threw right

Vargas played the 1949 season in the Negro League with the New York Cubans and played in Mexico in 1950. In 1952, he signed with Drummondville in the Quebec Provincial League for his only season in Canada.

- 1952 Drummondville Cubs—.282, 3 HR, 6 RBI

Roberto Vargas—Pitcher, 5'11", 175 lbs. Batted left, threw left

The Puerto Rican left-hander had just one season in the Negro League, 1948, with the Chicago American Giants. He moved to the Quebec League in 1949 with Drummondville, at that time not yet in organized ball. With twelve wins, he was one of the Cubs' top starting pitchers. After winning 18 games with the independent Lakeland Pilots in Florida in 1951, Vargas was signed by Cleveland and spent two seasons with the Indians' Class-A club in the Eastern League. Drafted by Milwaukee in 1954, Vargas pitched in 25 games in the major leagues with the Braves, without a decision. Later, he pitched in Montreal before ending his career playing in the Mexican League.

- 1949 Drummondville Cubs—Won 12, Lost 9
- 1957 Montreal Royals—Won 5, Lost 8, 3.48 ERA
- 1959 Montreal Royals—Won 0, Lost 1

Clemente Varona—Shortstop

The Cuban-born shortstop (advertised as a 20-year-old rookie) toured with the Brooklyn Cuban Giants in 1950, and suited up with the Indian Head Rockets of the Western Canada League in 1951. In 1952, Varona played a few games in organized ball with Porterville in the Southwest International League. He returned in 1953 to play for the Regina Caps.

- 1951 Indian Head Rockets—.310 (incomplete)
- 1953 Regina Caps—Statistics not available

Canadian Highlights: June 21, 1951, Varona produced three hits to lead Indian Head to a 7–5 win over Estevan and a share of first place in the WCBL. July 8, Varona suffered a broken leg in sliding home to try to beat a throw from the outfield in the final game of the Moosomin Tournament. He had five hits in six at bats in the tourney before the injury.

June 6, 1953, Varona had two doubles and a single and drove in a pair as Regina and North Battleford fought to a tie in a game called because of darkness.

Armando Vasquez—First Base/Pitcher, 5'8", 160 lbs. Batted left, threw left

Vasquez was born in Cuba and played with traveling teams (including the Cincinnati Clowns, Indianapolis Clowns and Havana La Palomas) from 1944 to 1947. He made his first appearance in Canada in 1947 when the La Palomas played an exhibition series in Winnipeg against the Cincinnati Crescents. In 1948, he started the season in the Negro League with the New York Cubans before jumping to the Brandon Greys in the Manitoba Senior Baseball League.

When he came to the Greys he first used the name of Bus Quinn. Using an alias was a common practice among some players of that era. Vasquez was a solid all-around player, hitting .324 his first season, third-best in the league, while winning 10 of 11 decisions as a pitcher. In 1949 he hit .289 and led the team with 16 triples. On the mound he appeared in 19 games, winning 12, losing just one. He was with the Greys for five seasons.

In a special ceremony in 2006, Vasquez was inducted into the Manitoba Baseball Hall Of Fame. He died in 2008 in New York.

- 1948 Brandon Greys—.324, Won 10, Lost 1, 11 G 9 GS, 9 CG *
- 1949 Brandon Greys—.289, 16 T, 4 HR, 13 SB, 84 RBI *, Won 12, Lost 1, G 19, GS 14, CG 11 *
- 1950 Brandon Greys—.244, 1 HR, 27 RBI, Won 1, Lost 0
- 1951 Brandon Greys—.279, 3 HR, 17 RBI, Won 0, Lost 1

1952 Brandon Greys—.314, 1 HR, 24 RBI, Won 2, Lost 4

All games—league, playoff, tournament, exhibition.

Canadian Highlights: June 7, 1948, in his first game with Brandon, Vasquez had four hits in an exhibition game victory over Rolla, North Dakota.

June 6, 1949, he had four RBI in the first game of a double header victory over Gilbert Plains. Vasquez won the second game going the distance in a 6–4 win. In a double header win over Walhalla, North Dakota, June 14, he had five hits including a home run and seven RBI. August 3, 1949, Vasquez knocked in four runs in a 5–4 win over Carman. The Free Press newspaper picked Vasquez as the all-star first baseman in 1949.

July 1, 1950, in the Dominion Day Tournament in Brandon, Manitoba, the Greys beat the Brooklyn Cuban Giants to reach the final. Vasquez led the way with a triple and three singles.

July 13, 1951, he had four hits and three RBI to lead Brandon to a 13–5 victory over Elmwood.

August 4, 1952, Vasquez was the hero in the Carman Tournament. In the bottom of the ninth inning he singled, stole second and third and scored on a wild throw.

Jose Vera—Pitcher

Vera pitched in the Saskatchewan Baseball League in 1953 with both Saskatoon and Regina.

Canadian Highlights: May 18, 1953, Vera allowed a run in each of the first two innings then settled down to hold Regina to three hits the rest of the way in a 5–3 win. June 10, in a superb relief effort, Vera pitched six innings of shutout ball as Saskatoon topped Prince Albert 15–4 at the Prince Albert Tournament. June 28, after pitching six innings of relief in the first game of a double-header, Vera hurled a one-hitter in the second game as Saskatoon and Prince Albert split the twin-bill.

Isaac Walker—Catcher/Pitcher, 5'10", 173 lbs. Batted right, threw right.

Isaac and his brother Oscar (below) attracted notice in 1963 while barnstorming with the Satchel Paige All-Stars. After a brief spin in pro ball in 1964, the pair traveled north to play for St. Lazare in the Manitoba Senior League. Isaac was squeezed out of a job after just one season as the league reduced the number of imports each team was allowed to carry.

1964 St. Lazare Athletics—.289, 13 RBI

Canadian Highlights: June 19, 1964, Walker fired a four-hitter and fanned 12 as the A's topped Souris. July 20, he had four hits, including a homer and double in a 20–2 trouncing of Dauphin.

Armando Vasquez, the Cuban pitcher-first baseman, spent five years in Canada with the Brandon Greys. In his first two seasons, the lefty hurler, won a combined twenty-two games while losing just two (photograph courtesy Lil Lowe).

Oscar Walker—Second Base, 5'9", 160 lbs. Batted right. threw right

In 1965 he led the Manitoba Senior League with a .452 average in 93 at bats. He also topped the loop in triples, 5, and runs, 35. He finished in the top ten in 1964 with a .352 mark. The little second sacker was selected to the all-star team both seasons.

>1964 St. Lazare Athletics—.352, 12 RBI
>1965 St. Lazare Athletics—.452, 4 HR, 22 RBI

Canadian Highlights: June 14, 1964, Walker had three hits in the first game of a twin-bill and added a triple, double and single in the nightcap as the A's took a pair from Brandon. August 4, he had three hits and was brilliant in the field as he figured in eight putouts and started three double plays as St. Lazare topped Brandon in playoff action.

In a double-header June 5, 1965, Walker had three singles in the opener and hit for the cycle in the second game—a single, double, triple and homer—as St. Lazare won 8-7 and 12-5 over Riverside.

George "Junior" Walton—First Base. Batted right

Walton arrived in Canada with the touring San Francisco Sea Lions in 1948 and 1949 and came back to play with the Estevan Maple Leafs in 1950.

Canadian Highlights: July 17, 1951, Walton had a double and two singles in a loss to Medicine Hat. The next day he had three hits as the Leafs advanced at the Indian Head Tournament with a win over the Ligon All-Stars.

Archie Ware—First Base, 5'9", 160 lbs. Batted left, threw left

Ware played in the Negro League from 1940 to 1950. Most of his Negro League career was spent with the Cleveland Buckeyes. In 1951, he joined Farnham in the Quebec Provincial League and, in 1952, he closed out his career in the Western International League with Lewiston.

>1951 Farnham Pirates—.257, 10 D, 1 T, 6 HR, 48 RBI

Howard Warfield—Center Field

The fleet center fielder was another of the Philadelphia-area players who suited up with the Rosetown Phillies of the 1954 Western Canada League. Warfield, a semi-pro veteran, was one of the league's leading run producers (5th in runs batted in) and provided sensational defense. Late in the season he took over as playing-manager of the Phillies.

>1954 Rosetown Phillies—.261, 7 T, 4 HR, 10 SB, 41 RBI

Canadian Highlights: May 19, 1954, Warfield was outstanding in center field for the Phillies making six putouts and adding two assists in Rosetown's 6-2 win over North Battleford. May 25, he popped a triple and double as Rosetown lost 18-15 to Saskatoon. June 15, he singled and scored the winning run in the 10th inning as Rosetown won its opening game at the Lloydminster Legion Tournament. He also contributed a double. June 20, Warfield had a homer, double and single in a 10-9 loss to Moose Jaw. July 4, he added a homer and single as Rosetown fell to Lloydminster in 11 innings. July 16, a bases-loaded triple was the difference as Rosetown beat North Battleford 6-4. July 26, Warfield was the hero as Rosetown shaded Moose Jaw 5-4 in ten innings. He knocked in three runs including the winner in the 10th and made eight putouts in the outfield. July 28, his towering homer keyed a four-run 3rd inning as Rosetown blanked Colonsay in the opening round of the Rosetown Tournament. August 3, Warfield accounted for all four runs for the Phillies in a victory over Lloydminster. A bases-loaded triple was the key hit. August 4, he made a brilliant throw from center field to nab Jose Valladares at the plate in the all-star game at Saskatoon.

John Washington—First Base, 6'2", 185 lbs. Batted left, threw left

Washington had an extended stay in the Negro League playing from 1933 to 1950 with seven teams. He joined the Elmwood Giants in 1950 in the new ManDak League and would have four productive seasons in Canada. A solid hitter, he was regarded as an excellent fielding first baseman. He closed out his career in 1954 with the Carman Cardinals.

1951 Elmwood Giants—.359, 16 D, 6 HR, 45 RBI
1952 Winnipeg Giants—.265, 7 D, 2 HR, 28 RBI
1953 Brandon Greys—.327, 12 D, 1 T, 4 HR, 45 RBI
1954 Carman Cardinals—.277, 11 D, 2 T, 1 HR, 36 RBI

Canadian Highlights: June 14, 1951, Carman beat the Giants 10–6. Washington led the Giants with a double and three singles. June 29, he punched out five hits in a 13–6 victory over Carman. The next day he hit a home run, two singles, scored twice and had two RBI as the Giants beat the Winnipeg Buffaloes 10–3.

May 24, 1953, Washington had four hits in a 12–4 Brandon win over Carman. September 14, in a playoff game against Minot, Washington was suspended for the remainder of the playoffs for attacking an umpire. When Brandon failed to field their team after the rhubarb, the contest was awarded to Minot.

Ross Washington—Outfield

Washington was a mid-season addition to the 1954 Indian Head Rockets, from the Jacksonville Eagles.

Canadian Highlights: July 23, 1954, Washington had a triple and two singles as the Rockets dropped an 8–6 decision to Moose Jaw. July 26, Washington's 4th inning triple proved to be the key hit as Indian Head shaded Lloydminster, 4–3

Murray "Skeeter" Watkins—Infield, 5'4", 135 lbs. Batted left, threw right

The diminutive infielder played in the Negro League from 1941 to 1949 with the Philadelphia Stars, Indianapolis Clowns and Newark Eagles. He also toured with the Jackie Robinson All-Stars. In 1950, he joined the Brandon Greys and played three seasons in the ManDak League.

1950 Brandon Greys—.222, 0 HR, 13 RBI, 10 SB
1951 Brandon Greys—.262, 1 HR, 26 RBI, 19 SB
1952 Brandon Greys—.225, 0 HR, 13 RBI, 12 SB

Canadian Highlights: July 12, 1950, Watkins had three hits in a Greys' loss to the Winnipeg Buffaloes. July 24, he placed a bunt perfectly down the first base line that scored manager Ian Lowe with the winning run in the tenth inning to give the Greys an 8–7 victory over Minot. Watkins was involved in a triple play August 24. Ian Lowe, at third base, scooped up the ball and fired it to Watkins at second base, who threw to first in time for Armando Vasquez to touch base and fire home to catch Carman's Bob Johnson trying to score from third. August 30, Watkins stole home with the winning run that gave Brandon a 2–1 opening game victory over the Carman Cardinals.

Watkins had three hits and two RBI in a 6–2 win against the Elmwood Giants on June 9, 1951. In games on July 13, against Minot and July 18, against Carman he had three hits in each game. Watkins was the story on July 19, as he led Brandon with four hits, scored once and drove in the tying and winning runs in a victory over the Winnipeg Buffaloes. That gave Watkins eleven hits in his last sixteen plate appearances. September 11, in the second game of the league final, Watkins paced the Greys at the plate with three hits as the Greys beat the Buffaloes 17–8 in a wild game.

Sherman Watrous—Catcher/Outfield. Batted left, threw right

Watrous spent three seasons with Saskatoon, Saskatchewan, clubs in 1950, 1951 (after a tryout with the Winnipeg Buffaloes) and 1953. In 1952, he was one of the top hitters in the Negro American League with the Memphis Red Sox. He was the clean-up hitter for the West in the '52 East-West All-Star Game.

1950 Saskatoon Cubs—.277 (led the league with 16 SB)
1951 Saskatoon 55s—Statistics not available
1953 Saskatoon Gems—.286

Canadian Highlights: May 31, 1950, the burly catcher had three hits, a triple and double included, and a steal of home, to lead Saskatoon to a 9–6 win over Colonsay. July 5, Watrous had two hits, but it was his base running which had the fans applauding. He stole home twice and had four other steals. August 17, in playoff action, his three hits paced Saskatoon to a 7–5 triumph over North Battleford. He had a homer and triple, August 20, in the second game of the series. The next day, Watrous belted a two-run homer.

June 16, 1951, Watrous had seven hits in eleven trips to the plate over two games as Saskatoon 55s won the Kenaston Tournament. July 13, he had three hits, one of them a triple, to pace Saskatoon 55s to a 4–1 win over Kamsack Cyclones to take top money in the Kamsack Tournament.

July 8, 1952, in a Negro League game played at Winnipeg, Watrous belted a homer and single as the Memphis Red Sox shutdown the Chicago American Giants 6–0. The following day, he singled and scored in the first inning as Memphis again downed the Giants, 3–0.

June 19, 1953, Watrous provided the firepower with a two-run triple and homer as Saskatoon Gems downed Moose Jaw 7–2. July 30, he clouted a grand slam homer to lead the Gems to a 10–2 win in the semi-finals of the Rosetown Tournament. August 8, Watrous had three hits and knocked in a pair as Saskatoon whipped Regina 10–2. The previous day, Watrous had three hits as Saskatoon beat Indian Head to capture the National Baseball Congress provincial title.

Amos Watson—Pitcher, 6'0", 170 lbs. Batted right, threw right

Watson, from Lakeland, Florida, played in the Negro League from 1945 to 1947 with the Indianapolis Clowns, Kansas City Monarchs and Baltimore Elite Giants. He joined the Elmwood Giants in 1949 as one of their import players in the Manitoba Senior League. He stayed with the Giants in 1950 when the team played in the ManDak League.

> 1949 Elmwood Giants—Won 8, Lost 4, 17 G, 12 GS, 10 CG
> 1950 Elmwood Giants—Won 1, Lost 2, 7 G, 6 GS, 1 CG

Canadian Highlights: July 14, 1949, the headline right across page 20 of the Winnipeg Free Press read "WATSON SHINES IN GIANT SWEEP." Watson fired a two-hitter to win the opener 2–0 and pitched into the 4th inning of the second game, allowing just one run, as the Giants won 8–4.

Harry Watts—Second Base, 6'0", 172 lbs. Batted right, threw right

Watts kicked off his career in organized ball in 1958 in the Cardinals farm system at the Class-B and Class-D levels. He joined the Winnipeg Goldeyes in 1959 and hit for power, leading the team in home runs, with 22. He advanced to Triple-A before wrapping up his pro career in the Texas League with Dallas-Fort Worth, a Chicago Cubs farm club.

> 1959 Winnipeg Goldeyes—.296, 28 D, 4 T, 22 HR, 83 RBI

Canadian Highlights: May 10, 1959, Watts had a big day as the Goldeyes split a doubleheader with Minot. He went three for four in the first game and three for five in the nightcap. The Winnipeg Free Press reported on June 29, that Watts helped Dick Hughes the Goldeyes' pitcher by making a super-human effort behind second base to rob Chuck Hinton of a two-run single. It reported that Watts also handled six other chances, several of the tough variety as the Goldeyes nipped Aberdeen 1–0. August 11, Watts clubbed a grand slam homer to highlight a come-from-behind, 11–10, win over Minot.

Joe Webb—Catcher

Webb Came from Hot Springs, Nebraska, to suit up with the independent Swift Current Indians in 1950.

Canadian Highlights: In his initial game with Swift Current, May 13, Webb had three hits and scored a pair in a win over Shaunavon. Webb was a key as the Indians took top money in the Sceptre Tournament. June 17, Webb clouted an inside-the-park homer, a single and had three walks for the Indians in an exhibition match against Muskogee Cardinals.

> "Throughout the day, Webb, Indians catcher was the sparkplug of the team, and drew rounds of applause from the crowd" [*Regina Leader-Post*, May 27, 1950].

Dan Webster—Pitcher/Catcher

Webster had played semi-pro ball in his hometown area of Detroit. In 1950, when Red House took over as manager of the Carman Cardinals he brought Webster to Canada.

When Carman got off to a slow start, Webster was one of the players released, along with House.

1950 Carman Cardinals—Won 0, Lost 2, 5 G, 2 GS, 1 CG

Ira Wells—Pitcher, 210 pounds. Threw left

Wells, a Texas native, had pitched briefly with the Memphis Red Sox in 1948 and played on the West Coast in the late 1940s with teams in Oakland. He joined the Regina Caps of the Southern (Saskatchewan) League in 1950.

Canadian Highlights: June 14, 1950, Wells gave a sterling performance at the Brandon Tournament, but still came away with a loss.

> Ira Wells, giant Regina mound ace, turned in one of the best individual performances of the day, when he all but stopped the potent Buffs single-handedly. Wells fashioned a five-hitter, fielded brilliantly and collected two of the seven hits by Regina off veteran Spoon Carter of the Buffs. However, costly errors by his mates accounted for four of the Buff runs and kept him in trouble most of the way [*The Leader-Post*, Regina, June 15, 1950].

Willie Wells—Infield/Pitcher/Manager, 5'8", 160 lbs. Batted right, threw right

Regarded by many as the greatest shortstop in Negro League history, Wells was inducted into the National Baseball Hall of Fame at Cooperstown in 1997.

He had a starry Negro League career from 1924 to 1949 and 1954 in which he played in eight East-West All-Star games. Wells was a member of the Newark Eagles' "Million Dollar Infield" (which included Mule Suttles at first and Ray Dandridge at third) in the late 1930s.

In 1949, with Jackie Robinson having integrated the major leagues, and the Negro League in decline, the 43-year-old Wells turned to Canada to extend his career. He joined the Elmwood Giants of the Manitoba Senior League and hit .333 in limited play.

In 1950, the ManDak (Manitoba-Dakota) Baseball League was starting up and Winnipeg Buffaloes' owner Stanley Zedd hired Wells as his playing manager. Wells constructed a squad mainly of players from the Negro League. Under his guidance the Buffaloes captured the first ManDak League championship. He was back at the helm of the Buffaloes again in 1951. Early in the season the St Louis Browns sent their head scout to Winnipeg looking for African-American talent. The scout was pleasantly surprised. When he left town he had Leon Day, Charlie White and Butch Davis signed to organized ball contracts.

The signings seriously hampered the Buffaloes' chances to repeat. They did reach the final before losing to Brandon. Zedd became disillusioned and disbanded the team. This left Wells looking for another baseball home. Brandon approached and Wells guided the Greys in 1952 and 1953. During his time in the ManDak League he added some mound duties as he would pitch in tournaments when his team was shorthanded or take the hill in mop-up roles. He closed out his career in 1954 back in Negro ball, when he managed the Birmingham Black Barons. Wells died in 1989.

At ages 45 and 46, Willie Wells hit .304 and .314 in his two seasons as playing-manager of the Winnipeg Buffaloes of the ManDak League. The top Negro League shortstop of the 1930s and 1940s, Wells was honored in 1997 with selection to the Hall of Fame at Cooperstown (photograph courtesy the National Baseball Hall of Fame Library, Cooperstown, N.Y.).

1949 Elmwood Giants—.333 (incomplete)
1950 Winnipeg Buffaloes—.304, 0 HR, 22 RBI
1951 Winnipeg Buffaloes—.314, 3 HR, 17 RBI, Won 1, Lost 0
1952 Brandon Greys—.667, 0 HR, 1 RBI *
1953 Brandon Greys—.234, 0 HR, 4 RBI

*Just six at bats.

Canadian Highlights: August 9, 1949, Wells was a star both on offense and defense in an exhibition match against the New Orleans Creoles.

> Wells of the Giants drew the applause from the fans as he assisted in no less than nine putouts, powdered a home run and walked twice [*Winnipeg Free Press*, August 10, 1949].

August 10, he punched out a double and two singles in a victory over the Creoles. August 24, Wells smashed a clutch home run to break up a four-all ball game as Elmwood beat an all-star team.

May 27, 1950, the Buffaloes played their first home game and Wells, playing right field, had three hits in a 6–5 loss to Brandon. The Buffaloes beat Minot 11–5 on June 12 and Wells led the way with a double and two singles. June 28, Wells hit three doubles to lead the Buffaloes over Brandon, 9–3. July 12, Wells knocked in four runs in a wild and woolly, 22–8 lambasting of Brandon. September 14, the Buffaloes won the league championship with a 1–0, seventeen inning victory over Brandon. Wells was tossed from the game in the tenth inning after a disputed call involving John Kennedy and two Brandon runners. He was given two minutes to leave the field by umpire Mark Van Buren and when he didn't depart he was ejected. The Buffaloes win gave Wells his first and only ManDak League championship

July 20, 1951, the Buffaloes were down 3–2 to Brandon in the bottom of the ninth inning with Buddy Owens on base. Wells then inserted himself into the game as a pinch hitter for Cy Morton and promptly hit a two-run homer to give Buffaloes the victory.

Wells managed the Greys into the semifinals in 1952 only to be beaten by Minot.

September 16, 1953, he was at the helm of the Greys when they lost to Minot in the league final.

Willie Wells, Jr.—Infield/Outfield, 5'3", 158 lbs. Batted right. threw right

Wells, Jr., had a Negro League career from 1944 to 1949 with the Memphis Red Sox. When Willie Wells, Sr., took over as manager of the Winnipeg Buffaloes in 1950, he brought his son with him to Canada.

1950 Winnipeg Buffaloes—.214, 1 HR, 15 RBI

Canadian Highlights: May 24, 1950, he was loaned to Elmwood as some of the Giants' players had not yet arrived. Wells Jr. singled in the winning run in the tenth inning that gave the Giants a 4–2 victory over the Carman Cardinals. June 14, Wells Jr. and Joe Taylor each drove in two runs to help the Buffaloes to first prize in the Brandon Tournament. July 24, he singled in John Kennedy with the winning run in the thirteenth inning to give the Buffaloes a 3–2 win over Elmwood.

Dave Whatley—Outfield, 5'10", 170 lbs. Batted left, threw right

The speedy outfielder had a solid Negro League career beginning in 1936 with the Birmingham Black Barons. He was with the Homestead Grays during their championship years of the late 1930s and early 1940s. He wound down his Negro play in 1945 with the New York Black Yankees and 1946 with Pittsburg Crawfords. Whatley ended up in Saskatchewan in 1949–50–51 as a star for the Kamsack Cyclones of the Manitoba-Saskatchewan League. Early in the 1951 season he took over as manager of the team.

1949 Kamsack Cyclones—Statistics not available
1950 Kamsack Cyclones—Statistics not available
1951 Kamsack Cyclones—.301, 9 D, 3 T, 2 HR

Canadian Highlights: June 18, 1950, Whatley had three hits and made two magnificent catches in the outfield in a 2–1 win over Yorkton.

Arstando Artemis "Ladd" White—Pitcher. Threw right

Imported from California to help the Ligon All-Stars at the inaugural Indian Head Tournament in 1947, Ladd was instrumental in the Ligon's first place showing. He had played Negro League ball in the late 1940s with the Memphis Red Sox and Indianapolis Clowns. He returned to Canada in 1950 with Drummondville in the Provincial League

> 1950 Drummondville Cubs—Won 9, Lost 12, 3.77 ERA

Canadian Highlights: August 6, 1947, Ladd tossed a three-hit shutout over six innings as the All-Stars won their tourney opener 9–0. The next day he went the distance with a three-hitter in besting former major leaguer Bert Shepard as the barnstorming club advanced to the semi-finals with a 1–0 win over Williston.

Charles White—Third Base, 5'11", 192 lbs. Batted left, threw right

White started his career in 1950 with the Philadelphia Stars. At age 22, he was one of the younger players on the Buffaloes in 1951. After just two months, White was snapped up by the St. Louis Browns and assigned to Toronto of the International League where he was converted to catcher. White graduated to the major leagues in 1954 with the Milwaukee Braves. He appeared in 62 games over two seasons. White ended up playing eight years in Canada, the last six with Vancouver Mounties in the Pacific Coast League.

> 1951 Winnipeg Buffaloes—.330, 1 HR, 19 RBI
> 1951 Toronto Maple Leafs—.283, 10 D, 2 T, 4 HR, 27 RBI
> 1952 Toronto Maple Leafs—.260, 9 D, 0 T, 2 HR, 13 RBI
> 1957 Vancouver Mounties—.277, 14 D, 4 T, 1 HR, 48 RBI
> 1958 Vancouver Mounties—.291, 18 D, 3 T, 2 HR, 38 RBI
> 1959 Vancouver Mounties—.273, 7 D, 2 T, 1 HR, 16 RBI
> 1960 Vancouver Mounties—.259, 16 D, 2 T, 3 HR, 46 RBI
> 1961 Vancouver/Portland—.268, 14 D, 1 T, 2 HR, 37 RBI
> 1965 Vancouver Mounties—.000 *

*Just six at bats.

Canadian Highlights: May 19, 1951, before 6,000 opening day fans at Osborne Stadium, Winnipeg, White had three hits as the Buffs dumped Brandon 11–4. White stroked two doubles and triple and had a stolen base. July 3, he drove in four runs with a home run, triple and a double as the Buffaloes crushed Elmwood 16–4.

Roy White—Pitcher

White traveled the West with Ligon's All-Stars on their 1947 and 1948 barnstorming tours.

Canadian Highlights: June 24, 1947, White tossed a five-hitter with ten strike outs as Ligon's topped Moose Jaw Canucks 7–1. August 7, White fired a four-hit shutout to give the All-Stars a 13–0 win in the final of the Indian Head Tournament.

June 23, 1948, White pitched a four-hitter to blank Winnipeg Reos 4–0 at the Brandon Invitational Tournament. He fanned eleven and walked two. June 28, he allowed just five hits while fanning 16 as Ligon's trounced Regina Red Sox 12–1. White had three hits at the plate. August 16, the 21-year-old White held Brandon to four hits as the All-Stars topped the Greys 5–1.

Sammy Lee White—Pitcher, 6'2", 180 lbs. Batted right, threw right

White was a mainstay of the mound staff of the Indian Head Rockets in 1953 and 1954. He had a brief pro career in the Florida State League in 1955 and 1956.

Canadian Highlights: July 16, 1953, White's three-hit, 1–0, shutout of Moose Jaw carried the Rockets into the final of the Indian Head Tournament.

July 7, 1954, White scattered seven hits as Indian Head topped Rosetown 7–2. July 12, he fired a three-hitter, with eight strikeouts, and belted a two-run homer in a Rockets' win over North Battleford.

Frank Wickware—Pitcher. Batted right, threw right

Wickware was one of the early stars of Negro ball. He played from 1909 to 1925. During the 1921 season, he pitched for the Calgary Black Sox on their Western Canada tour. (In spite of their name, it's believed the Black Sox were based in Chicago.)

> Frank Wickware is another negro pitcher who would rank with the Walter Johnsons, Joe Woods and Grover Alexanders if he were a white man. Wickware performed some marvelous feats in around Schenectady, N.Y., and has since moved on to Chicago where he has become a sensation among the semi-pros.
>
> Wickware has marvelous speed, a weird set of curves and wonderful control. And he has a trick that has made him feared among batters. He throws what seems to be a "bean ball" but his control is so perfect that he never yet has hit a batter in the head. But when the batters see the ball, propelled with mighty force, come for their heads, they jump away—and the ball, taking its proper and well-time curve, arches over the plate for a strike [*The Janesville Daily Gazette*, June 18, 1915].

Bill Wilder—Pitcher

Wilder came to the Regina Caps in 1953 after having played in Canada with a touring Brooklyn Cuban Giants squad in 1950. He had earlier pitched for the Raleigh (North Carolina) Tigers. The Louisiana native went to college with Rollie Miles, who came to Regina to play baseball and stayed on as one of the greats of the Canadian Football League.

Canadian Highlights: May 24, 1953, Wilder, a new recruit by the Caps, scattered 8 hits and allowed just two earned runs in his winning debut with Regina.

Joe Wiley—Second Base/Third Base

Wiley played the 1945 and 1946 seasons with the barnstorming Cincinnati Crescents before two seasons in the Negro League with the Baltimore Elite Giants and Memphis Red Sox. At Baltimore, Wiley was relegated to a reserve role by the second base play of future Dodger Junior Gilliam. Wiley was back on the road in 1949 with the New Orleans Creoles and in 1950 joined the Elmwood Giants of the ManDak League. He was traded to Carman in 1951.

1950 Elmwood Giants—.331, 1 HR, 21 RBI, 8 SB

1951 Elmwood/Carman—.249, 0 HR, 22 RBI

Canadian Highlights: May 31, 1950, Wiley had a homer and double in a loss to Minot. June 5, he belted a pair of triples in Elmwood's 7–4 triumph over Winnipeg. June 10, Wiley had three hits in an 18–6 trouncing of the Mallards. He had another three-hit game on July 24, and, again, on August 2.

June 28, 1951 saw Wiley get four hits in five at bats in a 7–6 Elmwood loss to Brandon. June 30, Wiley collected five consecutive walks, and scored a pair, as Elmwood beat the Buffaloes 10–3.

James E. "Jimmy" "Seabiscuit" Wilkes—Outfield, 5'8", 160 lbs. Batted both, threw right

Wilkes' speed earned him the nickname "Seabiscuit" (after the famous thoroughbred of the same era). Wilkes was a Negro League veteran who was a prominent member of one of the last great Negro League teams, the 1946 Negro League Champion Newark Eagles (the one with Larry Doby at Second Base and Monte Irvin at Shortstop). He played with the Eagles from 1945 to 1950 (including the season the Eagles played out of Houston).

He was signed by the Brooklyn Dodgers in 1950 and assigned to Elmira of the Double-A, Eastern League. July 28, 1950, the Elmira Star-Gazette reported that Wilkes and outfielder Bob Wilson would be the first two blacks to wear the Elmira Pioneers uniform. Wilkes was batting .281 with four home runs and fourteen RBI when the Dodgers sent him to Three Rivers Royals in the Can-Am League.

In 1951, he started the season back in Elmira, but after a short time was sent to the Lancaster Red Roses in the Class-B, Interstate League. In 1952, Wilkes started the season with Great Falls in the Pioneer League, but quit organized ball and returned to the Indianapolis Clowns.

With dwindling opportunities with American teams, Wilkes came north in 1953 to join the Brantford Red Sox of the Intercounty League in Ontario. He was so popular, he never left. He played for ten seasons (leading the Sox to the league title five consecutive years from 1959–1963), getting a job with the City of

Brantford and settling down in the Canadian community. After his playing days he became an umpire and stuck around the local diamonds for another decade.

Wilkes, whose forte was sparkling outfield defense, was no slouch on offense. He led the league in hits, doubles, runs and walks in 1956, runs scored in 1961 and 1963, and stolen bases in 1960. He had his uniform number (5) retired and he was inducted into the City of Brantford's Hall of Fame. Wilkes died in 2008 at the age of 82.

Canadian Highlights: July 6, 1955, Wilkes belted a two-run homer to help the Red Sox downed London 5–3. July 21, he had a big day at the plate with a homer, two doubles and a walk in five trips as he scored four times and knocked in a pair in a Brantford loss to Kitchener. July 30, Wilkes crushed a grand slam homer and a single to lead Brantford by Galt 5–3. August 29, in a sudden-death match to decide the final playoff spot, Wilkes knocked in the winning run in the 9th inning as Brantford topped London 2–1.

Alex "Wolf" Williams—Pitcher

Williams joined the mound staff of the Indian Head Rockets in 1950.

Canadian Highlights: August 9, 1950, Williams allowed just five hits as the Rockets topped Wilcox 4–1 at the Estevan Tournament

Babe Williams—Pitcher, 6'1", 175.
Threw right

Williams was recruited by legendary Fresno State baseball coach Pete Beiden, but most of Williams' success at Fresno came on the basketball court where he was an all-star. He had starred in baseball in the Oakland area in high school and semi-pro ranks. He spent one summer with Regina Braves of the Western Canada League.

> 1957 Regina Braves—17 G, 7 GS, 3 CG, Won 3, Lost 7, 3.67 ERA

Canadian Highlights: July 11, 1957, Williams went the distance, scattering eight hits, in a 7–3 win over Lloydminster.

Claude Williams—First Base, 5'9", 235 lbs.

Williams, from Austin, Texas, toured Western Canada with the barnstorming Ligon All-Stars in 1947 and 1949 and later suited up with the Regina Caps of the Southern (Saskatchewan) League in 1950. He led the loop in batting with a .413 mark.

> Williams, rotund first sacker for the Stars carried the top role as funster and at the same time showed amazing ability and dexterity with his "claw" at the corner sack. Donning catcher's equipment in the 8th inning of the twilight tilt, he caught in various positions including lying flat on the ground with his mitt a target that pitcher Rufus Ligon hit with unerring aim [*Flin Flon Daily Miner*, August 1, 1949].

> 1950 Regina Caps—.413, 29 RBI

Canadian Highlights: August 7, 1947, Williams had five hits to lead Ligon's to a 13–0 win over Wilcox in the final of the Indian Head Tournament.

July 19, 1950, Williams' three-run homer was the difference as Regina Caps downed Sceptre 5–3 to take top money in the Nipawin Tournament

Coney (Koney) Williams—Shortstop

Williams was a member of the powerful Brandon Greys of 1948–1949. He returned to barnstorming in 1950, with the Brooklyn Cuban Giants, but early in the season jumped to the Estevan Maple Leafs of the South Saskatchewan League. He returned in 1951 and played on three teams—Elmwood Giants, Saskatoon Gems and Kamsack Cyclones.

> 1948 Brandon Greys—.304
> 1949 Brandon Greys—.327, 31 D, 7 T, 3 HR, 71 RBI, 20 SB*
> 1950 Estevan Maple Leafs—.429 (incomplete)
> 1951 Elmwood Giants—Statistics not available
> 1951 Kamsack Cyclones—.339, 5 D, 3 T, 3 HR
> 1951 North Battleford—.394 (3rd)

*League, tournament & exhibition games

Canadian Highlights: June 11, 1948, in his debut with Brandon, Williams had three hits, a triple and double included, in a 10–9 win over

Gilbert Plains. July 5, Williams belted a pair of homers, one in each game, as Brandon split with Minot. July 7, Williams went 4 for 4, stole three bases and scored both Brandon runs in a 2–2 tie with Elmwood.

May 29, 1949, Williams led the Brandon offense with four hits, four stolen bases and two runs as the Greys downed Rolla, North Dakota 5–2. June 4, Williams knocked in a pair of runs with four hits in an 8–1 Brandon win over Elmwood. June 8, Williams had three runs and drove in three to pace Brandon by Carman 10–3. June 29, the Greys shortstop had three hits as Brandon topped Ligon's All-Stars 14–5. July 4, four hits by Williams led Brandon to an easy 14–1 win over Neepawa. July 8, Williams added four hits in a 5–0 shutout over Minot. The next day he drove in three runs in an 11–0 trouncing of Winnipegs. July 12, in a 2–0 blanking of Carman, Williams scored the insurance run after reaching on a single, advancing on a base on balls, then stealing third and home on the next two pitches.

> The Greys presented a snappy exhibition of "shadow ball" and several other novelty acts, but the sparkling work of Coney Williams at shortstop eclipsed the other displays. Williams got better as the game went on. He robbed the leadoff man in the first inning of a hit by moving several steps to his left and leaping high in the air to snare a line drive. In the fifth, he raced right across second base to field a bounder and make the play at first and he climaxed the night in the ninth by leaping high into the air to grab a sizzling drive which had base hit written all over it [*Brandon Sun*, July 14, 1949].

July 28, 1949 at the Indian Head Tournament, Williams bashed a pair of homers in a 17–3 win over Notre Dame Hounds.

August 19, 1950, Williams had three hits in Estevan's playoff victory over Notre Dame. He'd punch out another three hits in the next game, and a pair in the following one. In the first game of the final series, August 30, he had three hits and he wrapped up the season with five hits as Estevan won the final in five games.

May 24, 1951, Williams led Elmwood with three hits as Elmwood dropped an 8–7 decision to his old team, Brandon. June 17, now with Kamsack in the Manitoba-Saskatchewan League, Williams had an inside-the-park homer, triple and two singles against Saskatoon 55s. August 19, with his third club, the Saskatoon 55s, Williams clouted four hits, including a homer in a win over North Battleford. August 20, again he had a four-hit day this time in a playoff win over Eston. August 22, he added a triple and two singles in another playoff triumph. He finished third in hitting with a .394 mark.

Jeff Leroy Norldan Williams—Outfield/First Base, 5'10", 180 lbs. Batted both, threw right

Williams, who used both Jeff and Leroy as first names at different stops along his baseball trail, had Negro League experience with the Newark Eagles in 1947–1948. He moved to the Southern Negro circuit in 1949 before signing on with the Kansas City Monarchs in 1950. In his early years he played the middle infield.

Williams took his introductory course in organized ball at Springfield in the Mississippi-Ohio Valley League in 1950 hitting .280 in 69 games after leaving the Monarchs. He moved as high as Triple-A in his seven minor league seasons. His best campaign was in 1955 in the Class-C, Longhorn League when he batted .325 with 35 home runs and 121 runs batted in. In 1959, at age 32, he joined the Saskatoon Commodores of the Canadian-American League for his only season in Canada. He died in 1994 in Orlando, Florida.

1959 Saskatoon Commodores—.282, 3 HR, 24 RBI

Canadian Highlights: July 22, 1959, newcomer Williams clubbed a three-run homer in the 2nd inning and a two-run shot in the 7th as Saskatoon whipped Regina 11–2.

Jesse Williams—Shortstop, 5'11", 160 lbs. Batted right, threw right

His Negro League career ran from 1939 to 1951 with the Kansas City Monarchs and Indianapolis Clowns. In 1952, he played in Vancouver in the Western International League, his lone season in Canada. Williams closed out his career in 1954 when he played briefly in the Texas League. He died in 1990 in Kansas City.

1952 Vancouver Capilanos—.251, 18 D, 4 T, 0 HR, 42 RBI

Jim "Big Jim" Williams—Outfield/First Base/Manager, 6'1", 200 lbs.

Big Jim had an extensive career in Negro ball, beginning in 1936 with the New York Black Yankees. In the late 1930s, Josh Gibson, Buck Leonard and Williams were the middle of the order hitters for the Homestead Grays.

He played and managed for a dozen years in the United States before coming north with his Jacksonville Eagles (to be reborn as the Indian Head Rockets) in 1950.

"Big Jim" ran the Rockets for three seasons (1950–1951–1952) and then piloted the Regina Caps for one summer (1953) even inserting himself into the lineup to help deal with a rash of injuries. He was back for a brief stint with the Rockets in 1954.

Canadian Highlights: In 1951, he managed the Rockets to a 33–12 first-place record and the Saskatchewan semi-pro title. His team featured a 22-game winning streak. June 4, 1951, Williams belted a pair of homers as Indian Head swept a four-game weekend series at Delisle and North Battleford. July 31, Williams was suspended for six games and fined $50 for assaulting an umpire on a street in Medicine Hat. The attack occurred following the first game of a double-header against the hometown Mohawks. It was in the aftermath of a 9th inning rhubarb when Williams disputed a called strike by umpire E.C. Terry and was ordered to leave the ball park. When Williams refused to leave, the game was forfeited to the Hawks. A short time later, Terry said he was walking down the street away from the park when the Rockets' bus pulled up and Williams got out and crossed the street where he used violent language and threw a punch at Terry. August 22, Williams had a double and two singles as Indian Head evened a playoff series with Moose Jaw with a 6–2 victory.

June 21, 1953, the president of the Western Canada Baseball league announced that Williams had been fined $25 and suspended for 14 games as a result of a rhubarb in a game at Saskatoon June 14. Williams was reported to have struck umpire Bill Sawusch of Chicago. August 8, in the lineup because of injuries to three of his key players, Williams had a double and single and drove in a run. Three days later he was even better with a double and two singles, driving in three runs. August 12, Williams had a three-run homer and the following day he had a double and two singles.

Johnny Williams—Pitcher

In 1953, Williams pitched in the Saskatchewan Baseball League for the Saskatoon Gems.

May 22, 1953, Williams, the winning pitcher, crushed a grand slam homer and a single as Saskatoon whipped Moose Jaw 11–6.

Junior Williams—Pitcher. Threw right

Williams came to the Estevan Maple Leafs in 1950 after beginning the season with the barnstorming Brooklyn Cuban Giants. He started the 1951 season with Elmwood.

1950 Estevan Maple Leafs—Statistics not available
1951 Elmwood Giants—Won 0, Lost 2, 5 G 3 GS, 0 CG

Canadian Highlights: August 9, 1950, Williams had a four-hitter as Estevan topped Wilcox 8–1 at the Estevan Tournament.

Marvin "Tex" Williams—Second Base, 6'0", 190 lbs. Batted right, threw right

Williams played in the Negro League from 1943 to 1950 with the Philadelphia Stars and Cleveland Buckeyes. From there he went into organized ball and played up to 1961 with various teams. He was a consistent .300 hitter. In 1954, he was with the Vancouver Capilanos of the Western International League.

1954 Vancouver Capilanos—.360, 32 D, 9 T, 20 HR, 90 RBI

Canadian Highlights: 1954, Williams captured the league's batting crown and was selected to the WIL all-star team as the second baseman.

Roy Williams—Second Base. Batted both, threw right

The switch-hitting second sacker played just one season in Canada, with the 1953 Regina Caps of the Saskatchewan Baseball League.

1953 Regina Caps—.320

Canadian Highlights: May 15, 1953, Williams bashed the first homer of the season as Regina dropped a 9–6 decision in the league opener. He also had a single and scored a pair of runs. May 19, Williams clubbed two doubles and a single and scored twice in a loss to North Battleford. June 15, it was deuces wild for Williams in an 11–5 win over Moose Jaw as he had two hits (one of them a double), drove in a pair, scored twice, swiped two bases, made two putouts and had two assists. July 13, Williams belted a grand slam to give Caps a 12–7 win over Moose Jaw

Samuel C. Williams—Pitcher, 5'11½", 175 lbs. Batted right, threw right

Williams was a solid performer in the Negro League in his tenure with the Birmingham Black Barons, 1941 and 1947 to 1950. He lost three seasons to military service. The right-hander went 13–7 in 1950 with Birmingham before moving to the Mexican League. He started the 1952 season back with the Barons, but jumped to the Brandon Greys of the Man-Dak League. However, after just three league games, he left to join Licey of the Dominican Summer League.

Williams, decided to try out organized ball in 1953 and he pitched for another six years compiling some outstanding numbers. In 1953, with Pampa of the West Texas–New Mexico League, Williams appeared in 52 games, with 25 complete games, winning 25 of 37 decisions. In 1956, he went 15–9, 3.10 ERA, with 19 complete games with San Jose of the California League.

Williams died in 2007 at the age of 84.

1952 Brandon Greys—Won 1, Lost 2

Canadian Highlights: August 5, 1952, Williams beat Elmwood 9–0 on a three-hitter in the Winnipeg Tournament.

Willie "Curly" (Curley) Williams—Shortstop/Third Base, 5'10", 175 lbs. Batted left, threw right

His superb baseball skills and engaging personality made Williams "Mr. Baseball" in Lloydminster in the 1950s and 1960s.

He came to the prairies after a career in the

Willie "Curly" Williams became one of the prairies' most popular players over a ten-year stint, beginning in 1953. He had started his Negro League career in 1945 with the Newark Eagles and, after signing a contract in organized ball, reached as high as Triple-A. He spent nine seasons in the border community of Lloydminster, becoming known as Mr. Baseball in the area (photograph from the Mah collection).

Negro Leagues and a stint in pro ball with the Chicago White Sox organization where he reached the Triple-A level with Toledo (in his first game with the club Curly won three steak dinners and a savings bond for a triple which knocked in the first runs of the season). Williams seemed to have a knack to make a good, first impression. When signed by the White Sox and assigned to Colorado Springs he belted a two-run homer in the bottom the ninth inning for a season-opening victory.

As a teenager, Williams, and long-time friend Modie Risher, began playing with Negro teams in Charleston, Lakeland, Orangeburgh and Jacksonville in the 40s. He'd win a spot on one of the "major" Negro League teams in 1945.

Williams, then a shortstop, was a member of the Newark Eagles (and its successors) from 1948 to 1951. He was selected to play in the 1950 East-West All-Star game. He also played winter ball in the Dominican Republic and Puerto Rico. In late 1949 in Puerto Rico, Williams, on a homer spree (with something like six homers in seven days), attracted the attention of the Caribbean scout for the New York Giants. Then, after the 1950 All-Star game, the Chicago White Sox offered a contract. He gave organized ball a two-year trial before heading north to suit up with the Carman Cardinals of the ManDak League in 1953. Then after a season in the Dominican and a return to the Negro League with Birmingham, Williams became a fixture on the prairies.

In his first season in Lloydminster, he hit .280 and, as a third baseman, led the league in fielding. The following year, he was the team's leading hitter and, again, he'd lead the league in fielding, this time at shortstop. He was a perennial all-star who also advanced to playing-manager of the club. In his first full month at the helm, in 1961, Williams led the Meridians to 25 wins in 32 games, including tournament victories in Lacombe and Lethbridge.

After the collapse of the Western Canada League at the end of the 1961 season, Williams returned to Lloydminster to head up the city's entry, the Green Caps, in the Northern Saskatchewan League. These two summers would be the final two years of his 20-year baseball career. Fittingly, he went out with a blast—a .391 batting average.

In 1997, the Sarasota, Florida Council declared "Curly Williams Day" in honor of his efforts to raise funds (through the Curly Williams Foundation) to provide college scholarships for needy students.

> Playing in Canada was like playing in Puerto Rico or the Dominican Republic, just wonderful people, man. You enjoyed playing. May not have made a lot of money but you really enjoyed it, the people were excited you know, they enjoyed you, and they would invite you to their homes. You know when I first went to Lloydminster, I think there was only one black in the area. They had a black lady there, she was an older lady, I met her. Just me and her there ... I cried so much, when I was in professional baseball. I tell you. It was a breath of fresh air to play in Canada. We were treated so well up there, that's why I stayed up there so long. It was really wonderful. We had so much fun up there, everybody was accepted" [Telephone interview, 2001].

> He was a real quiet guy. Didn't talk very much, but a real good ballplayer. He struck me as the kind of guy you didn't want to mess with him [Former teammate Walter McCoy. Telephone interview, 2008].

Slim Thorpe, who headed up the Lloydminster franchise, had high praise for his easy-going star.

> Curly Williams was one of the finest gentlemen that I ever met. [He] was always helping the kids. We'd get these young college boys and Curly was in there talking to them, showing them how to do it. Curly was a Triple-A ball player, and he stayed with us as long as our league lasted [Slim Thorpe, in *75 Years of Sport & Culture in Lloydminster*].

1953 Carman Cardinals—.286, 15 D, 1 T, 12 HR, 40 RBI
1955 Lloydminster Meridians—.280, 13 D, 4 T, 5 HR, 33 RBI
1956 Lloydminster Meridians—.314, 12 D, 3 T, 7 HR, 45 RBI
1957 Lloydminster Meridians—.343, 14 D, 3 T, 15 HR, 55 RBI
1958 Lloydminster/N.Battleford—.330, 11 D, 5 T, 5 HR, 41 RBI
1959 Lloydminster/N.Battleford—.260, 11 D, 3 T, 11 HR, 59 RBI
1960 Lloydminster Meridians—.309, 19 D, 2 T, 4 HR, 40 RBI
1961 Lloydminster Meridians—Statistics not available
1962 Lloydminster GreenCaps—Statistics not available
1963 Lloydminster GreenCaps—.391, 4 D, 1 T, 3 HR, 16 RBI, (Incomplete)

Canadian Highlights: July 27, 1953, Williams knocked in four runs with a two-run homer, a double and a single as Carman beat Brandon 12–7. July 29, he belted his third homer in three nights to push the Cards by Minot 9–4. August 5, his triple, double and single were not enough as Carman lost to Brandon, 8–7. August 9, he went four-for-five to lift the Cardinals to a 15–11 win over Minot. August 16, Williams had three doubles and scored the winner in the 11th inning as Carman shaded Brandon 6–5.

July 17, 1955, in the second game of a double-header, Williams had three hits, including a homer, in a 6–5 decision over Saskatoon. He raced around the bases to score the winner in the bottom of the 9th inning as an argument proceeded at second base. July 22, Curly punched out two triples in a 6–5 victory over Regina.

June 19, 1956, Williams collected three doubles, but Lloydminster lost, 5–4, to Saskatoon. July 1, Williams drew seven bases on balls as the Meridians swept a pair from Edmonton. August 19, in spite of his two-run triple and three-run homer, Lloydminster dropped a 9–7 game to the Eskimos.

July 30, 1957, the power-hitting third sacker had four hits, including two home runs, to lift Lloydminster to an 8–7 win over North Battleford. August 4, Williams clubbed a homer and three singles, but Beavers won a slugfest 19–13. August 10, Williams clubbed a homer and two singles and scored all the Lloydminster runs in a 3–1 triumph over Saskatoon. The next day, he knocked in three runs with three more hits in besting North Battleford 8–2.

June 11, 1958, it was three hits and three RBI as the Lloydminster–North Battleford Combines topped Edmonton 12–9. July 22, Williams added a triple and three singles in a 10–7 win over Moose Jaw. August 2, he belted a grand slam homer to help the Combines edge Regina, 12–11.

July 13, 1959, Williams drove in four runs with a homer, double and single in an 8–6 triumph over Saskatoon. July 23, he had a three-run homer and knocked in five runs over-all as the Combines beat Regina 9–3. July 24, he had a bases-loaded triple as Lloydminster–North Battleford shaded Regina 6–5. July 26, Williams blasted a grand slam homer in a 10–4 win over Williston. July 28, Williams belted a homer to give him fifteen runs batted in over his last five games.

June 26, 1960, Williams had a homer in the opener and a triple, double and two singles in the nightcap in a split of a twin-bill with Calgary. July 7, he had four hits and four RBI in a wild, 19–15 victory over Saskatoon. July 27, in three games at the Lacombe Tournament, Williams was on base in 14 of 15 plate appearances, with 10 walks, three doubles and a single. July 30, at the Lethbridge Tournament, his grand slam homer sent the Meridians into the final with a 7–2 win over Lethbridge. August 7, Williams led the Meridians to a doubleheader sweep of Saskatoon to stretch their winning streak to 14 games. He had three doubles in the first game.

July 3, 1961, with Cliff Pemberton sidelined with a fractured finger, Williams took over as Lloydminster's playing-manager. July 27, 1961, Williams led the Meridians to top money at the Lacombe Tournament as he had three hits and scored the winning run in the final and belted a homer, triple and double in the semifinal.

June 3, 1962, the playing-manager of Lloydminster's GreenCaps bashed a pair of homers in a 16–4 trouncing of North Battleford.

Bernard Willis—Shortstop, 6'5"

Willis was quite a sight back in 1950 when the San Antonio basketball star toured with the barnstorming Ligon All-Stars. A shortstop at six-foot-five was pretty unusual, especially back in the 50s. Willis had considerable experience even by then. He had begun with his hometown Hondo Bears and played with semi-pro teams in San Antonio before joining the Kansas City Monarchs and Satchel Paige All-Stars.

Army service interrupted his barnstorming for two years although he continued to play with the Brooke Army Medical Center Comets in baseball and basketball. One of his B.A.M.C. teammates in 1952 was Bob Turley (soon to become a star hurler with the Yankees). In 1951, his teammates forfeited a tournament game in Dallas by declining to play after tournament organizers refused to allow Willis, the only black player, to take the field on a city-owned park designated for use only by whites. After his military hitch, he returned to play with the Ligon All-Stars and teams in the San Antonio area before hanging up his spikes in the early 1960s. He died in October, 2007 in San Antonio. He was 81.

Canadian Highlights: June 10, 1950, the Regina Leader-Post noted both his height ("the sensational six-foot-five shortstop") and talent ("hefty home run to the right field fence").

June 24, Willis punched out a double and single and stole two bases in the Ligon's 4–2 win over Lumsden. June 29, Willis belted a pair of homers and a triple in a losing cause as

Ligon's lost in the final of the Melfort Tournament.

Isaac "Pee Wee" Willis—Shortstop

The Los Angeles native was recruited by the Swift Current Indians in 1950. He left the team in June saying he was needed at home to take care of his ailing mother. He did not return.

Canadian Highlights: In his first game, May 13, Willis, batting in the cleanup slot, clubbed a triple and single as the Indians scored an 8–3 victory. May 26, Willis went 7 for 12 as the Indians captured the Sceptre Tournament. May 27, Willis tripled in the tying run after having scored a key marker on a steal of home in a win over Sceptre. June 5, Willis crushed a home run, triple and two doubles to lead Swift Current to an 8–5 win over Saskatoon Legion.

Al Wilmore—Pitcher, 6'1", 180 lbs. Batted right, threw right

Wilmore's Negro League career began after he returned from Army service in the South Pacific during the Second World War. From 1946 to 1950 he pitched with the Philadelphia Stars and Baltimore Elite Giants. He ventured north in 1951 to join the Winnipeg Buffaloes of the ManDak League where he pitched with some success. It led to a contract with the Philadelphia A's, but an arm injury cut short his career.

1951 Winnipeg Buffaloes—Won 4, Lost 5, 13 G, 10 GS, 6 CG

Canadian Highlights: June 1, Wilmore beat Minot Mallards 8–3 in his first game with the Buffaloes. July 2, Wilmore beat Minot Mallards 2–1 in the Brandon Tournament, giving up six hits over nine innings.

Alfred Wilson—Pitcher/Outfield

In 1935 he was signed away from Chappie Johnson's barnstorming team by Granby. The Quebec League had no restrictions on signing black players as the team was not in organized ball and Wilson was allowed to play on the all white team, eleven years before Jackie Robinson played in organized ball.

While he was with Granby, all the clubs in the Quebec League were in financial trouble and Wilson arranged for league teams to play black barnstorming squads like the Cleveland Clowns, Boston Black Giants and Hawaiian All-Stars. He returned to the Chappie Johnson All-Stars in 1936. In 1945, he managed a team, organized by Chappie Johnson, in Montreal called the Black Panthers.

1935 Granby—Won 5, Lost 0, .392, 20 RBI

Canadian Highlights: Wilson hurled a five-hit shutout against Indianapolis ABCs and blasted the first home run ever hit out of the Granby Stadium.

Chuck Wilson—Catcher/Second Base/Outfield. Threw right

Following a season with the Indianapolis Clowns in 1948, Wilson journey to Brandon to play for the Greys in the Manitoba Senior Baseball League. He was back again in 1950 when Brandon moved into the new ManDak circuit. In 1953, he returned to the Greys and played both infield and outfield and spent time splitting catching duties with Jesse Douglas.

1949 Brandon Greys—.280, 11 D, 11 T, 8 HR, 69 RBI, 22 SB *
1950 Brandon Greys—.306, 1 HR, 21 RBI
1953 Brandon Greys—.259, 12 D, 7 T, 9 HR, 45 RBI, 6 SB

League, playoff, exhibition and tournament games.

Canadian Highlights: June 14, 1949, Wilson made an auspicious debut with Brandon belting five hits, including a homer, and six runs batted in as the Greys swept an exhibition double-header from Walhalla. The next night he drove in three runs as Brandon topped Elmwood 7–2. July 1, in a dramatic end to the Kinsmen tournament at Brandon, the Greys scored the game's only run in the top of the 9th then escaped a bases-loaded jam in the bottom of the inning to edge Minot 1–0 to take top prize money in the four-team event. With two out in the 9th, Wilson singled, stole second, advanced to third on an error and raced home on a wild pitch. July 17, the Winnipeg Free Press reported that Wilson made a sensational catch of a liner in the ninth inning that saved a 7–6 Brandon win. September 10, Brandon beat Minot Mallards 7–6 to win the Mallot Trophy, awarded to the winner of international play between the cities. Wilson and Rafe Cabrera led Brandon to the win with three hits apiece.

May 26, 1950, the Winnipeg Free Press reported that Wilson was the most versatile player in the ManDak League. May 27, Brandon beat the Winnipeg Buffaloes 6–5 on Wilson's game-winning single before 5,421 fans. May 30, Brandon split a double header with Minot as Wilson had three hits in game one and two more in the second. June 2, Wilson belted three home runs and a single, good for six runs batted in, as Brandon trounced Regina 22–1 in an exhibition game in the Saskatchewan capital. He scored five times. June 6, saw Wilson hit two, inside the park, home runs as Brandon beat the Ligon All-Stars 11–4 in an exhibition game. He finished the game with three hits and four RBI.

May 16, 1953, Wilson clubbed a pair of homers as Brandon downed Minot in the ManDak League opener in North Dakota. May 24, a first inning grand slam homer by Wilson led Brandon to a 12–4 win over the Cardinals at Carman. June 17, Wilson knocked in six runs as he hit for the cycle, with a homer, triple, double and single, as Brandon clobbered Winnipeg Royals 13–3. September 10, Wilson knocked in five runs as Brandon took the opening game of the ManDak League final 9–4.

Danny Wilson—Infield/Outfield, 5'10", 170 lbs. Batted both, threw right

Wilson was a two-time all-star during his Negro League play, from 1937 to 1947. In 1952, he played with the Winnipeg Giants in his only season in the ManDak League.

> 1952 Winnipeg Giants—.238, 1 HR, 16 RBI

Canadian Highlights: June 24, 1952, Wilson led the Giants at the plate with a home run, double and single as they beat first place Minot 8–3. August 11, he again had three hits and three RBI as the Giants again beat first place Minot 8–0.

Emmett Wilson—Outfield

Wilson played for five teams in the Negro League between 1937 and 1946. During his career he played for both the Satchel Paige All-Stars and the Jackie Robinson All-Stars. He was capable of playing all outfield positions. In 1952 he tried to extend his career with the Brandon Greys in the ManDak League but played very briefly and left the team.

Leon Wilson—Outfield

Wilson, from Vallejo Junior College in California, came up to the Western Canada League as a second baseman, but within a few weeks shifted to the outfield and during his two years in the circuit was one of the top hitters in the league.

He had a spectacular start in Canada, bashing five homers in his first four games. He played for North Battleford Beavers in 1957 and with the Combines in 1958 when North Battleford and Lloydminster shared a team. The speedy outfielder hit .371 in 1958, but had to settle for second place in the batting race behind future major leaguer Jerry Adair (.409). His 10 homers tied for the league lead and he was tops in runs batted in with 53.

> 1957 North Battleford—.319, 12 D, 8 T, 9 HR, 46 RBI, 10 SB
> 1958 Lloyd-N.Battleford—.371, 11 D, 6 T, 10 HR, 53 RBI

Canadian Highlights: June 8, 1957, in just his second game in Canada, Wilson hit the first pitch to him for a homer, then added two more four-baggers. He belted another home run the following day and then his 5th of the season the night after. June 30, Wilson had a homer and three singles to lead the Beavers to an 8–5 win over Moose Jaw. July 12, Wilson knocked in a pair with a double and two singles in a loss to Regina. July 15, Wilson pounded out a double and two singles to lead the Beavers by Lloydminster 8–6. July 24, Wilson pounded a homer and added two singles in an 8–2 win over Saskatoon.

June 15, 1958, Wilson clubbed two triples and a single to lead the Combines to 15–4 win over Moose Jaw. June 17, a two-run homer by Wilson helped the Combines beat Moose Jaw 9–8. June 20, he produced three hits in a 6–2 triumph over Regina. Wilson had another three-hit day June 23 against Williston and again June 30 in a loss to Saskatoon. August 2, he belted four hits in a 12–11 victory over Regina. August 3, Wilson bashed two homers and a single in a 7–1 triumph over Williston.

Robert Wilson—Third Base/Outfield, 5'11", 197 lbs. Batted right, threw right

Wilson came from the Negro League where he played from 1947 to 1950 with the Newark and Houston Eagles. During the 1950 season he signed with the Dodgers and was assigned to Brooklyn's Elmira franchise, hitting .299 and .313 in his two seasons. With St. Paul the following two years, Wilson hit .334 and .317, the latter season with 13 home runs and 117 RBI. From 1954 to 1957, he had four productive seasons with the Montreal Royals. He started the 1958 season with the St. Paul Saints and had a "cup of coffee" with the Dodgers. In 1959, Wilson was with both Montreal and the Toronto Maple Leafs and closed out his career in 1960 with the Leafs and Ft. Worth. He died in 1985 in Dallas.

- 1954 Montreal Royals—.306, 25 D, 4 T, 9 HR, 61 RBI
- 1955 Montreal Royals—.317, 41 D, 10 T, 9 HR, 85 RBI
- 1956 Montreal Royals—.306, 43 D, 3 T, 12 HR, 90 RBI
- 1957 Montreal Royals—.290, 30 D, 2 T, 8 HR, 57 RBI
- 1959 Montreal/Toronto—.325, 30 D, 1 T, 17 HR, 72 RBI
- 1960 Toronto Maple Leafs—.227, 1 HR, 8 RBI

Canadian Highlights: In 1955 Wilson led the International League in hits with 190. In 1956, he was selected to the International League All-Star team.

Robert "Bob" Wilson—Outfield

Wilson was reported to have attended the Brooklyn Dodger camp at Vero Beach before joining the Regina Caps in 1953. A speed merchant, he was the fastest man on the Caps' squad. In his limited action he even took a turn on the hill.

Canadian Highlights: May 18, 1953, Wilson had three hits to pace the Regina attack in a 3–0 win over Saskatoon. June 12, Wilson went 3 for 4 in a losing cause to Carman. June 15, Wilson allowed just one hit in four innings of mound work as Regina topped Moose Jaw.

Tom Wilson

Wilson played for the Grandview Maroons in 1952 as one of their import players.

John Wingate—Outfield

The Texas athlete joined Estevan Maple Leafs of the Southern (Saskatchewan) League for the 1950 season after a college baseball and football career at Prairie View A & M. He also toured with a Los Angeles barnstorming team in 1948–1949 and, in 1951, became the first black player in "organized" ball in Texas. Wingate also played with the Kansas City Monarchs and with professional and semi-pro teams in Texas. He wound up his baseball career with the Texas Jasper Steers at the National Baseball Congress tournaments from 1958 to 1960.

Johnny Wingo—Pitcher. 6'2", 195 lbs. Batted left, threw right

Wingo spent two summers in Canada, 1950 with Carman of the ManDak League and 1952 with Three Rivers, Quebec, of the Provincial League. In his pro career, which lasted until 1957, he reached as high as Triple-A with Columbus of the International League.

- 1950 Carman Cardinals—Won 5, Lost 4, 10 G, 9 GS, 6 CG
- 1952 Three Rivers Yankees—Won 16, Lost 10, 2.76 ERA

Canadian Highlights: August 3, 1950, Wingo fired a seven-hitter and won his own game with a two-run single in the 7th inning as Carman downed Elmwood 3–2. August 10, Wingo drove in Almer McKerlie with the winner in the 10th inning as Carman topped Winnipeg Buffaloes 5–4.

Lester Witherspoon—Outfield, 6'1", 190 lbs. Batted both, threw right

The Negro League had just begun its decline when Witherspoon came aboard in 1947. He played with the Indianapolis Clowns and Homestead Grays over a three year period, leaving in 1950 for the Minot Mallards of the ManDak League. After a brief stay in Minot, Witherspoon jumped to the Swift Current team in Saskatchewan, Canada. When he left Minot he was batting .356. In 1951, he was a big hit with the Indian Head Rockets, hitting .402.

In 1952, he went into organized ball with Porterville in the Southwest International League. He continued his hot hitting and at season's end was selected to the league's all-star team. He played in organized ball until 1955 and played seven games for San Diego in the Pacific Coast League. Witherspoon died in 1980 in Opa Locka, Florida. He was 53.

> 1950 Minot/Swift Current—Statistics not available
> 1951 Indian Head Rockets—.402 (incomplete)

Canadian Highlights: May 24, 1950, Witherspoon belted a triple and two singles to lead Minot to a 5-4 exhibition win over Regina Caps. July 19, he poked an inside-the-park homer along with a triple and double in Swift Current's 10-4 win over the touring Hollywood Beavers. July 28, Witherspoon had two triples, two singles, two runs and drove in a pair to lead Swift Current to a 5–2 win in the opening round of the Swift Current Tournament.

June 14, 1951, Witherspoon scored three times and had a triple and single as Indian Head topped Medicine Hat 6–0. He went 4-for-5 the next day. Indian Head and Estevan were tied in the eleventh inning on July 20, when he doubled in two runs to give the Rockets a 5–3 win. He also had a single to go with his double. August 15, Witherspoon had five hits, a homer, two doubles and a pair of singles as Indian Head captured the Saskatchewan semi-pro title in demolishing Dauphin 23–1.

Samuel Nelson "Buddy" Woods—
Pitcher, 6'2", 205 lbs. Batted right, threw right

Woods was involved in Negro ball for eight seasons, beginning in 1946, pitching for the Cleveland Buckeyes and Memphis Red Sox. In 1954, with little left of the Negro Leagues, he came to Carman of the ManDak circuit for his single season in Canada. He followed with three years in organized ball, two in the southwest with Pampa, Texas.

> 1954 Carman Cardinals—Won 5, Lost 8, 80 IP, 53 BB, 47 SO

Canadian Highlights: June 23, Woods scattered six hits and shutout Minot Mallards 6–0. He helped himself on offense with two hits.

Bob Wright—Manager

Wright managed the Regina Caps of the Western Canada League in 1951 and the independent Medicine Hat Phillies in 1953. From the Philadelphia area, Wright began his career with the Philadelphia Pats and later joined the touring Bacharach Giants before settling in as manager of the Philadelphia Colored Giants.

John Wright—Pitcher, 5'11", 172 lbs.
Batted right, threw right

There were some who thought Wright was the prize when he and Jackie Robinson signed with the Dodgers. Alexander Pompez, owner of the New York Cubans of the Negro National League, was one of them.

> Wright should win as many as 15 games in the International League this season ... I don't think Jackie Robinson, the shortstop from the Kansas City Monarchs, is ready for fast company [*The Sporting News*, March 7, 1946, p.2].

Wright had nine years of Negro League experience, most with the Homestead Grays, when he paired with Robinson to break the color barrier in organized ball. Both were assigned to the Triple-A, Montreal Royals. However, the taunts, the indignities, the pressure, much in evidence during spring training, got to Wright and after pitching in just two games (both in relief) he was sent down to Three Rivers, Quebec of the Canadian-American League. He pitched well at Three Rivers, winning twelve games, but after the season left the Dodgers to return to the Homestead Grays and more comfortable surroundings. He went on to play in Venezuela, Mexico and the Dominican Republic before a season back in the Negro League with Indianapolis to conclude his career.

1946 Montreal Royals—Won 0, Lost 0, 2 G, 6 IP, 5 BB, 3 SO, 6.00 ERA
1946 Three Rivers Royals—Won 12, Lost 8, 4.15 ERA

Steve Enloe Wylie—Pitcher, 6'0", 180 lbs. Batted right, threw right

Wylie began his baseball career as a teenager pitching for his hometown Clarksville, Tennessee, Stars from 1927 to 1930. Later, he played for the Crofton Browns, a team owned by a Crofton, KY, coal mine company. Players would suit up for baseball in the summer and work in the mines in the off season. It's believed it was while Wylie was with Crofton that he was scouted by Negro League clubs.

Then 33, the big right-hander, began his Negro League career in 1944 with the Memphis Red Sox. Soon he would be in the uniform of the fabled Kansas City Monarchs and a teammate of Satchel Paige and an infielder by the name of Jackie Robinson. Wylie pitched for the Monarchs until 1947.

In the summer of 1948, Wylie began the season as the ace of George Ligon's Colored All-Stars. Near the end of June, 1948, Wylie pitched the All-Stars to top money in the Brandon, Manitoba Invitational Tournament downing the host Brandon Greys 5–3. It wasn't long after that he would be in the uniform of the Brandon club and became recognized as one of the great "money players" on the tournament trail in Western Canada. In 1949, again he began the summer with Ligon's All-Stars then jumped to the Minot Merchants, an independent team playing in North Dakota. When Minot joined the new ManDak League, Wylie was off to a great start, then left the team for Swift Current, Saskatchewan. From 1951 to 1954, he played in North Battleford, Saskatchewan, Grandview, Manitoba, and Brandon, Manitoba. Wylie closed out his career in 1956 in the Intercounty Baseball League in Ontario, Canada.

I never could throw the screwball," said Steven Enloe Wylie. "I had a knuckleball, a curveball, a slider and a fastball." "I could throw from three angles. I would throw it overhand, from three-quarters and sidearm [*Clarksville Leaf-Chronicle*, June 10, 1990].

June 12, 1990 the City of Clarksville honored Wylie with an official proclamation recognizing the achievements of Negro baseball and specifically Steve Wylie, hometown hero.

"I played in a lot of different places," said Wylie. "I won a lot of them, and I lost a lot of them" [*Clarksville Leaf-Chronicle*, June 10, 1990].

Wylie died at Clarksville, October 23rd, 1993 at age 82.

Within a few weeks in the summer of 1948, right-hander Steve Enloe Wylie, with both Ligon's All-Stars and Brandon Greys, gained a reputation as a great "money" pitcher as he pitched the winning game in three tournaments and in the deciding game of the Manitoba Senior League playoffs. Wylie had come to Canada after a tour with the Kansas City Monarchs, playing alongside such stars as Satchel Paige and Jackie Robinson (photograph courtesy Lil Lowe).

1948 Brandon Greys—Won 13, Lost 1, G 16, GS 14, CG 13 *
1949 Minot Merchants—Won 15, Lost 6
1950 Minot Mallards—Won 3, Lost 2, 6 G, 4 GS, 3 CG
1950 Swift Current Indians—Statistics not available
1951 North Battleford Beavers—Won 6, Lost 1, 7 G, 6 GS, 6 CG
1952 North Battleford Beavers—Statistics not available
1953 Grandview Maroons—Statistics not available
1954 Brandon Greys—Won 1, Lost 2, 6 G, 1 GS, 0 CG
1956 Galt Terriers—Statistics not available

League, playoff, tournament and exhibition games.

Canadian Highlights: June 23, 1948, the Brandon Greys signed Wylie after he had pitched the Ligon Colored All-Stars to victory in the Brandon Tournament. He didn't disappoint as he pitched brilliantly at times during the 1948 season. July 22, he fired a two-hitter and fanned twelve in an 11–1 victory over Muskogee in another Brandon Tournament. July 28, he pitched another two-hitter in beating the Elmwood Giants 9–0 in a league game. July 31, he beat ANAF Vets 12–3, giving up five hits and striking out sixteen. August 25, he scattered eight hits and fanned twelve in pitching the Greys to the league championship.

July 1, 1949, Wylie blanked Transcona 6–0 on a two-hitter to advance Minot to the final of the Kinsmen Tournament at Brandon. July 28, Wylie pitched two shutouts, one a one-hitter, the other a four-hitter to lead Minot Merchants to the top prize at the Indian Head Tournament. August 7, with the temperature at 108 degrees. Wylie (who received a gold watch as fans held Steve Wylie Day) held Brandon to four hits and fanned 11 in eight innings of work as Minot topped the Greys 3–2. He had to leave the game in the 8th after a beaning.

July 18, 1950, Wylie fired a one-hitter over five shutout innings in an exhibition tussle against the Nashville Stars.

June 6, 1951, Wylie pitched North Battleford to top money at the Lloydminster Tournament. The Beavers topped Morinville 11–1 in the final as Wylie fired a six-hitter. July 15, he pitched the Beavers to a 2–1, 10-inning victory over Prince Albert. He walked and scored the winner in the extra frame. September 7, Wylie fired a three-hitter as North Battleford captured the league title with a 2–1 playoff victory over Saskatoon.

Leopoldo Xiques—Outfield/Second Base

Xiques was one of nearly two dozen Cubans who formed the Indian Head Rockets in 1954.

1954 Indian Head Rockets—.283

Canadian Highlights: June 27, 1954, Xiques had a double and three singles as Indian Head trounced Rosetown 11–2. July 23, he drove in a pair with a triple and double in a loss to Moose Jaw. August 13, he had a double and two singles to lead the Rockets to a 7–1 win over Saskatoon. August 19, Xiques bashed two doubles and two singles in the Rockets' loss to Rosetown. The following day, he had two doubles and a single in a victory over Moose Jaw.

Clarence York—Shortstop/Third Base

York, of the Jacksonville Eagles, was a late season addition to the 1954 Indian Head Rockets.

Canadian Highlights: July 26, 1954, York had three hits to help the Rockets edge Lloydminster 4–3. August 9, he led the Rockets with two doubles and a single in a 10–7 win over North Battleford.

Francisco "Chico" Zayas—Pitcher, 6'0", 152 lbs. Batted right, threw right

Zayas started his career in 1955 and 1956 in Class-C and D ball in the New York Giants system. He had a cameo in 1959 with the Winnipeg Goldeyes appearing in just three games. He closed out his career in 1960 in the Mexican League.

1959 Winnipeg Goldeyes—Won 0, Lost 1

Luis Zayas—Utility, 5'8", 160 lbs. Batted right, threw right

Zayas had a strong second season in pro ball, hitting .328 with 24 doubles and 34 home runs in 1956 for Nogales of the Arizona-Mexico League. But that was the best of his 11 seasons. He reached as high as Triple-A with Havana and Montreal and spent his last seven seasons playing in Mexico.

1959 Montreal Royals—.119, 0 HR, 1 RBI

Roberto "Jeronimo" Zayas—Outfield, 5'8", 160 lbs. Batted right, threw right

Zayas had an eye opening introduction to Canada when he arrived from Cuba in 1953. "We were staying at the YMCA and the next morning we all got up and saw all this snow," said Zayas. "The newspaper phoned and they came over with hockey equipment and things like that and took pictures of everybody, in this park across from the YMCA." Zayas said he skipped the photo opportunity. "I didn't go because it was too cold. I stayed in my room. It was the first time I had even seen snow."

He played six seasons in the Western Canada League before settling down in Moose Jaw and playing and managing in the Southern Saskatchewan League. He was one of few imports to make his permanent home in Canada. He died in 2006 in Moose Jaw, Saskatchewan.

1953 Saskatoon/Moose Jaw—.273
1954 Lloydminster Meridians—.213, 3 HR, 17 RBI, 18 SB
1955 Lloydminster Meridians—.234, 1 HR, 12 RBI, 9 SB
1956 Lloydminster Meridians—.246, 2 HR, 12 RBI, 10 SB
1957 Lloydminster Meridians—.288, 2 HR, 27 RBI, 18 SB
1958 Lloydminster–NB/Moose Jaw—.232, 0 HR, 14 RBI, 6 SB
1959 Moose Jaw Mallards—.273

Canadian Highlights: In just his second game in Canada, May 16, 1953, Zayas pounded a homer to help Saskatoon to a win over long time rival, North Battleford.

July 12, 1954, he had two hits and three stolen bases in a 5–2 win over Rosetown. July 29, the speedster belted a pair of triples as the Meridians downed Kamsack 5–0 at the Rosetown Tournament. August 19, he clubbed a homer on the first pitch of the game to pace the Meridians to a 15—5 romp over Moose Jaw.

July 2, 1957, Zayas singled with one out in the ninth inning to spoil Charlie Piper's bid for a no-hitter. August 8, he had a homer, RBI single, walk and scored as Lloydminster topped Moose Jaw 10–7.

June 15, 1958, the little Cuban had a triple and three singles to pull Lloydminster–North Battleford Combines into first place with a 15–4 win over Williston Oilers. He tied for the league lead in stolen bases, with 18, in 1958.

Cuban Roberto Zayas had a cool reception on his first trip to Canada—snow in the spring of 1953. A highly popular player, Zayas settled down in Moose Jaw, Saskatchewan, following his career (photograph from the Mah collection).

Bibliography

Bjarkman, Peter C. *Baseball with a Latin Beat.* Jefferson, N.C.: McFarland, 1994.

Brown, William. *Baseball's Fabulous Montreal Royals.* Montreal: Robert Davies, 1996.

Chadwick, Bruce. *When the Game Was Black and White.* New York: Abbeville, 1992.

Clark, Dick, and Larry Lester, eds. *The Negro League Book.* Cleveland: SABR, 1994.

Clifton, Merritt. *Disorganized Baseball, Volume 1: The Quebec Provincial League.* Monroe, Conn.: self-published, 1991.

Creamer, Robert. "Conversation Piece, Subject: Don Newcombe." *Sports Illustrated,* August 22, 1955.

Dixon, Phil, and Patrick J. Hannigan. *The Negro Baseball Leagues, 1867–1955: A Photographic History.* Mattituck, N.Y.: Amereon, 1992.

Gardner, Robert, and Dennis Shortelle. *The Forgotten Players.* New York: Walker, 1993.

Garfield, Henry. *Tartabull's Throw.* New York: Simon & Schuster, 2001.

Golenbock, Peter. *Bums: An Oral History of the Brooklyn Dodgers.* New York: G.P. Putnam, 1984.

Hack, Paul, and Dave Shury. *Wheat Province Diamonds.* Regina, Saskatchewan: Saskatchewan Sports Hall of Fame and Museum, 1997.

Holway, John. *Blackball Stars.* Westport, Conn.: Mecklermedia, 1988.

Humber, William. *Diamonds of the North.* New York: Oxford University Press, 1995.

_____ and Spider Jones. *A Sporting Chance.* Toronto: Dundurn, 2004.

Johnson, Lloyd, and Miles Wolf. *The Encyclopedia of Minor League Baseball,* 2nd ed. Durham: Baseball America, 1997.

Kahn, Roger. *The Boys of Summer.* New York: Perennial Library, 1987.

Kelley, Brent. *The Negro Leagues Revisited.* Jefferson, N.C.: McFarland, 1998.

Kirwin, Bill. *Out of the Shadows: African American Baseball from the Cuban Giants to Jackie Robinson.* Lincoln: University of Nebraska Press, 2005.

Mann, Arthur. *The Jackie Robinson Story.* New York: Grosset & Dunlap, 1950.

McNeil, William F. *Dodgers Encyclopedia,* 2nd ed. Urbana, Ill.: Sports Publishing, 2000.

Menary, David. *Terrier Town: Summer of '49.* Waterloo, Ontario: Wilfrid Laurier University Press, 2003.

Mendham, Dan. *The 1948 London Majors: A Great Canadian Team.* Unpublished academic paper, University of Western Ontario, December 7, 1992.

Moffi, Larry, and Jonathan Kronstadt. *Crossing the Line: Black Major Leaguers 1947–1959.* Jefferson, N.C.: McFarland, 1994.

Peterson, Robert. *Only the Ball Was White.* Englewood Cliffs, N.J.: Prentice-Hall, 1970.

Riley, James A. *The Biographical Encyclopedia of the Negro Baseball Leagues.* New York: Carroll & Graf, 1994.

Robinson, Frazier and Paul Bauer. *Catching Dreams: My Life in the Negro Baseball Leagues.* Syracuse, N.Y.: Syracuse University Press, 2000.

Rygelski, Jim. "Lightnin' Len." *St. Louis Cardinals Game Magazine.* June, 1997.

Selter, Ron. "Minor League Slugging Champions." *The Baseball Research Journal.* Society for American Baseball Research, Number 28, 1999, 101–104.

Shury, Dave. *Batter-Up: The Story of the Northern Saskatchewan Baseball League.* North Battleford, Saskatchewan: Turner-Warwick Publications Inc., 1990.

_____. *Saskatchewan Historical Baseball Review.* Saskatchewan Baseball Hall of Fame and Museum Association, 1996.

Stroschein, Joan, ed. *Minot Mallard/Merchants Reunion Weekend.* August 1, 2, & 3, 1997.

Swanton, Barry. *The ManDak League: Haven for Former Negro League Ballplayers 1950–1957.* Jefferson, N.C.: McFarland, 2006.

Thorn, John, and Pete Palmer, eds. *Total Baseball.* New York: Warner Books, 1989.

Thorpe, Slim, as told to Leslie Rendel and George K. Ross. "Slim Thorpe's Story" in *75 Years of Sport and Culture in Lloydminster, 1903–1978.* Compiled by the Lloydminster History of Recreation and Cultural Activities Committee. Lloydminster, Alberta: Lloydminster Senior Citizens Society, 1979.

Trudeau, Christian. "Integration in Quebec." *Dominion Ball.* The Society for American Baseball Research, 2005.

Bibliography

Newspapers

Associated Press
Austin Dailey Herald, Minnesota
Baltimore Afro-American, Maryland
Battlefords Telegraph, Saskatchewan
Bismarck Tribune, North Dakota
Brandon Sun, Manitoba
Brawley News, California
Calgary Herald, Alberta
Camrose Canadian, Alberta
Charleston Daily Mail, West Virginia
Charleston Post and Courier, South Carolina
Chester Times, Pennsylvania
Chicago Defender, Illinois
Chicago Tribune, Illinois
Claresholm Local Press, Alberta
Clarksville Leaf-Chronicle, Tennessee
Cullman Banker, Alabama
Detroit News, Michigan
Edmonton Bulletin, Alberta
Edmonton Capital, Alberta
Edmonton Journal, Alberta
Fairview Post, Alberta
Fergus Falls Daily Journal, Minnesota
Flin Flon Daily Miner, Manitoba
Fort Wayne Journal-Gazette, Indiana
Fresno Bee, California
Galveston Daily News, Texas
The Globe, Toronto, Ontario
The Globe and Mail, Toronto, Ontario
Helena Daily Independent, Montana
Herald-Press, St. Joseph, Michigan
Indianapolis Star, Indiana
Janesville Daily Gazette, Wisconsin
Kamsack Times, Saskatchewan
Kingston Daily Freeman, New York
Kokomo Perspective, Indiana
Lacombe Globe, Alberta
La Crosse Tribune, Wisconsin
Lethbridge Daily Herald, Alberta
Lethbridge Herald, Alberta
Lloydminster Times, Saskatchewan
Los Angeles Daily News, California
Medicine Hat News, Alberta
Minot Daily News, North Dakota
Moose Jaw Times-Herald, Saskatchewan
Nashua Telegraph, New Hampshire
New Castle News, Pennsylvania
New York Times, New York
News-Palladium, Benton Harbor, Michigan
North Battleford News-Optimist, Saskatchewan
Pacific Stars and Stripes, Military
Paris News, Texas
Pittsburgh Courier, Pennsylvania
Pottstown Mercury, Pennsylvania
Progress-Index, Petersburg, Virginia
Red Deer Advocate, Alberta
Regina Leader-Post, Saskatchewan
Sarasota Herald Tribune, Florida
Saskatoon Star-Phoenix, Saskatchewan
Sexsmith Sentinel, Alberta
The Sporting News, Missouri
Swan River Star Times, Manitoba
Syracuse Herald Journal, New York
Toronto Star, Ontario
Traverse City Record Eagle, Michigan
Tri-City Herald, Washington
Tucson Daily Citizen, Arizona
Uniontown Evening Standard, Pennsylvania
Vancouver Province, British Columbia
Victoria Advocate, Texas
Victoria Colonist, British Columbia
Washington Post, Washington DC
Waterloo Daily Courier, Iowa
Winnipeg Free Press, Manitoba
Winnipeg Tribune, Manitoba
Winona Republican-Herald, Minnesota
Wisconsin State Journal, Wisconsin
Yorkton Enterprise, Saskatchewan

Internet Sites

Alberta On-Line www.ourfutureourpast.ca
Complete List of Minor Leagues, Mike McCann www.geocities.com/big_bunko/minor.html
Cuban Baseball, Cesar Lopez www.cubanball.com/
Legends of the Negro Leagues www.legendsofthenegroleagues.com
Major League Baseball www.mlb.com
Minot Mallards, Bill Guenthner www.minotmallards.com/
National Baseball Hall of Fame and Museum www.baseballhalloffame.org
Negro Leagues Baseball Museum www.nlbm.com
Negro League Baseball Players Association www.nlbpa.com
New Jersey City University www.njcu.edu/programs/jchistory/Pages/H_Pages/Hague_Frank.htm
Paper of Record www.paperofrecord.com
SABR, Quebec http://quebec.sabr.org/
The Newspaper Archive www.newspaperarchive.com/
The Society for American Baseball Research, Minor Leagues Database http://minors.sabrwebs.com/cgibin/index.php
UCLA Baseball http://uclabruins.cstv.com/sports/m-basebl/
Vancouver Baseball http://www3.telus.net/jgbennie/
Western Canada Baseball, Jay-Dell Mah www.attheplate.com/wcbl/

Personal Interviews

Nat Bates, Charlie Beene, Lyman Bostock Sr., Sherwood Brewer, Reg Chopp, Sherman Cottingham, Wilmer Fields, Emile Francis, Dirk Gibbons, Cleveland Grant, Pumpsie Green, Jim Lester, Marvin Ligon, Walter McCoy, Ira McKnight, Steve Molinari, Cliff Pemberton, Modie Risher, Sterling Slaughter, Roy Taylor, Ron Teasley, Len Tucker, Armando Vasquez, Bill Walasko, Jimmy Wilkes, Dewey Williams, Ed Williams, Willie "Curly" Williams, and Roberto Zayas.

Programs

1951 Saskatoon 55s
1951 Kamsack Tournament
1951 Carman Cardinals
1952 Carman Cardinals
1953 Winnipeg Royals
1959 Lethbridge White Sox
1960 Lethbridge White Sox
1960 Calgary Buffaloes
1960 Saskatoon Commodores
1960 Lacombe Tournament
1960 Lloydminster Meridians
1961 Lethbridge White Sox

Index

Numbers in **_bold italics_** indicate pages with photographs.

Aaron, Hank 93
Abe Saperstein's All-Stars 28
Aberdeen 174
Abilene Eagles 143
Acme Giants 124
Acosta, Jose 15
Adair, Jerry 186
Adams, "Smokey" Joe 15
Albuquerque Dukes 156
Alexander, Grover 109, 178
Alexander, Ted "Red" 16
Alexander, Wally 16
Allan, Harold 16
Almendares 46
Almendariz, Lou 17
Almendro, Jamie 11
Alston, Tom 14, 17, 142
Alston, Walter 19
Altman, Jack 9
Alvarez, Higinio 18
Amaro, Mario 18
American Association 12, 15, 28, 127, 131–132
Amoros, Sandy 19
A.N.A.F. Vets 137, 148, 190
Anderson, Bill 19
Anderson, Orinthal "Andy" 19
Anderson, Stanley Robert "Gabby" 19
Andrews, Curly 20
Andrews, Herb 12
Andrews, John "Sonny" 20
Andux, Orlando 21
Anthony, Tex 21
Appalachian League 74, 146
Argudin, Dionisio Cesar 21
Arias, Rudy 21
Arizona-Mexican League 16, 48, 98, 191
Arizona-New Mexican League 18
Arizona-Texas League 123, 167
Armenteros, Juan "Army" 21
Arnett, Barry 9
Ashby, Earl 22
Atkins, Joe 22
Atlanta Black Crackers 77–78, 151, 158
Atlanta Stars 31
Auburn Yankees 113
Austin, Frank 23

Bacharach Giants 188
Bailey, Andy A.Q. 23
Bailey, Brack 9
Ballestro, Miguel "Pedro" 23
Baltimore Black Sox 102
Baltimore Elite Giants 24, 26, 28, 41, 45, 52, 57–58, 67, 72, 102, 122, 127, 143, 145, 150, 155, 174, 178, 185
Baltimore Orioles 41, 53, 93, 131, 141, 150, 159–160, 163
Bankhead, Dan 23, 91
Bankhead, Fred 24
Bankhead, Sam 24, 71
Banks, Ernie 34, 135
Banks, Fred 84
Banks, Jim 24
Banks, Norman 24
Barbee, Quincy "Bud" 24
Barbon, Roberto "Chico" 25
Barnes, Frank 25
Barnes, Tom 25
Barnhill, Herbert 26
Barrow, Wes 26
Barrow, Wesley 105
Basin League 34, 66
Bassett, Lloyd "Pepper" 26
Bates, Nathaniel "Nat" 9, 26–27, 44, 75, 120, 137
Baton Rouge Hardwood Sports 30, 105, 146
Bauer, Paul 58
Bauman, Joe 89
Baxes, Mike 147
Beamon, Charlie 27
Beckley Black Bingles 91
Becquer, Julio 27
Beene, Charlie 9
Beiden, Pete 179
Belleville, Ontario 67
Benson, Baldy 27
Bentley, Lois 9
Bentley Brothers 38, 68, 78
Benton Harbor Buds 118
Bergeron, Tom 9
Berkley Tigers 124
Bernier, Carlos 27
Berra, Yogi 19
Berry, Mike "Red" 28
Beverley, Bill "Fireball" 28
Big Six League 7
Big State League 42, 145
Birmingham Black Barons 16, 22–23, 29–30, 32, 35, 41, 48, 52, 54, 58, 60, 78, 81, 91, 99, 106, 117, 121, 124, 128–129, 132, 137, 145, 150–152, 155, 182–183
Bismarck 6, 11, 108, 111–112, 165, 166
Bismarck Barons 85
Bismarck Corwin-Churchills 32, 117
Black, Joe 28
Black Spinners 151
Blackman, Jesse 17, 28, 49, 102

Blanco, Herberto "Henry" 29
Bob Feller All Stars 57, 91, 109
Bogal, Ted 9
Boise Yankees 89
Bolden, Jim "Fireball" 29
Bond, Monte 29
Boney, Marshall 30
Bonilla, Julio 30
Booker, Nathaniel "Legs" 30
Border League 8, 21, 112–113
Bostock, Lyman, Sr. 9, 30
Bostock, Lymon, Jr. 30
Boston Black Giants 185
Boston Blues 110
Boston Braves 13–14, 50, 92, 127, 135
Boston Red Sox 7, 14, 75, 92, 159
Boston Royal Giants 115
Bouza, Roberto 31
Bowen, Chico 31
Bowman, Duke 136
Bowsfield, Ted 67
Bowsman, Manitoba 53, 86, 97
Bowsman Maroons 130
Boyd, Lincoln 31
Brandon 169, 172
Brandon Greys 16–21, 24–26, 29, 31, 35–37, 39–40, 42, 47–49, 50–52, 56–60, 62–65, 67, 70, **_71_**, 73–74, 77–78, 86–88, 91–93, 95, 98, 100, 107–109, 113–114, 116–117, 127–130, 133–135, 138, 140, 143, 145, 147, 149, 152–154, 157–158, 168–169, 170, 173, 175–180
Brandon Invitational Tournament 67, 150, 155
Brandon Kinsmen Tournament 16
Brandon Tournament 38, 47, 90, 124, 152, 156, 175–177, 185, 190
Branham, Luther 31
Brantford 109
Brantford Hall of Fame 179
Brantford Red Sox 51, 65, 119, 138, 164, 178–179
Brathwaite, Hiram Alonso 32
Brazzle, Jabe 32
Brechner, Len 9, 89
Bremmer, Eugene 32
Brewer, Chet 17, 26, 32, 34, 40, 49, 110, 117, 124, 134–135, **_162_**, 165, 167
Brewer, Sherwood "Woody" 9, 34
Bridgewater Coyotes 89
Bristol Owls 28
Britton, John 35, 121
Broadview, Saskatchewan 6, 32
Broadview Buffaloes 58
Broadview Red Sox 118

195

Index

Broadway Clowns 97
Broady, Ken 35
Brookins, Dick 2, 13, 35, 68
Brooklyn Brown Bombers 161
Brooklyn Brown Dodgers 72
Brooklyn Cuban Giants 29–31, 49, 53, 61, 85–86, 98, 116, 130, 158, 169–171, 178, 181
Brooklyn Dodgers 1, 12–13, 19, 24, 50, 57, 64, 69, 72, 86, 94, 112, 114, 120–122, 128, 144, 146–147, 154, 157, 161, 167, 178, 187–188
Brooklyn Royal Giants 30, 102
Brost, Leola 9
Brown, Barney 35, 91, 169
Brown, Ben 37
Brown, Boyd 37
Brown, Eddie 38
Brown, Raymond 56, 111
Brown, Tom T.J. 38
Brown, Willard "Home Run" 39, 91
Brown, William 12
Bruton, Jack 40
Bruton, Nip 40
Bryant, Allen "Lefty" 40
Bryant, Clay 149
Buchanan All Stars 101, 123
Buffalo 126, 142
Buffalo Harlem Giants 151
Buford, Don 40
Bumpus, Earl 41
Burbage, Buddy 41
Burke, Ernest 41
Butts, Harry 1, 42
Butts, Thomas "Pee Wee" 42

Cabrera, Louis 42
Cabrera, Rafael "Rafe" 42, 66, 186
Cain, Marion "Sugar" 43, 85, 113, 118
Cairo Dodgers 117
Calgary 104, 117, 160, 184
Calgary Black Sox 177
Calgary Bronchos/Stampeders 7
Calgary Buffaloes 87
Calgary Dodgers 87
Calgary Elks' Tournament 87
Calgary Tournament 87
Calhoun, Walter 44
California Angels 95
California League 17, 27, 80, 111, 154, 182
California Mohawks 64, 83, 90, 136, 157
California Negro Leagues 44
California Winter League 33
Calvert, Charles 44
Calvin, Winters 26, 44, 75, 120
Cameron, Mark 9
Cameron, Henry "Red" 44
Campanella, Roy "Campy" 22, 44–45, 121, 147
Campos, Antonio "Tony" 46
Campos, Frank 45
Campos, Tony, Jr. 9
Camrose Tournament 25, 67, 116, 128
Can-Am League 87, 178

Canadian American League 7, 30, 70, 115, 126, 180, 188
Canizares, Avelino 46
Cardenal, Pedro 46
Carlisle, Sylvester "Pee Wee" 47
Carlsbad Potashers 89
Carlson, John 68
Carlyle, Saskatchewan 83
Carman Cardinals 15–16, 20–21, 23, 29–31, 33, 39, 41, 43, 47, 51, 53, 55, 57–58, 60–62, 64, 66, 74, 77–78, 81–82, 85, 88, 90–93, 99, 105–106, 108–113, 116–117, 120–121, 125, 130–131, 133, 138, 144–145, 147–148, 152–154, 156, *161*–163, 166–169, 171, 174–176, 178, 180, 183, 186–188
Carman Invitational Tournament 16
Carman Tournament 171
Carmangay Eagles 72
Carmangay Tournament 101
Carnegie, Herb 113
Carnegie, Ossie 113
Carolina League 98, 124, 138, 150
Carolina Negro League 28
Carr, Wayne "Pappy" 47
Carswell, Lindsay 47
Carter, Ernest "Spoon" 47, 175
Casas, Edel 69
Cash, Bill "Ready" 47
Castille, Irwin "Chuck" 48
Central Alberta All-Stars 49
Central League 98
Central Texas Vocational College 32
Cepeda, Orlando 55
Cesar, Jose "Bobby" 48
Chacon, Mario 48
Chadwick, Dave 49
Chandler, Happy 126
Chandler, Homer 49, 133
Chandler, Spud 57
Chappie Johnson Colored All Stars 44, 102, 124, 185
Charles, Ed 49
Charles, Johnny 49
Charleston Baseball Hall of Fame 140
Charleston River Dogs 140
Chatham All-Stars 9
Chattanooga Choo Choos 78
Chavez, John 154
Chicago American Giants 16, 19, 23, 26, 30, 32, 41, 60, 68, 70, 84–86, 91, 105–106, 111, 114, 116, 124, 127–128, 133, 137–138, 141, 151–152, 154, 156–157, 159, 163, 170, 174
Chicago Brown Bombers 73, 106, 119
Chicago Cubs 34, 60–61, 80, 134, 174
Chicago Palmer House Stars 16
Chicago White Sox 29, 40, 47, 53, 56, 108, 134, 182–183
Chopp, Reg 9
Christopher, Thad 49
Chunichi Dragons 122
Ciefuegos 46

Cincinnati Buckeyes 90, 92, 145
Cincinnati Clowns 26, 56, 96, 105, 114, 153, 170
Cincinnati Crescents 30, 47, 86, 97, 109, 137, 154–155, 170, 178
Cincinnati-Indianapolis Clowns 56
Cincinnati Reds 48, 132, 149, 160, 164
Cincinnati Tigers 90
Cisco, Randy 50
Claresholm Meteors 72, 101
Clarkson, James "Buzz" 50
Claxton, Jimmy 50, 68
Clemente, Roberto 50
Cleveland All-Stars 148
Cleveland Bears 26
Cleveland Buckeyes 22, 29, 32, 39–40, 46, 54–55, 63, 68, 85, 90, 92, 130, 165, 172, 181, 188
Cleveland Clowns 185
Cleveland Indians 32, 63, 92, 95, 125, 131–132, 144, 159, 162–163, 166, 170
Clevenger, Truman 119
Clifford, Luther "Shanty" 51
Clifton, Merritt 23
Clipper, Bob 51
Clovis, New Mexico 31
Cobb, Lillord 51
Coben, Murray 79
Coffee, Howard 52
Colas, Jose 52
Coleman, Emory 52
Coleman, Major 52
Coleman, Johnny "Lefty" 52
College World Series 41
Colliery League 115
Collins, Fred 57
Collins, Hubert Pee Wee" 53
Colonial League 28, 41–42, 80, 88, 133
Colonsay 68, 172–173
Colorado Springs 132
Colored House of David 97
Columbus 148
Columbus Blue Birds 102
Conley, Buford "Tex" 53
Conley, Howard "Butch" 53
Consuegra, Sandalio "Sandy" 53
Cooper, Tom 53
Corbin, Ace 128
Cottingham, Sherman 9, 54, 125
Cowan, John 54
Crofton Browns 189
Crowder, Edward Lee 55
Crue, Marty "Matty" 55
Crumpton, Bennie 55
Cuban Baseball Hall of Fame 69, 92
Cuban Giants 30–31, 68, 95
Cuban Stars 36, 47
Cuidad Trujillos 78
Culbreth, Doug 9
Cunningham, Bob 55
Cy Young Award 91

Dallas Eagles 149
Dancy, Nate 55
Dandridge, Ray 175
Danville, Ontario 68

Index

Danville All-Stars 30
Danville Dans 39, 88, 156
Dartmouth, Nova Scotia 66
Dauphin Red Birds 34, 63, 97–98, 102, 116, 120, 130, 151–152, 161, 171, 188
Davenport, Lloyd "Ducky" 56
Davidson, Keith 9
Davidson, Saskatchewan 158
Davis, Butch 30, 43, 58, 175
Davis, Edward "Peanuts," "Nyasses" 56, 91
Davis, Johnny Howard 56
Davis, Tommy 57, 95
Day, Leon 30, 57, 65, 175
Dean, Dick "Lefty" 58
Dean, Les 151
Decuir, Lional 58
Delisle, Saskatchewan 38, 127, 181
Delisle Gems 68, 78–79
Delorimier Stadium 12
Dennis, Wesley "Doc" 58
Dent, Carl 59
Denver Bears 19, 155
Denver White Elephants 101
Derwores, Jan 9
Detroit Clowns 100
Detroit Motor City Giants 62–63
Detroit-New Orleans Stars 126
Detroit Stars 62, 86, 95, 98, 100, 130, 163
Detroit Tigers 138
Detroit Wolves 74, 85, 93, 109
Devil's Lake 124
Dials, Bill 59
Diaz, Ezequiel 59
Diaz, Vincente 59
Dickinson 112
Dihigo, Martin 148
Dixon, Phil 9
Doby, Larry 178
Dominican Republic 48
Dominion Day Tournament 171
Dominion Hawks 115
Don Newcombe All-Stars 44
Donaldson, John 6, 59
Dothan Cardinals 123
Douglas, Jesse 14, 60, 185
Doyle, Dan 9
Doyle, Pat 9
Drake, Sammy 60–61
Drake, Solly 60–61
Drummond, Charlie 62
Drummondville 46
Drummondville Cubs 21, 23, 25, 27, 32, 56, 85, 102, 112, 114, 128, 132, 152, 166, 170, 177
Drummonville Royals 24, 127
Drummonville/St. Hyacinthe 153
Drummonville/St. Jean 22, 32
Drummonville/St. John 23
Duany, Claro 62
Duluth Dukes 46
Duluth-Superior White Sox 164
Duluth Travelers 47
Duncan, Mel 62

East West All-Star game 26, 39, 55–56, 62, 113, 132, 136, 140, 150, 156, 173, 175, 182

Easter, Luscious "Luke" 62
Easterling, Howard 63, 91
Eastern League 54, 58, 107, 162, 170, 178
Eastern Negro League 67
Eastern Ohio League 114
Eau Claire Braves 47, 55, 74
Edmonton 108, 128, 140, 143, 150, 165, 169, 166
Edmonton, Alberta 87
Edmonton Eskimos 7, 30, 41, 58, 98, 115, 120, 160, 169, 184
Edmonton Oilers 133
Edmonton Pontiacs 88, 115–116
Edmonton Tournament 49
El Cerrito High School 26
Elite Café 3, 9
Elliott, Gordon 9
Elmira Pioneers 178
Elmwood Giants 2, 26, 28–30, 35, 39, 49, 54–55, 58, 60–62, 66, 71, 77, 81, 85, 87–88, 90–93, 98–99, 105, 107–108, 112, 114, 116, 118–119, 125–126, 129, 131, 133, 135–137, 146, 148, 152–153, 155–158, 162, 165, 169, 172–174, 175–181, 190
Enalls, Bob 63
Endriss, Al 9
Estevan Maple Leafs 20–21, 27, 40, 47, 53, 74, 76–77, 97, 101–103, 105–106, 109, 112–113, 115, 118–119, 124, 129, 151–152, 158, 162, 170, 172, 179, 181, 187–188
Estevan Tournament 151, 179, 181
Eston, Saskatchewan 64, 180
Eston Ramblers 122131–132, 136
Ethiopian Clowns 23, 26, 49, 56, 153–154
Evans, Frank 63
Evansville Dodgers 41

Fabre, Sergio 63
Fairbault, Minnesota 77
Fairley, Ron 147
Fargo-Moorehead Twins 47, 157
Farnham Black Sox 80, 119, 131
Farnham Pirates 24, 32, 39, 72, 88, 99, 106, 109, 125, 127, 131, 144, 148–149, 160, 163, 165, 172
Farnham Red Sox 22–23
Feller, Bob 56
Fennell, Ralph 64
Fernandez, Humberto "Chico" 64
Ferro, Amancio 64
Fields, Wilmer 9, 65, 99
Finch, Rayford "Ray" 66, 169
Finney, Ed 67
Florida Cubans 8, 21–22, 25, 30, 44, 50, 59, 67, 82, *103*, 128, 132, 151, 165–166
Florida Gators 153
Florida Giants 137
Florida International League 46, 53, 69, 74, 110
Florida State League 74, 82, 91, 113, 117, 138, 177
Flynn, Mark 9
Foam Lake Tournament 44, 102
Foothills League 7, 72–73

Foothills-Wheat Belt League 7, 87, 101
Ford, John 9, 67
Ford, Whitey 27
Fornieles, Mike 67
Fort Wayne Capeharts 105, 149
Fort Wayne Dairymen 99
Fort Wayne General Electrics 140
Forten, Carlos 67
Fouste, Luis 68
Fowler, Johm "Bud" 6, 13, 23, 68
Fowlkes, Sam 68
Francis, Emile 9
Fredericton Capitals 113
Free Press All-Stars 162

Galloway, Hippie 13, 68
Galt 89, 179
Galt Terriers 51, 62, 92, 106, 151, 155, 163, 190
Garcia, Juan Rene 68
Garcia, Oswaldo 69
Garcia, Rolando 69
Garcia, Silvio 69
Gardella, Danny 126
Garrett, Jim 9
Gaston, Hiram "Mike" 69
Gatenby, Bill 9
Gee, Sammy 70
George, Eric 70
Gibbons, Dirk "Bubblegum" 9, 70
Gibson, Josh 39, 71, 181
Gibson, Josh, Jr. 71
Gilbert Plains, Manitoba 152, 171, 180
Gilkerson's Union Giants 59
Gilley, Napoleon "Nap" 80
Gilliam, James "Junior" 72, 147, 178
Gladstone, Granville "Happy" 72
Gladu, Roland 164
Glen, Hubert "Country" 72
Glenn, Stanley "Doc" 73
Global Word Series 29, 63, 66, 76, 78–79, 82, 84, 99, 150, 159
Godinez, Manual 73
Goliat, Mike 149
Gomez, Ruben 163
Gonzales, Hiram 73
Gonzales, Wilfredo 74
Goshen/Greensboro Red Wings 17
Gotay, Julio 74
Granby, Quebec 185
Granby Phillies 47–48, 70
Granby Red Sox 24–25, 77, 117, 122, 126, 140
Grand Forks Chiefs 55, 146
Grandview Maroons 148, 187, 189–190
Grandview, Manitoba 41, 52, 119–120, 130
Grant, Darryl 74
Granum White Sox 120
Graves, Morrell 74
Gray, Chappie 74
Great Fall, Montana 52
Green, Elijah "Pumpsie" 2, 9, 14, 26, 44, 75, 120, 137
Green, Shaeffer 76
Greene, James Elbert "Joe" 77

Index

Greene, Wilbur "Willie" 77
Greer, J.D. 77
Gregory, Leroy 9
Griffith, Bob "Schoolboy" 7
Griggs, Acie "Skeet" 78
Griggs, Benjamin L. "Bennie" 78
Guelph Maple Leafs 6
Guelph Merchants 89
Guelph Royals 89
Guenthner, Bill 9

Haas, Curly 28, 60
Hague, Mayor Frank 11
Halifax and District League 8, 120
Halifax Cardinals 135
Hall of Fame Cooperstown 91, 38–39, 45, 50, 124, 175
Hamman, Ed 80
Handy, George 80
Hankyu Braves 25, 35, 121
Hanson, Fritzie 127
Harding, Stephen 10
Hardy, Walter 80
Harlem Globetrotters 28, 34–35, 47, 58, 70–71, 73, 80, 85, 91, 96–97, 109, 114, 116, 137, 172, 155–157, 162
Harris, Wilmer 80
Harrisburg Senators 67
Harrison, Gary 9, 154
Harvey, Bob 80
Havana Cubans 53, 69, 74
Havana La Palomas 73, 114, 179
Havana Reds 48
Havana Sugar Kings 18, 48, 53, 74, 136, 149
Hawaiian All-Stars 185
Hawthorn, Tom 1, 10, 106
Heard, Jehosie "Jay" 81
Henderson, Arlington 81
Hendley, Bob 95
Henry, Al 81
Hernandez, Jose "Hippy" 82
Herrera, Mario 82
Herrera, Rick 122
Herrera, Roberto 82
Herzog, Whitey 27
Hester, Elmer (Jim) 84
Higginbotham, Carl 84
High Point Pointers 15
Hill, Benny 84
Hill, Sam 84, 99
Hinton, Chuck 174
Hodges, Gil 19
Holly, Stamp J. 85
Hollywood Beavers 188
Hollywood Stars 155
Holoway, John 156
Homestead Grays 13, 16, 19, 22, 26, 38–39, 47, 49, 51, 55, 63, 65, 69, 71, 119, 124–125, 127, 131, 138, 155, 164–165, 181, 188
Hondo Bears 184
Honus Wagner All-Stars 119
Hooker, Leniel "Lennie" 85
Hoover, Bill 10
Horne, Billy 85
House, Charles "Red" 74, 109, 174
House of David 68, 124, 157
Houston Colt 45's 128

Houston Eagles 56, 80–81, 85, 109, 178, 187
Howard, Elston 14, 25, 85
Howard, Percy 86
Huber, Otto 170
Hughes, Dick 174
Humber, William 14
Hunt, Art 86
Hurd, Marty 87
Hutchinson, Willie 34, 87
Hyde, Cowan "Bubba" 9, 88

Iglesias, Antonio 88
Illinois-Indiana-Iowa League 55
Indian Head Rockets 8, 14, 17–18, 20–22, 24–26, 28–29, 31, 33–34, 37, 44, 47, 52–53, 56, 58, 63–64, 67–68, 76, 81–82, 88, 90, 97, 100, 102, 104, 110, 113–116, 118–120, 122–123, 128, 130, 132–133, 135–137, *142*, 151–152, 158, 165, 167, 169–170, 173, 177, 179, 181, 188, 190
Indian Head Tournament 17–18, 30, 49, 52, 68–69, 75–76, 79, 82, 89, 100, 102, 104–105, 110, 116, 119, 123, 129, 132, 136–137, 146, 156–157, 172, 177, 179–180, 190
Indianapolis ABCs 59, 185
Indianapolis Clowns 2–3, 16, 31, 34, 39, 42–43, 52, 56, 70, 72, 86, 95, 107–108, 112, 114–119, 122, 128, 130, 138, 157, 170, 173–174, 177–178, 180, 185, 188
Ingram, Lee 88
Intercounty League 8, 16, 20, 37, 51, 62, 65, 67, 89, 91–92, 109, 111, 119, 138, 155, 178, 189
International League 8, 12, 15, 18, 25, 28, 41, 48, 93, 125–126, 128–129, 144, 147–149, 152, 165, 187, 188
International League All Stars 93, 141
Interstate League 178
Iowa Colored Ghosts 95, 109
Irvin, Monte 91, 178
Isnor, Marlene 10

Jackie Robinson All-Stars 24, 56, 169, 173, 186
Jackson, Alvin 89, 153, 168
Jackson, Daniel "Thumper" 89
Jackson, Isiah "Ike" 9, 89
Jackson, Reg 90
Jacksonville Eagles 8, 17, 28, 47, 52, 76, 102, 118, 135, 140, 181
Jacksonville, Florida Stars 76
Jacksonville Red Caps 26, 135
Jacobs, Gene 90
The Janesville Daily Gazette 60
Jean Braves 42
Jefferson, Willie 90
Jenkins, Daniel 90
Jenkins, Ferguson "Fergie" 91
Jenkins, James "Pee Wee" 91
Jessup, Gentry 91, 99
Jethroe, Sam 14, 32, 92
Jimenez, Felipe "Jimmy" 93

John Donaldson All-Stars 59
Johnson, Bob 93, 173
Johnson, Clifford "Connie" 93, 110
Johnson, Ernest 94
Johnson, Frank 94
Johnson, Harold 94
Johnson, Lou "Sweet Lou" 94
Johnson, Ollie 95
Johnson, Rufus 95
Johnson, Tom 95
Johnson, Walter 178
Jolles, Jaqueline 33
Jones, Aaron 95
Jones, Clarence 96
Jones, Collins Chesterfield 96
Jones, Paul 9
Joplin Cardinals 38
Joyner, Frank 98
Junior World Series 144

Kaiser, Cecil 98
Kamsack 51, 119, 191
Kamsack Cyclones 84, 165, 169, 174, 176, 179
Kamsack Tournament 67, 122
Kansas City A's 49, 133
Kansas City Monarchs 12, 16, 21, 24–26, 28–29, 32, 34–35, 39–41, 44, 51, 54–55, 58–60, 62, 68, 74, 77, 80, 83, 86–87, 89, 93–94, 105, 110, 112–113, 117, 124, 141, 143, 145, 152–156, 158, 160, 163, 166, 174, 180, 187–189
Kansas City Stars 97, 156, 162
Kemp, Dave 10
Kenaston Tournament 174
Kennedy, John 14, 99, 176
Ketchur, Tommy 49
Kindersley, Saskatchewan 54
King, Clarence "Pijo" 99
Kings, Don, Lionel, Ralph 100
Kingston Colonials 8
Kingston/Poughkeepsie 42
Kinsmen Tournament 190
Kintetsu Buffaloes 25
Kirwin, Bill 10, 156
Kitchener 51, 66, 89
Kitchener Panthers 62, 106, 163
Kittle, Hub 9
Kitty League 117
Kiwanis Tournament 59
Knoxville Smokies 159
Koufax, Sandy 95, 147
Kyle, Gus 135

Laboy, Jose Alberto "CoCo" 6, 100–101
Lacobe Tournament 127
Lacombe (Alberta) Tournament 55, 86, 106, 113, 147, 183–184
Lafleche, Saskatchewan 110
Lakeland Pilots 170
Lakeland Tigers 140
Lancaster Red Roses 178
Lanctot, Neal 10
Landrum, Lee 101
Lanier, Max 126
Latham, Horace 102
Lattimore, Alphonso 102
Laurention League 38

Index

Lazaro, Medino 102
Leakos, Spero 113
Leal, Toribio 102
Leavenworth Braves 40, 86
Ledo, Roberto 102
Leduc Oilers 67
Leonard, Buck 181
Lester, Jim 9
Lethbridge 117, 125, 142, 183–184
Lethbridge Cubs 98
Lethbridge Rotary Tournament 25, 35, 67
Lethbridge Tournament 84, 96, 160
Lethbridge Warriors 62, 120
Lethbridge White Sox 62, 79, 166
Levingston, Bob 102–103
Lewis, Herman 103, 105
Ligon, George 104
Ligon, Marvin 6, 9
Ligon, Rufus 104, 179
Ligon's Colored All Stars 2, 6–8, 20, 23–24, 32, 35, 38, 71, 74, 76, 79, 83, 86, 88, 94, 104, 106, 112, 120, 127, 129, 152, 159, 167, 172, 177, 179–180, 184–186, 189–190
Lillie, Dr. Andrew 9
Linck, Bob 9
Lincoln Giants 59
Lipscomb, George 104
Littles, Cecil 105
Lloyd, Johnny 105
Lloyd.- N. Battleford Combines 29–30, 94, 121, 142
Lloydminster 52, 81–82, 84, 89–90, 97, 103, 115, 122, 128, 130, 132, 158, 165, 179, 186
Lloydminster 1955 batting order 96
Lloydminster Green Caps 160, 183–184
Lloydminster Legion Tournament 172
Lloydminster Meridians 37–38, 59, 69, 108, 135, 138, 140–141, 150, 151, **168**–169, 183–184, 191
Lloydminster/North Battleford 40–41, 132, 140, 183
Lloydminster Tournament 22, 79, 190
Locke, Eddie 105
Lockett, Lester 105–106
Lombard, Buddy 106
London 179
London Majors 16, 91
Long, Avery 106
Long Branch Cubans 15
Longhorn League 34, 83, 89, 108, 123, 129, 136, 180
Longley, Wyman "Red" 107
Lopez, Cezar 10
Lopez, Hector 107
Los Angeles Dodgers 48, 61, 141
Los Angeles Red Devils 10
Lott, Benjamin "Honey" 2, 34, 107–108
Louden, Lou 108
Louisiana Black Travelers 21
Louisiana Travelers 129, 151
Louisville Black Colonels 168

Louisville Buckeyes 24, 31, 98, 125
Louisville Colonels 12
Lovelace, Jimmy 109
Lowe, Ian 173
Lowe, Lil 10
Luke Easter All Stars 149
Lumsden, Saskatchewan 184
Lyall, Gord 127

Maddix, Raydell 56
Maddox, Flash 109
Magic City Stars 27
Maglie, Sal 126
Mah, Jay Dell 2–3, 9–10
Mahaffty George 34
Malone, Willy 109
ManDak All-Star Team 57
ManDak League 2, 5, 8–9, 14–16, 18–19, 20–21, 23–24, 26, 28–30, 33, 35, 37, 39–41, 43–44, 47–49, 51–52, 54–57, 60–61, 62, 64, 66–67, 70, 73, 80–82, 84–86, 88, 90, 92, 98–100, 106, 108, 110–113, 116, 118–121, 124, 126, 129–131, 133, 136–137, 140, 143, 149, 151–155, 157–158, 162–163, 166, 169, 172–176, 182, 185–189
ManDak League All-Star team 62, 92
ManDak Tournament 91, 155
Manitoba Baseball Hall of Fame 70, 170
Manitoba Free Press 36–60
Manitoba Invitational Tournament 189
Manitoba-Saskatchewan League 8, 41, 53, 63, 98, 119–120, 148, 166, 176 180
Manitoba Senior League 8, 13, 16, 20, 30–31, 42–43, 49, 51–52, 58, 69–70, 93, 114, 119, 127, 135, 148, 153, 155, 161–162, 170–172, 174–175, 185
Manley, Effa 121
Manning, Max 92, 109
Mantle, Mickey 107
Marcell, Everett 109
Marichal, Juan 147–148
Maris, Roger 107
Maroto, Enrique "Ricky" 109
Marshall, Hiram 110
Marshall, William "Jack" 110
Martin, Billy 19
Martinez, Sergio 110
Massingale, Mac 110
Matchett, Jack 110
Mays, Willie 93, 129 145
McCabe, Ken 10
McCann, Kevin 10
McCoy, Ray 111
McCoy, Walter 9, 14, 111, 183
McDaniels, Fred 112
McDougald, Gil 19
McDuffie, Terris 112
McGowan, Curtis 112
McGraw, John 60
McGuigan, Chuck 9
McHenry, Henry 112
McIntyre, Vincent "Manny" 113
McKinnis, Gread 113

McKnight, Ira 9, 55, 113–114
McLean, Lil 10
McNary, Kyle 10
McNeal, Clyde 114
McNeil, William F. 11
Means, Winslow 114
Medicine Hat 116, 118, 157, 160, 168, 172, 188
Medicine Hat, Alberta 94–96
Medicine Hat Mohawks 44, 56, 75, 90, 102, 136–137, 181
Medicine Hat Phillies 100, 167, 188
Medicine Hat Superiors 34–35, 142
Medicine Hat Tournament 87, 102, 135, 153
Medina, Leonardo "Lazarus" 114
Melville Millionaires 114, 160
Memphis Red Sox 23–25, 39, 42, 54, 62, 80, 87, 104, 107, 112–113, 127, 149, 151, 163, 168, 173–178, 188–189
Menary, David 13, 65
Mendham, Dan 16
Merritt, Eli "Skip" 115
Metz, Nick 104
Mexican Baseball Hall of Fame 131
Mexican League 18–19, 25, 29, 46, 53, 69, 83, 95, 125–126, 133, 148, 164, 167, 170, 190
Mexico City 129
Mexico City Reds 150
Miami Clowns 16
Miami Marlins 125–126
Michaels, George "Whitey" 115
Michigan City Cubs 33
Michigan-Indiana League 33, 118, 140
Midland Indians 89, 129
Midwest League 69
Miles, Roland "Rollie" 115, 178
Miles, Zell 116
Mill City Tournament 115
Miller, Jim 9
Milon, Harold 116
Milwaukee Braves 40, 95, 128, 135, 144, 177
Milwaukee Brewers 127
Minneapolis-St Paul Gophers 35, 96
Minnesota Twins 30, 132
Minot Mallards 9, 19, 24, 37, 39–40, 42, 44, 52, 55, 57–58, 60, 62–63, 67, 70–71, 73–75, 77, 85, 88, 90–91, 93, 99, 102, 106, 109, 113–114, 117, 119–120, 124–125, 128–131, 136–137, 144, 146–147, 149, 151–154, 156–158, 163, 166–167, 170, 173–174, 176, 183, 185–186, 188, 190
Minot Merchants 40, 76–77, 157, 189–190
Minot Tournament 31, 43
Miranda, Miguel 116
Mississippi-Ohio League 52
Mississippi-Ohio Valley League 39, 64, 86–87, 119, 124 180
Mississippi-Valley League 66
Mitchell, Joe 56, 116, 158
Mitchell, Ken 116

Index

Molinari, Steve 9
Monteiro, Juverno Joseph 117
Monterrey, Mexico 129
Montreal Black Panthers 185
Montreal Expos 100–101
Montreal Royals 8, 11–12, 19, 24–25, 28, 44–45, 50, 57, 63–64, 68, 72, 92, 113–114, 120–121, 125–126, 128, 141, 144, 146, 148,-150, 167–168, 170, 187–188, 191
Moody, Lee 117
Moose Jaw 37, 48, 59, 53, 64, 66–68, 77, 83–84, 88–89, 97, 116, 118–119, 123, 133, 137–138, 150–151, 158, 166–167, 169, 172, 174, 181–182, 184, 186–187, 190
Moose Jaw Canucks 18, 40, 52, 150, 177
Moose Jaw Exhibition Tournament 40
Moose Jaw Mallards 94, 104, 135, 147, 167, 191
Moose Jaw Maples 81, 95, 100, 163–164, 167
Moose Jaw Purity Canucks 38
Moose Jaw Tournament 76–77, 115, 135, 151, 157
Moosomin Tournament 170
Morciego, Santiago 117
Moreau, Guy 146
Morgan, T. Kent 10
Moriarty, David 9
Morris, Barney 117
Morris, Ed "Santa Fe" 118
Morrison, Felton 118
Morrow, Jim 118–119
Morton, Bubba 138
Morton, Sydney Cy (Sy) 119, 176
Motor City Giants 98
Mouton, Claude 100
Mulcahy, Tom 9
Mullin, Arch 10
Munatones, Conrad "Connie" 9
Muskogee Cardinals 21, 53, 84, 101, 150–151, 174
Muskogee Colored Cardinals 76, 161

Napier, Eudie 119
Naranjo, Pedro 119
Nash, Ray 120
Nashville All-Stars 150
Nashville Cubs 26
Nashville Stars 58, 190
National Baseball Congress 32, 118–119, 150, 187
National Congress Tournament 106
Neal, Charles "Bomber" 120
Neal, Charlie 64, 120
Neal, Emmett 120
Neal, Ted 12
Neal, Tilbert 120
Nears, Henry 120
Necker, Rich 10
Neepawa, Manitoba 152, 180
Negro American League 13, 28, 39, 92, 130, 150, 173
Negro League 8, 19, 22–24, 26, 28–32, 35, 39, 42–44, 47–48, 50–52, 54–56, 58–60, 63, 65, 68–71, 73, 77, 80–81, 84–86, 89–91, 93–94, 96, 98, 104–106, 109, 111–112, 114, 119, 121–122, 124–128, 130, 132–133, 136, 138, 140–141, 143, 148, 150–152, 155–156, 159–161, 168–170, 172–176, 178, 181–182, 187
Negro National League 188
Negro Southern league 72, 98
Neilburg Monarchs 138, 140
Nemec, Ray 10
New England League 121
New Orleans Black Pelicans 26, 85
New Orleans Creoles 16, 26, 29, 78, 85, 94, 106, 130–131, 151, 155, 158, 176
New Orleans Crescents 26
New Orleans Eagles 55, 81, 107, 112, 149
New York All Stars 110
New York Black Yankees 3, 13, 16, 36, 49, 70, 80, 105, 107–108, 112, 125, 127, 133, 153, 176, 181
New York Cubans 19, 23, 29–30, 55, 62, 70, 78, 80, 91, 122, 124, 127, 148, 170, 188
New York Giants 53, 73, 99, 129, 150, 163, 183, 190
New York Komedy Kings 2
New York Mets 49, 60, 101
New York–Penn League 29, 94, 113
New York Yankees 14, 19, 25, 73, 94, 107, 113, 132
Newark Eagles 13, 16, 22, 32, 49, 57, 85, 109, 121, 127, 145, 155, 173, 175, 178, 180, 182, 187
Newberry, James Lee "Jimmy" 87, 121
Newcome, Don "Newk" 45, 58, 121
Newkirk, Alex 122
Nipawin Tournament 179
Nixon, Red 123
Noce, John 9
North Battleford 48, 64, 68–69, 78–79, 82, 90, 95, 97–98, 100, 102, 105, 108, 119, 130–131, 133, 135, 141, 151, 164–167, 169–170, 172, 174, 179–182, 184, 189–190
North Battleford Beavers 23, 28–29, 54, 68, 76, 78, 83–84, 101, 110, 122, 125, 137, 159–160, 186, 190
North Battleford Eagles 52–53
North Battleford/Lloydminster 76
North Battleford Tournament 59
North Western League 15
Northern League 8, 38, 69, 74, 83, 86, 89, 99, 123, 136, 145
Northern League All-Stars 101
Northern Saskatchewan League 8, 30, 51, 54–55, 59, 83, 114, 122, 140, 159, 183
Northern Senior League 59, 151
Northwest League 79–80 103, 120
Notre Dame, Saskatchewan 53
Notre Dame Hounds 17, 180
Novak, Tim 10

Oakland Beavers 74, 77
Oakland Larks 74, 109
Oakland Oaks 50
Oakville, Ontario 95
Oashawa Merchants 163
Oates, Phil 11
O'Farrill, Esteban Orlando "Chico" 122
Olivares, Ed 122
Oliver, Al 101
Oliver, John Henry 123
Oliver, Reinaldo 123
Olyslager, Art 10
Omaha Rockets 16
O'Neil, Buck 21, 74, 91
Order of Canada 91
Osborne Stadium 9, 20, 34, 131
Oshawa 107
Oshawa Merchants 65, 67, 111–112
Osorio, Pedro 34, 123, 133
Ottawa A's 23, 107
Ottawa Athletics 8, 63, 131, 165
Ottawa Nationals 39
Ottawa Nationals/Senators 8
Owens, Alfonso "Buddy" 123, 176
Owens, Jesse 97

Paar, Royce 10
Pacific Coast League 7, 17, 23, 28, 50, 56, 62–63, 72, 93, 95, 129, 133, 141, 146, 150, 160, 167, 177–178
Page, Jake 124
Page, Ted 124
Pages, Pedro 124
Paige, Satchel 6, 15, 32, 34–35, 37, 40, 56, 58, 110, 113, 117, 124–125, 136, 144, 160, 165–166, 189
Pan-Am Games (Winnipeg) 102
Papillon, Daniel 10
Paquel brothers 164
Parker, Joan 10
Parker, Tom "Big Train" 125
Parris, Jonathan Clyde 125
Partlow, Roy 126
Pascual, Lauro 126
Patterson, Andrew "Pat" 126
Patterson, Gabe 126–127
Pearson, Dave 127
Pearson, Frank 127
Pearson, Leonard "Lennie" 91, 127
Peatros, Maurice "Baby Face" 127
Peete, Charles "Mule" 128, 162
Pemberton, Cliff 9, 184
Penalver, Mario 128
Pendleton, Jim 128
Pendleton, Reg 159
Peninsula Grays 124
Peoria Chiefs 55, 69
Pepitone, Joe 157
Perez, Conrado 128
Perranoski, Ron 29
Perry, Alonzo 128
Peterson, Armand 10
Peterson, Bill 100
Petrolia, Ontario 68
Petrolia Imperials 6
Pettus, Lee Roy 129
Philadelphia Meteors 67
Philadelphia A's 14, 107, 132, 160, 165, 185
Philadelphia Black Meteors 84

Philadelphia Colored Giants 98, 115, 188
Philadelphia Hilldales 63
Philadelphia Pats 188
Philadelphia Phillies 14, 61, 99, 117, 132, 163
Philadelphia Stars 23, 32, 52, 58–59, 62, 72–73, 80, 106, 112, 122, 124–125, 127, 145, 151, 173, 177, 181, 185
Pickens, Frank 129
Picture Butte 1956 Mound Staff 154
Picture Butte Tournament 153
Piedmont League 15, 42, 117
Pigg, Leonard 130
Pilato, Francisco "Chico" 130
Pine, Felix 130
Pinkston, Alfred 130
Pioneer League 16, 41, 64, 89, 95, 138, 157, 164, 178
Piper, Charlie 191
Pittsburg Crawfords 26, 47, 49, 119, 124, 127, 133, 176
The Pittsburgh Courier 13
Pittsburgh Pirates 28, 49–50, 137, 155, 163
Plaxin, Lorne 10
Podres, Johnny 19
Pompez, Alexander 188
Pony League 20, 70
Pope, Dave 131
Pope, Willie 131
Portage La Prairie, Manitoba 35, 124
Porter, Andy "Pullman" 131
Porterville Comets 47, 90, 134, 166, 170, 188
Porterville Padres 33
Portland Beavers 167
Portland Rosebuds 26
Powell, Kelly 10
Power, Victor "Vic" 86, 126 132
Prats, Juan 132
Prescott, George "Bobby" 18, 34, 123, 133
Preston, Al 133
Preston, Joe 133
Price, Harold "Hal" 133–135
Pride of Michigan 163
Prince Albert 51
Prince Albert, Saskatchewan 111, 190
Prince Albert Bohemians 30
Prince Albert/Delisle 38
Prince Albert Imperials 88
Prince Albert Tournament 171
Prior, Jim 35
Provincial League 28, 91, 94, 122, 127–128, 131–132, 152, 155, 165, 177, 187
Psome, Creon 135
Puerto Rican Hall of Fame 148

Quarterman, Isiah "Ike" 135
Quebec Braves 49, 73, 95, 135
Quebec Carnavals 101
Quebec City 144
Quebec League 114, 185
Quebec Provincial League 8, 21–24, 26–29, 31–32, 38–39, 41–42, 46–47, 49, 54, 56, 62, 67, 69–71, 73–74, 80, 85, 93–94, 99, 102, 106, 109, 112, 114, 117, 119, 124–126, 130–131, 140, 144, 148–149, 153, 162, 170, 172
Quebec Senior League 38
Quinn, Bus 170
Quintana, Patricio 136

Rackley, Marv 11
Radcliffe, "Double Duty" 6, 26, 60, 136
Radville, Saskatchewan 59
Raisen, Joshua 10
Raleigh Tigers 178
Ramos, Pedro 27
Ramsay, Art 133, 136
Randolph, Jimmy 136
Redd, Hickey 136–137
Reed, Gary 10
Reed, Willie 26, 44, 75, 120, 137
Reese, Pee Wee 19
Regina 98, 123, 129, 135, 140–143, 169, 171, 174, 184, 186–187
Regina, Saskatchewan 105
Regina Bone Pilers 2, 35–36
Regina Braves 6, 18, 31, 48, 89, 117, 158, 179
Regina Caps 16–17, 24, 31, 40, 47, 49, 52, 59, 63, 67, 69, 76–77, 84, 90, 94, 98, 101–102, 108–110, 115–116, 118, 120, 129–130, 136, 150–151, 157, 159, 161, 164–167, 170, 175, 178, 179, 181–182, 187–188
Regina Caps/Red Sox 150
Regina Exhibition Tournament 31, 158
Regina Red Sox 152, 177
Regina Rough Riders 127
Regina Royal Caps 82, 100
Regina/Saskatoon 153
Revel, Dr. Layton 10
Rex, Clark 9, 98
Reyes, Leopoldo 137
Rhodes, Harry "Lefty" 138
Richards, Paul 44
Richardson, John 138
Richardson, T. W. 140
Rickey, Branch 69, 144, 161
Ricks, Bill 140
Riddle, Marshall 140
Risher, Modie 9, 140, 182
Risinger, Phil 9
Ritchey, John 141
Rivers, Bill 141
Riverside 172
Roberts, Curt 141
Robinson, Eloyd 17, 141, 143
Robinson, Earl 141
Robinson, Frazier "Slow" 9, 58, 143–144
Robinson, Humberto 144, 107
Robinson, Jack "Jackie" 1–2, 6–7, 11–14, 24, 64, 68–69, 72, 75, 80, 86–87, 92, 126, 154, 156, 161, 185, 188–189
Robinson, Norm 143
Robinson, Rachel 11

Robinson, Ray 145
Robinson, Rogers 146
Robison, O. B. 146
Roblin, Manitoba 53, 59, 130, 148
Rochester 100
Rochester Red Wings 122
Rochester Royals 77, 84–85, 88, 113, 152
Rodriguez, Fernando "Freddy" 146
Rodriquez, Ramon 66, 147
Rodriquez, Ruben 147
Rogosin, Donn 6
Rolla, North Dakota 171, 180
Roseboro, John 147–148
Rosetown 59, 75, 100, 116, 122, 128, 177, 190
Rosetown Phillies 37–38, 41, 52–53, 81, 90, 94, 118–119, 158, 167, 169, 172
Rosetown Riot 137
Rosetown Tournament 29, 67, 76, 79, 82, 84, 91, 119, 135, 137, 151, 172, 174, 191
Roswell Rockets 89
Roy Campenella All-Stars 58, 149–150
Rust, Art, Jr. 6

SABR 31
Sada, Ed 147
St. Boniface 49
St. Cloud 99
St. Hyacinthe A's 32, 130–131, 160, 165
St. Hyacinthe Saints 80, 93, 107
St. Jean 125
St. Jean Braves 24–25, 28, 32–33, 42, 50, 73, 80, 112, 122, 163
St. Jean Canadiens 163
St. Jean Canadians 95, 106, 132, 155, 163
St. Joseph Auscos 138, 150
St. Lazare Athletics 69–70, 127, 171–172
St. Louis Black Cardinals 16, 71, 147, 151
St. Louis Browns 15, 39, 42, 57–58, 81, 99, 121, 175, 177
St. Louis Cardinals 14, 16–17, 21, 25, 31, 82, 122–123, 128, 142 157, 160, 164, 166, 174
St. Louis Stars 163
St. Thomas 92, 130
St. Thomas Elgins 73
St. Thomas, Ontario 66
Sakatchewan Baseball League 90
Sakatchewan League 69, 141
Salas, Wilfredo 148
San Antonio Black Missions 109
San Antonio Missions 104
San Diego Padres 17, 111, 141
San Francisco Cubs 40, 44, 72, 77, 118–119, 129
San Francisco Giants 158
San Francisco Sea Lions 27, 31, 47, 58, 71, 101, 123–124, 172
San Francisco Tigers 27, 74
San Juan Senadores 163
Sandel, Warren 11
Sanders, Bill 133, 148

Index

Sanders, Neill 10
Santurce Crabs 39
Saperstein, Abe 80
Sardinas, Oscar 148
Sask. & District Baseball League 23
Sask. Exhibition Tournament 119
Sask. Optimist Tournament 79
Saskatchewan Baseball League 24, 59, 78, 81, 83–84, 128, 165, 171, 181
Saskatchewan League 7, 47, 59, 69, 77, 79, 81, 90, 94, 105, 110, 122, 152, 167
Saskatchewan Southern League 74
Saskatoon 64, 69, 76, 97, 100, 118, 130, 141–143, 151, 164, 167, 171–173, 184, 186–187 190
Saskatoon & District League 8
Saskatoon Commodores 55, 70, 89–90, 103, 113–114, 142, 147, 160, 180
Saskatoon Cubs 83, 173
Saskatoon Ex. Tournament 137
Saskatoon 55s 83, 131, 173–174, 180
Saskatoon Gems 35, 40, 47, 50, 59, 63, 69, 78–79, 82, 88–89, 94, 109–110, 118–119, 129, 137, 165–166, 169, 173–174, 179, 181
Saskatoon Legion 38, 55, 59, 110, 159, 185
Saskatoon Optimist Tournament 165
Satchel Paige All-Stars 54, 57, 60, 74, 86, 91, 109, 112, 145, 171, 184
Sawchuk, Terry 49
Sawusch, Bill 181
Scantleberry, Pat 148
Sceptre, Saskatchewan 133–134, 151, 174, 179
Sceptre Nixons 33, 90
Sceptre Saskatchewan 174
Sceptre Tournament 55, 185
Schaumburg Flyers 136
Scott, Gladwyn 9
Scott, Joe B. 149
Scruggs, William "Willie" 149
Scull, Angel 149
Searcie, Joe 150
Searcy, Kelly 150
Seastrom, Greg 9
Seattle Giants 15
Seattle Mariners 160
Seattle Steelheads 34, 97, 109, 116
Seoane, Pedro 151
Shaunavon, Saskatchewan 55, 164, 174
Shaw, Dave 151
Shelton, Jeff 151
Shepard, Bert 177
Sheppard, Freddie 151
Sherbrooke 38
Sherbrooke A's 164
Sherbrooke Athletics 23, 29, 46, 62, 69, 74, 112, 124, 126, 148
Sherbrooke Canadians 113
Shields, Fergie 134
Shreveport Acme Giants 118
Shuba, George 11
Shury, Dave and Jane 10
Simms, Fate 151

Simms, Toby 152
Slaughter, Sterling 9
Smith, Gene 152
Smith, Hilton 6, 40, 91, 110
Smith, Lloyd 152
Smith, Taylor 73, 152
Snead, Sylvester "Cy" 153
Snowden, Tom 154
Sooner State League 34, 46
Souell, Herbert 154
Souris, Manitoba 127, 171
South Atlantic League 53, 57, 78
South Dakota State League 89
South Minnesota League 100
South Saskatchewan League 129, 179
South Western League 89
Southern Alberta League 7, 34, 95, 120, 142, 160, 168
Southern League 16, 47, 53, 76–77, 103, 109
Southern League All-Stars 31, 52, 94
Southern Minnesota League 77
Southern Minnie League 19, 84, 113
Southern Negro League 28, 47
Southern Saskatchewan League 31, 40, 150, 158, 175, 179, 187, 150
Southwest International League 17, 33, 47, 134, 167, 170, 188
Southwest League 29
Southwestern League 34, 166
Southwestern Minnesota League 34
Sparrows Point Giants 143
Spearman, Al 154
Spencer, Joe 155
The Sporting Chance 14
The Sporting News 12, 45, 56, 58
Spyhalski, Paul 10
Steele, Ed 155
Stephenson, Wayne 9
Stevens, R. C. 155
Stewart, Don 9
Stilwell, Ron 9
Stivers, Wayne 10
Stone, Tony 106
Stovey, George Washington 155–156
Strong, Othello 136, 156
Strong, Ted 156
Suarez, Arnaldo "Chico" 26, 157
Sullivan, Wilson 158
Suttles, Mule 39
Swanson, Roy 158
Swanton, Barry 2–3, 9–10
Swick, Jules 9
Swift Current 49, 90–91, 123, 129, 133–134, 188
Swift Current Indians 55, 59, 164, 174, 184, 189
Swift Current Maple Leafs 157
Swift Current Tournament 34, 53, 58, 91, 118, 135, 164, 188

Tampa Smokers 28
Tartabull, Jose Milages 158
Tasby, Willie 159
Tate, Curtis 9, 50, 159
Tatum, George 159
Tatum, Goose 39

Taylor, Joe Cephus 159
Taylor, Ron 9
Taylor, Tommy 55, 160
Taylor, Travis 160
Teasley, Ron 9, 161, ***162***
Tennessee Stars 189
Terrell, Marvin 162
Terry, E. C. 181
Texarkana Bears 149
Texas Black Spiders 104, 112, 145
Texas Colored Giants 110
Texas Jasper Steers 32, 89, 129, 153, 187
Texas League 50, 112, 180
Texas-Okl-Louisiana League 143
Thetford Mines Miners 25, 28, 38, 62, 94, 145–146
Thomas, Fred 162–163
Thomas, Valmy 163
Thomas, Walter 163
Thompson, Hank 91
Thompson, Johnny 163–164
Thompson, Tommy 164
Thorne, Carlos 164
Thorpe, Norman 10
Thorpe, Slim 183
Three I League 78
Three Rivers 91, 144
Three Rivers Phillies 54, 117
Three Rivers Royals 70, 126, 140, 178, 188–189
Three Rivers Yankees 26, 117, 187
Thurman, Robert Burns "Bob" 164
Tillman, Frank "Spike" 164
Tillotson, Thad 160
Tisdale Lions Club Tournament 34, 133
Tisdale Tournament 52
Tomlinson, Roger 9
Toronto Blue Jays 8
Toronto Maple Leafs 8, 21, 25, 46, 58, 65–67, 86, 92, 95, 122, 125–126, 131, 144, 146–147, 149–150, 155, 168, 177, 187
Torres, Jorge 164
Torriente, Cristobal 7
Towns, Walter 164
Townsend, Dan 133, 165
Trail Smoke Eaters 67
Tribune ALL-Stars 162
Trice, Bob 14, 165
Trimont, Percy 165
Trouppe, Quincy 6–7, 9, 91, 165–166
Trudeau, Christian 10
Tucker, Len 17, 89, 142, 166
Tucker, Ron 9
Tulsa Blackballers 143
Tulsa Oilers 108
Turley, Bob 184
Turner, Bob 166
Twin City Colored Giants 60, 133
Tyler, Walt 17, 167

Underwood, Henry "Big Train" 167

Valdes (Gutirrez), Rene 167–168
Valdez, Chino 7
Valdez, Felix 7

Valdivielso, Jose 27
Valentine, James A. 36, 168–169
Valentine, Russ 169
Valladares, Jose 169, 172
Van Buren, Mark 66, 169, 176
Vancouver 104, 149
Vancouver Beavers 15
Vancouver Canadians 7, 63
Vancouver Capilanos 7, 42, 98, 105, 141, 174, 181
Vancouver Mounties 23, 27, 53, 62, 93, 136, 150, 159–160, 177
Vargas, Guillermo 170
Vargas, Roberto 170
Varona, Clemente 102, 170
Vasquez, Armando 9, 170–171, 173
Vauxhall 87, 142
Vera, Jose 171
Victoria Brown Bombers 8
Victoria Tyees 32, 72, 80–81
Vulcan, Alberta 87
Vulcan Tournament 153

Waco Tigers 89
Wadell, Rube 60
Walhalla, North Dakota 171, 185
Walker, Fleetwood 13, 156
Walker, Gene 68
Walker, Issac 171
Walker, Oscar 171
Walker, Weldy 13
Walton, George "Junior" 172
Ware, Archie 172
Warfield, Howard 172
Washburn, Ray 35
Washington, John 172
Washington, Ross 173
Washington Senators 15, 27, 46, 53, 67, 73, 93, 110, 159
Waterloo 163
Waterloo White Sox 108
Watkins, Murray "Skeeter" 173
Watrous, Sherman 173–174
Watson, Amos 174
Watts, Harry 174
Webb, Joe 174
Webster, Dan 174
Wells, Ira 175
Wells, Willie 42, 143, 159, 169, *175*–176
Wells, Willie, Jr. 176
Wellsville Braves 78
Weremy, Joe 9
Weseca Braves 77
Wesley, Gord 9
Wesley Park, Winnipeg 34
West Coast Negro League 109, 116, 155
West Contra Costa Junior College 26
West Minnesota League 97
West Texas Colored League 89
West Texas-New Mexico League 25, 159, 182

Western Association 40, 86
Western Canada League 5, 7, 9, 13, 18, 20–21, 28–31, 35, 37, 40–41, 48–49, 52, 70, 76, 79–80, 82, 84, 89, 94, 98, 103, 108, 112, 115, 117, 120, 132, 136, 150, 152, 157, 160, 166, 168, 170, 172, 179, 186, 188, 191
Western International League 7, 32, 42, 58, 80–81, 103, 105, 141, 172, 180–181
Western League 19, 42, 55, 89, 93
Whatley, Dave 176
Wheat Belt League 7
Whiskered Wizards 109
White, Arstando "Ladd 176–177
White, Charlie 175, 177
White, Roy 177
White, Sammy Lee 177
Whitman, Rod 110
Wickware, Frank 177–178
Wilcox, Saskatchewan 179
Wilcox Cardinals 104
Wilder, Bill 178
Wiley, Joe 178
Wilkes, James "Seabiscuit" 9, 178
Wilkes-Barre Barons 162
Williams, Alex "Wolf" 179
Williams, Babe 179
Williams, Claude 179
Williams, Coney (Koney) 179–180
Williams, Curly 9, 37, 79, 140, *182*–184
Williams, Ed 9
Williams, Eleanor 10
Williams, Jeff Leroy 180
Williams, Jesse 180
Williams, Jim "Big Jim" 181
Williams, Johnny 181
Williams, Junior 181
Williams, Marvin "Tex" 92, 181
Williams, Roy 181–182
Williams, Samuel C. 182
Willie Mays All-Stars 44, 150
Willis, Bernard 184
Willis, Isaac "Pee Wee" 185
Williston Oilers 46, 60, 71, 108–109, 140, 143, 177, 187, 191
Wills, Maury 48, 147
Wills, Ted 88, 97
Wilmore, Al 185
Wilson, Alfred 185
Wilson, Art 91
Wilson, Bob 178
Wilson, Chuck 185–186
Wilson, Danny 186
Wilson, Emmett 186
Wilson, Leon 186–187
Wilson, Lorna 10
Wilson, Robert 187
Wilson, Tom 187
Wilson Stock Yards Team 154
Wingate, John 187
Wingo, Johnny 187

Winnipeg 14, 32, 51, 56, 60, 70, 74, 95, 100, 118–119, 124, 165, 170, 174
Winnipeg Blue Bombers 116
Winnipeg Buffaloes 2, 26, 29–31, 35, 42, 47, 56–58, 61, 65, 67, 73–74, 81, 85–88, 91–92, 96, 98–100, 113, 116, 121, 124–125, 131, 133, *143*, 144, 146, 152–153, 156, 159, 162, 169, 173, 175–176, 178, 185–187
Winnipeg Free Press 2, 13, 16, 20, 42, 65, 58
Winnipeg Giants 40, 48, 60, 66, 88, 106, 109, 111–112, 125, 134, 136, 140, 154, 156, 173, 186
Winnipeg Goldeyes 8, 16, 21, 38, 46–47, 55, 69–70, 82–83, 101, 103, 142, 146, 157, 164, 174, 190
Winnipeg Reos 38, 43, 177
Winnipeg Royals 43, 48, 67, 70, 100, 108–109, 125, 134, 145, 154, 168–169, 186
Winnipeg Stadium 55
Winnipeg Tournament 182
Winnipeg *Tribune* 2, 34–35, 57
Winnipeg Vets 43, 114
Winnipegs 180
Winona Chiefs 34, 97
Winston-Salem Red Birds 123
Winston Salem Twins 98
Wisconsin All-Stars 78
Wisconsin State League 23
Witherspoon, Lester 17, 187–188
Woods, Joe 178
Woods, Parnell 32
Woods, Samuel "Buddy" 188
Woodstock, Ontario 68
Wright, John 188
Wrighy, Bob 188
Wyatt, Bernie 10
Wylie, Steve Enloe 58, *189*
Wynn, Bill 10
Wytheville Cardinals 146

Xiques, Leopoldo 190

Yakima, Washington 105
Yankton Terriers 34
Yankton Terry's 66
Yorkton, Saskatchewan 63, 98, 176
Young, Bill 9

Zayas, Francisco "Chico" 190
Zayas, Luis 190–191
Zayas, Roberto "Jeronimo" 9, *191*
Zedd, Stanley 175
Zeeben, John 9
Ziegler, Dale 9

www.ingramcontent.com/pod-product-compliance
Lightning Source LLC
Chambersburg PA
CBHW081159230426

43666CB00016B/2865